Women and Gender in Modern Europe

Women and Gender in Modern Europe

An Inclusive History

Jennifer A. Miller

BLOOMSBURY ACADEMIC
LONDON · NEW YORK · OXFORD · NEW DELHI · SYDNEY

BLOOMSBURY ACADEMIC
Bloomsbury Publishing Plc, 50 Bedford Square, London, WC1B 3DP, UK
Bloomsbury Publishing Inc, 1359 Broadway, New York, NY 10018, USA
Bloomsbury Publishing Ireland, 29 Earlsfort Terrace, Dublin 2, D02 AY28, Ireland

BLOOMSBURY, BLOOMSBURY ACADEMIC and the Diana logo are trademarks of
Bloomsbury Publishing Plc

First published in Great Britain 2026

Copyright © Jennifer A. Miller, 2026

Jennifer A. Miller has asserted her right under the Copyright, Designs and Patents Act, 1988, to be identified as Author of this work.

Cover image: Woman training for a Republican militia in Barcelona,
1936 © Wikimedia Commons

All rights reserved. No part of this publication may be: i) reproduced or transmitted in any form, electronic or mechanical, including photocopying, recording or by means of any information storage or retrieval system without prior permission in writing from the publishers; or ii) used or reproduced in any way for the training, development or operation of artificial intelligence (AI) technologies, including generative AI technologies. The rights holders expressly reserve this publication from the text and data mining exception as per Article 4(3) of the Digital Single Market Directive (EU) 2019/790.

Bloomsbury Publishing Plc does not have any control over, or responsibility for, any third-party websites referred to or in this book. All internet addresses given in this book were correct at the time of going to press. The author and publisher regret any inconvenience caused if addresses have changed or sites have ceased to exist, but can accept no responsibility for any such changes.

A catalogue record for this book is available from the British Library.

A catalog record for this book is available from the Library of Congress.

ISBN: HB: 978-1-3501-5327-1
PB: 978-1-3501-5326-4
ePDF: 978-1-3501-5328-8
eBook: 978-1-3501-5329-5

Typeset by Newgen KnowledgeWorks Pvt. Ltd., Chennai, India
Printed and bound in Great Britain

For product safety related questions contact productsafety@bloomsbury.com.

To find out more about our authors and books visit www.bloomsbury.com
and sign up for our newsletters.

To my parents, my first teachers, and to my students—past, present, and future

CONTENTS

List of Figures	viii
Introduction	1
1 The Beginnings of the Long Twentieth Century	5
2 The Turn of the Century and the Great War	29
3 The Modern Woman and Rise of Extremist Politics	53
4 The Second World War and the Holocaust	75
5 Women in Divided Europe	99
6 Fighting for Expanded Rights	123
7 Revolutions and Rebirth	149
8 The New Millennium	173
Conclusion	193
Notes	199
Bibliography	239
Index	259

FIGURES

1.1	Mary Jane Seacole, approximately 1850	7
1.2	First women bicycle race in Brittany at the velodrome in Brest, France, June 1897	24
1.3	Tessie Reynolds, English cyclist, 1893	24
2.1	Natalia Goncharova in makeup for an actress of the Futurist theater, September 12, 1913	30
2.2	"Remember Belgium—Buy bonds—Fourth Liberty Loan," 1918	37
2.3	Dorothy Lawrence in uniform, 1915	45
2.4	"The Parents" by Käthe Kollwitz (1921–22). Woodcut on paper	47
3.1	American entertainer Josephine Baker (1906–75), in costume for her famous "banana dance," *circa* 1925	58
3.2	"There is no room in our Collective Farm for Priests and Kulaks." Soviet propaganda poster, 1930	66
3.3	House of the German Mother, Elgersburg. Girls being prepared for their later role as mothers in Elgersburg, Thuringa, 1930	73
4.1	"Ready for ATS Parade." Lance Corporal Adina Williams of the British Auxiliary Territorial Service (ATS) gets ready for a parade on October 26, 1942	80
4.2	West Indian ATS Recruits of the British Auxiliary Territorial Service arrive at camp in an army car, Britain, 1943	81
4.3	*Einsatzgruppen* soldier murders Jewish mother and child, Ivanhood, Ukraine, 1942	87
4.4	"Women of the HeHalutz Movement Captured with Weapons," May 16, 1943	91
4.5	Jewish resistance fighters, 1943, from right, Małka Zdrojewicz, Bluma Wyszogrodzka and Rachela Wyszogrodzka	92
5.1	The Soviet Union 1963 stamp commemorating the "Second 'Team' Manned Space Flight" with a portrait of Valentina Tereshkova	107
5.2	September 1954: Full length evening two piece with mink cuffs, by Dior	115
5.3	Cover of *Screenland* featuring Brigitte Bardot, March 1959	116
6.1	British nurse and embryologist Jean Purdy (1945–85) hands physiologist Robert Edwards a dish containing fertilized human egg cells in their research laboratory in Cambridge, February 28, 1968	126

6.2	Dolle Mina protest with a giant penis at a public toilet on Dam Square, April 30, 1970	133
7.1	Women form a chain around Greenham Common US Air Force base, December 12, 1982	158
7.2	Chernobyl evacuees in a newly built village, Ternopilske, near Kiev	163
7.3	Fatima Achaboun, a young French-Tunisian girl, is surrounded by friends on October 9, 1989	170
8.1	Pussy Riot performs at the Day for Night festival in Houston, Texas, December 16, 2017, in front of the message, "Virgin Mary please get rid of Putin"	176
8.2	"Italian Troops Work Alongside and Train Afghan Security Forces in Shandand." August 29, 2011	185
8.3	*A Surge of Power (Jen Reid) 2020*. "Statue of BLM Protester Placed on Colston Plinth in Bristol," July 15, 2020	189

Introduction

Women's and gender history has not neatly followed a traditional chronological tack because European women have not equally participated in such narratives. Indeed, societies have historically assigned and maintained separate roles and spaces for women, including along ethnic, class, racial, and religious boundaries. This book examines a tumultuous chunk of that history, telling the story of women and gender in the long twentieth century, roughly from the 1850s to the 2020s. It considers the social, political, and cultural changes navigated by diverse groups of women from across Europe as they faced unprecedented historical challenges.

When a century ends and begins is a tricky question. The long-held belief in a "long nineteenth century"—that starts with the French Revolution and ends with the First World War—overlooks how dramatically many women's lives changed in the final decades of the 1800s. For some European women, the push for new political, economic, and social rights in this period defined the beginning of a new age. "Feminism" as a term and concept entered common usage during the 1890s, signaling a new prominence of the "woman question" in public discourse. With this new terminology, a new generation of theories, theorists, and political leaders emerged across Europe. Moreover, the dramatic changes of the nineteenth century would have an enduring and reverberating influence on the course of women's history throughout the twentieth and twenty-first centuries.

This period spanning the late 1800s through the early 2000s brought significant changes for European women: the ability to vote; to earn money and keep it; to work while married or pregnant; to divorce and also legally marry any gender; to hold a passport and travel; and to serve in the government and military (among others). The long twentieth century traces the ebbs and flows of women's lives through revolutions and world wars, pre- and postwar periods, and the rise and fall of welfare states, the Cold War and decolonization, Europe's demographic shift toward more ethnic and religious diversity in the twenty-first century, and technological advances that altered women's lives for better and for worse. This book takes these shifts as jumping-off points for illuminating European women's long twentieth century.

This is not a story of triumph, however. All histories of change are challenged by signs of continuity. As women achieved steps toward greater freedoms and mobility, they were met with recurring limitations. Women's experiences are neither continually improving nor declining but rather fluctuate according to regional, class, ethnic, racial, and philosophical delineations. Moreover, the changes that did occur were inequitable, and historians debate exactly how revolutionary much of the nineteenth and twentieth centuries were for the majority of European women. The fact that many saw innovation and improvements in their lives also highlights those left out of those advances, as rifts persisted and deepened along lines of race, ethnicity, religion, and income. The idea of a singular "women's experience" becomes especially meaningless when considering these inequalities.

Indeed, defining a "European woman" is a tricky thing, particularly in light of the scientific racism, colonialism, and migrations that shaped this period. The colony of Algeria, for example, was declared part of France in 1848, so Algerian colonial subjects were told that they were now French, that France was their motherland, and that French history was their history. France occupied Algeria for 132 years and administered it as a French department. Were the French citizens and subjects living in Algeria "European"? Moreover, if part of France was in Africa, where exactly were the boundaries of Europe itself? Post-decolonization emigration to the metropole in the 1960s answered these questions: even with formal citizenship, the ethnic French population did not consider north African immigrants to be French citizens—socially or culturally—despite their legal status. Many parameters are in play in women's history, including what it meant to be a woman verses a man in different contexts. For many women, class, race, nationality, or sexuality was a more prominent part of their identity and experience than their gender. Although the category "women" could be necessary, for example, in the fight for women's right to vote, in many key historical moments, "women" as a unified group simply did not exist.

Just as "European women" are hard to define, a book on women's and gender history is multiple books. It is a history of feminism(s), a history of gender and sex, a history of how different groups have defined womanhood, and the historical challenges to this category. When the field emerged in the 1970s, women's history pioneers started asking questions about research disparities—the lack of women in historical narratives—and determined that women had a hidden history that scholars had ignored or at least not sought out. Their fix was to make women of the past visible—to "add them" back into existing historical narratives by telling their stories or using different sources to access them. Soon, women's historians began revising these existing narratives not just by adding women but also by broadening the idea of what "counts" as history itself. Insisting that topics like sexuality, the family, gender roles, and social relationship between men and women were historically significant, women's history offered new insights in broader historical narratives of politics, economics, conflict, society, and culture.

However, by the 1980s, it became clear that the field often problematically reinforced some of the same presumptions that had excluded women before—namely, overlooking the larger diversity of women, including non-white women, poor women, and those who might not even identify as women. Feminist scholars of color in particular challenged the extent to which the field had prioritized gender as a category of analysis that could be separated from race and ethnicity. Introducing the concept of intersectionality, they argued that women's history must explore how multiple factors—not only gender but also race, ethnicity, class, sexuality, citizenship status, and region—interact in women's lives.

Finally, the field of women's history expanded once again to incorporate and refine the concept of gender. Far from being a synonym for "women," gender describes the social meanings attributed to the sexes, to distinctions between them, and to the ways that these meanings influence society, culture, politics, and private life. Gender history argues that history cannot be understood without exploring how gender ideologies structure social organization and hierarchies of power, and how they combine with race, class, region, sexuality, and citizenship to create diverse experiences among women. A history of gender in Europe thus complements and supplements women's history.

Accordingly, many parameters must be at least provisionally established in an attempt to write an inclusive history that considers what being a woman meant in different parts of Europe, at different times, and depending on race, class, religion, and other relevant factors. As new research emerges about women in Eastern and Southern Europe, the history of twentieth-century European women diversifies, changing and transitioning from more familiar narratives. Former colonial holdings and postcolonial migrations have and continue to shape European history, politics, and society. Furthermore, including accounts from Iceland to Algiers fleshes out the picture through essential regional diversity. While I have aimed to include as much new research and as many perspectives as possible, it must be acknowledged that a fully inclusive history of European women is aspirational and inevitably highlights those omitted. While this book cannot hope to resolve all of the issues around European women's complex identities, it can hopefully start new conversations.

The chapters of this book are organized chronologically and marked with familiar milestones and recognizable historical events as their anchors, as well as, surprises and reinterpretations. Each chapter centers gender as integral to these periods' defining characteristics. At times, attention to gender illuminates and clarifies a period and in others it complicates. In addition, four interconnecting themes emerge and reemerge. First, different aims and shapes of activism defined European women's experiences—in political and cultural revolutions; in campaigns for the vote in the early twentieth century and fights against legal patriarchy sixty years later; in postcolonial, nationalist, and fascist uprisings; in gay rights, Black liberation, feminist, peace, and environmental movements. Second, we see women's bodies continually put on the line in actual and rhetorical battles, used in a variety of ways for political purposes—as symbols, mothers, and reproducers for the nation; during Cold War consumerist battles; and graphically during military rape campaigns. European women were combatants on the frontlines, perpetrators of genocide, and also used their bodies for peace, ecological, and political protests. Third, women's labor—inside and outside of their home, in overseas colonies, and during twenty-first century globalization—disrupted the category of work. Socialist, communist, and conservative women struggled for control over women's production as well as its meaning and value. Lastly, the theme of women making themselves heard rings out throughout the book. Diverse groups of European women, broadly defined, found voice and self-expression through both traditional and innovative means, ranging from intellectual nexuses among the African diaspora in Paris in the 1920s to consciousness raising groups in the 1960s. Women reported as war correspondents disguised as male soldiers or were killed in action as photojournalists. Protestors—ranging from suffragettes to antinuclear activists to Black Lives Matter and Pussy Riot—shouted, danced, and performed their demands and expectations of their states, refusing to be ignored. Women, rich and poor, religious and secular, conservative and progressive, and of diverse ethnicities and sexualities, found both moments of solidarity and hardened boundaries between them. Studying these women as a group creates an overwhelming but extremely rich and vital narrative.

1

The Beginnings of the Long Twentieth Century

Introduction

In 1854, Mary Seacole, a British Jamaican nurse with decades of experience treating cholera and yellow fever, longed to go to the battlefront in the Crimean Peninsula, where the Crimean War (1853–56) raged between Britain and Russia. Located on the Black Sea, Crimea was on the cusp of what was considered Europe. France, Britain, the Austrian Empire, and the Russian Empire were battling for access to the lucrative ports of the Mediterranean Sea. When Britain joined the war on March 28, 1854, Seacole decided to leave right away: "No sooner had I heard of war somewhere, than I longed to witness it."[1] She was confident in her expertise—a combination of traditional Caribbean healing and Western medicine—writing in her published memoir: "I have never been long in any place before I have found my practical experience in the science of medicine useful."[2] Seacole, the daughter of a Scottish army officer and a free woman of mixed race, traveled from Jamaica to the Crimean front by herself to help the British. At a time when few colonized people or women had professional opportunities, Seacole made a name for herself.

Also working on the Crimean front was Florence Nightingale, the well-known British nurse who pioneered nursing as a profession. Nightingale led battlefield nursing units in modernized warfare, notably prioritizing sanitation when treating soldiers. Despite her renown, Nightingale was not necessarily beloved; according to a Welsh nurse also appointed to Crimea in 1854, "Florence was an arrogant and cold-hearted petticoat, out for power and glory at the expense of the sick."[3] Moreover, Nightingale's work was constricted by regulations and restrictions set by the government and medical profession, as well as Victorian propriety. Seacole, in contrast, was more freewheeling. She was almost fifty years old, stout, dark-skinned, and wore bright, colorful clothing, such as red, yellow, and blue dresses, scarves, and hats. Seacole used herbal medicines from her mother's Jamaican heritage as well as contemporary Western nursing practices. In addition to caring for the wounded, Seacole ran a business in Crimea—the Hotel Britain—that Nightingale falsely inferred might be a brothel because it was known to be jovial and served alcohol.

Few knew what to make of Mary Seacole. As a colonial subject, Seacole saw herself as British. She also saw herself as a national icon, businesswoman, and intrepid travel writer.[4] Like Nightingale, she sought what men want from war—glory, adventure, to serve their empire, and to be significant. Even as contemporaries doubted her, Seacole was confident and independent, published a bestselling memoir in 1857 to cement the legacy she felt she deserved and proclaimed herself a "heroine of Crimea."[5] Mary Seacole helps redefine ideas of what constituted a European woman during this era (Figure 1.1).

Although Seacole and Nightingale's experiences are not necessarily representative of many women's lives in the nineteenth century, radical shifts in the 1800s made their careers possible and set the stage for the rapid changes of the twentieth century. Revolution, industrialization, and imperialism marked the nineteenth century as a groundbreaking and transitional period for women. The French Revolution (1789–99) promoted the idea of equal rights that, while not extended to women at the time, galvanized feminist concepts and later movements. Beginning in the mid-1700s, industrialization and urbanization irrevocably altered the landscape of Northwest Europe as new forms of productive power replaced animal and human strength, and factories mass-produced goods and drew workers to crowded urban centers. Indeed, the Industrial Revolution (1760–1848) set the stage for labor movements and socialist feminism, as it transformed women's work in ways that were often dangerous, grueling, and exploitative. These nineteenth-century innovations, opportunities, and cultural changes produced profound shifts in women's lives and conceptions of gender and womanhood that would have lasting impacts into the twentieth and even twenty-first centuries.

The Industrial Revolution

In 1750, women and children rarely worked outside the home unless they had positions as servants inside someone else's household. Yet a hundred years later, British women and children were regularly competing for jobs in mills, mines, and factories as well as in upper-class mansions.[6] The introduction of the power loom in the 1780s revolutionized cotton manufacturing, ending handweavers' trade and bringing large numbers of women and children into factories. New forms of technology and a new managerial class made factory work both more productive and increasingly stressful for women workers. While managers considered them "docile" compared to male cotton spinners prone to agitate for better conditions and wages, growing numbers of foremen, engineers, and supervisors interfered

FIGURE 1.1 *Mary Jane Seacole, approximately 1850. Public domain.*

with workers, demanding sexual favors, for example, for women to keep their jobs.[7] Later in the nineteenth century, mechanization took over many branches of industry. In France, mechanization and the appeal of lower wages resulted in women taking over the boot, shoe, and tobacco industries as well as increasingly popular bicycle workshops.[8] In Britain in the early 1800s, women and young children (sometimes under the age of six) hauled coal trucks through dark, cramped passageways in coal mines for up to fourteen hours a day, risking death from explosions, roof falls, deadly gases, and machinery accidents.[9]

An 1842 government investigation into British mine conditions interviewed eight-year-old Sarah Gooder, who noted not only her fear at work but also her loss of childhood, "I'm scared … I would like to be at school far better than in the pit."[10] In France, activist Julie-Victoire Daubié investigated women workers at a silk factory in 1866 and found women suspended from straps for fourteen hours a day so they could use their arms and legs simultaneously, pulling thread from silk cocoons in basins of boiling water, and working in temperatures up to 104 degrees.[11] As these examples demonstrate, these new industrial workers, including girls like young Sarah and many working mothers, faced arduous, repetitive tasks with few if any safety measures, protections for economic downturns, sick pay, childcare, housing, or healthcare options. Given the poor conditions and serious risks involved, many women tried to leave factories as soon as they were married and get by with piecework, such as sewing, especially when they had children. Those who had to continue working outside the home found childcare extremely difficult to obtain and infant mortality rates were high, especially for those who could not afford wet-nurses and unwittingly fed their babies from unsterilized bottles.[12] Moreover, despite such hard work, women industrial workers were paid about half of what a man earned, and children even less. At a time when women began competing with men for jobs in factories, manufacturers preferred hiring women because of their cheaper wages. Paradoxically, women's labor was both essential to industrialization and valued much lower.

As industrialization and urbanization boomed in Northwest Europe and parts of Germany and France, much of Eastern and Southern Europe remained rural. In these slow to industrialize areas, agricultural work, piecework, and domestic service defined women's working lives, and changes took place more gradually or in different forms. Nineteenth-century rural Spanish women mostly worked in service (domestic service, wet-nursing, and washing) as well as domestic manufacturing (food and textiles).[13] The development of industries like textiles did increase the demand for female labor in factory towns such as Barcelona but also undermined women's hand spinning, which had been essential work for centuries.[14] Likewise in Italy, feudal-aged practices of women gathering and grazing animals were outlawed, while other women's work decreased as new markets arose and introduced ideas about bourgeoise domesticity.[15] Within the Austro-Hungarian Empire, industrialization further excluded Roma and Sinti communities, who were already considered outsiders, as their artisanal or cultural work became less relevant. Female healers within these communities also lost work alongside the professionalization of nursing.[16] Cultural biases could also interfere with accurate census data collection on "workers," which did not always include all women in this category, making it difficult for historians to truly assess women's labor participation.[17]

Most women of the poorer classes in the eighteenth and nineteenth centuries faced a fragile economic existence with dwindling options. Despite access to new industrial jobs, most European women worked in domestic service, living within a household as a cleaner, cook, nanny, lady's maid, or dairy girl. Forty percent of the British female labor force worked in domestic service—more than twice the number working in factories.[18] A third of women aged fifteen to twenty-four worked as servants in London in 1860, and female servants made up 32 percent of women workers in 1885 Berlin; however, these numbers declined significantly by the early 1900s.[19] Women working in domestic service were not allowed to marry, had little privacy, and little time off. Unlike women who worked in crowded factories or mills, women in service often worked alone in a large house where they were more vulnerable to sexual advances, coercion, or assault.[20] In fact, women in domestic service had higher rates of premarital pregnancy than factory girls because they lacked protection from sexual harassment, support networks, and sufficient wages. Illegitimacy rates ranged between 30 and 50 percent in parts of rural England, Sweden, the Austro-Hungarian Empire, and the Netherlands.[21]

The Industrial Revolution transformed the European labor landscape. Urbanization and new forms of wage labor codified the separation of men and women's work and altered the relationship between the family and the economy. As economic actors, wives and daughters working outside the home disrupted traditional family life, allowing some wives a measure of autonomy from their husbands, and daughters independence from their parents.[22]

New Social Classes

The Industrial Revolution also created new economic and social categories that would have a lasting impact: the "working class" and the "middle class." This terminology was first used in the nineteenth century amid industrialization, urbanization, and the significant changes they generated. Those who worked in the new factory system—men and women—now comprised the working class, and they developed a sense of common interests, problems, organizations, and eventually solidarity through activism. Yet as working-class identity hardened into a political movement, it did so in a gendered way, with male resentment over competing with women and other gendered concerns resulting in misogyny and exclusions within organized labor.

Indeed, working-class men advocated for the "family wage" and the virtues of domesticity to drive women out of certain kinds of work. This male breadwinner model—the assumption that men provided for their families and women only supplemented their income—meant that employers could increase profits by paying women less. Despite the ideal of domesticity, most women had to work. Histories of working women often center on their mobilization through trade unions, socialist and labor parties, charity work, and other acts of either resistance or reform, but it is worth noting that the vast majority of women had to put job security over solidarity in their own economic, emotional, and familial choices.[23]

Some women of the new middle class also worked—those whose husbands or fathers were skilled laborers or held corporate, managerial, or professional jobs. Some middle-class women worked with their husbands in their businesses, but many more moved into "respectable" white-collar jobs, such as shopgirls at newly introduced department stores in the Czech lands, Denmark, England, Finland, Germany, and Spain. However, like most women workers, they could not make a living wage or necessarily live independently. In Paris at the Bon Marché department store, women salesclerks lived on the premises so they could be supervised—to prevent male visitors, for example. They also ate their meals at the store and were not allowed to leave until after closing.[24] Department stores also shifted the image of the consumer, as middle-class women would eventually become their primary customer base as well as their employees. According to historian Erica Rappaport, shopping in urban spaces disrupted cherished boundaries between public and private spheres (i.e., masculine and feminine spaces) and blurred the lines between supposedly respectable and immoral women. Referring to London, Rappaport notes, "By the 1880s new images of middle-class womanhood celebrated rather than condemned women's identification with consumption."[25]

Unlike working- and many middle-class women, those of the wealthy upper class did not work for pay. Instead, upper-class women managed their staff, their households, and saw to their children's upbringing and education. They also sought to make their superior status recognizable in contrast to working women and wore increasingly elaborate and constrictive clothing such as corsets, and bustles under layers of skirts. Their corsets, for example, exaggerated feminine shapes while also making physical activity extremely difficult, reinforcing the idea that women could not do the same things as men. This belief in sexual difference reflected an ideology of female domesticity that gained prominence in the nineteenth century. According to this ideology, the sexes were fundamentally distinct, and men and women should therefore exist in "separate spheres": men, in the public world of paid work, politics, and intellectual thought; and women, in the home as devoted wives and mothers, exerting their purportedly innate moral influence. While this ideal was generally only possible for upper-class and sometimes middle-class women, it impacted all classes and served to further cement distinctions between them.

Midcentury Reform

Mid-nineteenth century European women were among the vanguard of organizing for democracy, civil rights, voting rights, socialist welfare, limiting economic exploitation, and national unification and liberation from European empires. Collective organizing and early workers' unions were a crucial workers' response to the "social question"—asking what responsibility society had toward those negatively impacted by industrialization. In 1843 (five years before the publication of the *Communist Manifesto*), one of the most indefatigable socialist activists, Flora Tristan, called for a Universal Workers' Union for both sexes for the right to work and the right to organize. In addition to appealing to working women to join the union, Tristan also addressed women of all classes: "Women, will you remain silent ... when the most populous and useful class, your proletarians brothers and sisters, working, suffering, weeping, and moaning, come and beg you to help them?"[26] Tensions arising from workers' movements, such as the socialist feminists, as well as from government repression and censorship, crop failures, widening gaps between the rich and the poor, and a lack of social safety networks erupted into revolts that spread from Paris, to Prussia, Vienna, Prague, Budapest, Milan, and Sicily in 1848. Both socialist and liberal women were active participants during demonstrations, for example, in Sicily, where women helped to construct barricades from stones, earth, lumber, and furniture, as well as in combat by heaving furniture, stones, and boiling oil at government troops.[27] Indeed, from 1848 to 1865, women across Europe were political actors at a time when men of all classes had blocked or limited all women's political possibilities.

The factory system dramatically transformed workers' living and working conditions. In addition to the hazardous industrial environments described above, urbanization's mass migrations led to slum conditions where many people lived together in cramped quarters with limited access to clean water, suitable ventilation, and waste collection—some lived near cesspools that collected raw sewage dumped into the streets. These issues became the object of study and concern, especially among middle-class and upper-class women involved in charitable work. Philanthropy was akin to both a profession and a pastime for Victorian reformers—well-to-do women who made it their business to address slums' conditions and vices. In France, Pauline Kergomard, an activist and school reformer, cofounded the French Association for Child Rescue that aimed to help abused children, including children who were "morally endangered" by parents who "live in a notoriously uproarious and scandalous state" and other conditions deemed unseemly.[28] With charity and social reform organizations, their advocacy stood in for what would later be covered by national legislation. Interestingly, these reformers used the ideology of separate spheres to justify their public works. Claiming their moral fortitude as caregivers, charitable upper- and middle-class women sought to help beyond the home but in roles deemed naturally suited to them.[29]

Reformers often looked down on slums and their working-class residents, citing high illegitimacy rates, alcoholism, and prostitution, and proposed moral uplift and individual responsibility over economic reforms or investigations of underlining causes. Some traveled across town not just to offer relief and assistance but also to gaze upon the other half's squalor and poverty as a "charitable adventure" known as "slumming."[30] A key issue for these reformers was "fallen women"—those engaged in sex work, even if intermittently. Prostitution was common as female wages could be too low for survival, and women who lost their jobs or homes had nowhere to turn for support. Poorer women who worked in factories or as domestic servants, dressmakers, milliners, laundresses, and dairywomen sometimes moved in and out of prostitution temporarily out of desperation when they could not find work.[31] In her study of French silk laborers, Daubié noted a high rate of suicide among destitute workers who saw prostitution as their only alternative for income. One woman left a suicide note stating, "I would rather die with integrity than live in sin."[32] Economic instability and the expansion and contraction of business cycles also forced women into other criminal activity—mostly theft—in alarming numbers. Middle- and upper-class reformers did not advocate for government intervention to aid the poor, however, as they believed in laissez-faire economics, but, at the same time, they supported the idea of the state as a paternal caregiver for women workers.[33]

Despite not offering aid to unemployed women, many states instead attempted to regulate prostitution throughout Europe with different motivations. In the early 1860s, Italy's first prime minister Camillo Cavour believed that controlling prostitution was necessary to ensure public health, order, and morality—key aspects of modernizing and civilizing the new Kingdom of Italy.[34] His Cavour Law of 1860 strictly regulated prostitution by organizing state-run brothels, requiring sex workers to register with the police, and requiring health checks and involuntary hospital stays for treating venereal diseases.[35] France had similar policies in place in the late nineteenth century, while Germany imposed stricter controls and Russia criminalized prostitution altogether between 1845 and 1866.[36] In general, though, most European governments tolerated prostitution with various regulations, viewing it as a necessary evil.

In the mid-1800s, the British introduced laws to regulate prostitution as part of imperial legislation, designed to strengthen the British Empire. The Contagious Diseases Act (CDA), passed in 1864 and extended in 1866 and 1869, was enacted to monitor prostitutes in order to mitigate health risks;

namely, to safeguard soldiers and sailors in colonial holdings, such as Hong Kong, India, and Australia, and in English and Irish port towns, against venereal diseases.[37] The new law was not designed to protect sex workers, however, and often had dire consequences for them, subjecting prostitutes and even women just deemed suspicious to mandatory pelvic examinations, treatments, and confinement. Like other policies concerning the poor and urban environments, the state saw a need to punish "polluting women" and shield "respectable men and women" from their corrupting influence. Thus, the CDA did not target the men who visited prostitutes, but rather the "carrier" women.[38] Within the context of Victorian values and social reforms, the CDA was a messy combination of uplift and control.

However, some women reformers recognized the risk inherent in such politics. Notable British reformer Josephine Butler saw the CDA's damaging impact firsthand while conducting rescue work among prostitutes in Liverpool. Butler published a "Letter to My Countrywomen" that reported on how the law endangered innocent women, explaining that they were powerless against the police and the courts: "On the oath of ... one policeman, who only needs to swear that he *suspects*, not that he knows her to be leading a vicious life, may order her to submit to the [pelvic] examination, periodically for twelve months, and if she does not obey can send her to prison for three months."[39] Butler drew the radical, natalist conclusion that police power over women's bodies was dangerous, arguing that excessive police power made ordinary men "weak" and, therefore, threatened the nation's "racial health."[40] Butler established the Ladies National Association for the Repeal of the Contagious Diseases Act, which in 1871 presented a petition with 25,000 signatures to Parliament. Due in part to her campaign, the Contagious Diseases Act was repealed in 1886.

As the sex work example suggests, women's bodies and sexual activity were central to nineteenth-century reform campaigns that conceptualized women as either potential mothers or potential "fallen women." Bourgeois reformers and legislators applied this idea to their advocacy for labor protections, leaving working women and children caught in the turbulent middle of their belief in an unregulated free market on the one hand and the urgent need for moral transformation on the other.[41] Reformers in Sweden questioned the morality of women working with men, working at night, and even the appropriateness of their clothing.[42] In addition, new regulations cast women as a distinct type of worker that needed paternalist protection because they were seen primarily as mothers.[43] For example, the Netherlands drew on the 1847 British Ten Hours Act (that limited women's and children's working hours) when drafting their own protective legislation, addressing women's health for the "prosperity of their families." One Dutch legislator also pointed out the prudence of protecting women workers because they were likely to replace recently restricted child labor.[44] In the 1880s, Germany also drew on contemporary ideas of sexual difference to define their burgeoning welfare states' policies, aligning a sexual division of labor with social policy.⁴⁵ The laws' equating of women workers with children in need of protection would have a lasting impact, preventing women from gaining equal access to professions and equal wages for equal work. It was not until the late twentieth century that protective legislation was overturned in many countries, after women sued for the same job opportunities afforded to men.

Educational and Career Advances

Perhaps the most significant reform for European women in the nineteenth century was access to higher education. Indeed, involvement in philanthropy, charity, and social reform spurred women's career, educational, and political ambitions, which they would later tie directly to suffrage. The latter half of the century saw the expansion of primary and secondary education for girls across the continent. In Eastern Europe, Jewish girls' enrollment in schools, including higher education, increased from the 1860s onward.⁴⁶ In Serbia, the Higher Women's School in Belgrade, a secondary school for girls, opened in 1863; and by 1883, Serbia had introduced six years of compulsory education for girls and boys into law—already the standard in France, the UK, and the United States.⁴⁷ Even so, laws and practice were two different things and in 1900, Serbia had the lowest female literacy rate in Europe. However, by 1905, female students in the newly established University of Belgrade outnumbered female students at other universities, prompting historians to write: "The exercise of the right to an education, even before it was granted to girls in the Habsburg and German empires, was the first victory of the Serbian women's movement."⁴⁸ Many Eastern European women saw the campaign for education as more significant than the fight for the vote and attended universities abroad if they were not accessible to them at home. The increased availability of secular literature in Eastern European Jewish communities influenced women and girls' behaviors, and some ran away from home to seek education in addition to refusing marriages, questioning traditions, and joining revolutionary movements.⁴⁹

While large numbers of women did not earn an advanced degree in this period, they campaigned for the right to do so and many universities across Europe began admitting women for the first time. The University of Heidelberg started by allowing women to audit classes, the University of Göttingen granted American physicist Margaret Maltby a PhD in 1895, and the University of Berlin conferred a doctorate upon German physicist Elsa Neumann in 1899. During the final quarter of the nineteenth century, universities in Denmark, France, Italy, Russia, Switzerland, and Sweden opened their doors (to varying extents) to women.⁵⁰ Educational access allowed European women to challenge what they knew and explore the unknown, including new careers.

Midcentury technological advancements in transportation and communication, such as expanded rail systems and telegraph cables, changed

Europeans' perceptions of distance, time, and speed in ways that drastically impacted women's opportunities. Trains allowed passengers to travel speeds and distances previously unimaginable, and European women began to leave their homes in search of not only education but also the newly available jobs in nursing, teaching, and civil service that accompanied the expansion of bourgeois society.[51] Telegraph cables shrank the world by transporting messages across vast distances in minutes instead of weeks or months, revolutionizing the stock exchange and creating integrated national and international markets.[52] The field of telegraphy hired women in increasing numbers in the mid-nineteenth century, providing an important case study of women's roles at work and in society, their relationship with emerging technology, and challenges to existing business models. The example of the telegraph shows how industrialization offered women new possibilities for independent living and meaningful work outside the home.

In the 1850s, young women, generally in their late teens and early twenties, began to work at private telegraph agencies in Britain, such as at the Electric Telegraph Company.[53] Scandinavian countries and Switzerland also began to employ women in the telegraphic service in the 1850s, while France, Germany, Prussia, and Russian followed suit by the late 1860s. When the International Telegraphic Union (ITU) was established in 1865, twelve of its original twenty-two member nations employed women.[54] By 1900, women worked in almost all European telegraph administrations and in many around the globe.[55] A higher percentage of women in Europe worked as telegraphers than in the United States. In the 1870s, 31 percent of operators in England were women, and by 1882, women comprised nearly half of all operators in the Paris Central Télégraphique, though they earned only half the pay of male operators.[56] Moreover, the rise and expansion of European colonialism in the late nineteenth century owes much to the development of the telegraphic system (as well as new railway and shipping networks). Colonial governments hired women telegraph operators to control their far-flung empires, for example, in the British Cape Colonies (now South Africa), in the Portuguese colonies, and in French West Africa.[57]

Telegraphy offered respectable employment for educated, middle-class women seeking financial independence. It also required a significant level of skill. To be a good telegrapher, one had to be not just literate but also a good speller, adept at Morse code, and have some knowledge of electricity and telegraphy. Indeed, many telegraphers had to pass entrance examinations as well as training courses. The Telegraph School for Women, established in London in 1860, required applicants to train for six weeks without pay. If they did not achieve the compulsory standard of eight words per minute by the end of this training period, they were dismissed. In France, single, widowed, and childless trainees between the ages of sixteen and twenty-five were accepted if they could pass an entrance exam that included writing, penmanship, arithmetic, geography, and knowledge of the metric system.[58]

Women took on management roles in telegraphy as well—in bookkeeping, inventory, filing, remittances to corporate headquarters, and maintaining ledgers of expenditures and payroll. Some smaller rural offices were managed by women. In addition, women's capital played a significant role in financing the nineteenth-century industrial economy, as those with means invested in telegraphy.[59] Some female telegraph operators also became active in labor movements. Norwegian telegraphers, for example, petitioned their parliament for a wage increase on multiple occasions, despite being consistently rejected—a problematic response considering the tasks men and women performed were largely indistinguishable. There were also a handful of strikes in other places, such as Manchester, England, where workers succeeded in securing higher wages for male and female operators in 1881. On the whole though, middle-class women were less engaged in labor movements than their working-class counterparts, which led the Italian Telegraph Administration to comment: "The women do not generally concern themselves with political questions, and are strangers to the struggles of parties and interests. This endows them with the best qualities requisite for the telegraphic service, namely, patience, discipline and application."[60] While the administration was correct in characterizing these women as good at their jobs, it was sorely mistaken about their lack of political interest. In fact, women's push for new political, economic, and social rights was a defining feature of the late nineteenth century, with impacts lasting well into the following century.

Women's Movements and Activism

Feminism—the idea that men and women are equal—entered common usage by the 1890s (though some had used it as early as the 1820s), signaling a new prominence of the debate around the equality of the sexes, known at the time as the "woman question." In 1872, Dutch feminist pioneer and novelist Mina Kruseman used the term in a letter to Alexandre Dumas, introducing it into public discourse in France and the Netherlands.[61] With this new terminology, a new generation of theories, theorists, and political female leaders emerged. Indeed, as the nineteenth century was drawing to a close, the "woman question" and debate over women's emancipation spurred women's movements in the UK, France, Germany, the Low Countries, the Austro-Hungarian territories, Switzerland, Scandinavia, Russia, Italy, Spain, Portugal, and Greece, as well as in North and South American, the Middle East and Asia. Political and economic activism by working women for fair wages and by middle- and upper-class women for suffrage and other civil rights launched social movements that would have success in the twentieth century.

However, the majority of women's campaigns in the nineteenth century did not necessarily identify themselves as feminists or as "suffragettes," as activists for women's enfranchisement in the UK would later be called. Advocates for women's rights varied by class and societal position. Middle-class women were concerned with white women's unequal access to political rights, education, and professional careers. At the same time, socialist feminists continued to see workers' rights and women's rights as inseparable, with the struggle for a living wage more important than the liberal political rights that bourgeois women campaigned for. In Eastern Europe, nationalist movements for ethnolinguistic nations within European empires intersected with and were often inseparable from women's rights movements. A broader view of European women's activism and concerns—across Europe—illuminates and redefines women's rights campaigns at the end of the nineteenth century.

Working women's relationship with the labor movement evolved over the course of the 1800s. Working-class socialist feminists were distinct from bourgeois reformers, who campaigned for protective legislation for moral reasons rather than against capitalist exploitation. Working women, on the other hand, organized around the gendered impacts of industrialization. In Germany, socialist feminists criticized police regulation of prostitution alongside protests against sexual harassment at work, in both cases arguing for more rights for working women and girls.[62] Women's additional responsibilities outside of work—childrearing and household maintenance—restricted their political participation, and their lower wages decreased the likelihood that they could pay union dues, not to mention few unions welcomed women since their lower wages made them unwelcome competition for men. Still, working women joined the unions that would have them as well as workers' political parties (though in small numbers) to seek social and political change. In the 1870s, after the failed Paris Commune—the short-lived revolutionary French government—and national unification in Italy and Germany, women's working-class movements became part of larger socialist political parties.

In Britain, women's participation in labor activism increased in the 1880s through New Unionism—an effort by organized labor to broaden its scope and agenda. For the first time, women workers, like matchgirls, were included as part of a mass labor movement organized around specific issues. In 1888, the Matchmakers Union mobilized matchgirls into a strike of at least 700 women over a proposed tax increase.[63] Their grievances included police harassment; dangerous conditions such as phosphorus poisoning; and being charged for brushes, for spoiled matches, for lacking childcare, and for being late.[64] While the strike resulted in both successes and concessions, the transition from helpless girls to advocates was a significant part of a larger wave of women's activism in the late 1880s.

Middle- and upper-class feminists had different concerns. Earlier in the century, many became involved in dress reform, protesting restrictive corsets and cumbersome dresses. An American women's newspaper called *Lily* crossed the Atlantic and published an article in 1851 decrying dangerous and constricting clothing: "[God] did not command us to wear long petticoats or girt our vital organs."[65] In 1861, English feminist Harriet Martineau wrote an article titled "Dress and Its Victims," noting, "There are a good many people who cannot possibly believe that dress can have any share in the deaths of 100,000 persons."[66] Affirming that indeed it could, she continued by outlining the dangers of corsets: "The ribs are pressed out of their places, down upon the soft organs ... the heart is compressed ... the stomach and liver are compressed, so that they cannot act properly ... Grave ailments are the consequence."[67] As a result of such arguments, some women began attracting unwanted public attention and hostility by wearing trousers. Their campaign against fashion contrasted with working-class concerns, demonstrating the diverse intentions, goals, and methods of women's activism.

In Northwestern Europe and Scandinavia, diverse campaigns for middle- and upper-class women's equality blossomed in the last quarter of the century. During this period of political foment, both failures and successes broaden the conversations on the "woman question." French women's right to suffrage was first discussed during the French Revolution from 1789 to 1793, but was unsuccessful as governments across Europe tied women's lack of property rights to their inability to vote. Freemasons and authors Maria Deraismes and Léon-Pierre Richer formed the French League for Women's Rights in the 1870s. Richer was just one of many male feminist pioneers in the nineteenth century. In 1878, The First International Congress on Women's Rights was held in Paris, and French feminist Hubertine Auclert challenged the omission of woman suffrage from the agenda, though she did not garner much support. Finally, in 1884, divorce was reintroduced into French law (after its abolishment in 1816) but it was still limited to cases of adultery, cruelty, desertion, and other causes that needed to be proven.

Women's campaigns in England were the most visible and have received the most scholarly attention, though they were not necessarily representative of most European women's experiences. In 1866, at the age of eighteen, Millicent Fawcett gathered signatures for a petition to Parliament for propertied women's suffrage. Fawcett persisted in her political actions and became the leader of the National Union of Women's Suffrage Societies. In 1928, at 62-years-old, she saw women's full right to vote in the UK realized.[68] In 1870 British author, Barbara Bodichon drafted a petition to the British Parliament—the Married Women's Property Act, which called for women to control their own wages. After much debate, the landmark legislation was enacted in 1882, and allowed married women the right to own, buy, and sell property.

Contemporaneously, after German unification in 1871, German feminist and writer Hedwig Dohm argued for women's suffrage—writing pamphlets, articles, short stories, and novels that supported women's right to vote, but her efforts did not garner much support. In the mid-1890s, women in Berlin—aware of French and British suffragettes—bravely spoke out on behalf of suffrage. Lily von Gizycki and Minna Cauer founded a periodical

Die Frauenbewegung (*The Women's Movement*) in 1895 that called for women on the left and right to cooperate for women's rights and suffrage, signing and submitting a petition to the government.[69] Finally, in Sweden, the Married Woman Property Association, active between 1873 and 1896, was the first organized Swedish women's rights organization and worked successfully to reform laws in favor of women's equality. The Swedish Marriage Code was reformed in 1874 and allowed for contracts to be drawn up before marriage to protect wives' or husbands' property, though the husband's legal domination over assets continued. Scholars see these marriage contracts or "settlements" as an important step toward Swedish women's legal emancipation.[70]

Inescapable historical contexts made Eastern and Western Europe more distinct in the nineteenth century; while industrialization shaped Northwest nations, nationalist movements dominated life in the east. In Eastern European countries such as the Czech and Hungarian lands and Poland, feminist concerns were generally couched within larger and more prominent nationalist and anticlerical movements. For example, amid the struggle for an independent Polish nation-state, activists prioritized nationalism over issues like women's rights, and all social resources were directed toward the nationalist cause first. Even so, in late-1860s Poland, after military actions and uprisings had quieted down, more women took on public roles in response to economic and political changes and, within the broader context of feminist debates across Europe, the "woman question" entered public discussion.[71] Likewise, in late-nineteenth-century Ukraine, women practiced what historian Martha Bohachevsky-Chomiak calls "community feminism" (even if they denied being feminists) through effective organizing for women's self-help, self-improvement, and greater participation in national causes.[72] Emancipation meant many things to women in Eastern Europe, who found themselves subjugated primarily as imperial subjects or as ethnic minorities within states.

Still, diverse women's movements spanned across Eastern Europe from the Balkans to the Baltics. These movements included philosophers, peasants, teachers, social workers, and scientists; Catholic, Protestant, Orthodox, and Jewish activists; and nationalist, liberal, and socialist feminists. Feminism was not brought to Eastern Europe as a Western idea, and Eastern European feminists did not necessarily aim to change patriarchal structures. Rather they addressed the issues most relevant to them according to their circumstances and national contexts. Nevertheless, many middle-class feminist movements in Eastern Europe were in step with Western European ones in their claims for educational and political rights.

Moreover, women's movements were not just popping up across Europe, but also interacting with each other in new ways. Features of the modern era, such as improved transportation and communication, helped create an international women's movement, or at least connected with the ones that existed. For example, the International Council of Women, an American suffrage organization, had a majority of European members. Women traveled with increasing ease via steamships and trains to international conventions in major European metropoles in both the East and the West, connecting and disseminating their particular feminist viewpoints.[73]

Women for Empire

Innovations in transportation and communication, in addition to women's broadened public roles, led many women to seek new opportunities abroad, especially in European colonial holdings. The latter part of the nineteenth century was a heyday for modern European imperialism. From the late 1870s through 1914, European colonial powers participated in the "Scramble for Africa," where nations competed to claim land for exploitation and direct control of large parts of the continent. European nations also claimed colonial holding throughout Asia, Latin America, and virtually every corner of the globe. Europeans had been involved in colonialism for centuries, but the nineteenth century ushered in a new form known as "high imperialism." High imperialism changed the nature of colonialism in important ways, particularly regarding race and gender. Now, the practice was characterized by more indirect forms of economic exploitation, an emphasis on political control, and attempts to reform colonial people to align with their own conceptions of "civilization."

Industrialization influenced the shift toward high imperialism, with its modern forms of communication, transportation, medicine, and weaponry; during a period of intense nationalistic fervor and jingoism; and amid a surge of new pseudoscientific ideas about race and evolution. These three factors intertwined in dangerous ways. Science assumed a new authority during the period, and starting in the 1850s, scientific "progress" involved the precise measuring and classification of all life, including human beings. Heavily influenced by Charles Darwin's theory of evolution and the new "science" of eugenics, people could be defined and categorized by race, nationality, sex, class, and psychological profile. The pseudoscience of Social Darwinism and scientific racism used the intersection of racial and sexual characteristics to construct what proponents claimed were clear, biologically confirmed boundaries between the "races." Despite the concept of "race" being constructed through earlier colonial endeavors, contemporaries were quick to apply hierarchies to this categorization, with European superiority built in as a given and data on diverse peoples collected in ways that supported these ideas. Spurred on by pseudoscientific notions of race and evolution and a fascination with comparing and ranking other people, Europeans claimed to be remaking colonial subjects in their own "civilized" image.

European women's presence in the colonies advanced the colonial agenda in various ways and also facilitated women's access to new roles and power. Indeed, European women found more career opportunities abroad than at home, and many relocated to colonial sites to become missionaries, writers, civil servants, anthropologists, or ethnographers. Nursing, for example, provided a way for German women to serve their country, support empire, and work in an elite (and increasingly feminized) profession. In 1888, a women's volunteer organization was established for secular nurses to serve Germany's colonial holdings in Africa, China, and various Pacific Islands. Though a minority in the colonial movement, these German nurses were able to take on leadership positions within their narrow realm.[74]

European women also engaged in the "civilizing mission" as missionaries, educators, or as wives of missionaries or colonial officers, and focused their attentions on colonized women. Armed with pseudoscientific racial concepts and ideologies of domestic and religious virtue, they sought to introduce European ideals of women's education, health care, and domestic training. British, French, and Dutch women set up schools for native girls to impart this education, though they rarely included vocational training that could have offered them a path to independence.[75] Rather, even those who showed interest in and sensitivity toward different cultures sought to "improve" local women's lives by insisting upon their own notions of European domesticity. Their goal was to create proper wives, mothers, and daughters in the colonies. Their message had a fundamental paradox, however: while lessons in religious and basic literacy were intended to free women from the restrictions imposed on them, they simultaneously prepared them for the inherently restrictive lives of European wives and mothers.

Likewise, European women sought to help each other further the civilizing mission. In 1888, Flora Annie Steel and Grace Gardiner published *The Complete Indian Housekeeper and Cook* as an (opinionated) domestic manual for English ladies managing colonial households in India. The guide outlined duties, described the nature of Indian servants, and provided recipes for local foods, among other things.[76] Steel lived in Punjab for twenty-two years with her colonial officer husband and, though she championed uplift and purportedly immersed herself in the local culture and language, the manual reflects the offensive premises and goals of imperialism. Steel and Gardiner present Indian culture as degenerative, Indian mistresses as slovenly and dirty, and Indian servants as infantile, including advice to readers such as, "The Indian servant is a child in everything save age, and should be treated as a child."[77] *The Complete Indian Housekeeper and Cook* demonstrates European women's active role in the imperial mission, as many sought to create a microcosm of Empire in their own homes.

At the same time, European women in colonial holdings around the globe occupied a wholly different role as members of the supposedly inferior sex within the supposedly superior race.[78] In 1851, the British census collected data on marital status that confirmed concerns about "surplus women"—that is, the large number of unmarried women. Unmarried women, especially those unable to support themselves, posed a moral threat to themselves and society as potential "fallen women" with no access to respectable motherhood, and fueled fears of population decline if they did not have children at all. "Surplus women" were a problem to be solved. One way to make them productive for the nation was for them to emigrate and aid in colonial rule.

In the colonies, white European women could help "preserve the race" by providing a responsible outlet for white men's sexual drives—an ironic notion considering the anxieties about "fallen" women.[79] Once seen as a sexual outlet, labor source, and local liaison for European men abroad, concubinage with colonized women became less acceptable in light of the new theories about racial difference and superiority. White European women's presence in the colonies was designed to reinforce racial separation by keeping white European men from sleeping with "native" women.[80] Policing sex along class, race, and gender lines in this way secured the boundary between colonizer and colonized, as sexual access and reproduction, class distinctions, racial policies, and imperial rule intersected around women's bodies.

Far from benefiting from domestic education, uplift, or the "civilizing mission," colonized women suffered multiple losses. When Europeans introduced mass-produced goods from Europe such as textiles, it eliminated many women's sole labor source. In addition, colonial leaders had both financial and political reasons to curb education in the colonies, and they stymied local advancements in colonial women's education and training. During the British occupation of the Near East, for example, colonizers scaled back Muslim women's labor and educational opportunities. When schools were present, they were considered an effective way to assimilate new colonial subjects rather than sites of academic rigor. French women in Africa were viewed as powerful influencers for both "civilizing" colonized Muslim girls and guaranteeing their submission to colonial authority. Education was a primary way to instill European values and beliefs, and this was especially true in determining women's place in colonial holdings.

Colonization was supposed to be a high point of technology and innovation, but it was also a dark period of moral degeneration. This context demonstrates the complexity and troubling juxtaposition of women's lives—the rich and the poor, the colonized and the colonizers. For some women, colonization offered exciting new opportunities, adventure, and advancement, while others experienced distressing transformations of their homelands. Under foreign rule, colonized women ostensibly became European themselves, but the violence and persistent inequality of colonialism made this new identity a complicated and not necessarily a welcome one.

Women on the Move

As the sun was rising on September 10, 1893, sixteen-year-old Teresa "Tessie" Reynolds set out for London on her bicycle from the Brighton Aquarium. Her 120-mile roundtrip journey took her 8 hours and 38 minutes, setting a new cycling record and establishing her as a world-class cyclist. Reynolds was emblematic of both the massive cycling trend that took off in the late nineteenth century and the "New Woman" who represented it. The great cycling craze of the Victorian Era included men too, but once a more skirt-friendly, drop-frame bike, known as the "ladies' bicycle" was invented, women's cycling boomed. Peaking in popularity around 1896–7, cycling was highly fashionable for "respectable" women and later for the working class as well. This trend occurred primarily in western Europe, particularly in the UK, but was a symbol of change to varying degrees for women around the globe from the Ottoman Empire to Asia.[81] The popularity of women's cycling was a clear sign that a New Woman had arrived and, among other significant developments, marked the start of the long twentieth century.

Visibility and public image were key aspects of this New Woman—as much an idea to revere as to fear. New Women were recognizable as they biked in more practical clothing, with fewer petticoats and looser corsets. They might have lived apart from their families, perhaps even openly with a lover, and often supported themselves financially. Just as Tessie Reynolds set out on her 120-mile journey, European women turned to cycling and travel with a new sense of personal independence and spontaneity. New passenger trains in Northwestern Europe allowed passengers to travel speeds and distances previously unimaginable, and European women began to leave their homes in search of excitement, education, and pleasure, traveling alone, with other women, or their families, while others migrated out of necessity.[82] Indeed, the women able to travel for adventure and leisure were rarely representative of the majority of European women in the nineteenth century.

Women's cycling was not just for leisure but, as Reynolds's record-setting ride exhibits, also for sport (see Figure 1.3). Female cyclists were interested in racing from the outset; the first documented account of women's racing is the velocipede race from Paris to Rouen in 1868, an event for women and men (Figure 1.2). Women across Europe from Belgium to Russia cycled competitively, ranging from clandestine groups to exhibitions before large crowds in the UK. Such events made women's cycling both profitable and accessible to large audiences in the 1890s and early twentieth century. In 1896, an exhibition paid a group of French women to perform cycling demonstrations of speed and skill at the Royal Aquarium in London. The excitement and commerce associated with women's cycle racing meant that in some cases female racers could earn more money than their male counterparts. According to historian Clare Simpson, the popularity of women's cycle racing at the turn of the century was much more than Victorian curiosity. It was also part of a mutually beneficial relationship between audiences, racers, investors, entrepreneurs, cycle retailers, and manufacturers.[83] Cycling connected the industry to a female market while connecting women to international professional sports.

FIGURE 1.2 *First women bicycle race in Brittany at the velodrome in Brest, France, June 1897. Getty Images.*

FIGURE 1.3 *Tessie Reynolds, English cyclist, 1893. Public domain.*

However, cycling also incited outrage alongside changes in women's dress, practices, beliefs, and values. Some saw cycling as a threat to women's (supposedly) traditional focus on the home and family. Medical professionals worried that exercise, especially cycling, might damage women's reproductive organs. The fact that experts saw women's cycling as alarming and linked it to women's reproductive health underscores the continued significance of these gendered tropes. Indeed, cycling was just one of many new developments surrounding the New Woman—such as educational and employment opportunities, participation in public activism and reform, and innovations in birth control and sexology—which contemporaries found distressing.

Sexuality

Practices and debates regarding female sexuality, desire, marriage, and reproduction shifted in light of significant cultural changes. With the rise of scientific authority and amid a secular turn in many European countries during the last decades of the nineteenth century, Victorian morality lost its prominence, and sexuality entered the realm of objective study. In the 1890s, sexology—a field that scientifically studied sex—proposed new ways of thinking about sex and sexuality. A boom in research, discussion, and distribution of sexual knowledge caused sexological concepts and ideas to enter the vernacular. Some sexologists considered the New Woman to be problematic for rejecting marriage in favor of education and career, labeling such women as unnatural and linking them to lesbianism.[84] But there were also sex advocates—writers, doctors, and social activists—that promoted the idea that sexual activity supported health and creativity.[85] Though not a majority, feminist ideas about sex sprouted across Europe and some younger feminists who wanted to study female sexual pleasure published key works. In Sweden, Ellen Key wrote that sexual desire was noble and that traditional sex roles were unnecessary and restrictive. In Britain, Edward Carpenter and Stella Browne challenged conventional middle-class morality, discussed topics like masturbation, and debated the merits of monogamy versus "free unions."[86] Additionally, many sexologists affirmed that women's pleasure was unconnected to reproduction and, rather, found in the clitoris.[87]

At the end of the nineteenth century, the field of sexology developed modern sexual classifications and nomenclature, particularly the research of the German psychiatrist Richard von Krafft-Ebing and the British-French physician Havelock Ellis. Both doctors played a primary role in cataloguing sexual instincts, such as solidifying heterosexuality as the norm, homosexuality as deviant, and defining particular types of people in the process. Gender was foundational to these new concepts, such as the theory of gender inversion that posited attraction to members of the same sex was merely a side effect of the overall inversion of the person's gender role.[88]

Indeed, "lesbian" was a modern sexological construct related to women who lacked "femininity" or took on roles considered to be masculine. In 1897, Ellis underscored this defining feature of lesbians in *Studies in the Psychology of Sex*, claiming the chief characteristic of the sexually inverted woman is a certain degree of masculinity: "When they still retain female garments, these usually show some traits of masculine simplicity, and there is nearly always a disdain for the petty feminine artifices of the toilet."[89]

Interestingly, advocates for homosexual rights often drew on sexology—including the concept of gender inversion—to argue against discrimination and toward acceptance. Feminist activist, Theodora Anna Sprüngli known under the pseudonym Anna Rüling was part of a flourishing homosexual rights movement in Germany in the 1890s and gave a speech publicly identifying herself as a lesbian and feminist at a time when the women's movement was ignoring lesbian women's involvement.[90] Rüling's 1904 speech in Berlin explained that homosexual women have "masculine proclivities" and were "more objective, energetic, and goal oriented than the feminine women; her thoughts and feelings are those of a man."[91] She also asserted that lesbians suffered more stress than homosexual men, as they endured acute familial and societal pressure to become wives and mothers. In this way, even negative studies and theories about homosexuals, same sex relationships, and gender "deviance" provided a new terminology that resonated with many individuals and enabled the development of queer communities that would aid homosexual rights activists into the twentieth century.

In fact, although homosexual communities were still rare in the 1800s, lesbians did find each other and forge relationships. As in normative heterosexual culture, lesbianism also differed by class. Sexuality also codified class distinctions. Domestic servants, seamstresses, and day laborers often shared rooms and beds out of financial necessity, creating a homosocial culture that could lead to same-sex relationships. Some working-class women worked in male-dominated trades and took on traditional male roles in their relationships as "female husbands."[92] In contrast, upper-class Victorian women had passionate friendships, often expressed in detailed letters that mentioned erotic desire and were, for some, part of an emerging lesbian subculture.[93]

Despite the dissemination of sexology and increased discussions about sexuality in certain circles, most women in this period had little access to knowledge about sex. Authorities continued to censor medical information about it and many still viewed female sexual desire as dangerous or pathological. Consequently, it was difficult to regulate reproduction and the most common forms of birth control were abstinence and withdrawal, which required the man's cooperation.[94] Medical advancements in birth control moved slowly; precursors to the modern diaphragm included using lemons; in 1827, scientists discovered the existence of the female egg; and in the 1930s doctors recommended the "syringe methods" or postcoital douching.⁹⁵ Women of all classes also sought abortions, some turning to herbal remedies or dangerous mechanical methods, at the risk of being severely punished.⁹⁶ Before vulcanized rubber, condoms were made from sheep guts or fish bladders and mainly used in brothels and considered too expensive for widespread use. When Charles Goodyear, an American chemist, perfected the vulcanization process in 1839, rubber condoms could be mass produced and contraceptive devices for both sexes followed, although the new diaphragms were illegal and condoms remained expensive for most.⁹⁷ Some women learned about these options from neighbors, and those who could afford it from pamphlets and advice books.⁹⁸ A limited survey of 150 French physicians in 1890 can shed some light on which methods couples preferred, reporting that 70 percent chose the withdrawal method, 26 percent used postcoital douching, and the remainder chose condoms, sponges, or diaphragms.⁹⁹

Starting in the late nineteenth century, information on birth control became more available, but still illegal. In England, Charles Bradlaugh and Annie Besant stood trial for pornography in 1877 for publishing information on birth control.¹⁰⁰ In contrast, pioneering Dutch doctor Alette Jacobs was on the forefront of preventative medical contraception. Jacobs believed that advising women on contraception was more medically, economically, and ethnically sound than simply encouraging abstinence.¹⁰¹ In 1882, she began fitting women for diaphragms and in 1898 published *Women, Her Structure and Internal Organs* to provide basic knowledge of female anatomy for general readers.¹⁰² Her work was controversial, however, in rural areas, especially Catholic ones, where the celebration of virgins and puritanical sexual practices remained. As with many of the topics discussed in this book, the question of sexual autonomy on the cusp of the twentieth century leaves historians to wonder how revolutionary this period was when considering most European women's experiences.¹⁰³

Conclusion

The end of the nineteenth century introduced both new opportunities and new restrictions for many European women. By the 1880s, women's lives were distinctly different—economically, politically, and culturally. For some, new educational opportunities led to new careers; for others, migration within Europe and abroad changed their worldviews. A swell of reform and activism empowered more women to become politically active, including for their own rights and livelihoods. Sport and leisure activities such as cycling offered a new sense of freedom, while the advent of sexology and revolutions in birth control irrevocably changed women's private lives.

The long-held belief in a "short twentieth century" that sees the First World War as its true beginning—a definitive start to a new, modern era—does not consider how dramatically many women's lives changed in the final decades of the 1800s. By the 1890s these shifts were consequential. What started as a quest for citizenship and women workers' rights evolved into political movements for suffrage, the right to unionize, and access to birth control, among other major transformations in the twentieth century. The modern age for women emerged from radical, revolutionary changes, and hard-won fights for economic, social, political, and sexual rights. The next chapter demonstrates that many of these challenges led to explosive conclusions as well as troubling continuities in the era of the First World War.

2

The Turn of the Century and the Great War

Introduction

The *Futurist Manifesto*, penned by artist F. T. Marinetti in 1909, called for a new philosophy to accompany the new century, one that challenged tradition and celebrated modernity and innovation with a cleansing, combative—and overtly sexist—aggression. He proclaimed, "We will glorify war—the world's only hygiene—militarism, patriotism, ... and scorn for women. We will destroy the museums, libraries, ... [and] fight feminism."[1] Marinetti's manifesto proved inspirational to many artists, yet he could not control Futurism or shape it to his jingoistic and misogynistic vision. Women were also drawn to Futurism, and the movement's female leaders shaped its progressive modernism. French dancer, writer, and painter Valentine de Saint-Point formally joined the Futurist movement in 1912 and after meeting Marinetti, penned her own manifestos: *The Manifesto of the Futurist Women* (1912) and the *Futurist Manifesto of Lust* (1913). De Saint-Point's writing addressed women's struggles in society and, drawing on Nietzsche, called for a superior female race. She connected women's driving force to lust: "Women are Furies ... warriors who fight more ferociously than men; lovers who incite."[2] Despite the broader philosophy's disdain for the modern woman, Futurism sought to insult public tastes and mock tradition, while celebrating change, originality, and innovation. As such, it was the perfect ideology for modern, feminist thinkers.

In 1913, Natalia Sergeevna Goncharova, self-identified Futurist and leader of a Russian avant-garde group, grabbed public attention by parading through the streets with hieroglyphs painted on her face and sometimes on her topless body. Her spectacle was meant as a statement to discard traditional art and customs with a return to tattooing and ancient Egyptian eye adornment (Figure 2.1). In an open letter to women in 1913, Goncharova, like De Saint-Point, encouraged them to see themselves as significant and heroic: "Believe in yourself more, believe in your strengths and rights before mankind and God, believe that everybody, including women, has an intellect

FIGURE 2.1 *Natalia Goncharova in makeup for an actress of the Futurist theater, September 12, 1913. Getty Images.*

in the form and image of God, that there are no bounds to the human will and mind."³

Other key female artists and writers, such as Edyth von Haynau of Austria, were also attracted to Futurism's imagining of women's emancipation beyond formal political recognition. Yet while many historians describe the onset of the First World War within the context of the Futurist movement—especially its glorification of war, violence, and technology—few recognize the movements' female leaders, their influence, or how they saw themselves within it.

This chapter explores the gendered impact of the turn of the century and the First World War on European society. Women's emancipation came to the fore during this period, not just artistically but also politically, economically, and culturally. As we saw in the last chapter, many of these changes in women's lives began in the late nineteenth century and, despite continuities, took on new forms in the early twentieth, especially during the upheavals of the Great War. The war's events—from mass mobilization to starvation on the home front—altered women's spaces, roles, and self-perception in varied ways. Just as the war blurred the lines between the home front and battle front, so too did it blur women's and men's roles and boundaries between the public and private sphere. Class divisions began to dissolve as well—even if contemporaries could not see it. But despite all of these blurred lines, the war ultimately hardened traditional understandings of gender. War propaganda exalted masculinity in battle, while the home front was meant to preserve women's roles as homemakers, mothers, and caregivers whenever possible. It is thus difficult for historians to definitively proclaim that the First World War altered the majority of European women's lives in lasting ways.⁴ Even so, the war had immediate impacts in the postwar period, such as the expansion of the right to vote and more economically and socially independent women. This chapter considers these emancipatory changes as well as gendered continuities for European women in the early twentieth century.

Political Action and Migration at the Turn of the Century

Before the Great War, the early twentieth century saw expanded political and economic power among European women—liberal, socialist, and nationalist—prompted by political, social, cultural, and economic changes brewing since the late nineteenth century. Women throughout Europe championed voting rights as a particularly important issue. In 1903, Emmeline Pankhurst and her daughter Christabel led the British Women's Social and Political Union (WSPU) to fight for suffrage, making their demands through militant protests such as breaking windows, cutting telegraph and telephone lines, slashing artwork in the National Gallery, and destroying mailboxes. On November 18, 1910, London police attempted to suppress 300 WSPU marchers with violence; suffragists had their arms and thumbs twisted, were beaten and pushed, dragged by their hair, and thrown from one policeman to another.[5] In the aftermath of what became known as Black Friday, suffragist and victim of the violence Henria Williams asked: "How many more lives must be laid down ... before an elementary act of justice and reparation is done to the womanhood of the country?"[6]

In Western Europe, German, French, and Italian feminists pressed their campaigns as well. At the Second International socialist conference in 1907, German Social Democratic Party leader Clara Zetkin advocated for universal suffrage, connecting women's voting rights to the broader working-class struggle against exploitative capitalism.[7] In 1909, the French Union for Women's Suffrage worked with the International Woman Suffrage Alliance (IWSA) to fight for the right to vote, though they were unsuccessful. In Italy, socialist, Catholic, and liberal women's organizations, though differing on many issues, all pressed for women's civil rights before the war.[8] On the other hand, women in parts of Scandinavia and Eastern Europe found political successes earlier. Women gained full voting rights in Finland in 1906 and in Norway in 1913. In the Czech lands, the first women's suffrage society was founded in 1905 and by 1912 had convinced three Czech parties to run a female candidate. Božena Vitková-Kunětická won a provincial assembly seat, as Czech men voted for a woman as part of their larger struggle for democratic and republican reform.[9]

As some groups of women gained political rights, women of minority groups' political inequality stood in stark contrast. Communities living in Jewish ghettos in Eastern Europe, for example, saw emigration as a chance to find improved conditions. This was especially true for women who looked to break from conservative traditions such as arranged marriages. In 1913, seventeen-year-old Rakhel Peisoty prepared to run away after learning that her father planned for her to marry a man she found to be "not much to look at or listen to."[10] Peisoty was politically minded and wanted to devote her life to fighting for social justice, political reform, and the revolutionary cause in Ukraine. She recalled years later in her memoir the limited opportunities she had at home: "If I accepted my parents' plans, it would mean my marrying this returned soldier, keeping house, bearing children, and getting lost in the narrow life of a market town, as most girls I knew."[11] Like other politically charged women in the early twentieth century, Peisoty (later known as Rose Pesotta) went on to play an important role as a labor activist and union organizer in the United States, living out the life of politics and purpose she had envisioned for herself as a young girl in Ukraine.

In the early twentieth century, many women began to envision different paths for themselves, as evidenced by suffrage and other political campaigns as well as the movement of millions across borders, continents, and oceans. Migrants were inspired by political movements in search of economic welfare, or, as in Peisoty's case, to escape an undesirable marriage and stifling traditions. Of course, women had been migrating and immigrating for centuries, including as single women looking for work, but at the turn of the century more women than ever traveled great distances. Women left Eastern Europe by the hundreds of thousands. Indeed by 1900, women made up 37.7 percent of new arrivals to the United States.[12]

Women's experiences with migration were often difficult. While Peisoty travelled second class and with relative ease, the majority of migrating women faced countless obstacles, ranging from hard-to-acquire paperwork to sexual predators. Whether from Russia, Italy, Germany, or the Hapsburg Empire, women faced uncertainty. Many were Jewish like Peisoty, departing countries like Russia that saw them as unwanted minorities. Passports were difficult and expensive to obtain, and once a migrant left the country, they lost their citizenship and could not return. Even women traveling legally still risked becoming stateless if they were rejected at Ellis Island. Moreover, human traffickers preyed on women with limited resources, which, despite being sensationalized by the press and through famous trials, was a grim reality for many Eastern European peasant women who were delivered to American brothels as well as factories and mines for hard labor.[13] (It is also true that some women knowingly chose to immigrate to work in the sex trade, having previously worked as sex workers before leaving home.[14]) Trafficking women gained international attention because it lay at the intersection of sexual respectability, ideas of female vulnerability, and nativist fears about global migration.[15] Still, many European women braved such risks and hardships, determined to forge new lives at the start of a new century. Their plans would soon be irrevocably altered, however, by the First World War.

The Onset of the Great War

Escalating nationalism and colonial, industrial, military, and geopolitical competition provided the kindling for the explosive outbreak of war in 1914. When Gavril Princip, a radicalized Bosnian Serb, assassinated Franz Ferdinand, heir to the Austro-Hungarian throne, it set off declarations of war based on nineteenth-century military alliances. Mobilization commenced rapidly, and large armies with powerful, technologically advanced weaponry produced stunning death tolls. Automatic weapons previously used during European colonial expansion in Africa were now trained on Europeans. A long, bloody, traumatizing war of attrition ensued. Despite the seemingly logical steps to war, the reality was messier, especially when seen through the lens of gender. Civilians and combatants of all genders, ages, and nationalities across the globe were drawn into the conflict, shifting political priorities, national borders, and daily life for all.

Depending on the context, the First World War stymied, shifted, or spurred on movements for women's rights as national mobilization took precedence. Across Europe, patriotic feminists turned their attention from suffrage campaigns to nationalistic prowar efforts. British activist Christabel Pankhurst, who had championed radical protest in the WSPU, now called for an end to militancy, encouraging women to suspend their fight for enfranchisement and engage in war work. Women's wartime organizing often emerged from existing suffrage movements. Indeed, many saw pacificism as a logical extension of their crusade for suffrage and looked to key organizations that linked pacifism and feminism, such as the International Council of Women and the Women's International League for Peace and Freedom, founded in 1888 and 1915, respectively. Hungarian Róza Schwimmer, a passionate feminist and pacifist, cofounded the Association of Women Workers in Hungary in 1904 and was instrumental in organizing the International Women's Suffrage Alliance Congress in Budapest in 1913, the organization's first meeting outside of Northwest Europe.[16] Schwimmer sought an end to the war as soon as it began, by any means necessary—an unpopular stance.[17] She traveled extensively promoting the pacifist cause and even met with US President Woodrow Wilson in 1914, imploring him, with great foresight, "If you do not help us end the war in Europe before the militarists end it, you too will be drawn in."[18]

Schwimmer was not alone in her quest for peace. From April 28 to May 1, 1915, she joined 1,200 delegates from twelve different countries at the International Congress of Women at The Hague. Dr. Aletta Jacobs, the Dutch birth control advocate seen in the previous chapter and cofounder of the Dutch Association for Women's Suffrage, organized the conference as an opportunity for women's organizations to discuss peace proposals.[19] Participants drafted a resolution that linked pacifism with the feminist struggle for equal rights, arguing that women's equality, gendered solidarity, and international peace must be prioritized simultaneously: "One of the strongest forces for the prevention of war will be the combined influence of the women of all countries ... Upon women and men rest the responsibility for the outbreak of future wars. ... [Women] can only make their influence effective if they have equal political rights with men."[20] The document also refuted propaganda that used the guise of women's protection as a necessary motivation for war: "This International Congress of Women protests against the assertion the war means the protection of women."[21] Schwimmer proposed that the resolution be presented to various heads of state—both neutral and belligerent.[22]

In addition, the events of the Great War afforded marginalized communities the opportunity to act as de facto full citizens through patriotic service on the home and war fronts. Jewish citizens in Europe saw the war as a chance to demonstrate their loyalty and belonging to nations and empires that saw them as outsiders. Colonial subjects likewise believed that war service—in either fighting or labor cores—would lead to increased political and social rights. Yet while battling nations accepted their service, leaders simultaneously reinforced traditional gender roles and racial discrimination while paradoxically blurring the lines of both.

Wartime Propaganda and Gendered Violence

The surge in nationalism in many European countries at the onset of the First World War resulted in widespread messaging that glorified gender difference. Many men were excited for the adventure of war, the potential for heroism, and a chance to prove their masculinity. Women were encouraged to cheerfully send their men into battle, now viewed as the wives, mothers, sisters, and daughters of the fighting forces. Homosocial civilian youth groups, such as the Boy Scouts, took on militaristic and patriotic tones, focusing on health and fitness for budding soldiers. In Britain, girls too sought admission to the Boy Scouts but often used maternalist language to argue that athletic activities such as bicycling would prepare them physically for the "rigors of motherhood."[23] Nationalist rhetoric in support of the war remained couched in class, gender, and racial terms, such as protecting mothers and families as a stand-in for national security.

Despite the patriotic propaganda, European understandings of war were based on nineteenth-century conflicts that had been short and lacked modern industrialized weaponry. As a modern total war, the First World War militarized entire populations and drew men and women into war zones in new ways, especially as the lines between the home front and battlefront blurred, and as the war spread from Europe to the rest of the world. The war effort resulted in brutal hardships and peril for citizens on the home front, who were also under attack. Women, children, and the elderly were especially vulnerable at home when air raids began in London in 1915 and when the Allied forces bombed German cities in 1918. Aerial bombing raids devastated towns and left civilians injured physically and mentally, despite how far removed from the battlefront they were, and led to enduring trauma. In 1917, Elizabeth Huntley decapitated her own daughter, and the doctor testifying on her behalf in court attributed this heinous act to a nervous breakdown due to "air raid shock."[24]

As in wars past, invading armies occupied territories—such as in Belgium, and parts of France, Serbia, and the Russian Empire—and devastated the lives of men, women, and children. Disturbing rumors of gendered atrocities committed against civilians during invasions and occupation, including rape and sexualized bodily mutilations (such as cutting off breasts), were reported in the British and American press shortly after the German invasion of neutral Belgium in 1914.[25] News of this widespread brutality during the assault earned it the name "The Rape of Belgium," and thereafter served as a symbol of the German forces' general barbarism. The Allies employed this reputation to publicize horrific stories vilifying the enemy—of children's severed hands, for example—but reliable eyewitness accounts of brutal sexual violence accompanied the propaganda.[26] A Belgian refugee in London recounted the atrocities committed against his family: "I have lost my wife ... [We] had five children, and we have not one left. Four of the little ones were trampled to death under the feet of a German regiment, and my little girl ... fourteen years old, was given to the German soldiery, who misused her before my eyes. Afterwards they took her away with the regiment."[27] Scholarship shows that women on all fronts were raped.[28] In addition, official reports commissioned by the Belgian, French, and British governments verify violence against unarmed civilians. This included the deportation of citizens; in 1916, several thousand women and girls from Lille, France were seized for forced labor.[29] During the Russian occupation of Germany's East Prussia, civilians were also deported, including 6,500 women and children, on overcrowded cattle cars lacking sanitation and food for thousands of miles. Many never returned.[30]

Racialized attacks were also common, especially in the East. Russian invasions of Austro-Hungarian territories particularly targeted Jewish communities. In the summer of 1917, retreating Russian soldiers in Galicia (an area in today's Poland and Ukraine), including mutineers and deserters, engaged in monstrous atrocities such as the gang rape of a Jewish woman who was then shot with a machine gun.[31] Between 1918 and 1920, there were more 1,500 pogroms in Ukraine alone, devastating approximately 1,300 towns and killing between 50,000 and 200,000 Jewish people, not counting the tens of thousands injured or victims of mass rape campaigns.[32] Under the guise of war, the Ottoman Turkish state massacred Armenians in 1915, including women and children, leading death marches with habitual beatings and rapes. The marches ended in deserts where Armenians were left with insufficient food and water. Viewing them as an unwelcome "nationality" within their empire, Ottoman Turks also sought to eliminate Armenian communities through gendered forced assimilation. Between 100,000 and 200,000 Armenian women and children were made to convert to Islam and integrated into Muslim households, including forcing marriage or concubinage upon young women and adolescent girls.[33]

As the war went on and enthusiasm waned, governments launched new propaganda campaigns that utilized violence against women to bolster support for the war and encourage the public to adapt to the hardships of life on the home front, including rationing food and goods, restricting access to information, and conscripting husbands, fathers, and sons. All countries at war celebrated women as a symbol of their nation—and one that needed protecting. Drawing on this idea, new propaganda prominently featured rape and other violence against women, often depicting the enemy as ethnically and racially other to pit European cultures against one another.[34] The British and other Allies' propaganda printed imagery of German "Huns"—monsters committing sexual atrocities—in newspapers, pamphlets, posters, and cartoons.[35] During the First World War, Allied

Nations relied on propaganda to motivate their citizens to participate in the war effort. The United States adopted this tactic as well; a 1918 poster promoting war bonds featured the dark silhouette of a German solider

FIGURE 2.2 *"Remember Belgium—Buy bonds—Fourth Liberty Loan,"* 1918. Public domain.

(identified by his distinctive helmet) leading away a young girl struggling to break free. Against a background of burning buildings, large letters implored Americans to "Remember Belgium," urging support for war out of an ethical obligation to protect innocent women and girls as much as for geopolitical purposes (Figure 2.2). Yet although violence against women was used as a tool to generate animosity toward the enemy, many women's accounts of their own experiences with sexual violence were ironically and tragically disregarded or lost credibility, especially after the war.[36] Even so, women's bodies—their protection and their violation—continued to symbolize nations throughout the twentieth century.

Women at Work

Women's contributions to the war effort were not merely symbolic. As belligerent countries faced a labor shortage from mass deployment and large numbers of citizens wounded and killed, most turned to women as a temporary auxiliary labor force. Women had worked in the formal labor force before 1914, of course, but the First World War shifted occupations, opportunities, and wages for many.[37] Across Europe, they took up positions that were previously restricted for women, as the war increased both large-scale weapons production and assembly-line work. In Germany, employers encouraged training and education to enable women to step into these positions, and women comprised 40 percent of workers in defense industries. In Britain, 60 percent of defense industry laborers were women, and London's Royal Arsenal employed over 30,000 women who handled explosives, assembled weapons, and worked on cranes.[38] Russian women were 43.2 percent of the industrial workforce by 1917, while in French defense industries, women made up a quarter of employees at the war's start and a third of the munitions workforce by 1918.[39] Italian women worked in armaments factories under horrible conditions and for very low pay, as well as in offices, asylums, and hospitals; they also commonly worked as professional nurses, ticket agents, street sweepers, streetcar conductors, and telegraph operators. In addition, Italian women contributed from their homes, producing 1,000 field tents and 125,000 pieces of clothing for the war effort.[40]

Women's industrial labor was undeniably essential for warring nations. As French General Joseph Joffre hyperbolically remarked, "If the women in the factories stopped work for twenty minutes, the Allies would lose the war."[41] Yet female war workers also challenged dominant gender ideologies that placed their role in the home. Munitions factories were dirty, noisy, and dangerous, the shifts were long, and women's work with weapons of destruction contradicted their presumed natural affinity for caretaking. Indeed, this came as a shock to many middle- and upper-class women who had never worked before or endured such arduous conditions. Like General

Joffre, governments and employers throughout Europe praised women's new roles in the workforce as fulfilling their patriotic duty. For example, in 1914, the Austro-Hungarian state urgently appealed to women's "duty," "service," and "sacrifice" to "perform service in the time of war."[42] Encouraged to embrace their "inner bond" with other women, workers were instructed to put aside their differences—between noble, bourgeois, and working class; Christian and Jewish; German-speaking and others—all in service to the empire at war, even thought they were subjects and not full citizens.

In some ways, new opportunities for women's work did lessen class distinctions, with patriotism as the great unifier. In 1917, Naomi Loughnan, a young upper-middle-class woman who lived with her family, went to work for the first time in her life at a dangerous munitions job with 12-hour shifts. Though she described the work as dirty, smelly, noisy, monotonous, and exhausting, Loughnan admitted to feeling secretly proud. She recalled, "With the zest of doing work for our country," the job filled her with "inspiration."[43] It also facilitated her first interactions with women from other (meaning lower) classes, and Loughnan was shocked to learn of their poor living conditions: "The upper classes are having their eyes prised [sic] open at last to the awful conditions among which their sisters have dwelt." Loughnan also recognized the sexism of the job—another great unifier—which dictated that women not question instructions or offer improvements on the machinery, but merely act like "good children."[44]

There were countless women like Loughnan who took pride in their contributions to the war effort. In 1917, journalist L. Doriat interviewed a French factory worker in Brittany who displayed exceptional patriotic duty on the job after sustaining a serious injury. Unlike the male employees before her who had learned through apprenticeships, she was one of many women put to work after only a day or two of training. The worker noted how important it was to remain focused during her eight-hour shifts: "You must ... pay attention ... The factory never stops, day and night shifts of eight alternate. It's intensive production: no mawkishness here, we are not women by the arms of the machine."[45] Her job was tempering steel for shell casings—up to one thousand per day—and she used a buffing wheel to polish the steel on the big, heavy shells. One day, she brushed her arm against the buffing wheel by mistake and it instantly shaved her arm down to the bone: "Clothing and flesh were all taken off before I even noticed. They had to scrape the bone, [and] bandage me every day. I was afraid of amputation."[46] Once doctors concluded that they could save her arm, she was determined to return to work, explaining, "Our sense of present need, of the national peril, of hatred for the enemy, of the courage of our husbands and sons—all this pricks us on."[47]

Despite such examples of patriotic zeal and women's vital significance to the war effort, women workers often faced bitterness and harassment from male coworkers. Many men resented women's new roles in the workforce, especially since they were paid less—in some cases, half as much as a man in the same position—which made them more desirable for employers. Yet as Madga Trott reported in 1915, a German woman could attempt to use war work for professional advancement but would likely be thwarted by the lack of training and male coworkers' hostility: "Male colleagues looked askance at the 'intruder' who dared to usurp the position and bread of a colleague now fighting for the Fatherland ... and the lady found it difficult, if not impossible, to receive any instruction and was finally forced to resign."[48] Trott's account reflected a central tension: that while women's labor was essential and their employment unavoidable, these truths also made working women threatening. Many Europeans were torn between accepting the need for women workers and fearing they would undermine societal gender norms and returning men's ability to earn a living and support their families. In reality, though, new employment opportunities did not mean that women became financially independent. Most states paid allowances to families whose husbands and fathers were at the front, stepping in as patriarch in lieu of endorsing female breadwinners. But regardless, this assistance did not affect shortages or other home front hardships.[49]

Even so, the war forever altered women's prospects in scientific, medical, and technological fields.[50] By 1917, 90 percent of Britain's industrial chemists were women, although they were mostly assigned tedious, repetitive tasks for months on end.[51] However, this history of science, medicine, and technology—along with the context of the First World War—cannot be separated from the early-twentieth-century feminist movement, and women made tremendous strides in gaining access to these fields. As mentioned previously, suffragettes championed causes well beyond the right to vote, including professional advancement. Women in medicine campaigned for better access to education, to laboratory work, and to other professions, and women scientists couched their participation in the field within arguments for full citizenship. In this way, as many historians have shown, the women's suffrage movement was also a push for broadly conceived women's equality. The vote was important, of course, but so was the ability to enter professions and earn an equal salary. Moreover, the intersections between science and women's rights are particularly significant, as many contemporaries used pseudoscience to deny women access to jobs, education, and the vote. But as with Futurism, scientific innovation during this era ushered in a reverence for progress and modernity, and European women wanted to be part of it.

Some of the hardest working women during the war were in a much older profession: sex work. War and prostitution have long been linked, and the First World War was no different, as state and military authorities across Europe sought to control women's bodies—as well as men's—in the name of security, hygiene, and morality.[52] That is not to say that prostitution was discouraged; armies provided brothels for troops both on the front and behind the lines, while civilian women back at home were encouraged to remain faithful to their husbands, families, and nation. Yet at the same time, in the age before widespread antibiotics, venereal infections were a substantial concern; they were not only difficult and expensive to treat but also understood to weaken a nation's military. Since suppling millions of condoms during a rubber shortage in Europe presented a logistical issue, states intervened in more invasive ways to control venereal disease among enlisted men. Some soldiers underwent preventative assessments as well as pre- and postcoital exams.[53] However, states went to greater lengths to police women's bodies and sexuality. In multiple theaters, from France to Poland, women merely suspected of being prostitutes could be forcibly subjected to pelvic exams, while infected women—prostitutes or not—were imprisoned in specific hospitals.[54] In German-occupied Belgium, local authorities collaborated extensively with German military officials to regulate troops' access to prostitution in order to protect not just their men from infection but also the "biological body of the nation."[55]

Still many women turned to sex work, either full-time or as needed, when faced with dire wartime conditions such as a lack of food or becoming refugees. Jewish women and those from other minority groups were particularly vulnerable to prostitution on the fluid Eastern Front, where antisemitic discrimination excluded Jewish persons from multiple professions, and authorities were already engaged in attempts to forcibly remove Jews. While it was these antisemitic measures that generated large numbers of Jewish sex workers, military officials sought (unsuccessfully) to control prostitution and venereal disease with an eye toward the perceived racial other. A May 26, 1915, report issued by the Russian army's chief of staff, for example, warned soldiers about German Jewish "syphilitic prostitutes," claiming they had been paid to lure and infect officers.[56]

Finally, despite much historiographical emphasis on industrial labor during the war, in 1914 most Europeans still lived in the countryside. Rural agricultural production was crucial not just to family economies but also to nations' food supplies. When men were deployed to the front, family left behind had to take over physically exhausting and constant farm work. Soldiers urgently wrote letters to their wives with detailed instructions on how to care for their farms and bring in the harvest.[57] Historian Jay Winter emphasizes the importance of the 1914 yield, arguing, "Harvest failure would have stopped the war, not because of a shortage of food, but because farmer soldiers would have deserted by the thousands."[58] But women on the rural home front prevailed; during the 1916–17 season, Italian women were lauded for bringing in a better harvest than the previous year.[59]

Women workers appeared everywhere in wartime Europe and in some instances, they were there for good. Whereas heavy industrial labor reverted to its masculine status after the war, employment in the service sector, such as banking and commerce, remained more open to women. Since such service work was a growth sector in every economy, women had access to jobs more stable than those of male industrial workers in shipbuilding, housebuilding, or engineering after the war. Whether or not women's war work changed gender roles and identities in lasting ways, it was clear that the formal labor force appealed to women. This inspired some and threatened others, as war work both validated women's feminine nature and perilously undermined it.

Modern Warfare and Medical Care on the Battlefront

One of European women's most significant contributions to the war effort was through medical support. Though women were at first discouraged from working near the front lines, by the second year of the war nearly all nations sought women as nurses or volunteers, organized by the Red Cross and other humanitarian organizations or hired by armies for low pay. The women who worked in medical support positions were often between the ages of 18 and 35, middle- and upper-class, university-educated, single or childless, and independently wealthy. The war offered an exciting opportunity for many upper-class women who had rarely left their family homes in search of work before. Medical roles became the most common way women served on the front.

Women's medical corps were indispensable to battlefronts throughout Europe. A notable example is the work of Scottish physician Elsie Inglis. A member of the Edinburgh National Society for Women's Suffrage, Dr. Inglis approached the organization when war was declared to propose establishing independent, women-staffed medical units. Her idea developed into the Scottish Women's Hospitals for Foreign Services—a mission that attracted hundreds of doctors, nurses, and auxiliary staff including over 1,500 Scottish women and volunteers from as far afield as New Zealand, Australia, and Canada. When Britain's Royal Army Medical Corps refused to help, Dr. Inglis reached out to the French government. With French support, Dr. Inglis set up the Scottish women's hospitals, all-female units to aid the Allied forces—the French, Belgians, Romanians, Ukrainians, and especially the Serbs. She also sent fourteen ready-made medical units staffed by qualified women to Belgium, France, Serbia, and Russia. Dr. Inglis even led her own unit in Serbia, where she improved hygiene and reduced typhus and other epidemics. She was unfortunately captured when the Austro-Hungarian and German troops invaded and occupied the region in 1915, but after the war, she became the first woman to hold the Serbian Order of the White Eagle.[60]

Frontline conditions were harsh, violent, and gruesome. In the face of modern industrialized weaponry, traditional maneuvers such as the "cult of the offensive" injured bodies in new and grotesque ways. In addition to the stress of persistent shelling and the constant presence of rotting cadavers, combatants were in danger of being impaled by a man's exploding teeth or blinded by mustard gas attacks and drowning in their own secretions as the gas impacted their lungs.[61] Frontline medics like Inglis faced these horrors as large influxes of men arrived at their units with new types of injuries. A nurse stationed at a hospital in Calais, France described wounded men who had been trapped in no man's land for two or three days: "The flies had been at their wounds, and the maggots had hatched out. They were most repulsive but the Dakin treatment [bleach] soon killed them."[62] Ironically, sexism increased women's battlefront exposure on the Western Front. Because few leaders saw female nurses and doctors as combatants, they were allowed access to sites denied to men in their positions, such as a downed plane or tending to injured soldiers in no man's land. Some nurses capitalized their positions such as Edith Cavell, a British nurse who treated injured soldiers in Belgium. German authorities arrested Cavell for smuggling injured soldiers and civilians out of Belgium to neutral Holland. She admitted to helping the service men escape and on October 12, 1915, a German firing squad executed her in Belgium. The night before her execution, Cavell had no apprehension: "I have no fear nor shrinking. I have seen death so often that it is not strange or fearful to me."[63] Even if unrecognized by their contemporaries as such, many female medics were veterans in their own way in the face of gruesome combat and consequences.

Seeing such grisly combat and working to exhaustion marked a radical shift in many women's lives, and many frontline workers reported PTSD-like symptoms after the war's end. In a postwar poem, Vera Brittain recounted her grueling days as a nurse in France, writing in a poem of "the sights and smells of blood and wounds and death."[64] Her work challenged the mythology of the nurse as the "angel at the front," and instead exposed the agony of war and war-ravaged bodies. Nurses were traumatized by their inability to ease soldiers' suffering and their fear of personal harm in lasting ways, though few contemporaries or historians have studied women's trauma during and after the First World War.[65] Likewise, historians have long discussed male-bonding from the stress of life in the trenches, and nurses also reported in their diaries that close connections with other women helped them endure and survive.[66] In this way, the categories of civilians, war workers, and combatants fluidly overlapped within the experiences of female doctors and nurses during the First World War.

In the summer of 1918, an influenza pandemic swept the war weary world and killed an estimated fifty million people, many of whom were already in poor health due to wartime shortages and conditions. Pregnant women were especially susceptible not only to miscarriages and giving birth to children with congenital impairments but also to dying of childbirth in large numbers.[67] The birth rate plummeted in 1918 and did not rise again until 1920.[68] A nurse tending to influenza patients at a British military hospital noted years later her fear: "They called it influenza but it seemed to us to be some frightful plague."[69] Indeed, nurses were on the front lines of the pandemic as many hospitals on the home front were understaffed due to the war. Historian of the 1918 Pandemic, Guy Beiner, noted the vital role nurses played: "In a reversal of professional gender hierarchies, nurses stepped in to provide effective care ... and paid a heavy price for their selfless exposure to the virus." Eyewitness Dr. Basil Hood observed nurses in his London hospital treating patients in the face of their own death: "As the patients increased and the nurses decreased, coming down like ninepins themselves ... I can see some of them now literally fighting to save their friends then going down and dying themselves."[70] Civilian women who were not nurses also faced the pandemic as caregivers for sick family members and neighbors, community volunteers at quarantine centers, and by treating infected people at make-shift facilities all at great peril.[71] The pandemic highlighted the blurred lines between the home front and battle front for caregivers working to exhaustion in a dangerous environment.

Women in Combat

"It was in midsummer 1915 that an English girl cycled alone into ... the war zone ... fifteen miles from the firing-line near Paris ... I am that girl," begins Dorothy Lawrence's 1919 memoir, *Sapper Dorothy Lawrence*.[72] Lawrence was an aspiring journalist seeking a position as a war correspondent. When denied, she disguised herself as a man and joined the fight as Private Dennis Smith with the First Battalion Leicestershire Regiment (Figure 2.3). After taking a channel steamer to France, Lawrence cycled out to the Somme with her uniform hanging from her bicycle. She bound her breasts with cotton sacking and used cotton stuffing to make her shoulders appear more prominent. The front was so disorganized she was able to insert herself into a battalion with a forged military identity document. Although some of her fellow soldiers were not fooled, they were sympathetic and kept her secret. As Dennis Smith, Lawrence served on the Western Front for ten days with a mine-laying company. When discovered, military authorities were determined to suppress her story, sequestering Lawrence in a convent before escorting her back to England and making her swear to tell no one.[73] Her exposure would have had dangerous implications, revealing not only that the military had been duped but also the ease with which she had performed their masculinity. Lawrence was one of many women across Western and Eastern Europe who engaged in subterfuge to serve as combatants.

The most involved female fighters were Russian women, who began fighting as regular soldiers at the start of the war—with and without approval.[74] Some, like Lawrence, disguised themselves as men and joined male regiments. Anna Alekseevna Krasil'nikova fought in nineteen battles as "Anatolii" and was awarded the St. George's Cross for her bravery. Marfa Malko, another Russian combatant, concealed her femaleness so well that it was not discovered until she was captured and in a German prisoners of war (POW) camp. Indeed, Russian female combatants were not uncommon. Driven by patriotism and a desire to defeat the German forces, some male Russian soldiers helped female soldiers by outfitting them, arming them, and

FIGURE 2.3 *Dorothy Lawrence in uniform, 1915. Public domain.*

hiding their true identities. Even when discovered by authorities, these women were often permitted to continue fighting. This acceptance of Russian female soldiers distinguished them from their Western counterparts and fueled their large numbers. Moreover, female soldiers' persistent campaigning led to an official change in military policy that overrode the legal ban on women soldiers and allowed them to officially join the army as combatants. This policy change was significant, as Russia sustained serious losses of both soldiers and land at the hands of German troops, and government-organized all-female units, such as the Women's Battalion of Death, inspired other women's companies. Press coverage and women's memoirs reveal how these war experiences revolutionized ideas of patriotism, citizenship, gender, and class identity in Russia.[75]

In fact, throughout eastern Europe, women asserted citizenship claims and demonstrated their nationalism and patriotism through combat. In addition to Russian, Bulgarian, Romanian, and Serbian women served as combat troops. Romanian Ecaterina Teodoroiu volunteered for the army at age twenty-three because her brothers were fighting. Even though she was twice wounded and eventually died in battle, Teodoroiu was memorialized in a decidedly feminine manner as a "young girl and a virgin."[76] Despite their heroism, female combatants were typically unable to convince their contemporaries to see them as soldiers, and popular and scholarly accounts of the First World War have largely overlooked their stories.

Radical Protest and Revolutions

As conditions on the home front deteriorated and support for the war waned, many civilian women responded with radical political action. Women led significant waves of strikes, protests, and riots in France, Germany, Italy, and Russia between 1917 and 1918, and gained new value and visibility as political protagonists.[77] With increased entry into the workforce, women came to dominate labor activism, as well as consumer protests. A police report from Vienna noted that a typical day in 1917 saw up to 350,000 people waiting in 1,100 food queues and 47,000 sent away hungry. Police across Europe patrolled these queues, intimidated by the potential for public unrest or even outright violence bottled up in each crowd of women. In one Russian town in 1915, 200 soldiers' wives threatened to storm and loot a shop if it did not lower the price of flour; this tactic proved successful, and they repeated it at shop after shop.[78] In Italy, frequent anti-war protests sprang from strict rationing, food shortages, war work demands, militarization, and generally poor conditions in a nation not yet socially unified or even in agreement about entering the war. Transitioning from local to national politics, Italian women played key roles in actions ranging from petitions and peace marches to strikes, occupations, and armed street fighting.[79]

Women also expressed anti-war sentiment through powerful artistic expressions that emphasized grief and suffering in the face of relentless death. German socialist, feminist, and pacifist artist Käthe Kollwitz was well-known for her woodcuts, posters, charcoal drawings, engravings, lithographs, and sculptures, especially those addressing the loss of her son on the front during the First World War. In posters such as "Never Again War," woodcuts such as "The Parents" (seen in Figure 2.4), and lithographs such as "Death," Kollwitz drew on themes of mother and child to express the suffering and loss of war.

A December 9, 1914, diary entry describes her plans for her son's memorial: "My boy! On your memorial I want to have your figure on top, *above* the parents. You will lie outstretched, holding out your hands in answer to the call for sacrifice: 'Here I am'."[80] Likewise, pacifist feminist writer Vera Brittain was a prolific British journalist before the war and paused her career to volunteer as a war nurse. After losing her brother, her fiancé, and two close friends in the war, she reflected on the mass deaths in her published diary, *Chronicle of Youth*: "The value of human life becomes

FIGURE 2.4 *"The Parents" by Käthe Kollwitz (1921–22). Woodcut on paper. Getty Images.*

so cheap, so that while the loss of ten men under tragic circumstances amid ordinary conditions would fill the whole country with horror, the news of the loss of thousands is now regarded with a philosophical calm and an unmoved continence."[81]

The unrelenting death toll and terrible conditions on home fronts across Europe unleashed political revolutions with lasting impacts. Indeed, the First World War provided a new and significant context for nationalist movements that had been ongoing since the nineteenth century. As governments shifted their focus to war production and mobilization, many such movements seized the moment to press their claims for independence. Nationalistic and feminist organizing had long been connected in certain regions, especially in Eastern Europe and the Balkan states as well as Ireland. Many saw the war as an opportunity for national liberation and democracy that would secure a path to women's emancipation. Polish socialist reformer and nationalist leader Zofia Moraczewska, for example, joined the Women's League of Silesia and Galicia (formed in 1915) to not only support the Polish military on Austro-Hungarian territory but also to raise funds for the national struggle, promote nationalist ideas, and motivate more women to participate in the national independence movement.[82] After the war, the Women's League of Silesia and Galicia joined forces with the Women's League for War Alert and the Polish Women's League to form the largest women's movement in Poland, numbering as many as 16,000 members. Within this women's movement, nationalism remained the dominant cause. Likewise, Polish socialist, nationalist, and feminist activist Maria Szeliga took part in multiple international women's groups, including pacifist ones, yet when war broke out in 1914, she abandoned the pacifist movement, hoping the war could achieve Polish independence.[83] Although Poland would not achieve national liberation through the First World War, it did present the possibility of winning multiple forms of independence, some of which were successful; Polish women attained suffrage during the course of the war, as did those in Latvia and Ukraine as well as Western nations like Denmark and Germany.

Likewise, women's involvement in the Irish nationalist movement and the accompanying women's rights movement long predated the First World War. In 1907, Irish politician, revolutionary, and suffragist Constance Markievicz called on the women of Ireland to engage politically and publicly for an independent Ireland. Her appeal was one of revolutionary emancipation: "Fix your mind on the ideal of Ireland free, with her women enjoying the full rights of citizenship in their own nation." Markievicz encouraged Irish women to take up arms for the cause: "[If] the call should come for your body to arm, do not shirk ... May this aspiration towards ... freedom among the women of Ireland bring forth a Joan of Arc to free our nation!"[84] And indeed, when the Citizens Army was established in 1913, women were welcomed as equals (even if not all saw them as such), and they marched and drilled alongside male volunteers with an intense focus on freedom from British rule.[85]

By the start of the First World War, many Irish nationalists saw the war as potentially beneficial to their cause, hoping a British loss would aid their fight for independence.[86] On April 24, 1916, Easter Monday, a group of Irish nationalists capitalized on an opportunity presented by the war's disruption, attacked British government buildings, and declared an Irish Republic. Now a rebel leader, Markievicz was second-in-command and one of only two female officers in the Irish Citizens Army that led the six-day rebellion. On April 30, 1916, Easter Sunday, the British issued a surrender order, to which Markievicz reportedly declared, "Surrender? We'll never surrender!" But the rebels were out of options, and Markievicz allegedly kissed her revolver before handing it over. British leaders punished the rebels severely, executing fifteen and imprisoning many more. Constance Markievicz was tried on May 4, 1916, and, as a company commander, scheduled for execution by shooting. However, because she was a woman, the authorities converted her sentence to life imprisonment.[87] Like many nationalist women of the period, Markievicz saw the fight for Irish independence and women's equality as inseparable and continued the struggle. After two years of brutal fighting, the island was divided into two nations: the Republic of Ireland and Northern Ireland, which remained part of the UK.

Meanwhile, the hardships of the war were keenly felt in the Russian Empire. Large concentrations of laborers, especially women, worked long hours for low pay, food prices and infant mortality increased, and negative reports from the battlefront all created the perfect conditions for working-class unrest, solidarity, and protest. Throughout the war, factory women engaged in strikes, bread riots, and demonstrations against severe shortages of flour and fuel.[88] Industrial strikes had been building during January and February of 1917, and erupted on February 23, 1917—International Women's Day, a socialist holiday. Women workers marched out of their factories, demanded bread, and crowded Petrograd's streets.[89] The crowd grew to several hundred thousand, as Moscow workers, students, and large groups of urban lower-middle-class citizens joined in what became a two-day revolt known as the February Revolution. Many women remember the February Revolution as carefree, bloodless, and joyful.[90] Ekaterina Olitskaia and her friend Olia recalled jumping out of bed to experience the revolution firsthand: "All day long we just walked in the streets among the crowds … We shouted greetings to the soldiers who had joined the people. We yelled 'Never Again!' in front of burning police stations … I was very happy. I was also quite lucky. During the entire February Revolution, I never saw a single dead body."[91] Even so, Tsar Nicholas II sent soldiers from the front to Petrograd to quell the rebellion, but when ordered to fire into the crowd, it became clear that many soldiers shared the protesters' grievances. By February 27, 1917, the government had collapsed.[92] Lenin returned from exile and by November the Leninist Bolshevik (or "one of the majority") party had seized power.[93]

The February Revolution had significant consequences, granting Russian women the legal and political rights they had long sought. By the summer of 1917, women gained suffrage, the right to serve on juries and serve as trial lawyers, and equal access to civil service jobs as well as equal pay. But while Russian women declared that they were more fully citizens than women in other nations, peasant women in the countryside saw fewer changes in their lives, widening the urban-rural gulf.[94] Moreover, Bolshevik women were still stymied by a gendered division of labor that ranked women lower than men, even as their organizational work and drive sustained the movement.

On the surface, equality permeated Bolshevik ideology, and women did gain social and political influence. Socialist feminist Alexandra Kollontai returned from exile after the Bolsheviks gained power, and she was the first woman elected to the Central Committee of the Communist Party. As the People's Commissar for Social Welfare, she advocated for protections for working women, including maternity leave, nursing breaks, and pre- and postnatal care, all as part of the 1918 Family Code. The first post-revolution All-Russian Congress of Working Women drew over 1,147 delegates to Moscow. There Kollontai gave a speech titled "Women and the Family in the Communist State," outlining the new role the state would play in family life. In terms of childcare, Kollontai proposed, "There are homes for the very small babies; day nurseries, kindergartens ... free lunches at school ... warm clothing ... Does not all this sufficiently show that the child is ... being removed from the shoulders of the parents and on to those of the community?"[95] At this same congress, Lenin commented on women's significance to the Revolution, insisting, "There can be no socialist revolution unless very many working women take a big part in it. ... One of the first tasks of the Soviet Republic is to abolish all restrictions on women's rights."[96] Lenin personally called for an end to women's domestic drudgery, the freedom to divorce, and the liberation of peasant women through collective farming.[97] In 1919, together with communist activist and politician Inessa Armand, Kollontai founded the *Zhenotdel*, the Women's Department of the Central Committee, which was devoted to women's affairs in the 1920s. Stalin, however, dissolved it in 1930, heralding a post-revolutionary era in which many of the promises of equality and support for women went unfulfilled, as we will see in the next chapter.

Finally, on the German and Austro-Hungarian home front, the Allies' economic blockade of the Central Powers had devastating effects on civilian populations. The deprivation of food and other essential products left the home front on the brink of starvation. Pandering to the nation's women, German state propaganda declared them "soldiers" in an economic war—a "voluntary home front army."[98] In response, women led food riots in Berlin (and other populous German cities) and fought authorities over the high cost of living, rations, and limited supplies in general. In the winter of 1915, hungry, frustrated Berlin women stormed market stands and stole potatoes, some as many as 10 pounds.[99] A Berlin police report from October 17, 1916, also noted women violently taking matters into their own hands: "The crowd had already stormed several butter shops because of the prices ... Several large display windows were shattered, shop doors destroyed, and entire stocks simply taken ... Officers were completely helpless against the crowd."[100]

Conditions on the home front grew more catastrophic as the war progressed, and women's riots were impossible for the state to ignore, as strikes and mutinies plunged the country into rebellion. In 1917, 500 factory workers stormed a Berlin city council meeting; women demanded that the authorities address their needs, proclaiming they were "representatives of the people."[101] They succeeded and obtained extra ration cards for bread. Not only were these women political actors before securing the right to vote, but they also came to stand in for all German citizens' demands on and expectations of their state. In the summer of 1918, German women exercised this power in a momentous way and with historic results: they wrote to their husbands and sons on the front, telling them to come home. In Munich, women staged protests demanding an end to the war, and Berlin women followed suit, especially poor working women, and radicals stockpiled weapons and called for strikes. When German soldiers mutinied on November 3, 1918, German women had already been protesting for four years. On November 9, 1918, workers, students, and soldiers crowded the streets and police did not suppress the uprising. In many ways, the government had already collapsed days earlier; the German Revolution had begun. Two days later, on November 11, 1918, the First World War was over.[102] German women, like those in Spain, Russia, and other places throughout Europe, used what power they had to impact the political process. States could not ignore their popular protests against wartime living conditions, and through their efforts, European women widened their political engagement in ways significant enough to end wars.[103]

Conclusion

European women's citizenship unfolded during the First World War, and when the Allies drew up the Treaty of Versailles, suffragettes wanted their concerns addressed. Representatives of the International Woman Suffrage Association (IWSA), such as Mary Sheepshanks, made the following demands: women's suffrage, economic independence, raising the age of consent, marriage law reform, and stopping government-regulated prostitution.[104] A French IWSA affiliate even met with US President Woodrow Wilson on the opening day of the Inter-Allied Women's Conference, February 10, 1919, to present the organization's case. Allied leaders granted some of their demands in the treaty's final draft, including equal pay for equal work and women's inclusion in the International Labour Organization and the League of Nations.[105] In addition, between 1918 and 1920, some nations rewarded women's patriotism, contributions, and sacrifices for the war effort with the right to vote—with stipulations. For example, in 1920 Belgium specifically permitted mothers and widows of soldiers killed in the war to vote. Meanwhile, the newly created democratic states of Czechoslovakia, Austria, Hungary, and the Republic of Poland granted suffrage to both men and women in their constitutions, while the new Soviet Union offered progressive family and women's legislation in accordance with Bolshevik values of equality.

In addition to garnering some legislative successes, during the First World War women entered into direct relationships with their states more broadly. Throughout Europe, their labor was essential and their protests dangerous and consequential. The war also offered women access to gendered social experiences that were previously unimaginable; the feminized home front enabled unaccompanied women to go out for a meal, a coffee, or to listen to music in the public sphere, while female nurses and medics who had never socialized with men outside of their family circles gained a new familiarity with them, including male physiology and vulnerabilities, by treating soldiers at the front.[106] Yet historians remain divided on the extent to which the First World War created a radical break with the past for European women or only a temporary one. As we will see in the next chapter, the interwar period had a mix of consequences and continuities for European women's lives, even as radical extremism altered life for all.

3

The Modern Woman and Rise of Extremist Politics

"What started as a playful game in women's fashion is gradually becoming a distressing aberration," read a 1925 editorial to the *Berliner Illustrirte Zeitung*. Calling for an end to modern styles, the author decried a perceived turn from femininity as "gentle, delicate women cut their long tresses and bobbed their hair," and dresses denied "the curve of the hips." The solution to such a "distressing" development, according to this writer, was to put a stop to invasive new ideas: "It is high time that sound male judgement take a stand against these odious fashions, the excesses of which have been transplanted here from America."[1] In France, progressive journalist Jane Misme also acknowledged these new trends, writing in 1901, "While the traditional woman has not yet disappeared, she has been challenged by another, baptized the New Woman."[2] A moniker applied since the late nineteenth century to describe the pants-wearing, bicycling women of the late Victorian Age, as turn-of-the-century critics insisted that the New Woman "disrupted" contemporary society. By the interwar period, backlash against this new era for women became a centerpiece of the radical political movements that followed.[3]

The mood after the most destructive war on European soil led to social and cultural upheavals throughout the 1920s and 1930s. Many embraced the innovations that arose in every area of life, praising the avant-garde over tradition, which they believed had led to the war in the first place. In urban centers, jazz music, expressionist art and cinema, and new cultural and intellectual trends soared in popularity. Mass culture and advertising disseminated images of the New Woman to a broad audience, starting even before the First World War, and modern definitions of femininity, masculinity, and sexuality only grew during the postwar period.[4] Many women stayed in the formal workforce after war's end, enjoying the opportunity to earn money even as most remained employed to support their families. Significantly, four European empires collapsed after the First World War—the Russian, Austro-Hungarian, German, and Ottoman—and new democratic nation-states formed throughout Eastern Europe. Women took on new political power—both real and symbolic—as many countries authorized women's suffrage and postwar socialist and communist movements (especially in the burgeoning Soviet Union) pushed for gender equality.

These changes sparked tremendous anxiety in interwar Europe. After the blurring of traditional gender roles during the First World War, many feared modern women's rejection of the "natural" differences between the sexes. Moreover, the rise of the New Woman coincided with many women gaining the right to vote and becoming increasingly more politically and publicly visible. Colonial diasporas, ethnic and racial tensions, and the war's inconceivable death toll generated widespread pronatalist panic, as ideas of scientific racism and eugenics that came to the fore in the late 1800s expanded in dangerous ways in the 1920s and 1930s, merging sexism and racism with new pseudoscientific authority and state power. The US stock market crash of 1929 produced a global economic depression, plunging millions of Europeans into unemployment, hunger, and despair. Now women had to defend their right to work in capitalist countries, as campaigns to solve unemployment seized on opportunities to reject women from "men's" jobs. Losing hope, citizens across Europe began to turn away from democracy and toward more radical forms of government in the hopes of finding quicker solutions to pressing problems.

This chapter traces the gendered impact of the vast cultural, economic, and political shifts that shook interwar Europe. In terms of women's rights, protections, and autonomy, these changes set the tone for both successes and regressions in the 1920s and 1930s, as women navigated modernity, the Great Depression, and the rise of authoritarian states. In some countries, fascist family, work, and racial policies came to dominate many women's lives, providing some with new leadership opportunities (even while extoling women's domesticity) and severely repressing others. At the same time, women on the left in more progressive countries helped develop welfare states that helped women as mothers and as workers. In an era rife with contradictions, women were at the center of debates on sexuality, politics, employment, welfare, eugenics, and pronatalism, which intersected in increasingly troubling ways.

Interwar Sexuality

Experimentation in women's fashion and the anxiety it caused were a part of larger debates about sexual politics and women's roles in the 1920s and early 1930s. These decades both questioned and sought to redefine gender norms, with paradoxical results. On the one hand, the period saw increased fascination, study, and celebration of sexual expression and diversity, particularly in major cities such as Amsterdam, Berlin, Budapest, London, and Paris. As discussed in the first chapter, the 1890s boom in sexology prompted new understandings and debates of sexual practices that continued into the twentieth century and were heightened after the First World War. At the same time, such discourse highlighted a distrust of modernity among conservative forces, which sought to regulate sex work, sexually transmitted infections, same-sex sexuality, and notions of respectability.[5] But bringing women and sex under control was not merely a reaction to modern fashions and sexology; it reflected growing fears that altered gender norms would result in moral, national, and racial decline. In this context, women's sexuality, particularly their reproductive labor, took on immense political significance within pronatalist and eugenicist campaigns—with dire consequences.

Though a minority, the interwar Modern Girl, also known as the "flapper," loomed large and symbolized change more than ever before. These heterosexual, flirty women with bright lipstick and low-cut dresses dated freely, smoked, drank, and danced—an intimidating combination. Postwar bodies that had endured shortages were thin, and many flappers were known for their androgynous waif-like physiques, narrow hips, flat chests, and short pageboy haircuts. Fabric shortages and the dangers of long hair in factory work prompted these changes to a degree, but many women enjoyed the new styles and increased social freedoms. While this shift was alluring to some men, many more responded with alarm, as exhibited in the 1925 editorial that introduced this chapter. Conservative women also expressed unease about the ways in which the war had blurred gender lines—with women in uniforms, at work in male roles, and in postwar boyish fashions. British antifeminist and eugenicist Arabella Kenealy blamed feminism for making women more masculine and thwarting the necessary separation of the sexes that she claimed distinguished a more civilized "race."[6] Though Kenealy herself pursued a career as a doctor, researcher, writer, and public speaker, she wrote that "masculinizing" women would burden the "[British] Race by producing an ever-increasing number of neurotic, emasculated men and boys."[7]

Concerns about slipping sexual morality and blurred gender lines merged with fears of homosexuality and sexual perversion.[8] Homosexuality was often associated with crime and other ostensibly degenerate activities such as drug use, alcoholism, visiting nightclubs, race mixing, and prostitution.[9] However, knowledge about lesbianism as a concept or identity was mostly limited to sexologists and the police.[10] Still, some states sought to criminalize lesbianism, employing prior legislation pertaining to male homosexuality and more contemporary medical discourse. In 1921, the British House of Commons debated an amendment that stated: "Any act of gross indecency between female persons shall be a misdemeanor and punishable in the same manner as any such act committed by male persons," referencing a 1885 criminal law.[11] There was clearly no common parlance to discuss lesbianism, as one parliamentarian noted, "I can quite understand that many Members of this house ... may hesitate to believe such a thing exists," before referring to medical experts: "I have consulted many asylum doctors and they assure me that the asylums are largely peopled by nymphomaniacs and people who indulge in this vice."[12]

Such hearings as well as criminal trials, social commentary, medical research, and other menacing depictions introduced lesbianism to the public. This included portrayals in popular fiction, as stories of vampire lesbians or older women preying on younger girls or breaking up marriages thrilled and terrified readers.[13] This theme reflected contemporary fears of declining marriage and childbirth. For example, in his 1922 book *Difficulties: An Attempt to Help*, well-known British author and actor Seymour Hicks warned men to protect their wives from treacherous female seducers who might not be easy to spot: "The male, however subtle, will be to your observant eyes obvious ... but a woman who seeks your wife is difficult to demand an explanation from ... and you may hesitate to label her a Lesbian ... [If] she succeeds, [she] will wreck your home more thoroughly than you can imagine."[14]

In the German Weimar Republic (1918–33), however, sexual freedom enjoyed a short-lived high point. Visions of a harmonious and modern postwar society included dazzling new consumer goods, a golden age of cinema, and utopian beliefs from nudism to communism to forge a more prosperous life overall. New ideas about individual freedoms and citizenship also prompted progressive reforms and advocacy for abortion rights, birth control, easier divorce, and homosexual emancipation.[15] And as the science of contemporary sexology gained authority over morality, sex therapists and activists promoted a rich and fulfilling sex life for everyone.[16]

In 1923, inflation spiraled out of control due to unprecedented devaluation of German currency, and chaos ensued, especially with respect to sexuality.[17] In Berlin, already a tourist destination for pleasure, the economic collapse led to the complete discarding of middle-class mores. Hotels employed professional male dancers to entertain lady clients and sex work boomed. One observer noted men, women, and children prostituting themselves and a general "pathological" mood: "At the pervert balls of Berlin, hundreds of men dressed as women, and hundreds of women as men danced under the benevolent eyes of the police ... Young girls bragged proudly of their perversion. To be sixteen and still under suspicion of virginity would have been considered a disgrace."[18] In addition, lesbian subcultures and homosexual emancipation movements not only emerged but also included a coalition of doctors, intellectuals, and politicians.[19] With relaxed censorship laws, by the 1920s over twenty periodicals written by and for cross-dressers, homosexual men, and lesbians were for sale at newsstands in big German cities and by subscription in smaller towns.[20]

However, this frenzy of amorality and decadence imagined by foreign visitors to Berlin (and even some historians decades later) did not necessarily represent Weimar Germany's wider sexual culture. While Germany did have a laxer attitude on homosexuality, prostitution, and sexual content, these attitudes remained contained in a manner that appeased conservatives.[21] For example, the state sought to limit media that supported and affirmed lesbian subcultures. Though not included in criminal law, authorities made it clear that they saw lesbianism as a threat—or at least as an unwanted and transmittable condition.[22] In the end, conservative groups dominated public discourse and the public was not convinced that Weimar democracy could change traditional sexual mores, political realities for women, or women's employment patterns in a radical way. In fact, the development of sexology placed a new stigma on same-sex sexuality in much of interwar Europe, as psychologists began to both define lesbianism and warn against it as immoral, dangerous, or pathological. In the 1930s, Sigmund Freud's influential theories on female sexuality—which, among other things, negated the clitoris's long-accepted importance for women's pleasure—predominated within sexology and remained largely unchallenged until the 1950s.[23]

Fetishizing Colonial Bodies

Until the First World War, colonial citizens and subjects were not a common sight in European metropoles. However, wartime recruitment brought North African, Caribbean, Chinese, and Indochinese workers, soldiers, and auxiliaries to Europe in large numbers. Though most were deported after the war, not all left.[24] The interwar years saw a growing colonial diaspora in European metropoles such as Paris and London, particularly among African and Caribbean communities. As a result, these cities became social, cultural, and political hubs for Black anti-imperial and intellectual thought, such as the Negritude movement in Paris—an activist literary movement inspired by the Harlem Renaissance in America. At the same time, fascination with African American music and culture gained in popularity in urban areas. This included a focus on women's bodies, exoticism, and sexuality, perhaps best exhibited by jazz singer Josephine Baker's 1927 stage costume—a skirt made of artificial bananas (Figure 3.1). These trends were inseparable from renewed interest in colonial holdings after the war amid the growing popularity of eugenics and scientific racism in the early twentieth century.

Although migrant communities were overwhelmingly male, women from the colonies were also political and intellectual forces in European urban spaces. In Paris, the African population boomed just as women gained further access to the public sphere, especially outspoken feminist intellectuals and activists. In this context, Black women in Paris expanded feminist and intellectual narratives as popular representations of both women and Afro-Europeans blossomed around them. Moreover, while African and Caribbean

FIGURE 3.1 *American entertainer Josephine Baker (1906–75), in costume for her famous "banana dance," circa 1925. Getty Images.*

women were estimated to comprise just 2 percent of the Black population in Paris, they—like all French women—lacked the right to vote and other civil rights. Finding common ground with French feminist groups, their arguments for rights expanded and extended back to the Caribbean.[25]

Among Black diasporic intellectual circles, the Nardal sisters of Martinique fill scholarly accounts of interwar Paris in general and of the Negritude movement specifically. The seven sisters were educated in the French colonial system before moving to Paris, and in 1920, Paulette Nardal was one of the first Black women to study at the prestigious Sorbonne University. The sisters were extremely influential and well-connected to important politicians, artists, and intellectuals of the period, and played a significant role in shaping Pan-Africanism—a diverse political philosophy globally uniting people of African descent.[26] In the Nardals' Paris apartment, African American writers such as Langston Hughes crossed paths with award-winning Afro-French writers and Senegalese poets. The sisters produced a journal in 1931, *La Revue du Monde Noir (The Black World Review)*, which linked the French and English-speaking diaspora with articles in both languages. They also used their political connections to advocate for the "world's colored peoples"; for example, Paulette Nardal wrote a telegram to the League of Nations admonishing Italy's 1935 invasion of Ethiopia.[27] The Nardal sisters helped engender conversations in private, through journal circulation, and with public forums that connected Black scholars and activists and helped create a vibrant Afro-French public.[28]

Notably, in 1931—the same year the Nardals premiered *The Black World Review*—France hosted the Paris Colonial Exhibition. The display included "anthropo-zoological" exhibitions where live humans—colonial subjects—appeared alongside objects to engage French citizens in the country's colonial "civilizing mission." Male and female subjects from colonies such as Indochina, Senegal, French West Africa, and New Caledonia were meant to bring empire to life in reconstituted villages, gardens, and pavilions. This fetishization of colonial bodies extended beyond the exhibition, implicitly suggesting that all Afro-Europeans were on display in Europe, even if simply out grocery shopping. In London, representations of the Black male body as predatory and dangerous (to white women) stretched from the colonies to the metropole, a trope used to demonize and police Black men. Nevertheless, interracial relationships between Black men and white women were more likely in colonial metropoles, such as London, where British women helped African and Afro-Caribbean men navigate city life and engaged with them in both political campaigns and, at times, in personal relationships that led to marriages.[29]

Even though wealthy West African families had been sending their daughters to study in Britain since the 1800s, London's Black population was overwhelmingly male until the late 1950s. African and Caribbean women thus often lived on the margins of both male-dominated Black political organizations and white-dominated feminist movements, though they provided crucial support. Yet while small in number, Afro-British female intellectuals and activists, such as Una Marson and Constance Cummings-John, traveled, formed feminist networks, and broadened the scope of social justice movements. Entrepreneur and activist Amy Ashwood Garvey—wife of prominent Black nationalist Marcus Garvey—was particularly influential. Ashwood Garvey was Jamaican born and lived in the UK from the 1930s to the 1950s, where she launched a newspaper, ran a restaurant and night club, and helped put on theatrical productions. Through her businesses, she created alliances across racial, gender, class, and political boundaries. As a Pan-African activist, Ashwood Garvey worked alongside her husband for multiple social justice and civil rights causes, and like Paulette Nardal, launched a Black organization in the UK in defense of Ethiopia. Ashwood Garvey also built upon African and Caribbean feminist networks and forged connections with white feminists. She met British suffragette Sylvia Pankhurst in 1930 and mentioned her (among others) in her 1953 "The Rise of Woman" address in Barbados, establishing a link across the Atlantic.[30]

Before and after the First World War, white British feminists also made efforts to politically engage women across the UK's colonial holdings. In 1925, for example, the British Commonwealth League, dominated by middle-class white women, formed with the intention to promote women's groups within Commonwealth countries. Their concerns as feminists, however, did not mask their sense of cultural or racial superiority, as exhibited by the aim to "raise the status of women of the less forward races" included in the league's constitution.[31] Indeed, few white British feminists challenged the concept or institution of empire, missing an important opportunity for solidarity. Instead, in another mode of fetishizing colonial bodies, they remained focused on issues like prostitution and "the plight of Indian women" when engaging with women of color.[32] Still in the colonial diasporic communities blooming in Western European metropoles, diverse women from the colonies played an important role in political, cultural, and intellectual life, their contributions shaping feminist thought across the globe.

Maternalism and Interwar Politics

In the interwar period, European women entered the political sphere in new ways. In the aftermath of the First World War, many European nations secured women's right to vote, including Austria, Belorussia, Czechoslovakia, Estonia, Hungary, Ireland, Lithuania, Luxembourg, the Netherlands, Poland, Sweden, and the UK. In Spain and Portugal women had the vote intermittently or only for short periods of time; Spain from 1931 to 1935, for example. Scholars debate which factors most influenced securing women's suffrage: women's wartime work and sacrifices on the home front, engagement on the battlefront, feminist campaigning, or the expansion of mass politics generally. In any case, women built upon both wartime and prewar experiences to engage with formal politics to either advance women's societal positions, social welfare provisions, or both, as they were intrinsically linked. For example, those who had played an active role in volunteer organizations before and during the First World War continued to do so in the interwar period by joining political parties, as philanthropic work had taught them that state-level resources were required to address poverty's realities.[33] However, legal access to the polls did not guarantee equal electoral participation. Despite new political rights, however, many women remained economically and socially marginalized, and found themselves unable to access education, work, and the networks that accompany them.[34]

Suffragettes had envisioned that once women could vote, they would unite across party lines—as voters and as elected officials—to advance women's political agendas. Yet the feminist dream of equal representation in lawmaking and public office was not realized. Women did not even reach 10 percent of elected officials in many initial postwar elections. German women were the most successful, representing 9.6 percent of the National Assembly that drafted the Weimar Constitution in 1919. Despite their low percentages, many women did serve in cabinets across Europe, for example, in Austria (1919), Armenia (1919), Germany (1919), Poland (1919), Latvia (1920), Luxembourg (1919), and Lithuania (1920), with the most representation in Scandinavia and the developing USSR. Social democrat and Marxist Nina Bang became the world's first female cabinet member (outside of the USSR) when she was appointed Minister of Education in Denmark in 1924. However, Bang saw feminism as a distraction from her main concern—class struggle.[35] Bang was not an exception. Many elected women did not want to be seen as feminist or radical and supported a wider range of issues. Likewise, contemporary political parties—liberal, socialist, and conservative—wanted to engage women within their existing party platforms instead of creating new parties or platforms solely around women's issues, and they largely succeeded.[36]

In Eastern European democracies, such as the new state of Romania, governments were more concerned about fighting communism in the wake of the successful Russian Revolution than supporting women's equality. Interwar Romania did have a women's movement, however, which sought legislative protections for women and the right to vote. Dominated by aristocratic and upper-class elites and tied to conservative organizations, these activists were out of touch with the majority of Romanian women who lived in rural agricultural communities where family status, cultural rituals, and kinship gendered social interactions and hierarchies.[37] In addition, women in right-wing groups that had worked with the suffrage movement in the past moved toward maternalist and pronatalist rhetoric in the interwar period. These groups increasingly highlighted the significance of traditional women's roles and argued that women should not compete with men for economic and political opportunities.[38]

The ideology of maternalism thus shaped women's political participation in the 1920s and 1930s more than a commitment to women's equal rights. Maternalism proposes that as mothers, women had a special ability and propensity to help the vulnerable. In the post-suffrage period, women—as citizens, voters, and politicians—were often seen (or strategically chose to frame themselves) primarily as mothers and wives whose main responsibility to society was child-rearing.[39] Politically, they were therefore best suited to address issues of social welfare, family, and others considered to fall within women's interests.[40] Under the influence of maternalism and postwar societal recovery, women moved into the public sphere as volunteers to promote social policies such as marriage and sex counseling, as well as instructions for childcare.[41] In addition to concerns about low birth rates, a rise in venereal disease outbreaks, alcoholism, and crime (especially among youth) prompted states to roll out new social programs and domestic policies. Within parties that accepted female leadership, such as the British Labour Party, women politicians were expected to focus their activities on such social issues as well as labor market questions that primarily affected women and children.[42] British Labour Party officer Marion Phillips, for example, campaigned for male workers and women's unpaid domestic labor, subtly equating them in a 1920 address to women voters: "The Labour Party is the party of the workers and so it realizes the needs of women, for who are workers to such an extent as they? We need shorter hours in the workshop and the factory but still more do we need shorter hours and less anxiety for the woman in the home."[43] While many male citizens believed women should only have an opinion on social or women's issues—in Sweden some argued that women should not vote on temperance when they largely did not themselves drink, for example—maternalist politics became women's main entry into interwar political influence.[44]

Indeed, maternalism and the development of the welfare states in the 1920s and 1930s went hand in hand. In both democracies and fascist states, the Great Depression resulted in millions of unemployed, hungry, and disillusioned citizens who turned to their governments for solutions. Demand for improved state welfare granted women more employment opportunities and political influence. State welfare bureaus were, in a way, a continuation of the work women did during the First World War and as volunteers, and women played key roles in shaping welfare states. Moreover, in an age of pronatalism increasingly paired with eugenics, motherhood was not merely personal but a matter of national concern, placing women squarely in the center of political and public debates.

Thus, women's low percentages as elected officials should not obscure their political impact. As discussed in previous chapters, even before securing the right to vote, women influenced national politics, especially in terms of maternity benefits, family allowances, and family-centered policies.[45] Indeed, women had long been political actors in the public sphere, not only through maternalist social policies but also via significant collective action, as seen with the Berlin food riots during the First World War. Although suffrage changed little for most European women, who continued to lack autonomy in politics and employment, many were politically involved in the interwar period, whether they could vote or not. Women's political interests as well as employment rights increasingly became a topic of public and national debate in an era of mounting anxiety.

Women in the Workforce

Most Western European countries pushed women out of the workforce after the First World War ended, despite the large numbers of widowed and single women dependent on paid employment. Male workers had not found class solidarity with women workers and instead resented and felt threatened by their lower wages (20–50 percent less than men's). To offset employers' urge to replace male workers with cheaper female counterparts, French and German labor unions supported the idea of women's equality. Nevertheless, many men had trouble accepting women as their equals at work, and despite ebbs and flows in the need for women workers, the image of the worker as male persisted in Western Europe.

Indeed, tradition and outright resistance thwarted female competition for what were customarily men's jobs. After the First World War, many Western European and Scandinavian countries granted women equal employment rights in civil service jobs. By 1935, for example, women comprised 25 percent of the UK civil service, though they were still largely concentrated in clerical work. White-collar jobs in clerical, telephone, telegraph, and retail positions became increasingly feminized, or "pink-collar." As such, they were considered respectable, cleaner, and more appropriate than factory work, but these jobs offered low pay, long hours, and often shift work. Women were also expected to quit when they married and were generally excluded from supervisory roles, even if they had done them during the war.

Women did make some strides in the professions, however. In 1918, the UK Education Act raised the age at which students could leave school to fourteen years old, improving not just girls' education but also their career prospects. As more girls completed secondary education, their access to universities enhanced their professional opportunities, especially to become teachers, nurses, and even doctors. In Weimar Germany, women gained a foothold in the medical profession, including professional authority. Pediatrician Marie-Elise Kayser recruited colleagues to support breast milk collection and distribution to infants in need, noting her important influence not just as a physician but as a female doctor for female patients: "It would be particularly easy for us … as female physicians to persuade nursing mothers to cooperate in charity work that creates life-saving medicine for sick infants."[46] Kayser was one of many female doctors who saw themselves as valuable professionals in the 1910s and 1920s, claiming space in organizations and journals within an otherwise unwelcoming field for women. They used their supposedly innate connection to women and children's health to consistently buttress their professional reputations from 1919 to 1945.[47]

The Swedish case demonstrates the push and pull factors impacting women's employment, which was anything but linear in the twentieth century. Women in Scandinavia won the right to vote earlier than those on the Continent, and Swedish political debates about women's employment diverged during the interwar period as well. As in most of Western Europe, Sweden sought to remove women from paid employment immediately after the First World War, even though married women comprised only 10 percent of the Swedish workforce. Policies to fire married women were enacted in the 1920s, only a few years after they had gained equal access to civil servant positions.[48] In support of such policies, one conservative parliamentarian argued that women already had enough work in the home: "Married women who understand their tasks in the home can never be unemployed—there are always socks to mend."[49]

However, Sweden changed course in the 1930s. In 1933, the Swedish Social Democratic Party challenged restrictions on married women's labor, and in 1934, the government denied nine different motions to constrain married women's employment options—in the midst of an economic crisis, no less. In 1937, Parliament passed maternity leave, and in 1938, a commission studying married women's work resulted in a 1939 law stating that employers could no longer fire women upon marriage.[50] The 1939 law was not necessarily intended as a feminist statement though. During an era of pronatalist advocacy, it was a pragmatic decision, as they hoped making marriage for working women more attractive could help raise the national birthrate.

Male-dominated Swedish trade unions also countered restrictions on married women's employment. Yet as with most European labor unions, they were not necessarily feminist or altruistic; the labor market was sex-segregated to the extent that female workers were not in competition with male workers. The unions set job descriptions and corresponding wage categories, which differed by gender, and were not motivated to change this. As Swedish unions gained strength in the 1930s vis-à-vis employers (including bargaining rights), they had the power to fight employers' attempts to pay women less and thus undercut hiring more expensive men. In solidifying their power, male trade unions also subsumed what had previously been female trade unions, decreasing women's representation and leadership considerably.[51] As the Swedish example shows, women's interwar employment rights were rarely rooted in a sense of gender equality and more in service of national concern.

The New Soviet Woman

After the 1921 Bolshevik victory, the new Soviet Union continued its battle to win over the populace. In a nation in which women outnumbered men after the First World War's high death toll, especially in Moscow, state efforts promoted an image of the New Soviet Woman. A confident, independent worker and valuable contributor to the state, the New Soviet Woman was featured in recruitment posters (Figure 3.2) and reinforced through a New Economic Policy (NEP) that—among other things, such as agricultural reforms—wrote the revolution's promises for women's emancipation into law. In addition, divorce and family planning became more accepted, state welfare was (at least partially) available to assist families with childcare and education, and more women were able and encouraged to join the workforce.

The Eastern Europeans who became part of the Soviet Union or its satellite states saw many of the same revolutionary ideas in the 1920s. This meant new educational and career opportunities for women, leading some to work outside of the home for the first time and in new types of jobs. Working women could take advantage of social services such as basic daycare and guaranteed child support in cases of divorce. All who qualified could attend state-controlled universities for free and some women received stipends to help them finish high school first. Czech and Slovak women moved into the civil service, medicine, and university and high school teaching in large numbers, forming the first generation of women professionals.

The ideology of the New Soviet Woman resonated widely. Indeed, for the Soviet revolutionary and feminist Alexandra Kollontai, discussed in the last chapter, the New Soviet Woman was not an idea or a fashion but a fact. She was single, self-reliant, psychologically free, and, of course, fully engaged in modern economic and political life. Reflecting in her diary about how to live as an independent Soviet woman, one of Kollontai's contemporaries concluded that relationships with men would have to wait until the men could offer "comradely love" and not just physical satisfaction.[52]

Unsurprisingly, though, some women got lonely waiting for comradely love, as many Soviet men were not necessarily ready for the New Soviet Women.[53] Neither were employers. As in the West, women were frequently fired and replaced by male veterans, which was both an NEP policy and a preference. In 1923, women were 35.7 percent of workers in Moscow; by 1926, that percentage had dropped to 25.6. Employers were also hostile toward women workers and taunted them verbally, causing some to quit.[54] There was a fundamental tension between encouraging women to hold jobs and to focus on motherhood, as the nation faced both great industrial need and a massive population loss. Thus, the ideology of and contentious response to the New Soviet Women in some ways reflects many of the postwar ideals that did not come to fruition across Europe.

FIGURE 3.2 *"There is no room in our Collective Farm for Priests and Kulaks." Soviet propaganda poster, 1930. Getty Images.*

The New Soviet Woman proved to be a short-lived icon. Lenin died in 1924, prompting a power struggle that ensued until Joseph Stalin emerged as the new general secretary of the party in 1929. Everything changed in the 1930s under Stalin's leadership. He launched a brutal campaign of crash industrialization, collectivized farms, and continued horrific policies begun during the Revolution of punishing and killing dissenters.[55] He also abolished the Zhenotdel (Women's Department of the Central Committee) in 1930, which Kollontai had headed, arguing that it was superfluous. Moreover, officials claimed that women's growing economic and reproductive independence was having dire effects, including the breakdown of the family, a decline in fertility, the abandonment of children, and a rise in alcoholism and teen delinquency. In response, the state tightened its control over family life, including reproduction and gender relations, and encouraged women to return to traditional roles and limit family planning. Stalin passed laws restricting divorce options and outlawing abortion and homosexuality to both promote pronatalism and shore up "family values"—the official party line.[56]

Under Stalin, women had to navigate a new Soviet era, wholly unlike the revolutionary context discussed in the previous chapter. Diaries from the time show citizens grappling with their personal transformations, wondering if they were succeeding in becoming true communists. Seventeen-year-old Evgenia Rudneva reflected on how exactly to become a pure Soviet citizen, and especially what that meant for a girl, writing in 1937, "How can I not love my Fatherland, which gives me such a happy life? ... [What] would I have been, had I been born before the revolution? I would have been an ignorant girl, perhaps already a bride, who would harvest tomatoes in the summer and bake bread in winter."[57] Rudneva's rumination hints that girls expected to live happier, more fulfilling, and emancipated lives after the revolution. Although the regime forced rapid economic, social, and cultural changes, personal changes for women occurred more slowly.

As seen with Rudneva's reflections, Stalin's emphasis on traditional family life did not discourage young women from promoting the party line. On the contrary, young women (and men) were active recruiters for the Soviet state under Stalin. Antonina Solovieva, for example, was assigned by her local communist youth organization branch to promote collectivization and compel farmers to abandon a traditional peasant lifestyle.[58] Her job expanded beyond recruitment and encouragement, however, to include reporting on resisters, grain hording, and retaliatory attacks on machinery. She wrote in her diary in 1930 that her group was quite successful at infiltrating local communities: "Some of us would [arrive unannounced and] ... join the peasant girls at their evening get-togethers. Usually the boys would come, too, and sing quiet songs."[59] Solovieva was valuable to both promote Stalinism and gather intelligence. Solovieva was one of many young women working in the 1930s on behalf of Stalin's aggressive industrial agricultural campaign to modernize the USSR and allow it to compete on an international scale. Yet despite the zeal women expressed as state recruiters or in their private reflections, Soviet society underwent a masculinization that left them in subordinate roles as part of this process.[60] As the ideological dismissal of the New Soviet Woman demonstrates, the hope and opportunities of revolutionary rhetoric fell flat under Stalin's dictatorship—a common experience in Europe as authoritarianism gained political traction in the 1930s.

The Rise of Extremist Politics

As nations buckled under the ongoing strain of the Great Depression, the 1930s saw the ascent of right-wing fascist movements in Europe. Accompanied by pronatalist anxiety and backlash against the modern woman and other avant-garde trends of the 1920s, these movements put the party and a central leader above all else. Fascist leaders espoused traditional gender roles and denounced practices such as family planning and divorce alongside their extreme ethno-nationalist policies. Indeed, the rise of extreme right-wing politics used women as a basis for their attacks, curtailing women's participation in both political and economic life and recentering it on maternalism and pronatalism to suit the state. At the same time, fascist family, work, and racial policies (in Germany, Italy, and Romania, for example) provided some women with new opportunities even while severely restricting the lives of others.

The development of welfare states in these nations took on new political importance within this context. Welfare provided a way for right-wing parties to attract women, gain political consensus, and thwart unrest. All interwar states—fascist, democratic, and communist alike—made it clear that having children was a patriotic duty, and right-wing fascist groups touted their support for women through domestic policies designed to support families, especially mothers, and housewives—the roles they thought most productive for women. In Italy, the birthplace of fascism, welfare programs promoted the National Fascist Party with initiatives in which Mussolini urged all Italians to wage a "battle for births."[61] Holding a romantic view of Italy that praised peasant women as strong and fertile, the pronatalist campaigns allowed access to a larger community of people, such as in rural or poorer homes, and allowed women to play more active roles.[62] Additionally, Italian women had become accustomed to making personal sacrifices for the state—a key tenant of fascism—for example when they were encouraged to donate their weddings rings so the metal could be used for bullets during the invasion of Ethiopia (1935).[63] Many women found that their wartime experiences and nationalist beliefs merged when governments began to count on women's volunteer labor to instate programs such as sewing workshops, teaching childcare to teenaged girls, visiting pregnant women, distributing vegetable seeds and powdered baby formula, and running children's camps and nurseries.[64] While volunteers may not have seen themselves as overtly political, they furthered political aims with their work by preparing women and girls for their "maternal mission."[65] Moreover, as this example demonstrates, when women did find agency, autonomy, and authority under fascism (or in other authoritarian states such as the USSR), it was only really over other women. By conducting home visits as volunteers or social workers, fascist women taught skills infused with state ideology, such as childcare, health, and sanitation, while acting as the state's conduit into private homes.

Women's newfound authority also expanded into public political life as well. Fasci Femminili (Female Groups), the women's wing of the National Fascist Party, was able to work autonomously, organize their own conferences, and lobby for a mix of feminist and patriotic interests, such as the right to vote.[66] Although most male leaders did not take much notice of Fasci Femminili, fascist women also secured seats in provincial government bodies for the first time during this era. In sum, despite their circumscribed roles, millions of women joined Italy's fascist party and influenced the fascist state and women's roles and engagement with it.

In France, fascism gained strength but did not unify into a central party. "La Solidarité Française" (French Solidarity) formed in 1933 as both a fascist and paramilitary organization. Solidarity's women's sections recruited actively, and fascist Frenchwomen joined their male counterparts in radical action, such as taking part in the anti-Parliament riots in Paris on February 6, 1934, organized by various far-right groups. Lucienne Blondel was the most visible woman in French Solidarity as a leader and as a writer who contributed to a weekly column. She campaigned for women's right to vote but believed that depopulation was a more pressing issue.[67] Blondel cautioned: "France is dying of depopulation ... in thirty or forty years its population will be half of what it was before the war."[68] Blondel's politics were aligned with French policy that had long supported pronatalism. In 1920, the legislature passed harsh measures that criminalized abortion and birth control education with prison terms and fines. France also gave gold medals for women who bore ten children, and silver and bronze for fewer.[69] Insisting that women desired "to have children, make health, beauty, and elegance reign in their home," Blondel and other fascist women argued that women not only preferred motherhood and domesticity but also that the nation's future depended on it.[70]

There was a great paradox in right-wing fascist groups and how they utilized women. On the one hand, they promoted separate spheres in which women maintained a romanticized traditional lifestyle of caring for the home, children, their husbands, and by extension, the nation with its accompanying patriarchal structure. This included demonizing the modern woman with misogynist politics and rhetoric, such as Adolf Hitler's warning that the New Woman would thwart a modern state's potential with their degenerate, promiscuous ways.[71] On the other hand, women who supported fascist states and organizations did so by working outside of the home and in new leadership positions or in jobs similar to men, often under universalizing principles such as national service. In Nazi Germany, national service was mandatory for women and men but took different forms, with women's ad hoc programs in support of larger goals such as mass mobilization of the population, aligning the state and society, and mobilizing for war.[72]

A famous historical debate between two historians of Germany, Claudia Koonz and Gisela Bock, reflects this paradoxical relationship between women and fascism. Namely, were these women actors and agents who gained influence, professionalism, and leadership roles within the fascist states or were they state subjects whose lives were restricted and controlled?[73] Could fascism be feminist by offering ambitious women leadership and political outlets? Their activities were limited and always within the party's line of restricted roles for women, but they were also active leaders, operating with autonomy in a modern political organization. Such contradictions shaped women's participation in fascist and other extremist political movements in the interwar period.

Eugenics, Racial Nationalism, and the Nazi Regime

In Nazi Germany, fascism linked racism and sexism.[74] Drawing on eugenics, scientific racism, and theories of "racial hygiene," the Nazi state sought to create and preserve a national gene pool for what they believed would be a "superior race." Regulating reproduction was thus an essential task, implemented through pronatalist policies for women deemed "racially fit" and extreme, often deadly, measures for those deemed "unworthy of living."[75] Special hereditary health courts passed judgement on who could reproduce, with geneticists, psychiatrists, and anthropologists mandating an estimated 400,000 sterilizations. Tubal ligation was the most common method used on women, and the invasive procedure resulted in the deaths of hundreds of women.[76] Pronatalism and anti-natalism worked hand in hand in this context: the state compelled the "right women" to give birth while preventing "threats to humanity" from reproducing, via sterilization and eventually mass murder.[77]

The year 1932 marked a low point in the international birthrate, prompting many countries to blame women for a "birth strike" and invest in pronatalist programs that took eugenics seriously.[78] Eugenicists—on both the left and the right—believed they could and should produce "better" humans through social policies.[79] In Hungary and Czechoslovakia, for example, ideas about "national fitness" led to patriotic sports associations. More ominously, Germany and counterparts across Europe from Spain to Scandinavia to the USSR promoted racial hygiene—the idea that racial "purity" could be achieved by preventing "inferior" races from propagating coupled with positive policies to encourage fitness, and even compulsory motherhood, for the "desirable." The Russian Eugenics Office, founded in 1921, spearheaded collaboration with the US Eugenic Record Office, the German Society for Race and Social Biology, and the British Eugenics Education Society to fashion their ideal nations.[80] Thus, the Nazi regime was not alone in attempting to engineer their society.

Eugenicists believed in racial deterioration and thought they could impact evolution toward the fittest population. Nineteenth-century ideas of scientific racism, seen in the first chapter, used naïve pseudoscientific beliefs to initiate Social Darwinism into state policies, even in purportedly democratic nations, centered on women as the "mothers of the race."[81] The new state of Romania, which boasted vast ethnic heterogeneity, defined citizenship in its 1923 constitution without regard to ethnic, linguistic, or religious differences.[82] Even so, pseudoscientific ideas about "racially defined" ethnicity and the growing popularity of eugenics movements served to sharpen the blurred lines of who exactly belonged. Racial nationalists and eugenics supporters sought sterilization for some and pronatalism for others, and published articles chastising and cautioning Romanian women against miscegenation, for example, marrying Hungarian men. The government soon joined in the campaign to regulate women's bodies, passing restrictive measures such as criminalizing abortion, but with one notable exception— to prevent passing on hereditary defects.[83]

The implementation of such ideas about "racial purity" peaked in Nazi Germany. The Nazi revolution was driven by a need for "racial purity" that centered on the intersection of sex and race, through reproduction on the one hand, and sterilization and death on the other. In a progressive timeline, Hitler used legal means to slowly develop his racial nation. In 1933, Hitler passed the Law for the Prevention of Hereditarily Diseased Offspring, among other laws, to order the sterilization of those with certain psychiatric or physical conditions, hereditary illnesses such as epilepsy or blindness, criminal records, or undesirable politics.[84] In 1935, the Marital Health Law banned marriages between people considered "hereditarily healthy" and those deemed unfit. At the same time, the Nazi government opened the first concentration camps, starting with Dachau outside of Munich in 1933, to great fanfare in the press.[85] In 1935, the Nuremberg Laws formally denied all Jewish Germans their rights as citizens and established racial segregation, in ways that affected men and women differently as seen in the next chapter. Such laws restricting German Jews from social, economic, and cultural participation led to what historian Marion Kaplan has termed a "slow social death."[86]

Nazi laws began redefining an "Aryan" woman's responsibility to the state as well. Beginning in 1933, abortion was illegal for "racially pure" women, and by 1935, doctors and midwives had to notify the state in all cases of miscarriage for investigation. "Aryan" women with low birth rates were vilified and accused of "racial suicide." The 1935 Law on the Unification of the Health Care System established a network of heath care institutions as instruments of pronatalist Nazi policies, which included maintaining some Weimar initiatives, such as breast milk collection sites. German medical professionals lent eugenic and antisemitic policies legitimacy by endorsing the necessity of "cleansing" German society of threats to the folk's "racial body."[87]

"In my state, the mother is the most important citizen," Hitler declared in a speech on September 8, 1934.[88] Indeed, his government reinforced this priority with programs intended to prepare German women and girls to ideologically, socially, and physically serve the Reich. The German Girls' League (part of the Hitler Youth organization) was compulsory for all girls starting at age fourteen. Girls had to complete a year of farm or domestic service under the training of female guardians. The German Girls' League merged propaganda with leisure activities such as hiking, dancing, and song recitals that emphasized "national socialist values," comradeship, sacrifice, and duty—especially as wives and mothers.[89] Likewise, the Mother and Child Relief Agency (part of the National Socialist People's Welfare Organization or Reich Mothers' Service of German Women's Enterprise) offered courses on topics such as pregnancy, child rearing, housekeeping, and racial hygiene to girls and women alike (Figure 3.3). Like the German Girls' League, these initiatives were meant to encourage women to accept the roles of housewife and mother as their primary calling and strengthen the national community both ideologically and demographically. The organization also offered medical care and financial support to pregnant women and ran kindergartens to provide childcare. Such material benefits drew in many women who needed the support, whether they believed in the mission or not.

Nazi Germany was thus divided into a rigid hierarchy of "valuable life" versus "valueless life." The Nazi state endorsed motherhood and housework for "Aryan" women and sterilization and forced labor for those deemed racially "unfit" or "morally deviant." This hierarchy promoted social control and cohesion by purging "undesirables" from state welfare, the economy, and the society, ultimately resulting in mass incarceration and systematic execution.[90]

Conclusion

In the interwar period, women across Europe navigated a shifting cultural and political landscape. Some took on modern fashions and lifestyles, while the field of sexology turned a medical—and eugenic—gaze toward women's sexuality. Many seized new forms of political authority in meaningful but also purely symbolic ways, as the Modern Woman generated considerable backlash and maternalism shaped the boundaries of women's political participation. Indeed, a central contradiction in this chapter was how women both took on further public roles while also often supporting a return to traditional domesticity after the upheaval of the First World War.

FIGURE 3.3 *House of the German Mother, Elgersburg. Girls being prepared for their later role as mothers in Elgersburg, Thuringa, 1930. Getty Images.*

Moreover, responses to the Great Depression led to increased state planning and welfare, firmer racial and ethnic boundaries, and new ways to regulate and police women and their bodies. The overlapping identities of gender and class, and the conflicts between them, were particularly prominent during the economic crisis of the 1930s. At the same time, class distinctions between women softened as nationalist, communist, and eugenicist ideas hardened and led to a rise in extremist politics and authoritarian states. As scientific racism gained authority and state power, women's rights, protections, and reproduction became grounds for national debates and eugenic policies that were both pro- and anti-natalist, with fatal consequences. These changes and continuities provide important context for the gendered impacts of authoritarianism, the Second World War, and the Holocaust—subjects of the next chapter.

4

The Second World War and the Holocaust

Introduction

In 2021, France awarded Josephine Baker its highest honor by inducting her into the French Pantheon, the national mausoleum of heroes. Baker was the first entertainer and the first Black woman to be inducted.[1] Fleeing Jim Crow persecution in the United States, Josephine Baker moved to France in 1925 at the age of nineteen and became one of Europe's most celebrated artists, known for her singing, dancing, and provocative costumes. She was a member of the Paris intellectual and artistic elite, married a Frenchman, and became a French citizen in 1937, embracing France as her new homeland.[2] In 1939, when France declared war on Germany, Baker was recruited to work as a secret agent, conveying information about Axis troop movements to the Allies.[3] Speaking of her decision to join the French Resistance, she declared her passion for France: "The people of Paris … have given me their hearts. … I am ready, captain, to give them my life."[4]

As an international celebrity who performed abroad and entertained soldiers at the front, Baker could easily travel between the Vichy regime and the free zone in the south of France, as well as throughout Europe and North Africa.[5] She was often invited to diplomatic parties at the British, Belgian, and French embassies, where she eavesdropped for information useful to the French Resistance.[6] Baker made careful notes that she pinned to her underwear, confident that no one would search her and wrote secret messages in invisible ink in the margins of performance scores headed for London.[7] She also hid weapons, resistance fighters, and Jewish refugees in her Paris home.[8] After the war, France awarded Baker the Resistance Medal, the *Croix de Guerre*, and the Legion of Honor. Significantly, when she spoke in Washington DC at the 1963 March on Washington for Jobs and Freedom, she wore her French Resistance uniform with her medals across her breast. Baker not only impacted the war, but also the idea of who a French hero could be—in the middle of a genocidal race war.

This chapter delves into the complexity of women's lives during the Second World War, when the divides between traditional male and female roles and between civilians and combatants blurred in unprecedented ways. Often challenging gendered expectations, European women contributed on the home front and the battle front, took on both hidden and visible roles, and were both the persecuted and perpetrators. As seen in the previous chapter, different ideologies and belief systems—communism, fascism, liberalism, Catholicism, and Judaism—as well as class, race and ethnicity, also informed women's choices and constraints. Their experiences on the various sides of the war and in its immediate aftermath highlight women's commonalities and their differences.

The first part of the chapter explores women's new prominence at home and in combat. European women had essential roles as both noncombatants and combatants, commanding tank battalions, piloting bombing missions, and serving alongside men as nurses and auxiliaries. They worked in food production, provided first aid in emergency centers, and helped evacuate millions of children. Women like Josephine Baker—as well as those with far less cultural cachet—played key parts in formal and informal espionage and cracked crucial enemy codes with some of the world's first computers. Their labor and cunning were essential to the war effort, yet women's participation in wartime activities was inspiring for some and jarring and problematic for others.

Next, the chapter centers Nazi Germany and the Holocaust—a topic both separate from and intricately intertwined with the history of the Second World War. Considering women's distinct Holocaust experiences, this section addresses the gendered problems and trauma in extreme situations when faced with impossible choices for survival. Some women—Jews and non-Jews alike—resisted Nazi genocide and occupation in armed and organized groups as well as in more subtle ways. At the same time, women were also perpetrators of extreme violence both in official roles in Nazi camps and as civilians acting on their own accord. Resisters, survivors, and perpetrators all negotiated gendered spaces and positions during the Holocaust.

The chapter ends with a look at the war's final days and the first weeks of postwar Germany, when women's rebuilding efforts and a shift to a majority-female population generated a "crisis of masculinity." Finally, it questions when the war truly ended, as sexual violence persisted in the form of a widespread Soviet military rape campaign, while Holocaust survivors remained unmoored in Displaced Persons camps and would continue to reckon with the era's trauma throughout their lives.

European Women at War

Across Europe, the Second World War forced women to take on more prominent roles in the workplace, the war effort, and within their own families and communities. Although there were some commonalities among European women's wartime experiences, contrasting combatant nations and those occupied in the West versus those occupied in the East reveals significant differences as well. Moreover, as seen with the First World War, historians are divided on whether or not the war accentuated the boundaries between men and women's roles—merely interrupting prewar gender relations—or radically altered them in lasting ways.[9] Regardless, the war certainly changed women's daily lives for the duration.

Women on the home front became more economically and emotionally self-sufficient as they took over as heads of households, breadwinners, and protectors of property and children.[10] A commonality among many (though to varying degrees) was the challenge of managing their households under the constraints of rationing and shortages, similar to the First World War. Securing scarce ingredients, learning to utilize or preserve rations, and finding new recipes to maximize protein and other nutritional needs, while also seeking normalcy and maintaining traditions was a time-consuming effort.[11] When Britain was preparing for possible invasion in 1940, the Chiefs of Staff Committee addressed the significance of these tasks, using an image of the home to project a positive outlook and emphasizing that women's service relied on keeping their households running without their menfolk.[12]

Despite the persistence of such gendered ideologies, many women left their homes during the Second World War. Indeed, as mass deployment increased the need for workers, one consistency across combatant and occupied countries was the desire for women to provide cheap labor to support the war effort. In addition to running homes, cultivating food, and managing rations, many European women moved into full-time employment. They took jobs they had held during the First World War, such as nursing and clerical work, as well as new ones traditionally reserved for men, including carpentry, mechanical and electrical work, welding, telegraphy, policing, delivering mail, flying transport planes, and driving buses, ambulances, and fire engines.[13] By 1943, almost 90 percent of single women and 80 percent of married women in the UK were working in factories, on the land, or in the armed forces. While poor and working-class women had always worked, middle-class women more often held uncompensated charity positions or helped their husbands in family businesses. Wartime employment, both full-time work and traditionally male labor, was a cultural shift for many of these women.

In Nazi Germany, women of all ages, education levels, and classes faced a similar paradox. National Socialist ideology championed their role as unpaid caregivers (i.e., mothers and housewives) but also relied on women to work low-wage factory jobs in the nation's drive for full employment.[14] In 1943, the German Law for the Defense of the Reich required all women between the ages of seventeen and forty-five to work unless they were pregnant, worked in agriculture or health care, had a child under the age of six, or two or more children under the age of fourteen. (In 1944, the age range for women workers was extended to fifty years old.[15]) Likewise, as seen in the previous chapter, fascist Italy also outwardly supported traditional gender roles, yet women were prominent in factories and in public administration offices by 1943. States used their ideology to maximize women's double burden to their advantage, casting housework as a recreational break from assembly lines and family life as a sustaining motivator—a pattern emphasized even more during the postwar period, as will be seen in the next chapter.

In reality, though, there could be no "break" from war. The Second World War blurred the lines between the battle front and home front, between civilian and combatants, as the total war disregarded long-observed rules about who could be attacked. Aerial bombings put ordinary citizens on the frontlines, ravaging towns, destroying housing, and killing civilians at a higher rate than combatants. Both the Axis and the Allies engaged in strategic bombings of cities to not just disrupt industry and war production, but to also unsettle civilian life and undermine morale. In 1940, the German military bombed Britain for seventy-eight straight nights during the "Blitz," killing or wounding more than 100,000 civilians. On the Eastern Front, the Nazis declared that all civilians could be potential "partisans" (active conspirators, resistors, and saboteurs) and were therefore also combatants to be killed—women, children, and the elderly included. For instance, on October 10, 1941, field marshal Walter Von Reichenau sent a top-secret correspondence to Army Command stating that his troops were not taking their task of eliminating the "Jewish-Bolshevistic system" seriously enough; as an example, he noted that "unnatural women" were being taken prisoners of war instead of achieving "complete annihilation."[16]

Allied bombing raids preceded the 1944 land invasion on the German home front, intensifying in 1943 to kill about 400,000 German civilians, destroy 70 percent of housing, and leave 20 million homeless at the war's end.[17] Käthe Ricken was a young mother at the time, and recounted in her diary what life was like under the bombs and ensuing destruction in Hamburg, the site of a massive incendiary bombing campaign: "Some of the men who had gone outside ... told us that the whole of Hamburg was blazing like a torch. I held little Wolfgang close and just prayed to get out of that hell-hole alive."[18] In the bombing's aftermath, Ricken saw corpses littering the streets and was forced to live with her son in an apartment with no water, gas, or electricity: "I can't cook or wash, so the nappies can't be kept clean. I threw them in a nearby stream just to be rid of the smell. Now I'm having to cut up my own underwear for nappies."[19]

The lines between civilian and military employment were also blurred during the war as many European women worked in official military capacities. The British Auxiliary Territorial Service (ATS), established in 1938 as a women's branch of the British army, began employing women in clerical and driving positions but soon expanded their roles. Even so, women's labor was valued lower than men's, impacting their compensation and the institution of other discriminatory practices. Marian Orley of the Women's Auxiliary Air Force (WAAF) commented on the sexism in her job: "I began to get a bee in my bonnet about equal pay. I was posted to [the] Air Ministry Signals ... There were about twenty telephone operators on the switchboard—men and women. The NCO [noncommissioned officer] in charge of the watch was a woman sergeant and she was paid less than an ordinary airman on the switchboard."[20]

The British war effort relied on women across the empire, recruiting not just from the UK but also from the Dominions, India, and the Caribbean. One hundred West Indian women volunteered to serve in Britain during the Second World War.[21] The ATS allowed Black women to join after the Colonial Office requested a nondiscriminatory policy to both meet growing personnel demands and improve relations between Britain and the Caribbean. Figure 4.1 depicts Lance Corporal Adina Henrietta Williams, a nurse from British Guiana who worked as a mechanic repairing vehicles, smiling at the camera through a mirror for an official photo in 1942. The image was clearly meant to present a positive, inclusive view of women in the British military. Figure 4.2 shows a West Indian detachment of the ATS arriving at camp in an army car in November 1943, smartly dressed in uniform with mixed expressions of anticipation and excitement. Ena Collymore Woodstock's daughter recalled her mother's wartime experience abroad: "When they got there, they had them typing. ... [but she] didn't come to England to type; she wanted to be in the war."[22]

Indeed, women from throughout British colonial holdings actively participated in the war effort. In May 1942, the British Women's Auxiliary Corps (India) allowed Indian women to join the military in nonmedical roles for the first time, now permitted to work as typists, switchboard operators, and drivers anywhere the Indian army was posted.[23] Around 5,000 ATS enlistees served in the Middle East, 80 percent of whom were locally recruited. Women across the empire worked in factories to produce essential weapons and textiles as well as in positions of manual labor such as farming, road work, and even mining.[24] Such war practices transgressed gender and societal norms but did not translate into structural change, especially within an immutable imperial context. Although recruiting from colonial holdings was meant to reinforce the idea of Britain as the motherland, wartime experiences and training helped to prepare the future leaders of postcolonial nations.[25]

European women played crucial roles in military intelligence as well. From the 1920s until Hitler's defeat, the German military relied on an encoding device called an Enigma Machine, which allowed for billions of ways to encode a message. Cryptologists in Poland analyzed the German code and were eventually able to replicate and share their findings with France and Britain before the war started.[26] In Bletchley Park, 50 miles north-west of London, over 10,000 men and women, military and civilian, worked as code breakers for decades, sworn to secrecy and hiding their participation

FIGURE 4.1 *"Ready for ATS Parade."* Lance Corporal Adina Williams of the British Auxiliary Territorial Service (ATS) gets ready for a parade on October 26, 1942. Getty Images.

FIGURE 4.2 *West Indian ATS Recruits of the British Auxiliary Territorial Service arrive at camp in an army car, Britain, 1943. Getty Images.*

from friends and family.[27] Joan Clarke was an English cryptanalyst and numismatic expert who became an expert decoder of the German naval Enigma Machine. Though she started in clerical work, Clarke soon showed her expertise and was promoted to one of the few women codebreakers at Bletchley. Having been invited by her former geometry professor, she arrived at Bletchley on June 17, 1940, and by June 18 she had cracked her first code. Clarke cracked two more on June 22 and 26. Previously breaking such codes had taken around two weeks.[28]

At Bletchley, women in the Women's Royal Naval Service (WRNS), Women's Auxiliary Air Force (WAAF), or Auxiliary Territorial Service (ATS) also accounted for 75 percent of the clerical staff. Women hired for clerical work were typists, clerks, secretaries, and telephone and teleprinter operators, while others worked as translators, cryptanalysis, and record officers. Those skilled in Morse code had to build up a fluency of speed and accuracy. While the hiring process did not consider class distinctions, some women recalled class tensions at work: "Many of the girls recruited early were debs [debutantes] … Some were very grand and not at all friendly. Also, they smoked endlessly and often blew it at us." Despite such resentments, all worked at an intense pace, covering 24-hour shifts to decode, translate, collate, and forward messages as quickly as possible.[29]

As historian Janet Abbate notes, these women were founders of computer science. They were recruited to fill male positions at a crucial period in the development of computing, and many women were fascinated by the new work. Eleanor Ireland, for example, was transfixed when she first saw the Colossus, a large set of computers used for codebreaking: "All these whirring tapes ... and the noise of it all ... I was fascinated by it ... I thought, now *that's* where I'd like to be, not doing the other things. I wanted to be on *that* machine."[30] Prospective coders took placement tests that determined which machines they could operate, yet Ireland recalled that men and women were treated differently. Female coders had to march and do drills after working all night on machines and were burdened with additional housekeeping and low-level administrative tasks, none of which was expected of male coders.[31] Still, codebreaking was exciting work that exposed women to new forms of intellectual stimulation and freedom and enabled them to invent novel professions as the science of digital computing took shape.

The total war engaged European women on all fronts. As in the First World War, large numbers served in military hospitals and other medical capacities. They also fought in all branches of the military for different countries: 225,000 women served in the British army; 450,000 to 500,000 in the American army; 500,000 in the German army; and about 1 million in the Soviet army.[32] In fascist Italy, the government called on women to enlist on April 14, 1944 and 6,000 joined the Female Auxiliary Service.[33] Many of these women took on roles previously considered "men's jobs," and new titles had to be invented in languages that offered no female form for "machine gunner," "infantryman," or "tank driver."[34] Public opinion was divided on whether or not women should be in armed combat, but even noncombatant military positions put them in harm's way; they could be fired upon while manning search lights or in other supporting roles.[35]

In the Soviet Union, the 1941 Nazi invasion killed millions and almost captured Moscow, creating a military crisis. In this context, the Soviet Union recruited women into combat with a new fervor. Soviet women were heavily involved in combat as medical assistants, snipers, machine gunners, commanders of antiaircraft guns, and sappers (military engineers). Many had come to think of themselves as soldiers in the 1930s under Stalin and saw the German invasion as a chance to realize the notions of violence and modern womanhood they had merely conceived of during the previous decade. Indeed, historian Anna Krylova has argued that the Soviets "re-gendered" civic combat duty by presenting it as part of the social collective and including women in a new way.[36] The Soviet press featured encouraging stories of women, who, for example, did not need to prove combat readiness after graduating from horseback riding school, where they learned to vault and slash a saber.[37]

After she learned her father had been killed in action, Valentina Pavlovna Chudayeva of Siberia developed a patriotic urge to fight, asserting, "To die was too easy; you had to do something. To act. Thousands of people felt the same."[38] Pavlovna Chudayeva appealed to her division's commander, who arrived to find her with a heavy submachine gun hanging from her thin neck. She told him she wanted to shoot, and he allowed it.[39] Pavlovna Chudayeva was sent to an antiaircraft regiment and was terrified, feeling like the planes were headed right for her: "[It was] not really a young girl's job."[40] She returned from the front permanently disabled. Another Soviet soldier, Nadezhda Vasilyevna Anisimova, was a medical assistant in a machine gun company and recalled that "death was always close." One morning, she rescued a wounded man who had been left in no man's land, using a belt to drag him for 8 hours to safety. Anisimova was awarded a medal for her courage.[41] By 1944, official Soviet military language described women combat soldiers as "exemplary fearless soldiers of the Red Army," moving away from language of female sacrifice and other gendered stereotypes.[42] In this way, the context of the war allowed them to capitalize on the ideologies of gender equality and patriotism.

Conversely, the spyscape of the Second World War often required that women utilize more traditional gender stereotypes and expectations, as female spies were believed to pass more easily as civilian and thus avoid detection.[43] While Josephine Baker might be an extraordinary example due to her celebrity, ordinary women also played integral roles as spies, gathering and couriering information and weapons, hiding resistors, training in armed and unarmed combat, and "passing" as civilians or adopting alternate identities. In the world of espionage, "spy wives" (the wives of spies) also gathered significant information living alongside their husbands within the covert spaces of intelligence operations. Wives' actions could support or threaten their husbands' work as spies and their lives were often equally endangered, whether they knew it or not.[44]

A female spy's greatest disguise was "performing femininity" and drawing on perceptions of women as apolitical noncombatants. A 1944 British Special Operations file commented on women's utility as spies: "Girl couriers were used extensively, because it was a fact that women were rarely stopped at controls ... They provided excellent cover for their movements about the country by visiting friends ... [and] shopping."[45] Nancy Wake, a member of the French Resistance and a British Special Operations Executive, is perhaps the most well-known female spy. Wake was trained in killing techniques, traversed the Pyrenees, parachuted into Nazi-occupied France, conducted dangerous sabotage missions, and cycled over 300 miles in 72 hours through enemy territory, posing as a housewife out shopping.[46] In a 1999 interview, Wake commented, "What you've got to remember is that I was just a normal young woman."[47]

European women took on essential roles in their families, communities, and nations during the Second World War. They resourcefully maintained their households under the strain of shortages, rationing, absent men, and consistent danger. They worked in factories and military outposts, became crucial codebreakers and spies, and fought and died alongside men in combat.

Whether or not these experiences led to enduring postwar freedoms, women challenged traditional gender ideologies with labor and ingenuity that was indispensable to the war effort.

Women and the Holocaust

Scholars have debated the appropriateness of discussing a women's Holocaust history. One faction argues that the constructed racial category of "Jew" trumps distinctions between men, women, and children's experiences and worry that focusing on gender over "race"—what happened to Jews as a group—undermines the specificity of the Holocaust as primarily and uniquely antisemitic.[48] Placing the history of the Holocaust within a larger narrative of women's and gender history, they believe, could center other threads, themes, actors, and victims. Some even accused feminist Holocaust scholars of appropriating Holocaust history to pursue the feminist aim of researching female oppression by patriarchal societies across time.[49] In contrast, other scholars are concerned about the erasure of women and their marginalization within broader Holocaust narratives. They argue that gender-neutral statements privilege male experiences and do not allow space for accounts specific to women.[50]

It is indisputable that Nazi policies targeted Jewish people as a "race" regardless of gender. It is also clear, however, that Jewish women had unique experiences in the Holocaust—experiences that, as historian Marion Kaplan has argued, could mark the difference between life and death. Due to stress and insufficient nutrition, many women stopped menstruating or did so irregularly—neither of which necessarily prevented pregnancy. Pregnancy and childbirth were dangerous, often unpredictable, and even illegal for Jewish and other women deemed racially undesirable such as Roma and Sinti (as seen in the last chapter). Even in an emergency, a pregnant Jewish woman might fear medical aid or hospitals. In addition, some Jewish women who went into hiding tried to blend in as nannies or servants, but few mothers attempted this, knowing their chances of surviving with their children were slim to none.[51] Motherhood was also deadly in Nazi camps, as prisoners were selected for either work or death upon arrival. Pregnant women and mothers of small children were some of the first groups immediately designated for killing because they were considered "incapable of work." And older women in general were more likely to die during the Holocaust precisely because they were both women and of advanced age. In these and many other ways gender permeated Holocaust history. Moreover, since many women kept diaries of their experiences, they played an invaluable role in documenting it.

Patriarchal systems broke down as antisemitic policies progressed during the 1930s and into the 1940s, and German Jewish women took on roles that were novel for any German woman at that time: procuring paid employment to take over as the breadwinner, selling their homes and properties, and seeking new places to move for refuge.[52] Since women were often tasked with shopping for families, they were frequently in the public sphere when being there was incredibly dangerous.[53] When the government began to ration food, Jewish Germans received less, paid more, and had their shopping limited to certain stores and eventually to just one hour per day. Shoppers faced long lines and shortages and the list of forbidden foods for Jews grew, and women were disproportionally impacted by halting fabric sales and the closing of public laundries. When it was no longer safe for Jewish men to be outside, negotiating for return of property, delaying deportation, and other tasks that involved confronting German authorities fell to Jewish women. Any of these dealings risked beatings, arrest, or deportation.[54]

Indeed, Jewish women were not spared any physical violence. As Nazi authorities began evicting Jews from their homes to be relocated to crowded *Judenhäuser* (Jewish houses), the Gestapo abandoned taboos against hurting women and the elderly, kicking, slapping, and punching women of all ages. In 1942, Gestapo agents attacked women between the ages of seventy and eighty-five in Dresden's Jewish nursing home.[55] Sexualized violence was also more prominent against women of multiple communities, who continually risked sexual humiliation, brutality, and rape.

Gender also shaped life in the hundreds of "ghettos" created to force Jewish citizens from their homes and into concentrated urban areas in German-occupied Eastern Europe. Ghettos varied widely in their construction, duration, isolation, size, restrictions, and governance, but overcrowding and scarce resources invariably led to hunger and disease. Many women and girls sought out male partners and engaged in clandestine marriages to avoid facing their situations alone, and some turned to sex work for survival.[56] Women also knew that they could barter sex for a chance at survival for themselves or their families, to escape deportation, or to obtain food when facing starvation.

Just as women were activists within Jewish communities before the war, they also took on leadership and administrative positions within the ghettos, doing what they could to help their neighbors survive. Jewish women worked in soup kitchens, which were covert hubs for youth movements, meetings, secret schools, and also provided access to food and other valuable commodities.[57] Additionally, they served as nurses, doctors, and midwives in ghetto hospitals where they also struggled unsuccessfully to contain the epidemics that plagued ghettos.[58] Countless women risked their lives to help the resistance by transporting information, passports, people, and weapons in and out of the ghettos.[59]

Although women had been targeted and taken prisoner in previous wars, the systematic killing of unarmed civilians, including women and children, marked Nazi Germany's military campaign as distinct. The progression of concentration camps (open since Dachau's founding in 1933), labor camps, and finally extermination camps after the 1942 Wannsee Conference articulated the "Final Solution"—total annihilation of European Jewry and others who did not fit into the Nazi racial state—demonstrating the evolution of a larger race war. Germany's 1941 invasion of the Soviet Union encapsulates this war for race and space as envisioned by the ideology of *Lebensraum*—a living space for the "superior German race." Special *Einstazgruppen* (mobile killing units) followed on the heels of the military, killing all Jewish citizens without exception and often those deemed "partisans" (active conspirators, resistors, and saboteurs).[60] Jewish women and children were separated from men. *Einsatzgruppen* were unsure at first if women and children were included in their orders, but Schutzstaffel (SS) leader Heinrich Himmler assured them in an October 1943 speech that Jewish children must be killed so they could not grow up and attack Germany's sons and grandsons.[61] The SS also charged police units, soldiers, and local collaborators with killing civilians, including women, children, and the elderly.[62] In Pripyat, Ukraine, for example, Heinrich Himmler gave orders to clear out marshes where "partisans" were hiding, commanding, "All Jews must be shot. Drive the women into the swamps."[63]

Photo documentation, ostensibly taken by German officials (and later collected as part of the Main Commission for the Investigation of Nazi War Crimes), shows naked pregnant women, some with babies in their arms, being herded to a mass grave were they would be shot into by Ukrainian auxiliary police. *Einsatzgruppen* also killed at short range, including women and babies (see Figure 4.3). This mode of killing was also gendered, as there were more women left on the home front, especially the elderly who could not easily migrate, and those who stayed behind to care for family members.[64]

In other occupied countries in Eastern Europe, Nazis beat and sometimes killed politically affiliated women, including federal and state parliamentarians.[65] Jewish and non-Jewish women alike were targeted *as women*, their experiences both gendered and sexualized. When the German army invaded Poland in 1939, they sought to distinguish between Poles and ethnic Germans in the historically ethnically mixed region, criminalizing sexual relations between the two groups and even forbidding friendships. Despite these regulations, German men often sexually assaulted Polish women and, later in the war, German military authorities established brothels where Polish women were forced to serve men who fought for the Reich.[66] These women's diverse experiences demonstrate the value of considering Holocaust's history through women's experiences.

Resistance

The Holocaust was not hidden and resistance against the Nazi state and its actions took many forms. Scholars find resistance hard to define, with some counting only organized armed resistance and others including passive

FIGURE 4.3 Einsatzgruppen *soldier murders Jewish mother and child, Ivanhood, Ukraine, 1942. Getty Images.*

everyday acts. Women were engaged in both, as petitioners, letter writers, soldiers in underground armies, and as saboteurs—against military action as well as the genocide of the Holocaust. Jewish women across Europe—in towns, ghettos, and camps—engaged in both armed and unarmed resistance when and how they could, including mutual aid, morale-building cultural activities, underground operations, religious life, procuring food and supplies, and helping people hide and escape.[67]

Resistors and those engaged in opposition activities existed on all sides of the war; Jewish and Germans alike participated, including German teenager Ria Bröring. Seventeen years old when the war started, Bröring kept a diary that offers invaluable insight into everyday experiences during the Holocaust. On April 23, 1942, Bröring noted that she "once again" saw columns of Jews suffering, struggling, and collapsing, referring to the long, lethal "death marches" that Nazi prisoners endured. She made special mention of mothers, children, and the elderly, writing, "The suffering of these poor tottering figures is indescribable ... Mothers comfort crying children. Old men are helped along by sons and daughters. Sheer misery stares out of the eyes of every one of them." Significantly, Bröring also included an accurate portrayal of the Holocaust events: "The rumor here is that they are taken off to Poland and then killed." She went on to distribute a Catholic bishop's denouncement of the "euthanasia" campaign until she was arrested and interrogated by the Gestapo.[68]

Religious resistance, especially among Catholic women, in Belgium, France, Poland, and Germany, was prominent and dangerous. The Belgian resistance, though small, had networks that provided shelter to children of all ages, from seven-day-old babies to adolescents. Desperate parents had no choice but to trust strangers with their children, frequently with little knowledge of where they would end up. Catholic nuns took initiative and used convents and orphanages as one of the few relatively stable and secure rescue locations, even though children had to be moved often.[69] Once they were old enough, they could join the Committee for the Defense of Jews, an organization within the Belgian resistance network.[70]

Some Germans also made their opposition to the Nazi regime known, despite the risk. Sophie Scholl and her brother Hans, for example, participated in Hitler Youth activities as kids, but recognized the racism and militarism inherent in its ideology. As Christians, they felt they had a moral duty to speak out. When Sophie was a 21-year-old university student, she and Hans distributed anti-Nazi leaflets as part of a student-run resistance group known as the "White Rose" at the University of Munich. Their leaflets called on Germans to think ethically about their moral duty and the consequences of their actions: "Germans! Do you and your children want to suffer the same fate that befell the Jews? Do you want to be judged by the same standards as your traducers? Are we to be forever the nation which is hated and rejected by all mankind?" A university janitor reported them, and Hans and Sophie were convicted of treason and executed along with Christopher Probst by guillotine April 22, 1943.[71]

In Nazi-occupied countries in Eastern Europe, resistance was especially dangerous. Armed, organized resistance took the form of partisan groups. The largest were among the Soviets, the communists in Yugoslavia, and the Greek People's Liberation Army. Many of the women who fought in communist partisan groups did so out of a desire to achieve gender equality, especially in the postwar world. As in other groups, women initially participated primarily in medical capacities but in 1942, the People's Liberation Army of Yugoslavia made combat roles officially available to women. This did not, however, result in women being promoted to leadership positions either militarily or politically.[72]

Even so, Historian Jelena Bainić writes that women's mass participation in the Yugoslavian partisan resistance was one of the Second World War's most significant phenomena.[73] The significance comes from the fact that most of the female recruits had peasant backgrounds from underdeveloped areas with strong patriarchal traditions. Men with similar upbringings had to accept fighting with and against women on an unprecedented scale. Indeed, the German opposition was taken aback when they encountered female partisans in combat roles or women's uniformed corpses.[74] They also had to accept defeat by female combatants, which was difficult for a German commander who wrote of his disgust at losing to a woman: "Yesterday we had our second black day, we had to leave many dead and badly wounded ... And when you consider that we suffered these losses at the hands of a *female* Partisan company, it really makes you want to throw up."[75] Women combatants were also fodder for political and cultural debates, as anticommunist groups tried to discredit the partisans by making the female fighter a favorite target of their propaganda. Yet partisan leaders took pride in proclaiming a new era of equality.[76]

In addition, Zionist organizations attempted to aid Jewish refugees in escaping Eastern Europe. The Slovak Central Refugee Committee in Bratislava traveled to London with two other delegates to request (unsuccessfully) for British help in getting Jewish refugees out of Slovakia. Committee member Gisela "Gisi" Fleischmann went on to attend a conference in Paris to plead for refugees. When Hitler invaded Poland on the last day of the conference, Fleischmann traveled home to her family in Bratislava instead of escaping to London. There, she aided illegal emigration transports to Palestine during 1939 and 1940. This work included caring for refugees in an abandoned munition factory on the outskirts of Bratislava, raising funds from an impoverished Jewish community, and distributing aid while they waited for ships to take them down the Danube River to the Black Sea. Fleischmann personally delivered food, cared for children and organized cultural activities for the refugees, who were sometimes confined to the munition factory for months.[77]

The Slovak Central Refugee Committee worked through massive bribery campaigns and when discovered, they were ultimately traced back to Fleischmann. She was arrested, and her friends worked for four months to plan her escape. When they had finally secured a certificate of entry into Palestine for her, Fleischmann would not take it, refusing to leave her sick mother or her community. She was eventually killed in Auschwitz. Fleischmann's leadership and actions were unique in that they sought to rescue not only what was left of her home community but also Jewish people across Nazi-occupied Europe.[78]

Evidence such as German police records document other forms of Jewish resistance throughout the war. Men and women hid in woods, acquired explosives and weapons, fought as partisans, and revolted in ghettos and labor camps, despite having few chances of survival or success.[79] Hanna Lévy-Hass, a Jewish Bosnian teacher, joined the resistance as a paramedic when the Nazis took control of Yugoslavia. In 1943, seeking to join the partisans in the mountains, Lévy-Hass tried unsuccessfully to convince the small Jewish community where she taught to flee with her. Three young people came to her home begging her to stay, fearing that her absence would be noted and all the Jews in the community would be killed in retaliation. She agreed but was arrested by the Gestapo in 1944 and was later deported to Bergen-Belsen concentration camp. Incredibly, Lévy-Hass survived the war and documented it.[80]

During her six-month imprisonment and throughout her time in Bergen-Belsen, Lévy-Hass kept a diary, managing to secretly record entries. Her diary was eventually published in English in 1982 and provides rare insight into life within the camps, including remarkable examples of everyday resistance. Lévy-Hass noted that mothers were more likely to collaborate for the common good: "Because of the children they are responsible for, the women sometimes show more practical and collectivist tendencies. They stubbornly try to find a way out."[81] Upon noticing missing rations, her barracks of 120 women organized to confront the woman responsible for food distribution, electing delegates to ensure fair distribution and supervision.[82]

One of the most significant acts of Jewish resistance took place in the spring of 1943 at the Warsaw Ghetto in Poland. Lasting for four months, the Warsaw Ghetto Uprising was the largest armed opposition carried out by targets of Nazi genocide. In January 1943, when the SS attempted to liquidate the ghetto's remaining occupants (only 20 percent of the ghetto's original number), they were surprised by armed resistance. The resistance fighters were armed with gasoline bombs, hand grenades, pistols, rifles, and a few submachine guns hidden in an elaborate system of bunkers and underground passages.[83] Women made up only 15,000 of the remaining 60,000 residents, yet they played significant roles in sustaining the fight.[84] Twenty-nine-year-old Zivia Lubetkin and nineteen-year-old Masha Glajtman were among the leaders of the resistance. Glajtman led a group of ten fighters, three of whom were women. Emanuel Ringelblum, another participant, wrote in his diary about their varied tasks: "Three female fighters staying in the apartment prepared meals and carried out various sorts of dangerous missions and orders."[85] In addition, mothers attempted to hide their children and to escape through tunnels and sewer lines, as did 21-year-old Regina Fuden.[86] Fuden was considered an expert sewer guide and managed to lead forty people out of the ghetto before she died fighting the Germans.[87]

Nazi SS commander, Jürgen Stroop, who led the uprising's suppression in 1943, wrote a book-length account of the revolt titled *The Warsaw Ghetto Is No More*.[88] The leather-bound report was meant as a souvenir album of German victory, but it also highlights throughout the Jewish women's proficiency with weaponry, noting in one case that "women fired from pistols held in both hands" and hid pistols and grenades on their person. Stroop also included several striking photos of armed women, including one of two women resisters and one man with the caption: "These bandits defended themselves with weapons."[89] According to survivor Stefania Szochur, twenty-years-old at the time, Germans were "afraid of the 'Jewish bandits'."[90] Figure 4.4 likewise depicts three members of the Jewish youth organization HeHalutz: "Women of the Hehalutz movement captured with weapons." In Figure 4.5, an official photo shows the captured Rachela Wyszogrodzka (left, partially out of frame), Bluma Wyszogrodzka (center), and Małka Zdrojewicz (far right), who was the only one to survive the

FIGURE 4.4 *"Women of the HeHalutz Movement Captured with Weapons,"* *May 16, 1943. Stroop Report; source IPN (Institute of National Remembrance—Commission for the Prosecution of Crimes against the Polish Nation), National Archives (NARA).*

war. Though small in numbers, women's participation in the Warsaw Ghetto Uprising was crucial.

A year later, Warsaw saw another significant but unsuccessful uprising, this time within the city itself, when (non-Jewish) Polish patriots and the Home Army, Poland's principal resistance organization, attempted to drive out the German occupiers. Known as the Warsaw Uprising of 1944, it was the war's largest Polish military and civilian resistance effort, with men, women, and children, as well as the Polish Army in exile, taking part. As in the Ghetto Uprising, women also played key roles in the Polish resistance movement in general and the Warsaw Uprising in particular. Some worked in traditional gendered positions, such as cleaning, cooking, delivering food and messages, and acting as caregivers and nurses, while others were involved in heavy fighting.[91] The Home Army's all-female battalion of diversion and sabotage, the Dysk, was well-equipped and succeeded in securing a western district of Warsaw. On August 2, 1944, they attacked an SS depot that, significantly, had been a holding ground for Jewish citizens before deportation to the killing center Treblinka. They also created all-women sapper units known as *minerki* patrols, which saw hand-to-hand combat, participated in bombings, and used homemade flamethrowers to set German-occupied buildings on fire.[92] German forces responded brutally, making no distinction between soldiers marked with armbands and civilian populations of men, women,

FIGURE 4.5 *Jewish resistance fighters, 1943, from right, Małka Zdrojewicz, Bluma Wyszogrodzka and Rachela Wyszogrodzka. Stroop Report, NARA.*

and children.⁹³ They were instructed to see "enemy civilians" as anyone with a hostile attitude toward the Germans, collectively responsible for any act of the uprising, and German forces routinely raped Polish women fighters.⁹⁴

After the Germans suppressed the uprising, over 2,000 women were taken captive and the death toll for female soldiers was estimated at 5,000. The significance of women's participation in the Polish Home Army is evident in the number of medals and honors bestowed upon them: 20 percent of the Cross of Valour military decorations went to women, 40 percent of the Silver Cross of Merit with Swords, and 50 percent of the Bronze Cross of Merit with Swords.⁹⁵ Throughout, female resistors showed tremendous skill and courage in the face of violence, occupation, and genocide.

Perpetrators

While historians previously discussed women's wartime experiences only through victimhood and sacrifice, German women's complicity with the distinctly gendered spheres created under Nazism show that Nazi women did not merely conform to the regime. On the contrary, they were active participants and collaborators. These women carved out spaces for themselves, had special responsibilities as women, sought career advancement, crossed gendered boundaries, and took on "men's roles." There were female SS units that were typically tasked with communication duties and housekeeping, in addition to making themselves sexually available to other SS officers to produce "valuable children" for the Reich.⁹⁶ Women also policed Nazi camps as both high-ranking and lower-level guards. The hiring pool was large for lower-level unskilled and semiskilled workers. Authorities advertised these positions with promises of job security, high wages, and ample responsibility—an especially attractive offer for women in Nazi Germany. At the women's concentration camp Ravensbrück, German women were recruited through such ads, hired, and given a short training course. Women's camps typically had female guards and Ravensbrück employed about 2,000.⁹⁷ One guard, Irma Ilse Ida Grese, worked at Ravensbrück starting at age eighteen. After seven months there, she was transferred to Auschwitz in 1943 for a job as a telephone operator but was soon promoted to camp guard. Hungarian survivor Olga Lengyel remembered Grese, describing how she walked through Auschwitz with a whip in her hand and a strong scent of perfume.⁹⁸ Over 3,600 women like Grese worked in concentration camps, but only sixty stood trial after the war; of those, only twenty-one were executed.⁹⁹

In addition, hundreds of women who had lived and worked in Nazi-occupied Eastern Europe were called to testify during the war crimes tribunals conducted by the Allies after the war. While it was their husbands who were under investigation, there is ample evidence about the women who were recruited, volunteered, or otherwise accompanied their husbands to the East. Hundreds of thousands of German women joined the colonizing mission as teachers, nurses, clerical workers, social workers, resettlement advisors, and racial examiners in the Nazi Eastern settlements (Poland and the USSR's Western territories).[100] Some 400,000 were deployed to Eastern battle zones to work on train platforms and in field hospitals for the army and the SS. Over 500,000 German women took on support positions, such as radio operators, flight recorders, and wiretappers. As secretaries, they organized, tracked, and distributed supplies. And at least 200,000 of these women worked in the violent East keeping the war machine running.[101] In her role as a secretary, Liselotte Meier planned massacres in which thousands of Jewish citizens were marched to a killing site, forced to undress, and then shot into pits; Jewish workers were then forced to cover the bodies with quicklime and earth. Meier also attended more than one massacre.[102]

Other women were witnesses to mass shootings and killed civilians themselves in cold blood, including children, even though they were not required or expected to do so. As historian Wendy Lower points out, women who came of age in Nazi Germany were as exposed to ideological indoctrination, mass mobilization, and Nazi conquest as the era's boys and men. Thus, it is highly likely that many more women willingly participated in the genocide than reflected in documentation and prosecutions. According to Lower, they were also just as brutal: "[They] were not marginal sociopaths. They believed that their violent deeds were justified acts of revenge meted out to enemies of the Reich."[103] Erna Petri, for example, testified after the war that she had shot Jewish children who had escaped from a boxcar near her property. In addition to antisemitic motivation, she explained that she wanted to prove herself to SS men.[104] Likewise, on September 16, 1942, secretary Johanna Altvater accompanied her boss to a Ukrainian ghetto, but she was on her own when she called over two young children as if to give them a treat. When they approached, she violently killed a toddler in front of the child's father, who later testified that he had never seen "such sadism from a woman."[105]

The women who had lived in Nazi Eastern settlements were often unapologetic and coldhearted in their testimonies before the court.[106] But persecuting women was not a high priority and the International Tribunal at Nuremberg decided that clerical workers, secretaries, stenographers, and other low-level support staff—though making up 35 percent of all SS personnel—would be exempt from indictment. Judges falsely believed these women had been ignorant of criminal policies and had lacked authority to execute them.[107]

Postwar Germany

Germany's signing of unconditional surrender on May 8, 1945, marked the official end of the hostilities of the Second World War. However, suffering on the German home front continued unabated in the postwar period.

Orphaned children wandered past women picking over piles of bricks from bombed-out houses.[108] Helpless civilians trekked through blasted landscapes. There were not enough ambulances to carry the sick and the dead; they had to be transported in carts and wagons.[109] Lacking supplies and housing, surrounded by mountains of rubble in major cities, and flooded with refugees and displaced persons, the remains of much of Europe had to be rebuilt from the ground up—structurally, politically, economically, and socially. And it was German women—both *Trümmerfrauen* (women of the rubble) and occupying soldiers' girlfriends—who took on the task.[110]

Historian Elizabeth Heineman has referred to the immediate postwar period in Germany as the "Hour of the Woman," in which women's experiences and suffering stood in for a collective memory of the era. Indeed, the "Rubble Women" who gathered usable bricks and other materials from demolished housing loom large in historical representations and photos. The image of the *Trümmerfrauen* did not subvert traditional ideologies of women as housewives nor did it secure increased social or political freedoms for women in the postwar period. But it did reflect a larger demographic shift that left postwar Europe as a site of gender upheaval in which—due to wartime fatalities, long delays in returning from the front, and for German soldiers, detainment in POW camps—women greatly outnumbered men.[111] In 1946, the Soviet Union had 12.4 million more women (between the ages of twenty and forty-four) than men, who had been killed by the millions during the German invasion of 1941. In postwar France, there were 1.8 million more French women than men; in occupied Germany, 7.3 million more. About 11 million German soldiers became Allied prisoners of war, some not returning until as late as 1955, and German men who were not causalities of war or imprisoned in POW camps came back wounded, too weak to work, and psychologically shattered by wartime experiences. Haunted by what they had witnessed at the front, veterans now had to contend with social changes back at home as well.

This demographic shift to women making up the majority of the population as well as what some perceived as emasculated men created a social crisis for many observers in postwar Germany. Physicians and psychiatrists addressed the loss of sexual desire among starving German POWs recovering from psychological defeat as part of a larger discussion of their emasculation, their focus on German POWs as dehumanized victims of totalitarianism blurring the lines between (former) Nazis and their Jewish victims. Moreover, commentators concerned about this "crisis of masculinity" directed attention away from German men's recent past and instead credited the country's overwhelming presence of women. Divorce rates soared as soldiers returned to women who were more independent and autonomous (including sexually), leaving men feeling cheated or humiliated.[112] This narrative of a feminized Germany gendered the process of rebuilding, as restoring normalcy necessarily involved reconstructing traditional gender norms.

When Did the War End?

The Second World War did not have a clear ending for many women. Bombing raids and a lack of supplies left the majority-female German population searching for food, shelter, and clothing long after peace was declared in 1945.[113] Moreover, the final stage of German defeat was enacted upon women's bodies, as sexualized violence persisted in the form of large-scale rape campaigns by Soviet Red Army soldiers—especially between April 24 and May 5, 1945, when the Soviets finally and definitively held Berlin.[114] Soviet leadership did not discourage the rapes, which could include girls as young as ten, and noted: "Break the racial pride of the German woman. Take her as your legitimate booty."[115] They also took the rape campaigns across central and Eastern Europe, terrorizing women from Berlin to Budapest. Clinics and doctors in Vienna reported 87,000 women were raped by Soviet soldiers in the first three weeks following their arrival.[116] Budapest was under siege for 102 days without running water, electricity, or enough to eat, while Soviet soldiers looted private residences and carried out mass rapes of women and girls.[117] These women became combatants in a new way that meant the war had not officially ended for them.

Sexual relations more generally took on a new political significance in the context of postwar occupations. Sex—forced and consensual—negotiated or realigned power between occupied and occupier nations.[118] Even before the war's end, many women in occupied countries had to rely on their sexuality for survival. As Jewish women's situation became increasingly dire, some began selling sex for shelter or working in brothels, and by 1944 many Italian women were trading sex with US troops for food or cash.[119] These conditions did not simply stop when the Germans surrendered. Moreover, some women experienced postwar sexual backlash, such as in France, when girlfriends of Germans were forced to shave their heads to publicly mark and humiliate them for having intimate relationships with the enemy during the war.[120] In the postwar period, occupying soldiers (including African-Americans in a defeated Nazi Germany) were engaged with European women in relationships—that ranged from casual dating to marriage to prostitution—across Western Europe as these troops were well supplied with essentials and luxury items such as nylon stockings, cigarettes, and chocolate.[121]

Finally, determining how to qualify an "end" to the suffering of the Holocaust is difficult. For one thing, many Jewish concentration camp survivors still found themselves in camps after the war—this time for "displaced persons" (DPs), or stateless refugees. Allies established DP camps to not only feed, house, and care for refugees but also to work on repatriating people, many of whom had no documentation, families, or homes left.[122] A steady rush of Jewish weddings and a Jewish baby boom in the DP camps demonstrate how women were central to rebuilding families and the larger community of survivors.[123] The repatriation process continued until 1957, over a decade after the war's official end.[124] And even when survivors had resettled, the ongoing trauma of their wartime experiences followed them into their new lives and beyond, into the next generation.

Conclusion

War begins before the first wound is inflicted and its effects last long after treaties are signed. Its demands destabilizing social notions of gender, sexuality, family, and nation and so offers an opportunity to study gendered change. The World Wars irrevocably altered European women's lives, dividing them into segments of "before," "during," and "after." Paradoxically, they each also provide cases of both continuity and rupture—major shifts in gender relations in terms of status, expectations, and experiences. With the Second World War, gender ideologies and women's roles evolved, but this did not always translate into meaningful or lasting change. Indeed, whether or not the Second World War advanced women's equality is the subject of much historical debate. Women's war experiences were important for their educational and professional progress, especially regarding postwar demands for increased legal and political equality. But as discussed in the next chapter, European women also encountered static or regressive attitudes and policies in the war's aftermath.

The Second World War and the Holocaust brought a level of weaponry, destruction, and genocide previously unheard of on European soil. It left Europe utterly depleted physically, morally, and psychologically—a land of misery and desolation where women had both played a part in the destruction and were also left to pick up the pieces. The days of "Western Civilization" and European global dominance were over. In their stead, two new global superpowers emerged—the United States and the USSR—who would face off in a decades-long Cold War. As the next chapter will show, here too gender played a significant role, with women's bodies often at the center of Cold War debates.

5

Women in Divided Europe

Introduction

In 1951, French obstetrician Fernand Lamaze traveled to the Soviet Union where he witnessed a new technique for pain management during childbirth called the psychoprophylaxis method, or PPM. What he saw forever changed how he thought about pain during labor. Soviet doctors designed PPM to ease pain based on learned breathing patterns and Russian physiologist Ivan Pavlov's theories of psychological conditioning. The premise of PPM was that expectant mothers could condition themselves to both anticipate and respond to labor's onset through mental relaxation and patterned breathing, and thus thwart pain signals sent to the cerebral cortex.[1] When Lamaze returned home and introduced French women to the method, they were excited to try a modern, innovative Soviet technique. Indeed, many Western European women were interested in PPM *because* it was a Soviet technique, which many associated with state-of-the-art practices.[2] Now widely known as the Lamaze method, few know of PPM's Cold War Soviet origins.

Childbirth practices may seem like an unlikely Cold War battle, but PPM's history demonstrates the importance of gender and biopolitics, or the intersection of human biology and politics, at this historical moment. PPM marked not only a social and cultural shift in childbirth but also in the politics of it. Scholars often refer to a postwar "baby boom" due to high birth rates, yet rarely view it through the act of childbirth itself. Freely crossing the Iron Curtain, psychoprophylaxis provides an interesting case of how scientific practices and ideas did not always abide by Cold War borders. In fact, as with other modern advances, such practices were used as tools to demonstrate one side's appeal over the other. At a time when the Soviet pharmaceutical industry lagged behind the West, PPM was an affordable "communist scientific technique" presented to mothers abroad as an example of what the Soviet Union had to offer. In this way, discussions about childbirth, women's bodies, and gendered understandings of work, family, and nationalism became ideological battlegrounds, designed to entice citizens to choose between two opposing ways of life: capitalist versus communist, West versus East.

This chapter centers around women's experiences on both sides of the Iron Curtain. During the Cold War, women's roles and gender relations served significant ideological and political purposes in both domestic and international policies, which became increasingly inseparable as the rivalry between East and West progressed. Indeed, in what the Cold War constructed as "the East" and "the West," women's roles as both mothers and workers symbolized the states' principles and progress with opposing sides insisting that they provided women the most desirable options.[3] Whether it was the promotion of domesticity in the West or the ideal female worker and mother in the East, women's bodies quite literally defined these political battles. This was especially salient as both sides attempted to outnumber the other in demographic competition.

Eastern and Western Bloc nations expanded gendered policies during this period, including those addressing family life, sexuality, and women in the workplace and in politics. Women's responses to state assistance and control—regarding childbirth, childcare, housing, medical care, birth control access, and employment, to name a few examples—impacted key debates and policies. Their support and acceptance were key means of gauging the success of political propaganda, while feminist critiques and activism challenged the status quo with women's unique perspectives, especially those that addressed race, class, and gender. Women's new power as earners and consumers, especially in the West, was reflected in targeted advertising as well as broader cultural shifts in leisure activities, film, and television. Meanwhile their consumption practices were also meant to exhibit Western superiority. Finally, the end of both the Second World War and much of European colonialism sparked widespread migrations that changed who a "European woman" was, as growing minority populations dealt with racism and made new demands on both the state and existing feminist movements. In all these ways and more, gender is foundational to understanding the Cold War period on both sides of the Iron Curtain.

Pronatalism and Women's Roles in Western Welfare States

In both Eastern and Western Bloc nations, postwar rebuilding and the Cold War competition overlapped with conceptions of women's roles. Newly established welfare states in Western Europe emphasized motherhood, patriarchal authority, and nuclear families to promote nationalism and anti-communist agendas.[4] Implicit in these discussions was the role the state would play in family planning. Indeed, many postwar countries invested heavily in welfare policies—such as the National Health Service (NHS) in Britain and *sécurité social* (social security) in France—to support pronatalist goals. In Britain, married women had more social benefits than unmarried women to encourage this focus on motherhood and domesticity, while state welfare initiatives like affordable housing assisted young couples in marrying and starting a family.[5]

In addition to promoting motherhood and pronatalism, policies of "social democracy" were meant to address citizens' material concerns, especially those of poor and working-class women. Social democracy was based on easing anxiety about subsistence to thwart the appeal of radical movements like fascism and communism, as seen during economic crises in the 1930s.[6] European welfare states were not particularly difficult to implement because expanded wartime governments and ad hoc social benefits since the First World War were already in place, as were dire material conditions—a lack of housing and healthcare, for example. Programs such as expanded public schools, school lunch programs, old-age insurance, and veterans' pensions changed citizens' expectations and relationships to their government.[7] Increased government assistance in housing and healthcare was also seen as payment for wartime sacrifices of loved ones, especially for women.[8]

However, as pointed as these programs were toward what states believed women needed, they were not designed with women's equality in mind. The Western model was openly designed to keep men as the head of households and women as their dependents, especially in the interests of pronatalism. Lord Beveridge, architect of the British welfare state and longtime eugenicist, insisted that married women should avoid employment in order to "ensure the adequate continuance of the British race."[9] West Germany, Spain, Italy, and the Netherlands not only offered women fewer positions but also had a lack of childcare options and laws that kept stores closed on weekends, during the lunch hour, or after work hours making it impossible for two working parents to buy groceries.[10] For example, West German stores closed by 5 p.m.[11] Indeed, many Western states emphasized that a stable, democratic society required a traditional home with a male breadwinner, not only to counter communism but also to restore normalcy after the war's gender upheaval. To promote traditional domesticity, the 1952 West German Law for the Protection of Mothers excluded women from holding certain jobs and approved employer-paid maternity leave before and after pregnancy. Far from promoting working mothers, however, the paid maternity leave discouraged many employers from hiring women and encouraged them to fire women when they got married or when they became pregnant as a cost-saving measure.[12]

In contrast, France promoted women's employment and supported family allowances that funded children and families.[13] France—and many Scandinavian countries—prioritized working mothers, providing family allowances, prenatal and postnatal care, maternity benefits, and childcare. French stores also remained open until eight o'clock in the evening to allow shopping for households where both parents worked.[14] Even so, British, French, and West Germany trade unionists supported a "family wage" that put husbands in charge of family resources and preferred that women stay out of the labor market and not compete with men for lower wages.

In the Western Bloc, women's lived realities rarely matched the social and cultural messages about women's roles that states promoted. Unlike the single factory girls and domestic servants of the previous centuries, this female labor force also included women who were older and frequently married with children. In 1950, 25 percent of West German married women worked—a regressive shift, down from one in three in 1939—but by the 1970s, that number was up to 50 percent.[15] In Great Britain, 39.5 percent of women worked in 1960, the majority concentrated in clerical jobs. In Austria, women comprised 45 percent of workers in 1960; by the mid-1970s, the median age of marriage had risen to twenty-five.[16] Women's job opportunities were most abundant in Scandinavian countries such as Sweden and Denmark, while in much of Southern Europe, women's participation in the labor force lagged as many women continued to work out of their homes in traditional crafts. By the end of the 1960s, for example, women made up only 27 percent of the Italian labor force.

Furthermore, in postwar Western Europe, jobs in domestic service—such as live-in housekeeping—decreased as women increasingly found jobs in a more modern service sector, working in shops, offices, and professions like teaching and nursing. Additionally, state bureaucracies that administered the housing, health care, insurance, and other welfare programs continued to employ many women hired during the war. As lower- and mid-level public sector jobs underwent a "feminization," female bureaucrats effectively ran postwar welfare states in Western Europe. The concentration of women in the service sector relied on gendered assumptions that they could use their innate femininity to deal with difficult interactions, such as air stewardesses addressing drunk or belligerent passengers. Originally a male occupation, a female flight attendant's appearance became the most important feature in the 1960s, as airlines hoped to increase profitability by exploiting female sexuality and fashion trends.[17]

The need for female labor did not decrease, even if governments preferred women not work. Which women should work also became racialized in the postwar years. Migrant women's labor became a way to have both full employment and, in the words of a London magistrate, recognize that the "strength of the nation is built upon the strength of the home life of the citizens," a home life governed by wives and mothers.[18] In the years when married (British) women's employment was discouraged, Britain recruited African, Caribbean, Irish, and Italian women, among others, to work in the newly established National Health Service, in hotels and catering, as nurses and midwives, and in the textile industry. During the 1950s, Britain was one of the first countries to draw heavily on foreign labor for low-income jobs in hospitals, public transport, postal service, and education, a pattern many other Western European countries would follow in the 1960s.

Women's Lives at Work and at Home in the Eastern Bloc

As with PPM, the childbirth pain relief technique, the Soviet Union used gender and women's roles at work and at home to advertise communism as the most progressive and equitable of all societies. Eastern Bloc women's experiences were shaped by major ideological differences, and postwar Soviet states mandated gender equality in ways not matched in the Western Bloc— in family, work, politics, and education. In contrast to Western Europe, in communist countries the primary relationship was between the individual and the state, not within a nuclear family. According to historian Marina Kiblitskaya, Soviet women were "married to the state," meaning that their relationships to work, family, and personal life resulted from internalizing the state's ideas, replacing personal concerns with unquestioned loyalty.[19] Thus, in the eyes of the state, a communist woman's duty was both productive and reproductive, and only by fulfilling both roles would she be "emancipated." In turn, she would receive social welfare benefits from the state—at least this was the initial promise. Likewise, the state defined masculinity by assigning men roles as soldiers, leaders, managers, and workers. The state was to be the true, universal patriarch.

As expected, many more women worked in communist countries than in the West. In 1970, women were 51 percent of the *entire* labor force in the Soviet Union and 41 percent in Hungary.[20] Kiblitskaya uses the expression "bread winners by default," pointing out that women had to make up for the shortfalls of their husbands' salaries (and often compensate for their costly drinking problems) by getting multiple jobs.[21] While many women in Eastern Bloc countries were concentrated in boring, menial, low-paying jobs, women also gained access to traditionally male professions, such as law, medicine, and engineering, at a quicker pace than their Western counterparts. Indeed, by the mid-1970s, women made up 60 percent of workers in professional occupations. In addition, while the percentage of female doctors in the US only increased from 6 to 17 percent between 1950 and 1990, women comprised a mostly steady 70 percent of doctors in the Soviet Union during that period. However, after the 1917 Russian Revolution "proletarized" professions typically considered bourgeois or intellectual, those who worked in such fields became just another group of employees in a state-controlled organization. Scholars have pointed out that the loss of status for doctors and lawyers directly contributed to increased numbers of women in these roles.[22] Moreover, since the state controlled higher education and professional regulation in Soviet states, women had greater access to fields that were simultaneously losing both prestige and high-earning potential. In effect, these states feminized traditionally male, higher-class professions.

In consolidating the Eastern Bloc into communist republics, Soviet gender ideologies infiltrated a wide range of national cultures and policies.

In some places, legislation reinforced the communist commitment to gender equality. In 1946, the Soviet occupied zone of Germany, later known as East Germany, issued an equal pay order and instituted quotas for women's political participation, mandating that one-third of party members be female. In many ways, gender politics is an efficient way to track Soviet influence on traditional values in satellite states. For example, in Yugoslavia, socialist modernization projects impacted women's ability to inherit real estate, be seen as legal adults, and represent themselves in public affairs. Due to Yugoslavia's ethnic diversity, women's rights were subject to distinct sets of legislation: Serbian civil law, Sharia law for Muslim populations, and old Austrian and Hungarian civil laws. However, Yugoslavian sports policies had no gender-based divisions. Participating in sports was a new experience for many women, especially those from rural areas, which most of the Eastern Bloc was. Some believed that sports could provide a way to "penetrate Muslim communities" and discourage wearing the veil.[23] Eastern Bloc women's increased visibility in the postwar period—in the media, sports, construction sites, and more—was meant to create an image of a young woman able to compete with men under communism's ethos of gender equity.

Like the Soviet Union, Hungary passed laws granting women political and legal equality. In rural sectors of the country, land reforms ended private ownership that had privileged men, but also resulted in a managerial class that was mostly male.[24] At the same time, more men left agriculture to work in factories, which increased the number of women and elderly agricultural workers. In urban areas, the communist policy of equal access to education played a direct role in increasing women's employment opportunities. As in France and other Western welfare states, Hungarian state-funded maternity leave and free nurseries and kindergartens were designed to balance work and motherhood. These policies had a significant impact. In 1951, 7,000 children were enrolled in Hungarian nurseries; by 1970, that number had jumped to 40,000. In addition to top-down measures, economic necessity drove more women to find work. Access to state assistance—such as pensions, childcare, housing, and healthcare—was dependent on one's employment status. In Hungary, by 1970, 64 percent of women participated in the formal labor force, a greater percentage than in most capitalist countries, with a significant number working in historically male fields.[25] Statistics do not provide the whole picture, though, as some Hungarian policymakers struggled with the "unreliability" of working mothers with small children, who had to take unpaid leave for sick children or when nurseries shut down for illness or hire an expensive nanny. These working women's attempts to balance the demands of paid and unpaid family labor, caused problems for the Hungarian industrial sector specifically and the economy as a whole.[26] As in the West, though, the dominant ideology of the male breadwinner never really subsided despite the East's contrasting context. Even so, compared to their Western counterparts, most Eastern Bloc countries had substantial maternity leaves and childcare facilities, leading to women's increased participation in the workforce and greater independence, including for widows and single mothers.

Indeed, domesticity was not idealized as it was in the West, but rather seen as an ill of capitalist societies, especially in terms of gender equality. In fact, many nations in the Eastern Bloc legalized abortion to align with communist ideals of gender equality and to encourage women's full employment and because, outside of East Germany and Yugoslavia, few birth control options were available in the Eastern Bloc. Beginning with the Soviet Union in 1955, Central and Eastern European states including Poland, Bulgaria, Hungary, Yugoslavia, and Czechoslovakia relaxed their abortion laws during the 1950s. By 1960, a pregnant woman in the USSR, Bulgaria, and Hungary could have an abortion upon request; in Czechoslovakia, Yugoslavia, and Poland, the pregnant woman only had to demonstrate a hardship.[27]

Yet at the same time, the Soviet Bloc was interested in reestablishing more traditional families, not just in the interest of pronatalism but also because they envisioned a rational Soviet citizen governed by self-control.[28] The communist woman was a working mother—two distinct but inseparable roles that supposedly came naturally with state support. Historians are divided on the extent to which Eastern Bloc nations emphasized the nuclear family versus individual loyalty and contributions to the state. Nevertheless, women carried the burden of housework and childcare while also rebuilding their countries economically. Theirs was a distinctly communist "double burden," as states demanded a larger workforce with full employment for all citizens. This increased labor demand was not met with a serious reconsideration of women's domestic roles, however. Ironically, when declining birth rates troubled Soviet officials, many argued that employment had negative consequences on women's duty as mothers.[29] Their state-sanctioned equal economic responsibilities also did not change age-old assumptions about women's roles in society.[30] In a 1946 Yugoslavian newspaper, for example, a humor article mocked men for washing their own plates, blaming communist ideals of gender equality for this sad state of affairs—even though this ideal was rarely realized.[31] Nevertheless, Soviet propaganda continued to tout communist superiority on gender equality.

In addition to questions of women's roles and professions, gendered Cold War rivalries moved beyond countries and into space itself. One of the most striking ways Soviet women entered traditionally male professions was through the space program. During the Cold War, both the United States and the USSR sought to achieve significant "firsts" to demonstrate their technological prowess to the world. The Soviet Union struck first, making history on October 4, 1957, by successfully launching Sputnik I, the world's first artificial satellite. Sputnik's success was not only embarrassing for the United States but also intensified Cold War tensions and expanded the arms race into space. Both countries competed to develop new technologies to avoid feeling "left behind." When General Nikolai Kamanin, director of

Soviet cosmonaut training, heard a rumor that American women would begin receiving informal space training, the Central Committee of the Communist Party grew determined that the first woman in space would be from the Soviet Union. Officials even pushed for qualified women to begin training before their male counterparts. In 1962, Kamanin wrote in his diary, "We cannot allow that the first woman in space will be American. This would be an insult to the patriotic feelings of Soviet women."[32] As Kamanin's sentiment demonstrates, the Space Race again placed women at the center of Cold War competition.

During the application and selection process, Kamanin discussed what kind of woman he was looking for and why it mattered in the Cold War context in his diary: "I told them I needed girls who were young, brave, physically strong and with experience of aviation, who we can prepare for spaceflight in no more than six months." Most importantly, he insisted, "The central objective of this accelerated preparation is to ensure that the Americans do not beat us to place the first woman in space."[33] Since the Vostok space vessel had functions that could be controlled from the ground, Kamanin did not feel that extensive training was necessary. He was confident that he could train a new female astronaut for the mission in just four months. However, male astronauts, including accomplished Air Force officers with extensive flight records and training, were not at all pleased to have a woman join them—essentially cutting the line. That seat on the Vostok was coveted, and they felt it was rightly theirs. Many also did not believe that women belonged in space on principle, relying on traditional understandings of gender roles. As one of the annoyed cosmonauts asked, "Can we risk the life of a mother?" However, Kamanin's diary entries were very clear about the Soviet Union's mission: to be the first country to send a woman into space, no matter what.

Valentina Nikolayeva-Tereshkova, a textile mill worker and amateur parachutist who had completed over one hundred jumps, was selected from a pool of 400 applicants. Like many proud Russians, Nikolayeva-Tereshkova was swept up in a moment of national triumph following the flight of Soviet cosmonaut Yuri Gagarin and wrote a passionate letter volunteering her services "should a woman cosmonaut ever be required."[34] On June 16, 1963, Nikolayeva-Tereshkova orbited Earth forty-eight times and spent almost three days alone in space. As the first and youngest woman to fly a solo space mission, she was celebrated as a national hero. Her portrait appeared on the 1963 Soviet Union stamp titled, "Second 'Team' Manned Space Flight" (Figure 5.1). Although an extraordinary example, Nikolayeva-Tereshkov's role in the Space Race demonstrates the ways that ideas about gender and women workers—from menial laborers to career astronauts—held a central position in Eastern states' policies, economies, and the larger Cold War rivalry, even as communism's promised equalities were not realized for most Eastern European women.

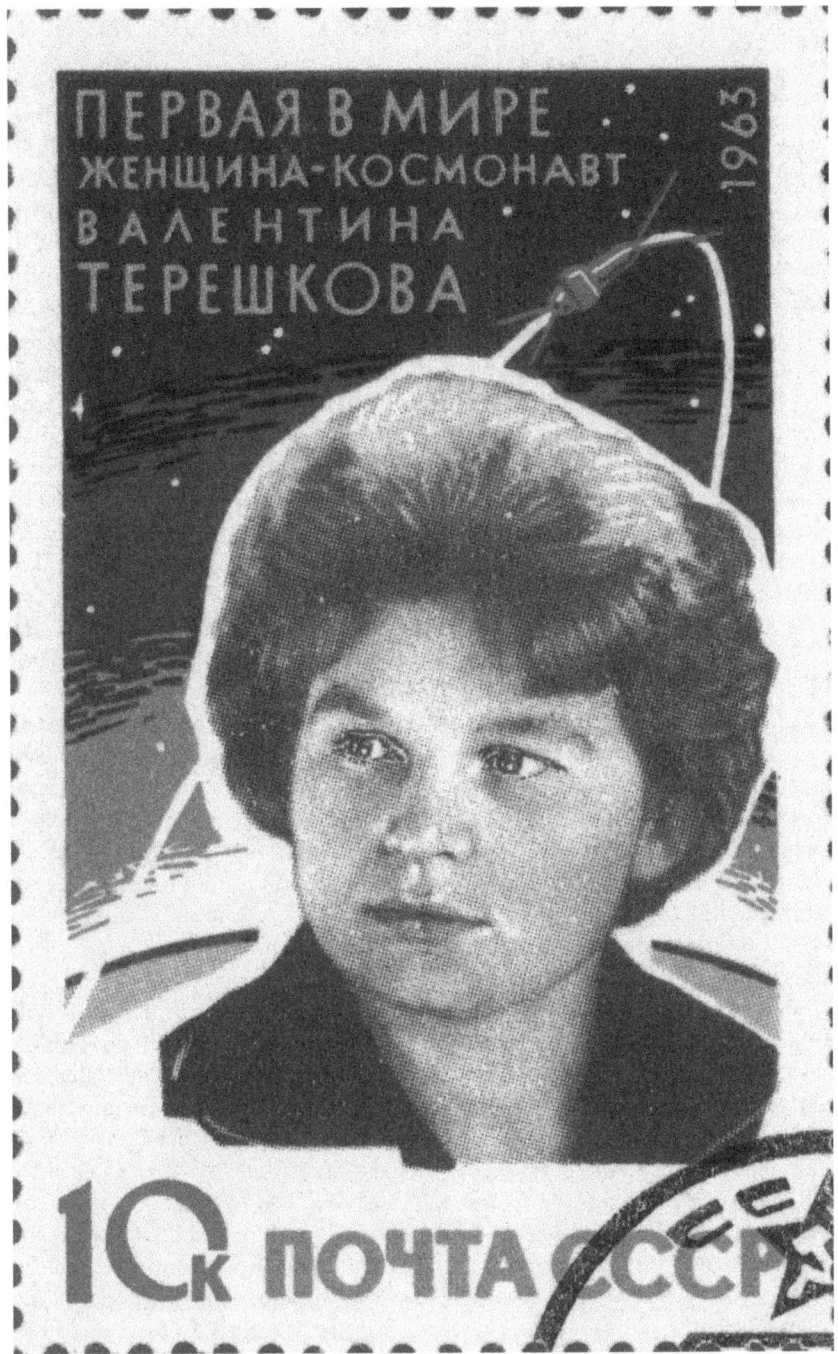

FIGURE 5.1 *The Soviet Union 1963 stamp commemorating the "Second 'Team' Manned Space Flight" with a portrait of Valentina Tereshkova. Public domain.*

Postwar "Guest Worker" Migration

Accompanying the rise in women's employment, migrations within and across European countries characterized the postwar period. From Iberia to Scandinavia, a combination of high fertility rates and unemployment numbers prompted vast relocations to more industrialized northwestern nations from rural areas with primarily agricultural economies in Southern and Eastern Europe as well as from former colonial holdings around the globe.[35] Often known as "guest worker" migration, these international labor programs in Northwestern Europe (as well as in the United States and oil-rich Middle East countries) launched a new era of migration meant to serve the social, economic, and national needs of both sending and receiving countries. By the 1970s, some countries such as Italy, Spain, and Portugal—which had been sending their citizens north to work—began receiving their own foreign workers from the Philippines, South America, Cape Verde, Tunisia, and Eritrea, including large numbers of female domestic workers.[36]

Female workers arrived in the earliest waves of guest worker immigration, and while they were in the minority of recruited workers, their numbers increased steadily over time and their participation was impactful. Migrant women's entry into the labor force supported Western European welfare policies. Host countries relied not only on their female citizens to fill menial positions but increasingly also on immigrant guest workers who would accept low compensation, often on a part-time basis. Both groups of workers lowered welfare states' costs. As a result, guest workers were recruited mainly for jobs that required no qualifications and were unskilled, unhealthy, monotonous, and poorly paid. Immigrant women were employed in domestic service as cleaners as well as jobs in electronics, textiles, tailoring, food packaging, and fish processing, sometimes with piecework arrangements. Guest worker women's biggest complaint was their low wages; a survey conducted in 1963 showed that only 30 percent reported satisfaction with their compensation.[37]

By recruiting migrant women to fill positions previously held by white Western European women, guest worker programs effectively enabled married women in host countries to embrace domesticity and the male breadwinner nuclear family model. In West Germany, for example, female guest workers were shuttled into "women's work"—a de facto term, as sex-based wage discrimination was now illegal—and other low-paying positions so that German women could leave the labor force to focus on home and family. In Belgium, female labor force participation reached its lowest level of all time in 1950, as working women became increasingly stigmatized and the housewife was presented as ideal. At the same time, the percentage of foreign women living and working across Western Europe increased, stepping in to fill positions native-born women did not. For example, the 1982 French population census reported that 43 percent of their immigrant population was women.[38]

Not all women migrating due to guest worker programs came as laborers. Many were also wives who joined their husbands abroad to start families in a new country.[39] Some of these women had difficulty obtaining necessary work permits, some did not speak the host country's language, and others simply had too much to do at home to also enter the formal labor force. Furthermore, not all women migrated by choice; some were pressured to marry men working abroad or to immigrate themselves and request to have their husbands join them later. Women who were coerced in this way often lacked the power to refuse.[40]

Different familial and cultural backgrounds could impact women's experiences abroad. Guest workers from Anatolia in central Turkey versus those from the more urban Istanbul, for example, could have had very different motivations for leaving. Women from urban areas in particular saw guest worker programs as exciting opportunities to alter their status not just financially but also socially and culturally. One Turkish woman from Istanbul was eager to go to West Berlin, recalling that she became friends with her German colleagues and spent some of her earnings on fashion and nightlife. In a 2003 interview, she recalled her arrival at the age of twenty: "It was an adventure. If I make it, it is okay, and if I don't, that's okay, too. I was single ... I had no children ... I was very, very self-confident and often very independent ... I have no regrets. I made the right decision."[41] In short, Western Europe's postwar economy offered women who had never thought of living or working abroad in an unknown place the chance to do so.

Many nations implemented policies that enabled migrants' families to reunite in their host countries.[42] The European Community's "free movement of labor clause" allowed, for example, Italian citizens to join family members abroad, bringing many men, women, and children to Northern Europe.[43] Article 19 of the European Social Charter of 1961 also guaranteed family reunification of migrant workers as a fundamental human right. These familial migrations, as well as an emerging north–south divide, prompted Southern Europeans to seek opportunities in northern Europe. The children of reunification who traveled to Northern Europe found their lives altered as well. Sixteen-year-old Spanish migrant Concepción Origuel wanted to become a physician's assistant in her host country of West Germany but was rejected each time she applied for an apprentice position. Noting that her other female classmates had found apprenticeships, Origuel hinted at the discrimination she faced as an immigrant. She commented that the doctors "always want to know first where I am from and what my parents do. We're not lepers or anything."[44] Reunification, when spouses, children, and other family members joined a worker abroad, irrevocably changed families' experiences as well as European demographics.

In addition, men's labor migration to Western Europe had a considerable effect on the women who stayed behind. Though based on the early 1900s, historian Linda Reeder's research on a small town in Sicily shows that mass male guest worker emigration impacted Sicilian women's ideas about motherhood, work, and national belonging. Rather than being passively left behind, women were actively involved in their husbands and sons' decisions to depart. Many of these women were integrated into the larger Italian state in new ways—beyond their local communities—because of the demographic shift. Now it was they who had to interact with government officials when registering births, for example, or otherwise negotiating their affairs. Postwar migrations created similar patterns in other places as well. In Greece in the 1960s and 1970s, both urbanization and emigration weakened traditional family relationships and altered Greek women's position in society. In many cases, elderly parents stayed behind when family members emigrated as guest workers. Nuclear families became more common, taking the place of traditional households comprising three to four generations. In this context, women and mothers took on more direct roles in household management and childcare as they lost their extended family networks.[45] In cases where both parents emigrated, the impact on children left behind could be severe. A Turkish woman lamented her parents' departure for West Germany, recalling, "I was dropped off at my grandmother's. It was the most painful day of my life. In Turkey everyone told us, 'Your mother and father are sweeping up money from the ground in Germany.' "[46]

Postwar labor migration was not just a Western European practice. East Germany (GDR) suffered a labor shortage due to low birthrates and losing millions of citizens who fled to Western zones before the construction of the Berlin Wall in 1961. In 1963, the first contract workers arrived in the GDR from Poland, Hungary sent workers in 1967, Algeria in 1974, Cuba in 1975 and 1978, and Mozambique in 1980. East Germany also allowed workers from their "socialist friends" in East Asia, prompting immigration from North Korea and Vietnam. Indeed, many Eastern Bloc countries saw the Socialist Republic of Vietnam (reunified in 1976) as an attractive labor source. In the 1980s, close to 300,000 Vietnamese workers traveled to the Soviet Union, Bulgaria, Czechoslovakia, and East Germany through bilateral agreements with "socialist friends."[47] Thirty-seven percent of East Germany's migrant Vietnamese labor force were women, mostly in their mid-twenties to early thirties, and about 60 percent of migrating laborers were married.

Female contract workers generally found positions in light industry, such as textiles, while men worked mainly in construction and mechanics. But with women migrants in the minority, the East German state gendered contract work male—a stance most evident in their controversial pregnancy policies for foreign laborers. Segregated from local communities, contract workers lived in crowded rooms divided by sex, with state officials monitoring the women for pregnancy.[48] (Some factory officials even distributed birth control pills.) Lacking family reunification programs, Vietnamese women who became pregnant while working in East Germany had to choose between abortion or returning to their country of origin to have the child. According to a 1980 agreement outlining state procedures regarding pregnant Vietnamese workers, "Pregnancy and motherhood change the personal situation of the affected female workers so profoundly that they are subsequently no longer able to realize the demands of temporary employment and training." Therefore, the state continued, "Vietnamese women—like women in the GDR—have the right ... to terminate their pregnancies cost-free." However, termination was less of a right and more of a requirement to stay in the country: "Vietnamese women who do not avail themselves of contraception or abortion must ... return to Vietnam."[49] The Vietnamese government considered these policies inhumane and the East German state ultimately abandoned them.[50] Such policies still applied to other groups, however, as Mozambican female laborers were sent home automatically if they became pregnant, and only Polish workers were allowed to give birth.[51] Contract work in the Eastern Bloc was thus gendered not just by segregated housing and wage discrimination but also in its tight control of fertility, mirroring other postwar obsessions with women's reproduction and sex lives. Even so, as in Western Europe, many migrants refuted the idea that they were solely exploited; as one woman reported, "I was young and excited to see and experience other places in the world!"[52]

Decolonization and Gender

In addition to guest worker programs and other labor migrations, decolonization prompted migrations that shifted both who European women were and where they lived. Amid failed political negotiations after the Second World War, many European colonial holdings—including those in South and East Asia as well as North and Sub-Saharan Africa—turned to wars of independence. By the 1960s, Britain, France, the Netherlands, Italy, and Belgium had been forced to surrender their colonial holdings. Colonial resistance was a consistent and inherent part of imperialism, and women were active resisters across the colonial world. But the world wars had bankrupted Europe morally and financially, creating a new colonial context that produced new leaders, allowed colonial troops to interact with each other, heightened political consciousness, and spurred on independence movements that had been developing for decades.

European nations did not give up their colonial holdings without a fight, however. Throughout these efforts, African women joined efforts to create independent nations, supplying weapons, food, and communication, as well as serving as combatants and enduring torture at the hands of European armies.[53] Algerian women were no different and engaged in intelligence gathering and terrorism, playing on gender stereotypes to smuggle bombs in their handbags or baby carriages. These women also endured brutal torture and sexual abuse when caught or merely suspected.[54] French civilians were horrified to learn that the French military used beatings, electroshock, waterboarding, and sexual assault and rape of Algerian women during the Algerian War for Independence (1954–62).

During the bloody war, what was "best" for Muslim women was a prominent point of debate. In challenging French imperial rule, Algeria's National Liberation Front (NLF) fought against French forces who claimed to be "saving" Muslim women and modernizing Arabs from traditionalism. From their point of view, the French authorities believed they could win over native Algerian women by promoting their emancipation; that is, by encouraging conformity to French standards of modern womanhood.[55] Yet this idea was more political than emancipatory, as it disregarded Algerian women's own nationalist, cultural, and religious views. But after all, the colonial project was never designed to be emancipatory.

The newly independent states that resulted from decolonization in Africa, Asia, and the Middle East were often politically precarious with authoritarian rule, ethnically diverse populations, and economic instability—a combination that frequently led to violence and waves of immigration that have continued into the twenty-first century. Tens of thousands of former colonial subjects, who had been trained for generations to believe that European metropoles represented possibility and democracy, flocked to European countries seeking employment, opportunity, and, in some cases, asylum and refuge. Belgium, France, the Netherlands, the UK, and Portugal all received significant numbers of migrants from former colonial holdings, many of whom were considered citizens.[56] Former colonial subjects were also recruited to work in economically thriving countries through guest worker programs. In a 2011 interview, "Julia" recalled her anticipation in 1968: "I was excited ...I'd never been anywhere." She went to work as a nurse, as one of thousands of young Caribbean women, and recalled the appeal: "I think [back then] nursing was the only way, really, for women to leave ... and forge a different life."[57] The migrations did not abate: by the end of the 1980s there were about 16 million foreign nationals residing in different West European states, some who had settled and stabilized over the past decade.[58] By the mid-1990s, women made up over 49 percent of the foreign population in many Western European countries, including Denmark, Greece, Iceland, Ireland, Norway, and Sweden.[59]

However, while settling in Europe could offer new financial and social freedoms, resentment, job and housing discrimination, violence, sexism, and xenophobia awaited many former colonial subjects upon their arrival. Despite these migrants' contributions to buoying welfare states, they reaped few of the benefits. Housing was especially difficult to find. Schools were resistant to immigrant children (often thought to be incapable of mastering the language or simply not smart) and did not foster their success as they did native-born students. Immigrant women suffering from abuse at work or at home could find few resources to help. Authorities were slow to react, possibly due to viewing domestic violence as a "private issue," but also frequently due to racist attitudes and language barriers. In sum, being an immigrant, a worker, a wife, and a mother intersected in ways that proved extremely stressful for many women in postwar Europe. Those who followed husbands with jobs in Europe were isolated from the family support networks they left behind. Many also felt conflicted about how to foster cultural heritage in second-generation children while also accepting that their children felt "European."[60] While no longer colonial subjects, such questions of acculturation were compounded by racism, xenophobia, and other longstanding biases that would shape many immigrants' experiences in Europe for generations.

Leisure and Consumption

In the West, consumption took on a political and gendered importance in the postwar period. Used to promote a democratic, capitalist, and carefree lifestyle, Western women's consumer practices were meant to contrast with Soviet women's austerity and androgyny. In 1959, US Vice President Richard Nixon and Soviet First Secretary Nikita Khrushchev squared off in an impromptu debate that exemplified this gendered rivalry—an exchange known as the "Kitchen Debate." While not as serious as the Cuban Missile Crisis, scholars consider the Kitchen Debate a crucial Cold War moment that seized the world's attention.[61] It took place at the American National Exhibition in Moscow, a demonstration meant to promote cultural exchange that also functioned as a de facto competition over the capitalist democratic versus communist lifestyle. Strikingly, the exhibition's model kitchen and its display of women's homelife was how the two opposing world leaders chose to emphasize how their respective states would fare in the future.

The American model kitchen was filled with modern, affordable, and supposedly labor-saving devices, such as a dishwasher, refrigerator, and range. These appliances represented not just American manufacturing success but also social and cultural success via the happy housewife. The message was not merely implied. Highlighting the kitchen's dishwasher, Nixon boasted, "This is our newest model. This is the kind which is built in thousands of units for direct installations in the houses. In America, we like to make life easier for women."[62] In response, Khrushchev scoffed at the idea of such gadgets' importance, stating that they were inferior to traditional methods. He teasingly asked if the United States also had a machine that "puts food into the mouth and pushes it down," and confidently declared that Nixon's grandchildren would live under communism. Nixon disagreed, insisting that an affordable dishwasher for every American woman proved that Khrushchev's grandchildren would live in freedom. This debate, hyper-focused on women's lives, marked one of very few face-to-face exchanges between leaders of the two global superpowers. Broadcast on the new medium of television for the world to see, the Kitchen Debate cemented consumption and women's roles as central to the Cold War competition and to each side's perception of superiority.

In the 1950s and 1960s, social welfare states generated economic expansion, making disposable income a reality in the West, replacing subsistence income as wages rose. The growth in mass consumer culture and production, and higher standards of living complemented the promotion of a capitalist democracy and increased women's consumer demands. As exhibited by the US model kitchen, purchases of televisions, radios, and "timesaving" technologies for the home like dishwashers increased greatly during this period. The new commercial products women could display in their homes both demonstrated membership in the middle class and supported the idea of women's role in the domestic sphere. Advertisers took note. Although the central unit of consumption was envisioned as the nuclear family—namely, young married couples with children—it was women consumers that advertisers targeted the most. Television programing and advertisements geared specifically toward women enabled consumption from within the home as well as in the public sphere.[63] Western women's eager participation in consumerism was a bit paradoxical; many invested in technologies that reinforced domesticity at a time when women began to question their own roles as housewives. Moreover, despite women's purchasing power, they were not equal earners and did not always have control over household finances.

As some historians have noted, Western women were also "purchasing their leisure" in new ways in the postwar period. Fashion magazines, travel guides, radio programs, record albums, and films all broadened their worldview. Women went to the movies more frequently, once a week even, accommodated by a boom in the number of cinemas built; for example, by 1941, there were more than 4,500 cinemas in Great Britain.[64] Films and other mass media also exposed women to new models of fashion and sexuality. Christian Dior's "New Look," for example, featured full skirts and constricting, cinched waists to highlight femininity that was at once uncompromising and bold in its message of feminine appeal (see Figure 5.2). Such Western fashion represented not just a "new look" but a new outlook on women after years of military uniforms and rationing.[65]

At the same time, French model and film star Brigitte Bardot became an international pop culture icon who used her gender and modernity to break taboos about women's sexuality both on and off the screen. Over the course of her career, Bardot appeared in forty-seven films and presented an overtly sexual, unambiguously heterosexual femininity. As France's first mass-media celebrity, young women imitated her hairstyle and clothes, and the paparazzi stalked her relentlessly. Figure 5.3 portrays Bardot with bare shoulders, arms, and neck in a suggestive pose with one finger on her signature red lips. Her hair cascades down her bare front in an image that represents what many considered her scandalous, hedonistic, and sexually free lifestyle. Historian Ginette Vincendeau notes that Bardot's rise to fame anticipated the societal and sexual changes of the 1960s and 1970s, even as a somewhat unrealistic role model when women were also battling for equal political, social, and reproductive rights.[66]

FIGURE 5.2 *September 1954: Full length evening two piece with mink cuffs, by Dior. Picture Post "Fashion's New Alphabet." Photo by John Chillingworth / Picture Post / Hulton Archive / Getty Images.*

Postwar Western popular culture and advertising promoted a new image of men as well. This new assertive masculinity emulated American cultural icons like the Marlboro Man, James Dean, and Elvis Presley in its rebellious, rough, confident, and sexually aggressive style. In contrast to postwar ideologies of womanhood, these men were perceived as independent from

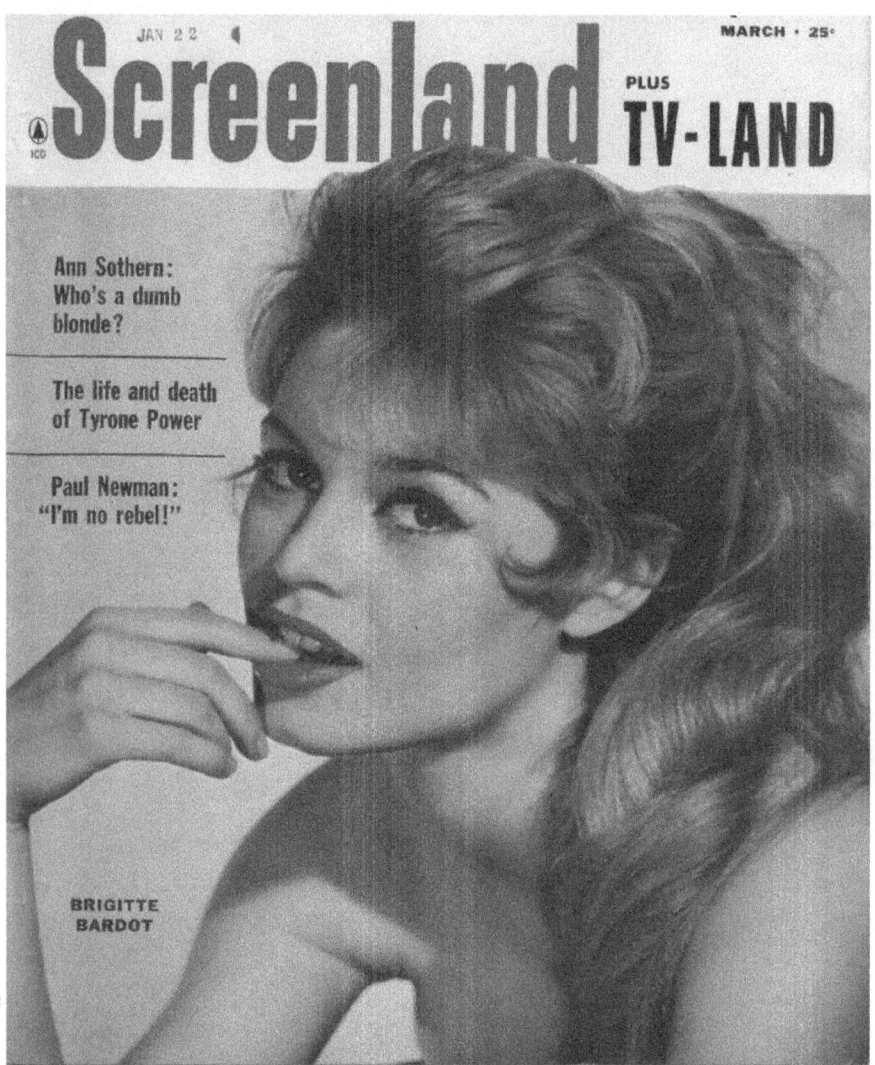

FIGURE 5.3 *Cover of* Screenland *featuring Brigitte Bardot, March 1959. Public domain.*

dull domestic life, as men's social and cultural citizenship now encompassed not just political and economic rights but also sexual freedom outside the restrictions of marriage. This included new forms of self-expression that were distinctly Western and capitalist. For German men in particular, embracing American styles provided a way to set themselves apart from their fathers' generation, which had actively participated in the Second World War and Nazism. Yet despite such dominant cultural images, there were only 1,000 men for every 1,400 women in West Germany in 1950, and one-third of households were headed by widowed or divorced women. Clearly the effects of the war were still palpable. Still, Western Europe embraced the postwar period as a new era, reveling in the consumerism capitalist prosperity made possible.

Meanwhile, Soviet leadership also began to address living standards and consumption within party rhetoric during the 1950s, known as the Khrushchev era. While the Eastern Bloc continued to privilege production (despite being dominated by shortages), consumption nevertheless became a gendered political battleground on which to compete with the West.[67] Using observation and data collection to monitor public opinion, consumer demand, and household budgets, authorities wanted to maintain control over consumer desires—to shape consumption in a Soviet way. This involved presenting the Soviet woman as a "rational consumer" who contributed to society's development and engaged in a tasteful, communist style of domesticity.[68]

At the same time, Soviet officials believed that women were influenced less by political reasoning and more by emotions and material appeal. But despite viewing them as ideologically inferior, historian Susan Reid notes that officials saw that as consumers, Eastern women wielded power.[69] Their consumption provided a way to counter the stereotype that the communist woman had lost her femininity through labor and equality. By encouraging women to dress fashionably and purchase cosmetics, perfume, and jewelry, Eastern Bloc nations also used gendered products and constructions of the consumer to assert communist superiority. In this way, women's bodies, identities, and consumption were at the center of Cold War debates, even as they did not fall neatly into the constructed dichotomy of East versus West.

Feminist Critiques

Real political change for women after the Second World War depends on how one defines politics and political participation. Some European women did see expanded political rights because of the war, including the right to vote: the Moldavian Soviet Socialist Republic (SSR) passed women's suffrage in 1940; Bulgaria in 1944; France, Italy, and Yugoslavia in 1945; Romania in 1946; Malta in 1947; Belgium in 1948; and Greece in 1952. Many Soviet republics had already granted women the right to vote in 1918 after the 1917 revolution. However, whether suffrage and other formal political gains translated into real political access and benefits for European women is debatable. In fact, women's new or expanded political rights did not have a large impact because women's political participation and influence declined during this period. As with the suffragists who had fought for the right to vote, many postwar women believed that their voices and concerns would best be heard within party politics, yet in France, West Germany, and the UK only 5 to 7 percent of elected officials were women. The USSR had women's councils that functioned as the state's official women's movement, unlike the single-issue, smaller, grassroots campaigns in the West.

Women, especially those in the Western Bloc, began to publicly critique gendered ideologies and roles during this period. French philosopher and novelist Simone de Beauvoir was the most prominent European challenger to assumptions of women's traditional roles. In *The Second Sex*, first published in 1949, she argued, "The man represents both the positive and the neutral, as is indicated by the common use of *man* to designate human beings in general; whereas woman represents only the negative [or that which is different]."[70] De Beauvoir insisted that women's oppression stems from this designation as "the Other" and not the norm. These ideas reflected the conflicting messages women received in Western welfare states. On the one hand, the rapid economic growth, full employment, and high wages for men provided the tax base to afford and promote the cult of domesticity—that white, European women should leave the formal workforce, marry, and reproduce. On the other hand, postwar women were working outside the home in greater numbers than ever, had more educational opportunities, increased personal ambition, and rising expectations. Were both realities possible?

These contradictory messages induced a stress that American feminist Betty Friedan termed "the problem that has no name." Friedan's 1963 bestseller *The Feminine Mystique* outlined this "problem": the expectation that women's satisfaction in life would be derived solely from the domestic sphere—housework, marriage, passive sexuality, and children—and turning away from political and economic engagement left many women deeply unhappy and confused. Based on fifteen years of fieldwork and numerous interviews, Friedan questioned, if a housewife achieved the life she had been socialized to idolize, one that was "truly feminine," then why was she deeply depressed? According to one interviewee, "The problem is always being the children's mommy, or the minister's wife and never being myself," echoing de Beauvoir's sentiments of women existing only in relation to others. Another woman likewise described her depression thusly: "I'm desperate. I begin to feel I have no personality ... [I'm] somebody who can be called on when you want something. But who am I?" Friedan argued that women's subservience to men financially, mentally, physically, and intellectually was what prompted their unhappiness. Furthermore, she insisted that women needed to become aware of their state—to recognize and explore the "problem that has no name"—by having their "consciousness raised."

Friedan's critique of postwar domestic ideologies resonated around the world. *The Feminine Mystique* was one of the most translated books of the 1960s, and won the Pulitzer Prize in 1964. It was the first feminist treatise translated into Catalan during Franco's dictatorship and inspired a similarly revolutionary essay on women in Catalunya, Maria Aurèlia Capmany's "La dona a Catalunya."[71] The translation of Friedan's book was emblematic of a shift toward more liberalizing measures in Spain that permitted the dissemination of more ideological and feminist texts. These translations and the publications they spurred lay the groundwork for a militant and committed Spanish feminist movement that took off after Franco's death in 1975.[72]

While Friedan was perhaps the most read of the time, other European women added their voices to articulations of women's postwar discontent. British psychoanalyst Juliet Mitchell published an essay in 1966 that explained the central paradox of women's lives as a structural problem rather than a personal one: "The situation of women is different from that of any other social group ... They are not one of a number of isolable units, but half a totality: the human species ... [Women] are fundamental to the human condition, yet in their economic, social and political roles, they are marginal."[73] In 1975, German sociologist Helge Pross surveyed West German housewives and concluded that while many enjoyed the flexibility in their workday, they missed the social contact they used to have with coworkers. They were also frustrated by being economically dependent on their husbands.[74] These Western feminist critiques once again placed women at the center of ideological battles. At the height of the Cold War, the very model of the nuclear family, male breadwinner, and women's consumer-driven domestic contentment—which was held up as a triumph of Western welfare states in direct contrast to the Soviet paradigm—was exposed as a sham.

These feminist challenges and arguments did not resonate as strongly with women in Eastern Europe. They saw Friedan's book as essentially claiming that women wanted to pursue careers rather than be middle-class suburban housewives. Bombarded with communist rhetoric celebrating women's roles as workers, they had very little basis to identify with the book's message, let alone view it as a foundational feminist text. After all, as Bulgarian scholar Kornelia Slavova asked, how could the "problem that has no name" be applicable in a society where the state has already emancipated women? Yet, as mentioned above, the "double burden"—women's paid labor outside the home combined with unpaid labor in the home—was common on both sides of the Iron Curtain, and communist ideologies of gender equality did not necessarily translate to Eastern women's lived experiences. As a result, "European feminism" is a tricky and ultimately diverse category as seen in the example of Afro-feminism.

Intersectional Feminism

As coalitions between different groups and identities, feminist movements are intersectional by nature. However, this intersectionality has not always been sufficiently factored into predominately white Western feminisms, which have often overlooked race and class. Partnerships between Black and white feminists have historically been weak, as white feminists are often viewed as at best ignoring the intersectional essence of Black women's experiences and at worst supporting dominant racial hierarchies. In the postwar period, gender, race, class, and international movements collided in significant ways that inspired critical Afro-feminist thought throughout Europe.

In August 1958, Majbritt Morrison, originally from Sweden, was arguing with her Jamaican-born husband Raymond Morrison at a London underground station. Onlookers attempted to intervene, prompting a fight between the bystanders and some of the couple's friends. The following day a gang of youths threw milk bottles at Majbritt Morrison and called her racial slurs for being with a Jamaican man. Later that night, a mob of three to four hundred white people attacked the houses of West Indian residents during what historians now call the Notting Hill race riots. Assaulting the interracial Morrison couple—an alarming but potentially minor incident— set off a wave of violence that impacted the larger immigrant community, tapping into white Londoners' racist anxieties that had been simmering beneath the surface since decolonization. The gendered aspect of the racism—a white woman with a black man—was as significant as it had been in the nineteenth century.[75] The passage of time changed little in this respect, as Brixton police and Black British residents would again clash violently in 1981 and 1985 partially over the wretched living conditions of their neighborhood.

Afro-British women served in important activist roles during this era, particularly in London. In 1953, a group of migrants formed the Nigerian Women's League (NWL) to address the plight of West African women in London, especially the lack of available services and general feelings of isolation. In a speech at a New Year's dance, the Nigerian women emphasized their membership in broader feminist movements as well as what was unique to them: "We believe that the women of Nigeria are capable of following in the courageous footsteps of the many brave women of other lands who have in the past fought against prejudice and overcome overwhelming obstacles … Ours is the cause of Nigerian women."[76] From London, these women called for global change.

Four months before the Notting Hill race riots, Claudia Jones, an influential communist feminist activist originally from Trinidad and Tobago, launched the *West Indian Gazette and Afro-Asian-Caribbean News*, Britain's first national, independent, and commercial Black monthly newspaper.[77] Jones was a significant leader in an intersectional movement for Black London. In response to the riots, she organized a Caribbean-style carnival in Notting Hill, televised by the BBC, meant to change public perceptions of the West Indian community and prevent harassment from white Londoners.[78]

Jones was one of many Black women migrants from the Caribbean, Africa, and Indian subcontinent who settled in Britain after the Second World War. The Black feminist movement they created was connected to both postcolonial activism and 1960s–1970s civil rights movements. These women's concerns about and experiences with race, gender, class, and sexuality intersected in ways unique from other British women. Some anticolonial activists emphasized gendered difference, pointing out that African women in precolonial societies had a higher and more favorable status than that of European women. They blamed British colonialism for degrading women with their introduction of gender hierarchies. Moreover, many Black feminists critiqued their marginalization within mainstream, white-dominated feminist movements, which did not address such colonial legacies or other issues, such as racialized poverty, that many Afro-European women faced. Some also accused white feminists of not just overlooking but also supporting the racial hierarchies shaping European society. Afro-feminist activism grew out of decades of abuse and discrimination, both under colonialism in their home countries and after they had established new homes in Europe. This group of Black feminists was just one of many significant political movements in the postwar period as we will see in the next chapter.

Conclusion

Ideas about women and gender directly impacted every aspect of Cold War politics and daily life. In both the West and East, women's employment, consumption, and fertility took on distinct political meanings, as opposing sides employed gendered ideologies to assert superiority in the competition between capitalism and communism. Their rhetoric and expectations often differed dramatically from women's lived experiences. The postwar period also saw women's employment skyrocket, while technological advances—from oral contraception to the first woman in space—shifted perceptions of women's private and professional lives. Moreover, the end of the Second World War and European decolonization resulted in vast postwar migrations to and throughout Europe. These demographic shifts significantly impacted geopolitics and culture as questions of assimilation, xenophobia, and cross-ethnic relationships redefined who a European woman was and could be.

Despite states' attempts to use female citizens as examples of their respective political and cultural virtues, Eastern and Western European women's lives were not necessarily as diametrically opposed as Cold War rhetoric claimed. In both the Eastern and Western Blocs, women's education and workforce participation increased; both found it difficult to combine family responsibilities with paid work; and in both places, women had little direct political power. But there were significant differences. Women in Eastern Europe complained of overwork, coercion, and oppression, so much so that many rejected the idea of equality as a goal and sought a more traditionally domestic lifestyle. In the Eastern Bloc, both gender equality and higher standards of living proved to be broken promises. Instead of earning women's loyalty to the communist state, official policies and unofficial realities called attention to the empty messages of Soviet propaganda. Consequently, many women in the Eastern Bloc moved away from considering women's rights and toward fighting alongside men for basic human rights. Women's activism, resulting from disillusionment with a conservative postwar order that did not meet their expectations, contributed to the downfall of the communist system, as we will see in later chapters.

In contrast, many Western European women experienced a growing independence from work, enjoying postwar prosperity and a higher standard of living. This was especially true in northern Europe, where states had more social welfare benefits, consumer products, and household technologies. At the same time, women began to question gendered expectations more broadly as a burgeoning second-wave of feminist movement (or movements) took root. Postwar feminists in both the East and the West argued that legislative changes alone were not sufficient to achieve equality. Instead, they sought to enact social and cultural changes, as well as end sex discrimination enshrined in law.

6

Fighting for Expanded Rights

Introduction

In a 1972 interview, pioneering French feminist Simone de Beauvoir reflected that the postwar period saw few real improvements in women's lives: "I realized that the situation of women in France has not really changed in the last twenty years."[1] As the subject of much historical debate, de Beauvoir's sentiment is both true and false. Women across Europe experienced tumultuous changes during the 1960s and 1970s, culminating in fundamental shifts in sexual mores, reproductive autonomy, legal parity, gender relations, and daily life. Attitudes and regulations fluctuated in new ways as politicians, religious leaders, and the mass media navigated this cultural upheaval. Indeed, the relationship between rights and culture is complex, leaving these changes uneven and incomplete, especially when considering the diversity of European women's lives. This chapter uses women's and gender history to explore this complexity and narrate an evolution of power relations in the extended postwar period.

Reproduction remained at the fore in these decades, with more open conversations about sex and advocacy for women's reproductive rights. While the previous chapter emphasized state policies to increase childbirth, many women rejected these pronatalist messages. By the 1960s, medical advances and campaigns for reproductive autonomy succeeded in creating new options for birth control as well as widespread, socially acceptable discussions of it. These innovations had the potential to change women's lives in revolutionary and emancipatory ways, though access varied greatly by country and class. Historians debate the extent to which women in the postwar period had easy and affordable access to modern birth control practices such as sterilization, barrier methods such as condoms and diaphragms, intrauterine devices (IUDs), and oral contraceptives. Moreover, state involvement in fertility persisted, with reproductive rights as a marker of totalitarian governments' control over women's bodies in fascist Spain and Romania, for example. In the context of the Cold War, how the two Blocs addressed reproduction and sexuality and positioned women and the family became points of comparison between authoritarian communist states and liberal market societies.[2] Still, the end of the baby boom was the beginning of a new era in many ways; even if women were not able to access birth control, most knew it existed and sought to limit their fertility (legally or illegally) to pursue other aspects of their lives. Family size decreased with a lasting impact, particularly in Northwestern Europe. This decline in births amid new ways to control fertility is one of the most significant aspects of twentieth-century women's history.

Relatedly, these decades saw extra-parliamentary activism not just for women's legal rights but also against deep-seated gender ideologies in Western, Eastern, and Southern Europe. Scholars refer to this postwar revival of organized resistance for women's rights and issues as the "second-wave" of feminism (pointing to the women's suffrage movements of the late nineteenth and early twentieth centuries as the "first"). European women expressed their frustrations with the limits of changing the legal landscape of the 1950s, and articulated new modes of individualism and democratized sexual attitudes that trumped traditional, elite mores in the 1960s.[3] Second-wave feminists organized to confront issues like abortion rights, equal pay, and gender discrimination, fighting the patriarchy through formal politics and international advocacy as well as public protests, marches, and other, sometimes violent, direct actions. By the 1970s and 1980s, their efforts resulted in significant cultural and legal shifts throughout Europe and ethnic minorities made new demands of their own.

However, women stood at the crossroads of new waves of local and global activism that extended well beyond "women's issues" and gender-based advocacy. Activism for labor and civil rights, women's and gay liberation, reproductive autonomy, and other social justice and prodemocratic efforts often converged within movements, including those fighting against authoritarian regimes. At times, these varied and multifaceted missions came into conflict, pulling women in multiple directions. Moreover, depending on national and political context, many activists were unable to focus on just one issue, such as childcare or equal pay, and thus folded "feminist" actions into larger demands for change.

As in earlier eras, European women's bodies, citizenship, demands, struggles, and successes intersected with national and global politics in the extended postwar period, but the radical activism and cultural and legislative shifts of the 1960s and 1970s could certainly be characterized as revolutionary. However, historians note that these transformations were not necessarily the start of a revolution so much as a culmination of decades of technological innovation, study, activism, and changing social mores. And as de Beauvoir implied, in some ways these events were emancipatory for women and in others, not at all.

Technology and Fertility

The contraceptive known as "The Pill" has been called the most significant scientific invention of the twentieth century. An artificial hormone supplement to be taken daily, the Pill was first approved for use in the

United States in 1960 and arrived in Germany and Britain in 1961. By 1967, when it became legal in France, nearly 13 million women used oral contraception worldwide, establishing family planning as a new norm.[4] Still, historians debate how truly revolutionary the Pill was for European women. On the one hand, many among those who could access the Pill found it life-changing, as the ability to control their fertility impacted career and other life choices. On the other hand, how transformative could it be when only a minority of European women had access to it?

Despite the Pill's revolutionary potential, women did not necessarily get to make their own decisions about birth control, and it was not readily available for all women due to both laws and customs. Class, social norms, and religion all impacted access to the Pill, which was primarily an option for Western married, middle-class couples due to both its cost and doctors' attitudes. As an American development, the USSR was uninterested in its dissemination and enacted policies and laws aimed at limiting its availability. On both sides of the Iron Curtain, doctors became the main gatekeepers of birth control.[5] In Western Europe, as prescribers of the Pill, physicians took on new authority over women's sexuality, family planning, and reproductive health. Additionally, it took researchers a decade to address the Pill's serious side effects. Even clinical trials for the Pill's safety and effectiveness did not always involve informed consent.[6] Moreover, in 1959, the British "Population Investigation Committee" of the London School of Economics conducted a nationwide study of citizens' conceptions of marriage, contraception, and family size. Questioning who made decisions about birth control in marriages, the report found that "contraception is still part of the husband's prerogative."[7] In a 1965 study, many British women still reported feeling uncomfortable raising the subject of contraception with their husbands because they saw it as his domain.[8]

Even if postwar family planning policies generated more public discussion of sex within marriage, Western Europe generally saw a return to more conservative sexual mores and ideas of sexual respectability.[9] A rise in church attendance reflected this shift. Churches had great influence in preventing the dissemination and use of birth control, as religious leaders and public officials in culturally Catholic countries heavily restricted and withheld information on contraception, making the issue both religious and political. In 1968, Pope Paul VI released the Catholic Church's official position on the Pill, declaring birth control (and abortion) to be sinful and unnatural. In Spain, run by fascist dictator Francisco Franco, the state could exert pressure and enforce its own policies on reproduction, and liberal welfare states in Northern Europe and countries in the socialist Eastern Bloc also regulated contraception and abortion.[10] It was not until the 1970s that young, single women (primarily in Northwestern Europe) gained legal access to the Pill. Yet despite restrictive policies, pronatalist messages, and religious censure, many European women used birth control even if it meant breaking the law, and more traditional forms of contraception, such as the rhythm method (avoiding intercourse during ovulation), abstinence, and douching continued.[11]

This period also saw reproduction medicalized in new ways with advances in sonograms, fetal monitoring, amniocentesis, and the final move from midwifery to hospital births in large numbers.[12] At the same time, scientific innovations aided women previously thought unable to bear their own children. In vitro fertilization (IVF) allowed wealthy women in Western countries to conceive, and the first "test-tube baby," Louise Joy Brown, was born in Great Britain on July 25, 1978. British nurse, embryologist, and pioneer of fertility treatment Jean Purdy worked alongside physiologist Robert Edwards and gynecologist Patrick Steptoe on Louise Joy Brown's successful birth and oversaw the conception of over 500 babies (Figure 6.1).[13]

FIGURE 6.1 *British nurse and embryologist Jean Purdy (1945–85) hands physiologist Robert Edwards a dish containing fertilized human egg cells in their research laboratory in Cambridge, February 28, 1968. Getty Images.*

Following the accomplishment in England, tens of thousands of women gave birth through IVF, though the procedure's high cost limited access. By creating possibility in previously impossible scenarios—such as deceased mothers or fathers being able to produce offspring, and new options for same-sex parents—IVF changed and multiplied the meaning of motherhood.

The practice was not devoid of critics, however. In the wake of Hitler's Germany, some feared IVF would allow totalitarian states to create children for their armies. Others thought IVF was shameful and unnatural and would usher in a social revolution alongside the scientific one by allowing single women and same-sex couples to conceive. Bioethicists debated the moral distinctions between "medically infertile patients" who are unable to have children biologically, and "socially infertile patients" who are unable to have children due to sexual orientation or lack of a partner.[14] Still others thought it reinforced the stigma of the "childless" woman as less worthy, while reaffirming traditional gender roles that implied all women should aspire to motherhood.[15] It was not until the early 1980s that IVF births became more commonplace and gained public acceptance (for married couples mostly), especially in countries that offered high reimbursement levels for the expensive procedure, such as in Scandinavia.[16] The history of IVF is an interesting case study in the strategic use of "rights" in issues of fertility.

A Sexual Revolution?

The postwar period saw significant changes in sex and sexuality in European societies and culture: the professionalization of sex research, discussions of selling sex, pornography's legalization and growth, greater representation of sexual minorities, and changing mores and laws. By the late 1950s, sex education texts and advice literature for improving intimacy in marriages were bestsellers, and the Pill's decoupling of sex from reproduction changed the sexual dynamics between men and women.[17] The increased use of birth control liberated many heterosexual women to enjoy sexual exploration with new excitement and new demands for satisfaction from their partners. In addition, the younger generation who had not lived through the Second World War began to challenge assumptions and images that promoted a traditional family. During the 1960s, increasing numbers (though still a minority) of young adults lived apart from their parents and took advantage of newly legal and available contraception and, later, decriminalized abortions. Media and advertising also promoted a "sexual revolution," encouraging young men and women to partake in individualism and sexual freedom through consumer goods and by featuring sex in movies, music, and advertising.[18]

In Western Europe, the idea of a generational shift toward a freer sexual culture was apparent in new hairstyles, makeup, higher hemlines, and more slacks for women. Notably, the younger generation had more disposable income than adolescents of previous eras, and popular culture turned to this younger crowd, featuring sex more prominently in movies, music, and other media. Beginning in the 1960s, advertisers embraced the notion that "sex sells" and used suggestive images to promote a wide range of consumer goods, playing on these generational differences.[19] The media publicized a sexual revolution to market products—even if the sexual revolution they were selling was not most people's lived reality. Indeed, while older generations believed that younger adults engaged in unconstrained sexual experimentation, surveys conducted at the time did not find that the majority of young adults were much different from the older generation, especially when compared to the first sexual revolution from the late nineteenth century through the "roaring" 1920s.[20] Much of the so-called sexual revolution heavily advertised was a façade.

Even so, sexuality was a popular consumer product, and erotica became a big business. The commercialization of sex in 1960s West Germany included illustrated magazines filled with suggestive images of women in alluring positions and outfits, sex surveys, and classified ads for mail order erotica. Before the expansion of the West German erotica industry, sexual conservatism, characterized by the 1953 anti-pornography Law on Youth-Endangering Texts, had ruled the day, and erotica entrepreneurs had to be careful not to surpass what the law and public opinion would tolerate. Older conservative attitudes proved increasingly irrelevant within a few years, though, as illustrated magazines brought sex into the public sphere and condom vending machines (in full view of children, some pointed out) accounted for up to half of all condom sales.[21]

Conversely, in East Germany, the state emphasized reproductive heterosexuality while also banning homosexuality, discouraging adultery, and making abortions nearly impossible to obtain.[22] The government also declared pornography decadent and profit-oriented, unlike socialism's "healthy sexuality."[23] Yet the East German state also used publications with sexual or erotic content—including photos of topless and full frontal nude women—to garner public interest, their own form of advertising for what they were selling ideologically.[24] Such widespread media attention demonstrates that while sexual behaviors and attitudes may not have been revolutionary, there was clearly a public appetite for sex in many postwar nations.

Gay and Lesbian Communities and Identity

However, cultural or attitudinal changes about sexuality generally did not extend to homosexual communities, and the discrimination and criminalization of the prewar years continued. In West Germany, homosexuals who had survived concentration camps could be arrested again as "repeat offenders" under a seventy-year law against homosexuality that was not officially repealed until 1994.²⁵ In fact, gay people were arrested at higher rates during this period than under the Nazi regime. In France, a 1946 law prevented homosexuals from taking jobs in public service, and in 1950s Sweden, an extreme social backlash against homosexuals resulted in police raids and witch hunts in the media. The Catholic Church also went on the offensive against a "homosexual peril," while in the West, gay people could be prosecuted as potential communists in addition to being arrested for homosexual behavior.²⁶ Significantly, lesbian sexuality and women's status within these legal codes were elusive and unclear, leaving the people and activities associated with homosexuality most often gendered male.²⁷

Movements to decriminalize homosexuality in some parts of Western and Eastern Europe were successful at the end of the 1950s and the following decades. By the late 1950s, Denmark, France, Italy, the Netherlands, Sweden, and Switzerland had eliminated criminal penalties against homosexuality.²⁸ In Hungary, repressive laws against homosexuality were reversed in 1958. The Hungarian Ministry of Health unanimously supported decriminalizing same-sex relations between consenting adults, based mainly on a switch to a medical definition of homosexuality as an innate biological phenomenon instead of a deviant personal choice.²⁹ In 1960, the Homosexual Law Reform Society was founded in the UK and same-sex activity was decriminalized in England and Wales by 1967. Although such legislative moves to decriminalize homosexuality were undeniably significant, predominant attitudes take much longer to transition. Consequently, gay men and lesbians continued to navigate social stigma and violence well beyond decriminalization.³⁰

Nevertheless, European women explored their sexual choices in ways that did not accept postwar sexual mores. A collective lesbian identity emerged, built on the vibrant communal lesbian bar culture of the interwar years, as well as new opportunities for same-sex intimacy that emerged during the war's single-sex environments, such as factories and the military. Parisian women who desired women, for example, claimed social spaces for themselves in their daily lives—at outdoor markets, movies, or on the metro. In many ways, the crowds and anonymity of urban life made such community building possible. One French woman from the countryside, Geneviève, noted that "dragging" (dressing in men's clothing) was more difficult in small towns where one could not "do what one pleased." Geneviève had met the love of her life while serving as an ambulance driver during the Second World War, noting, "Truly, one is free in the army."³¹ Like gay men, lesbians crafted their own worlds in bars and clubs in many European metropoles after the war. Patricia from Paris recalled that in the 1960s the only place to meet other women was in a club, despite their limited numbers. In London, the Gateways nightclub was a popular dance spot both before and after the war.³² In the postwar period, these clubs were not just part of a larger bohemian night scene as in the interwar era, but increasingly distinct, coherent, and physically discrete lesbian spaces.³³ Now, lesbians reserved areas within larger pubs for women to have private parties and to have "a place to go."³⁴ In the Eastern Bloc, women lived closeted lives but also carved out spaces for themselves, such as in Hungary, where lesbian women's meeting places were "tolerated," as discriminatory laws only applied to men.[35] Regardless, these communal spaces played a large role in the postwar development of a collective lesbian identity across Europe.

A significant shift in awareness and attitudes around homosexuality arose in the 1960s and 1970s, inspired in part by these evolving queer subcultures and spaces as well as the broader opening of views toward sex. Britain's first lesbian magazine, *Arena Three*, published its first issue in the spring of 1964 and by 1965 had over 600 private subscribers.[36] *Arena Three* sought to address negative attitudes in the general (and largely heterosexual) public about lesbian identity and culture, with articles about self-doubt, job discrimination, and joy at finding a lesbian community. The magazine also printed letters from the lesbians themselves, which offer insight into how these articles were received.[37] Mary L. of Petersfield, UK, wrote to *Arena Three* in 1965, thrilled to see the magazine's positive portrayal of lesbian love: "I ... was almost shocked to be actually seeing something so vitally applied to me—it was so unusual! I was delighted that the myth that lesbian loves never work, never last, was exploded." Not everyone celebrated lesbians' increased visibility, though. Miss A. M. A. J. and Miss T. H. wrote to *Arena Three* later in 1965 that the growing public awareness was making their lives more difficult:

> My friend and I have lived together now for four years ... Since these articles have been appearing in the Sunday press and on TV we have noticed an increasing (but Morbid) interest in our relationship with each other ... [Y]ou have caused lots of unhappiness and unnecessary embarrassment ... We do not wish to be the subject of curious speculation ... [We] do not need to fight a cause for the general public to be educated.[38]

These two contrasting letters highlight how debates, discussions, and ideas about sexual identity moved into the public sphere and took on new political importance as women navigated a new mode of lesbian identity in the 1960s. In the following decades, this attention to identity politics would politicize sexual orientation itself. Couched in larger, more assertive grassroots battles for homosexual recognition, rights, and decriminalization, conflicts emerged over the ostensibly apolitical culture of public leisure versus the political agenda and urgent activism of the gay liberation movement.[39]

Second-Wave Feminism

The postwar period saw a concentrated revival of feminist activism not just against legal inequality but also against de facto discrimination and misogyny in everyday life. In addition to fights for equal pay for equal work, rights within marriages, reproductive rights, and expanded political rights, feminist movements demanded changes in society and culture, including access to childcare to relieve women's double burden, challenging sexism in the workplace, and increased bodily autonomy. Many Western feminists in the 1960s and 1970s objected to what they saw as the heightened commodification, sexualization, and objectification of women's bodies.[40] Their fight for bodily control occurred within a larger context of other contentious struggles—such as battles for labor rights, gay liberation, and resistance to totalitarian regimes. These movements at times intersected and at times splintered, with national context playing a significant role.

Despite many gains, overall, the progressive shift in women's legal status in the immediate postwar years either fell short or slowed considerably. For many Western European countries, it was not until the 1970s that wives and mothers had full legal parity: French wives could first control their own property in 1965 and gained full parental rights in 1970, and in Italy, civil divorce and equal parental rights were first granted in the 1970s. Though West Germany repealed a law in 1957 that gave fathers sole control over legal decisions for children, West German women were still not legally equal to their husbands until 1977. Married women in Iceland were legally considered dependents of their husbands, and it was not until 1978 that the taxation system granted women some legal independence.[41] Lastly, it was first in the 1980s that Portuguese and Spanish women gained property and parental rights.[42]

Feminist activists often found solidarity, including across class boundaries, with single-issue concerns. For example, public childcare was a mobilizing issue in Sweden where feminists focused primarily on labor and economic equality.[43] Likewise, in 1967, in a communal kitchen in West Berlin, women founded the Action Council for the Liberation of Women (ACLW) to establish self-organized, anti-authoritarian childcare facilities known as Kinderläden (or day care centers).[44] The ACLW mobilized hundreds of students and working women who found that their roles as wives and mothers hindered their career opportunities, and they achieved tangible results.[45] Although men were not included in the organization, the ACLW attempted to work with like-minded (and often male-dominated groups), such as the popular West German Socialist German Student Union (SDS). Yet, reflecting a common experience among activist women, their male colleagues ignored them and dismissed their concerns, maintaining that feminist demands came second to socialist class-based issues. On September 12, 1968, at an SDS conference in Frankfurt, activist and filmmaker Helke Sander of the Berlin ACLW demanded that the group address women's oppression seriously and urgently. When her speech at the SDS conference was met with ignorance and arrogance, enraged audience member Sigrid Rüger pelted the SDS board members with tomatoes.[46] The thrown tomato became a symbol of women's rebellion and political awakening to articulate their demands.[47] Moreover, such experiences convinced many activist women of the need to establish their own autonomous feminist organizations.

Second-wave feminism, as with the first wave, pushed for women's equality with more than speeches. Like the thrown tomatoes, some protests took public forms designed to garner media attention to their causes. The Dutch socialist feminist group Dolle Mina (Mad Mina), founded in 1969, used playful and entertaining demonstrations as well as more aggressive ones. In 1970, they placed toddler-filled playpens in front of the Amsterdam stock exchange to highlight the deficiency of Dutch childcare services.[48] Later that year, while campaigning for equal access to public toilets (only urinals for men were available), they installed a towering papier-mâché penis labeled "Ladies Room" (Figure 6.2).[49] Dolle Mina members also crashed a gynecological conference and bared their stomachs, across which they had written: "boss of one's own belly."[50] Four years later in 1974, when the Minister of Justice attempted to close down an abortion clinic in Bloemenhove, Dolle Mina and other women occupied the space and prevented the police from entering for two weeks.[51] The clinic remained open, and the issue of women's right to abortion prompted a new coalition of women's groups named We Women Demand. Dolle Mina firmly believed that radical action needed a performative edge—a public spectacle—to attract the attention needed for change.[52]

In many Western European countries, public protests were more than playful: kidnappings and more radical forms of activism—even terrorism, such as planting bombs—became more common as activists felt their protests were not effective enough. Though these groups were not always specifically feminist, many women took on leadership roles within them, as in the West German organization the Red Army Faction, co-led by Ulrike Meinhof.[53] Another West German feminist group, Red Zora, also supported militant guerrilla action: "Our dream is that there are small gangs of women everywhere; and that a rapist, trafficker of women, wife batterer, porn dealer, creepy gynecologist must fear that a gang of women finds him, attacks him, and humiliates him in public."[54] Red Zora followed through with this vision, launching media campaigns and demonstrations that publicly humiliated those implicated in violence against women. The group also organized protests in sex shops, clogging the toilets and setting off small incendiary devices. Their actions escalated to include larger bombings, such as of a Karlsruhe court, after it ruled in favor of an anti-abortion law.[55] As with other second-wave feminist groups, Red Zora fought for access to safe, legal abortion, an end to violence against women, against sexism in the media, and in solidarity with international feminist movements—and went about it violently.[56]

Legal Abortion and Reproductive Autonomy in Western Europe

A women's right to control her body was a unifying element of feminist movements in the postwar period, culminating in the 1970s with legislative changes legalizing abortion. European efforts to decriminalize abortion

FIGURE 6.2 *Dolle Mina protest with a giant penis at a public toilet on Dam Square, April 30, 1970. Getty Images.*

differed based on political context, such as states that were politically stable versus unstable, and democratic versus authoritarian regimes. Abortion was and remains symbolic in many ways: it was not just a medical, social, or economic matter linked to women's sexuality, autonomy, and privacy, but also a highly politicized issue connected to morality, nationhood, and demographic decline.[57] Divergent political and nonpolitical groups weighed in, such as religious organizations, in ways that cut across established political constituencies and were equally significant to Western, Southern, and Eastern European women's lives. As mentioned previously, even in the age of revolutionary preventative measures like the Pill, most women still had to battle for access to older contraceptive methods.

Before the advent of the Pill and even beyond, abortion was simultaneously illegal, common, and difficult to secure. Mary Ingham, a British woman from a rural town, explained that the only options for unplanned pregnancies were undesirable ones: adoption, single motherhood, or a hasty marriage.[58] Ingham's memoir recounts a telling example in 1960s Britain in which a women's boyfriend deceptively provided false contraception pills and, once she was pregnant, arranged for an illegal abortion. During the procedure, the doctor used a saline injection to induce labor and then abandoned the woman to lay on dirty newspaper in agonizing pain for more than a day. She was eventually saved and taken to a hospital where unsympathetic nurses tended to her. Stories like this gave many women a sense of urgency in their fight for reproductive rights, as abortion was the leading cause of maternal deaths.

Obtaining the legal right to abortion in Britain had been an ongoing battle after bills proposed in 1953, 1961, 1965, and 1966 had failed.[59] At the same time, a tragedy involving a drug used to combat morning sickness was also unfolding. When the medication, thalidomide, was found to cause birth defects, abortion rights activists, including the Anglican church, campaigned for the right to legal abortion in case of risk to the mother's or baby's life and in tricky questions of birth defects. The successful UK 1967 Abortion Act changed many women's lives significantly.

By the 1970s, campaigns for reproductive rights that began in the 1960s saw real legislative changes in other parts of Western Europe. Denmark legalized abortion in 1973, West Germany in 1974, France in 1975, and Italy in 1978.[60] In 1902, Norway legalized abortion in cases where the mother's life was in danger, or the baby could be stillborn; and in 1969, the Norwegian Labour Party expanded access to the procedure even further. In the Norwegian case, abortion on request was included as part of a broader recognition of feminist politics on the party platform. This example shows how abortion was not necessarily just a "women's issue" but one that garnered attention from some mainstream political parties alongside other feminist demands.

Like most reform, though, the change was uneven: abortion was not legal in the Netherlands until 1984 and Belgium until 1990. Such divergent results make it difficult for historians to conclude whether or not the extended postwar period was truly emancipatory or revolutionary for European women, especially when considering such a diverse group of people. Indeed, nations such as Spain and Portugal were ruled by extremist right-wing dictators during this era, and abortion was not a legal right on request in Spain until 2010. In Portugal, as in many other countries, women mobilized for their collective agency around the issue of reproductive rights. Modern contraception was not available to most women, as the regime had forbidden it in line with restrictive pronatalist policies. Combined with limited sex education and few resources, these conditions resulted in many illegal and dangerous abortions. What's more, the regime rarely prosecuted illegal abortions and kept limited records in order to deflect attention from the issue. In this context, many of the practitioners that provided the procedure sought to punish the women seeking it and took advantage of their positions, including charging more for the use of anesthesia—a cruel proviso many had no choice but to accept.[61] One woman reported that doctors attempted to discourage abortions by treating women viciously: "When they arrive at the hospitals they scrape them in cold blood ... to demoralize women ... to not have any more abortions."[62] Unlike in other Western European countries, Portuguese women's movements that fought for abortion rights made the case that abortion was, above all, a social justice issue affecting poor working-class women as much as a gendered concern.[63] Under authoritarian rule, including reproductive freedom within political discussions of class inequality and private versus the state's rights placed women at the crossroads of Portugal's future.

Legal Abortion and Reproductive Autonomy in Eastern Europe

Some Eastern European states saw similar reforms in abortion access as the West, such as East Germany, Czechoslovakia, and Yugoslavia. However, birth control's impact and larger issues of reproductive autonomy in Eastern Europe have a complex history due to a central paradox of communist rule—the premise of gender equality and a substantial pronatalist drive. After the 1917 Bolshevik Revolution, the USSR legalized abortion in 1920. However, Stalin turned away from women's equality and recriminalized the procedure in 1936 amid an international decline in births.[64] Following Stalin's death, the Soviet Union again reversed restrictions on abortion in 1955 due to the medical risks of illegal abortions, which were on the rise. Other Eastern European countries followed suit, fearing dropping birthrates, and by the mid- to late 1960s, Albania, Bulgaria, and Romania had recriminalized abortion.[65] Despite these bans, limited access to contraception in the Eastern Bloc resulted in what scholars call an "abortion culture," where abortion became the most common method of preventing childbirth, leading to a spike in illegal abortions, maternal mortality, and overcrowded orphanages.[66]

The restriction of reproductive rights in Eastern Europe was most extreme in Albania and Romania, where dictators drew their pronatalist policies both from a desire to modernize as well as maintain traditional gender power relations. After the Second World War, mass employment and advances in education motivated many Albanian women to pursue interests outside of motherhood, but national rhetoric did not support them. Although Albanian women were legally equal to men under communism, the state also believed that the family was sacred. In the end, Albanian women had little of the Eastern Bloc's proclaimed gender equality, as strong patriarchal traditions trumped all other political ideals. Women's double burden was extreme, caring for their children, husbands, and in-laws and often doing housework, including laundry by hand, with little help. During the 1970s economic crisis, the Communist Party-sanctioned Women's Union campaigned for domestic assistance for women, and some did see increased help from male family members at home.[67] But in this same context, women had few rights within marriage and divorce was difficult to obtain; they could not cite being spiritually or sexually dissatisfied or even claim marital rape as causes for divorce, since husbands saw sexual access to their wives as their right.

Indeed, Albanian women's inequality in public and private were interlinked. The Penal Code of 1977 banned abortion and punished repeat offenders as well as providers who caused the mother's death through abortion.[68] The state's commitment to pronatalism also benefited from a dearth of modern contraceptives (pharmacies stopped selling condoms in 1981), and doctors not only received little training about sexuality and birth control, but were also not allowed to discuss family planning, even when economically distressed families pleaded for help.[69] In this context of desperation, maternal deaths due to self-induced illegal abortions ranged from 36 to 62 percent of all maternal deaths between 1985 and 1991. At the same time, Albania's pronatalist program provided incentives for women to become mothers. For example, women who gave birth to twelve or more children were given the title "Heroic Mother" (with little other reward).[70]

Romania had one of the most notorious pronatalist policies that repressed women and their offspring for generations. Romania granted the right to abortion in 1957, following the wave of liberalizing legislation in Eastern Europe. However, in 1966, communist dictator Nicolae Ceaușescu implemented a pronatalist policy based on the idea that Romania needed a large population of workers to rapidly develop the economy. Without warning, on October 1, 1966, abortion became only legally available to women over age forty-five, who already had four living children, or for whom pregnancy would put their lives at risk.[71] Decree 770 placed women at the center of Ceaușescu's regressive policies, declaring that it was their responsibility to provide a "great nation" with a large population and, echoing some of Hitler's eugenic ideas, encouraging ethnic minorities to emigrate. The Romanian woman's role was clear: to be a fruitful socialist mother.[72]

Instead of carrots, Romania chose sticks. In lieu of financial incentives or symbolic awards, propaganda negatively targeted childless women and the state banned all forms of birth control. Contraceptives were sometimes available on the black market, but they were cost-prohibitive for most women, even condoms.[73] With policies that indirectly forced pregnancies, Ceaușescu declared that "the fetus is the socialist property of the whole society. Giving birth is a patriotic duty. Those who refused to have children are deserters."[74] Accordingly, the government issued penalties for Romanians who did not procreate, increasing income taxes by 10 or 20 percent (depending on socio-professional category) for childless citizens over the age of twenty-five of any gender or marital status, even in cases of medically diagnosed infertility.[75] Employed women between the ages of sixteen and forty-five were subjected to periodic mandatory gynecological exams in the workplace or risked losing their healthcare, pensions, and social security.[76] State officials also made unannounced home visits to interrogate women about how often they had sexual intercourse with their husbands and why it had not resulted in pregnancy, accusing them of pursuing an unpatriotic boycott.[77]

Some Romanian women took matters into their own hands, waging their own war against the repressive pronationalist state. An underground abortion industry emerged, run by both amateurs and medical professionals.[78] Illegal abortion became women's primary method of birth control, with some claiming to have had between five and seven abortions. Even so, they were dangerous and expensive, and the state kept Romania's high maternal mortality rate a secret.[79] In ethnographies conducted after 1989, many Romanian women spoke out about the loneliness, vulnerability, and terror they associated with reproduction and sex under the totalitarian, patriarchal state.[80] Moreover, this repression had lasting consequences. With limited access to abortion, contraception, and resources to support their children, Romanian orphanages filled to overflowing, often with newborns. Generations of children were left to survive in inhumane conditions of violence, hunger, cold, sexual abuse, and rampant outbreaks of contagious diseases such as HIV/AIDS.[81]

As the Romanian case shows, women's bodies continued to be central to Cold War culture: in the communist ideology of production and reproduction; in state control and surveillance; and in burgeoning dissent movements that eventually ended the Cold War. Indeed, reproductive and marriage rights formed the core of many fights for increased democracy, as women demanded fundamental legal changes to achieve full citizenship. While many of these fights are framed as "women's issues" and many self-identified feminist organizations approached them as such (particularly in the West), women living under totalitarian regimes in the Eastern Bloc often saw concerns like reproductive freedom as integral components of larger movements.

Student Activism and Global Revolution

Throughout Europe, the renewal and evolution of feminism took place amid broader social and economic activism, particularly among younger generations. The year 1968 was of global revolution mobilized by young people and workers worldwide: university students shut down towns for days and months across the globe from Argentina to the Soviet Union to Japan and some were arrested and even killed.[82] Women were ardently involved in this diverse activism, including civil rights campaigns, antiwar protests, organized labor, and feminist demands. As seen in the last chapter, decolonization and national liberation movements in Africa, Asia, Central America, and the Middle East offered alternative models of radical social transformation. Many European activists, men and women, saw in these global revolutions what was missing in European activism, not only in idealism but also in their violence, as some would later turn to terrorism.[83] Women were central protagonists in these revolutions—as leaders and organizers, as protesters in the streets, and as negotiators of peace.[84]

Universities were the perfect breeding ground for student organizing and activism.[85] Enrollment in higher education rose dramatically in the postwar years, especially for women, and by the mid-1960s, more European women were attending universities than ever before. Unlike previous generations, female students could reflect upon what they were learning and experiencing without the pressure of children and marriage, and many developed a new political consciousness. Although most young people in Europe did not attend universities, student movements loom large in the historical landscape and define this period as one of hardening generational differences. Moreover, as student protests increased, their activism grew to include widespread issues and demographics well beyond university grounds. In France, for example, fed up university students joined the local workers' movement to enact large strikes that shut down Paris in May 1968. Women activists were on the frontlines of the police response, getting beaten and arrested alongside their male counterparts. But unlike male activists, some of these women were subjected to gendered sexual violence and raped in the back of police vans and at police stations, as happened in Prague in 1967.[86]

Student protests started with localized issues but quickly bloomed into larger critiques of the state. Some even expanded to have revolutionary global impact, as in Czechoslovakia after the lights in Prague's Strahov dormitory went out on October 31, 1967. To the students left in the dark, the building's consistent blackouts exemplified the poor conditions under which they had been living, and dormitory residents spontaneously gathered in the outside courtyard chanting: "We want light!" The police responded by using their patrol cars to herd the students onto the sidewalks and into the courtyard, where they attacked them with tear gas and beat them with their batons.[87] The protestors' chant for "light" was both literal and symbolic, reflecting demands for more democracy and transparency in the government. Unrest and discontent had been growing in Eastern Europe since the late 1940s, and much ensuing activism came after Stalin died in 1953, a period characterized by political liberalization known as "de-Stalinization." The 1967 student demonstration in Prague launched a wave of protests in Czechoslovakia that would result in a Soviet invasion and global response.

In 1968, the year after the dormitory protest, Alexander Dubçek became the new leader of the Communist Party of Czechoslovakia. Dubçek called for more political and social openness—"socialism with a human face." He abolished censorship, allowed competing political groups, and reinstated the secret ballot to protect citizens' votes. Cultural, social, and political liberalizations blossomed in this environment, during what scholars now call the Prague Spring. Community members began to speak out at local meetings, previously banned books became available, Western films were shown in cinemas, and some students were able to travel.[88] Many women were energized by the prospect of reforms, such as the extension of maternity leave, and there was much excitement around Dubçek.[89] According to one memoir, "[Women] would wait for Alexander Dubçek ... They brought pieces of homemade cake or bunches of flowers. Children gave him their teddy bears for good luck."[90]

The Soviet Union responded to Dubçek's changes by invading Czechoslovakia with 200,000 Warsaw Pact troops and 5,000 tanks on August 20, 1968, who were met with Czechoslovak resistance, especially by young men and women and university students. At 4:00 a.m., the morning of the invasion, journalist Vera Homolova received a call about the invading troops and rushed to the Czechoslovak Radio newsroom. When troops burst through both the barricades and the hundreds of people who had gathered to protect the radio, Homolova managed to escape to a nearby building that functioned as a provisional studio. Homolova and two colleagues received messages and broadcast until September 9, 1968, never leaving the studio. University students, such as Vera Roubalova, fought back by taking down street signs to confound the invading troops. They also painted signs that read, "Go Home Ivan!"[91] Despite brave resistance, the Soviets gained control and ended the uprising. Members of the Czechoslovak resistance were fired, assigned to menial jobs, and followed by Soviet officers. They continued their opposition work, however, but they had to move their operations underground—sometimes literally when meeting in basements. Moving to domestic spaces allowed women more access to resistance movements and to participate undetected, especially after the formation of Charter 77, discussed in the next chapter.[92]

Protests against the Soviet invasion of Czechoslovakia were intense and widespread, including a few key demonstrations by Eastern European women. In the 1968 Summer Olympics in Mexico City, the Czechoslovak gymnast Vera Čáslavská tied with a Soviet athlete and when sharing the podium with her, stood with her face down and head turned away from the USSR flag during their national anthem. "I longed to humiliate the Soviet flag and raise my humble nation," she said after.[93] In support of Czechoslovakia, the International Olympic Committee did not punish Čáslavská.[94] In Moscow's Red Square, Soviet dissent poet Natalya Gorbanevskaya, organizer Larisa Bogoraz, and six others protested publicly but peacefully against the Soviet invasion of Czechoslovakia, holding banners reading: "Shame on the Occupiers," "Long Live Free and Independent Czechoslovakia!" and "Freedom for Dubçek." The protesters were beaten, arrested, stood trial, and either imprisoned, exiled, or sent to psychiatric penitentiaries.[95]

While activists like Gorbanevskaya and Bogoraz demonstrated publicly and authored petitions and letters of protest, Gorbanevskaya was already being watched by Soviet security forces because she had been involved in a "self-publishing" movement across the Eastern Bloc also known as *samizdat*.[96] *Samizdat* involved clandestinely copying and sharing either typed or handwritten information, news, or fiction—poems in Gorbanevskaya's case—and asked the readers to themselves type or hand copy a version to continue the distribution. Indeed, since many women were professional typists, they were often the engine of *samizdat* and worked from their homes at great personal risk.[97] These *samizdat* copyists were crucial to the dissident movements and networks that eventually ended the Cold War across Eastern Europe. In Poland, for example, women were influential as editors, journalists, and communication strategists in illegal opposition press.[98] In the USSR, Gorbanevskaya founded and edited the journal *Chronical of Current Events* to publicly expose and denounce official responses, noting: "The [publication's] importance ... lies in the fact that we created this information, publicity, by our own efforts ... [including] information from the camps and prisons ... I know how difficult it is, how complex and almost impossible, and how it reaches us thanks to the gigantic risks."[99] The *Chronical* and her unrelenting protests led to Gorbanevskaya's eventual arrest and two-year imprisonment in a mental hospital; she lived the rest of her life in exile. Women like Gorbanevskaya, though a minority, remained significant leaders in dissident movements in the 1970s and 1980s, especially through their essential roles in *samizdat*.

Gay and Lesbian Liberation

In Western Europe, gay and lesbian activists who had long been involved in other cases—such as civil rights, third-world liberation, women's liberation, student activism, and workers' rights—now took up their own, inspired by radical protests in New York City. On June 28, 1969, police raided a New York gay bar, the Stonewall Inn, and a group of gay men, lesbians, and transgender women spontaneously fought back in anger. This was not a planned protest with a distinct political agenda, but a confrontation born of deep-seeded frustration that energized grassroots activism for gay rights globally. European gays and lesbians heard a new and radical voice from

New York in a period when police and societal harassment had continued despite legal reforms or in areas still seeking legal reforms. Taking their cue from the US gay liberation movement, organizations challenging homophobia and demanding gay rights emerged in London, Paris, and West Germany, and annual marches honoring Stonewall spread across Western Europe.[100] In 1968, gay rights movements across Europe held protests, and in 1971, the first Gay Power march was held in Öreboro, Sweden. In Germany and France groups dedicated to action and revolution—such as the Homosexual Action West Berlin (HAW) and the Homosexual Front for Revolutionary Action in Paris (FHAR)—formed in 1971 as well.

Yet in the cauldron of 1960s and 1970s activism, voices for gay rights—and especially lesbian rights—were often drowned out amid other protests for economic, social, and political change. Second-wave feminists did not necessarily fight for lesbian rights, seeing gender, not sexual identity, as the primary source of oppression, and civil rights activists prioritized racism over sexism. Indeed, competing demands pulled women in multiple directions. Lesbian rights groups often splintered from both gay liberation movements (that could be majority male) and feminist movements (that were majority heterosexual) even if they originated in them. In Great Britain, lesbian activists who had been involved in the Gay Liberation Front, an organizational movement hub, splintered off in the 1970s and 1980s. In 1982, West German lesbian groups formed the umbrella organization Lesbian Circle to articulate their specific concerns for equality.[101] In the 1980s, international activism picked up as well—the LGBT acronym and the rainbow flag were adopted—and saw increasing successes in European parliaments and with international bodies; for example, the World Health Organization removed homosexuality from its list of mental illnesses in 1993.[102] In 1994, sexual rights language was introduced to the UN Conference on Population and Development in Cairo, though it would take another decade for a resolution on sexual orientation to be drafted. Distinct lesbian movements and communities continued to organize independently, fighting discriminatory laws, police abuse, and other issues.[103]

Women's Labor Activism

European women have been active in labor movements since the Industrial Revolution, and in the 1970s, women's labor activism again reached a fever pitch when an oil crisis caused a global economic downturn. Heavily industrialized Western European countries had previously increased productivity by simply hiring more workers, but as factories became more mechanized, workers were either replaced with faster machinery or pushed to work at unprecedented paces. At the same time, despite new production speeds, inflation, and profit margins, wages remained low, especially for women and foreign workers.[104]

This tightening economy in the 1970s accelerated working women's demand for equal pay, more job security, and childcare.

Many immigrant women working in Europe also invested in these waves of labor activism and went on strike to fight for equal wages and better working conditions. These strikes constitute a crucial moment in labor history, women's history, and immigration labor history, as these categories intersect when resisting sexism and in the case of foreign-born women, poor housing conditions and policies in company-owned housing.[105] Foreign-born female workers were underrepresented in labor unions as well, leading many to conduct illegal (not union-sanctioned) wildcat strikes.[106] Between May 1970 and 1973, immigrant women at a West German auto parts factory continuously protested against being relegated to "Light Wage Category I"—a designation that carried a de facto "women's wage" in a country that ostensibly provided equal wages for equal work. Citing poor working conditions, unequal work distribution, and gender discrimination in raises, 800 foreign and German-born women signed a resolution requesting higher wages for all female employees in 1970.[107] In 1973, after two years of intermittent strikes, a German television reporter announced, "The public is astonished by the determination ... The foreign workers—women no less—threatened to disrupt the entire West German automobile industry." In these strikes, success came from solidarity between the foreign and domestic workers and support for their campaign to raise wages for all workers, male and female.[108]

This trend was apparent across Western Europe. In France in the early 1970s, women workers gained more support in trade unions as awareness grew about job discrimination. In 1972, women at Les Nouvelles Galeries in Thionville went on strike; in December 1978, French women occupied the Confection Industrielle du Pas-de-Calais; and women workers participated in meetings, demonstrations, strikes, and occupations in Lip, France.[109] In 1968 in Great Britain, women workers started several strikes for reclassification of their jobs and equal pay—a similar fight to the German women's—resulting in the 1970 Equal Pay Act, which saw some improvements but not full pay equity.[110] By the late 1970s, the UK was suffering from the effects of chronic economic problems such as underinvestment, managerial inefficiencies, and labor disputes over wages, leading to massive strikes from 1978 to 1979. Historians refer to this period as the Winter of Discontent, and women trade unionists, particularly from the female-dominated service sector, participated actively in the more than 2,000 strikes. The Winter of Discontent was both unsuccessful and unpopular. However, it was a key turning point for women not just in grassroots activism but also in union leadership.[111] British women's union membership increased throughout the 1970s, especially with West Indian and Asian women joining at higher rates and participating in strikes.[112]

In Eastern Europe, a higher percentage of women worked and engaged in labor activism, such as in the February 1971 Julian Marchlewski Cotton

Industry Plant strike in Lodz, Poland (a city where 87 percent of women worked), where 88 percent of the striking workers were women.[113] During the strike, the state was not sure how to respond to the women's nonviolent actions, such as sitting and crying or gathering in front of shop windows but not breaking any.[114] Many saw these women in gendered terms, as mothers who were justified in demanding the right to be fed and be able to feed their families.[115] After the fifth day, the strike ended successfully and price hikes were rescinded.[116]

In 1980, another strike against food price increases in Poland prompted the start of a major resistance organization known as "Solidarity" co-led by Anna Walentynowicz that would be influential in the 1989 end of communism in Poland, as seen in the next chapter.[117] The labor movement and the feminist movement were not distinct for these women, who had been engaged in resistance movements for more democracy since the 1950s. They took on leadership roles and infused feminism into a wide variety of causes, organizing meetings, networks, rallies, and protests well into the 1980s. Indeed, governments' failed responses to women's strikes, including their inability to address women's specific demands, added to Eastern Bloc states' growing woes in the 1970s and 1980s.[118]

International Advocacy in the 1970s

The 1970s were transformative for many European women, demonstrated by increased feminist consciousness and political agency. In Eastern and Western Europe, feminist scholarship burgeoned, and women moved into the public sphere politically, economically, and socially. Legal changes granted hard-fought reproductive rights and addressed wage equality, however incremental. By the mid-1970s, the international community took notice; the United Nations declared 1975 International Women's Year and Mexico City held the first World Conference on Women that same year. East Berlin hosted the UN World Congress of Women soon after the event in Mexico City. In 1976, the International Tribunal on the Crimes Against Women took place in Brussels, Belgium. As a result of these international symposia, significant institutions were established to address research and funding for women's issues, such as the International Research and Training Institute for the Advancement of Women (INSTRAW) and the United Nations Development Fund for Women (UNIFEM).[119]

These international congresses had local impacts as well, generating activism and advocacy in communities around the globe. In Iceland, for example, the percentage of women in the labor market had increased rapidly in the 1960s, from 34 to 50 percent.[120] After the UN declaration of International Women's Year, Icelandic women went on strike to protest earning less than 60 percent of what men earned in addition to doing unpaid housework. On October 24, 1975, 90 percent of Icelandic women participated in Kvennafrídagurinn

(Women's Day Off), refusing to work outside or inside the home, including childcare.[121] Five women's rights groups within Iceland organized the strike, and it had an immediate and significant impact. Women ran most of the telephone services and were typesetters for newspapers, and the strike shut down both. Schools closed because most teachers were women. Flights were canceled, as they could not operate without flight attendants, and banks slowed down due to the absence of tellers. Stores were running out of hotdogs as fathers scrambled to feed their children.[122] Businessmen were forced to take their children to work with them. When the strike's organizers scheduled a mass meeting in Reykjavik's city center, the 25,000 women attendees walked there, stopping traffic in the streets.[123]

Despite its immediate impact, it is hard to assess whether the strike was truly successful, because although Iceland's parliament passed the 1976 Comprehensive Equality Act, a wage gap persisted for decades. Still, the strike powerfully demonstrated that women's work was vital; it contributed to the first democratically elected female president in 1980; and it influenced a subsequent strike in Poland.[124] As with many movements in the 1960s and 1970s, Iceland's Women's Day Off strike was not necessarily a novel or revolutionary action but rather a culmination of earlier activism. Indeed, the first documented Icelandic women's strike took place in 1907, and the first women's trade union was founded in 1914.[125]

The recognition that housework was unpaid labor sparked further local, national, and international activism. At the 1972 National Women's Liberation Conference in England, Selma James introduced the demand that women receive wages for unpaid domestic labor. James and several others soon launched the International Wages for Housework Campaign (IWFHC), inspiring autonomous chapters that sought to make visible and advance the struggle for unwaged women.[126] The feminist group Lotta Femminista (Feminist Struggle) coordinated an influential IWFHC protest in Italy, where most women lacked financial independence, wages were low, unemployment was rising, and economic equality was a primary feminist and leftist goal.[127]

The IWFHC's international advocacy made it distinct from the national movements mostly discussed in this chapter. Fliers from the Wages for Housework Committee in New York announced that women's unpaid work was not a labor of love but a "crime against women internationally," arguing that women face a "life sentence of housework at home, and outside, servicing men, children, and other women, to produce and reproduce the working class. For this work we are never paid a wage."[128] Another flier emphasized the international scope of the campaign: "Notice to All Governments ... In return for our work, you have only asked us to work harder. We are serving notice to you that we insist to be paid for the work we do. We want wages for every dirty toilet, every painful childbirth, every indecent assault, every cup of coffee and every smile. And if we don't get what we want, then we will simply refuse to work any longer."[129]

However, the emphasis on class struggle put this movement at odds with many Western feminist groups. The World Conference on Women in Mexico City exhibited a division among the demands of predominantly white Western feminists and women of color, who did not necessarily see gender as their primary form of oppression. At the 1975 annual conference of the International Wages for Housework Campaign in London, a separate Black Women for Wages for Housework committee formed to specifically address intersectional issues of race, class, and gender with one branch in Brooklyn, NY and the other in Bristol, England. In 1977, the Brooklyn chapter published a newsletter, explaining their position: "If International Women's Year is to mean anything for Black women internationally, it must mean money to claim what has already been promised in treaty and in law, what has already been more than earned, and what has always been withheld."[130] Western socialist and communist feminists pursued wages for housework campaigns as economic and class issues, mirroring concerns found in Eastern Europe.

Violent Protest and Terrorism

In countries ruled by right-wing military dictators, such as Portugal and Spain, women fared worse than men. In Portugal, for example, not only did women have no control over their property or children, but husbands also received only light punishments for crimes such as killing wives suspected of adultery.[131] Women fought back against this repression in nationalist and resistance movements. Leading up to a 1974 coup that would displace the authoritarian regime, Portuguese women were involved in opposition movements that had been developing for decades, participating in demonstrations, strikes, and revolutionary action with student groups and unions. However, as overthrowing the totalitarian regime was opposition groups' pressing need, women's gendered concerns took a back seat. Furthermore, the diverse movements for democracy that emerged in Portugal after the coup did not initially support women's most immediate concerns (decriminalizing abortion, for example), as they felt it was secondary to the fight for democracy. They also did not want to risk backlash from the Catholic Church. Feminist workers prioritized securing a democratic society—one acceptable to the labor, environmental, and youth movements—before taking up abortion rights and other concerns they considered less urgent.[132]

In such contexts, feminist activism was just one piece of a larger nationalist struggle, some of which turned to violence. Following a similar path to Portugal, women's radical activism in Spain took off in this period, as nationalist separatists as well as prodemocracy groups fought for independence from the fascist regime. Within Spain, the Basque separatist group Euskadi Ta Askatasuna (ETA; Basque Homeland and Liberty) was founded in 1959 to promote Basque culture but became a prominent—and violent—nationalist and separatist organization. Women's participation in the ETA's first ten years coincided with a period when larger numbers of Basque women were working outside of the home, pursuing higher education, and encountering social organizations and political movements.[133] Other radical nationalist organizations soon developed around the ETA, merging feminism, motherhood, and armed political violence in interesting ways.[134] Over time, the ETA morphed into a terrorist organization that engaged in bombing campaigns, assassinations, and kidnappings all in the name of securing Basque independence. Women were active in all areas of the ETA, including the military front, and were subjected to sexual harassment and even rape by the police if captured.[135] The ETA was a patriarchal organization, influenced by conservative Roman Catholicism, and policed women's sexuality by expecting them to only marry Basque men.[136] Though few women were involved in the ETA's most dangerous actions, the media seized on ETA women and portrayed them as extremely dangerous; some were imprisoned and killed, their participation in violent protest at odds with stereotypes of women as peaceful and nurturing, invoking potent gendered anxieties.[137]

Women's involvement in political terrorism also stretched to Northern Europe. The island of Ireland is divided between the predominantly Catholic independent Republic of Ireland and the predominantly protestant Northern Ireland, which remains part of the United Kingdom. In Northern Ireland, the Irish Republican Army (IRA) took up the cause of the Catholic minority, seeking to create one unified nation in a violent conflict that persisted for thirty years. The two sides clashed from 1968 until the Good Friday Agreement of 1998, resulting in approximately 50,000 casualties over the three decades. Women were involved in the street fighting—as combatants and casualties—and also played a vital role in the peace process, especially in facilitating dialogue across the border.[138] Women organized mass protests, lobbied politicians, and supported victims of the violence. However, they were also subjected to sexual violence and harassment in this period in ways that men were not. The state used sexual violence to police women who became politicized and challenged authority and, therefore, transgressed gender norms by exerting political agency.[139] Women experienced violence ranging from everyday sexual harassment by soldiers on foot patrol to rape by prison guards; this violence against women was a weapon of war.[140]

In this era of terrorism, women were also leaders in negotiating peace. The middle-class organization Protestant and Catholic Encounter (PACE) established seventy community groups at its peak to encourage Catholics and Protestants to start a dialogue.[141] Likewise, the group Women Together emerged in 1970 to unite working class-women, Protestant and Catholic, to discourage violence, and to pressure local authorities to seek solutions. The group was founded after violent riots in Belfast among working-class communities, resulting in both increased British army presence and accompanying militant activism.¹⁴² According to one reporter, Women Together gathered tens of thousands of signatures for their 1972 peace petition, as well as arranged trips for children, organized women to form a human barrier between troops and rock-throwing protesters, and other small local actions.¹⁴³ There were important crossovers between women active in the peace movement and in the Northern Ireland Women's Rights Movement (NIWRM), a group established in 1975 to demand legislation for equal employment, welfare, and education rights.¹⁴⁴ However, Women Together used gendered assumptions about women as mothers and caregivers to define themselves not as political activists but as "natural peacemakers" in contrast to male violence.¹⁴⁵

Indeed, while women's work for peace aligned with traditional gender ideologies, their militant activism and violent terrorist acts were at odds with the common perception of women as peaceful and nurturing.¹⁴⁶ The disconnect between women and violence impacted media coverage and generated public shock at the actions of primarily white, middle-class women.¹⁴⁷ As with the ETA in Spain, women were often overrepresented in media coverage of European terrorist groups such as the Red Army Faction in West Germany and the ETA in Spain. Women's participation in violent political action threatened the existing gender order.¹⁴⁸

Conclusion

Trends in European women's lives cannot be neatly divided into eras, making for an uneven narrative of the evolution of women's rights in the extended postwar period. Successes—and what constituted them—varied by cultural and political context as well as by different movements' priorities. Some patterns do emerge, however. Fertility continued to play an outsized role in women's opportunities from the 1950s through the 1970s, with advances like the Pill and campaigns for reproductive autonomy looming large despite the persistence of pronatalist political efforts and concerns about changing sexual mores. In reality, it was not new sexual appetites that made contraception popular, but poverty that made it crucial. In addition, declining birth rates enabled more women to join the formal labor force, take on new leadership positions, and engage in new and diverse forms of activism.

Indeed, this era saw the emergence of a "second-wave" of feminism as well as a burst of different social movements with objectives both distinct and overlapping. From student groups and labor activism to radical and even violent resistance to authoritarian rule, women across Europe strengthened their political participation and consciousness. The decriminalization of homosexuality, introduced in some countries in the 1960s and 1970s allowed for changing attitudes and circumstances for gay men and lesbians.¹⁴⁹ Eastern European women challenged the state control of information—always a significant issue in women's history—by self-publishing and disseminating resistance materials. Reproductive rights and equal pay were consistent motivations for feminist activism, but women also pursued these issues within other movements for political and economic change that did not necessarily prioritize gender oppression, making feminist activism an elusive category—in Europe and elsewhere. While the legislative successes of the 1970s, especially access to legal abortion and moves toward wage equality, suggest that this period was emancipatory, historians remain torn. The relationship between legislation, rights, and cultural change is complicated, and as we will see in the next chapter, activists would carry their work through the 1980s and 1990s.

7

Revolutions and Rebirth

Introduction

As tensions rose and the lines between the Eastern and Western Bloc hardened, two sweeping forces defined the final decades of the Cold War for European women: state-level cuts, which decreased women's quality of life in different ways, and new activist coalitions to fight against environmental destruction, nuclear war, and the AIDS epidemic, as well as to end the Cold War. In the West, neoliberalism replaced postwar ideologies of social democracy and domesticity, and the European Union and individual states invested more in women's education, careers, and policies to help balance work and family. However, these attempts only chipped at the edges of women's double burden, and many struggled in new ways under the notion that they could "have it all."

The 1986 Chernobyl nuclear disaster sent shockwaves around the world, signaling not only the danger of nuclear power but also the harsh and corrupt realities of the Soviet system. Women played important roles in Chernobyl's aftermath as scientists, journalists, workers, and activists, pressuring European governments to address environmental crises. Concurrently, Eastern European dissident movements coordinated their actions against communist rule. The resulting revolutions for more freedom and democracy in the East culminated with the end of the Cold War in 1989 and the dissolution of the USSR in 1991. Surprising to many, the dismantling of the Eastern Bloc was largely peaceful, some even referring to the breakup of Czechoslovakia as the "Velvet Revolution."

The violent dissolution of Yugoslavia marked a notable and brutal exception, with women's bodies as a primary battleground in the ensuing genocide and civil wars. The gendered atrocities of the Yugoslav Wars of the 1990s, such as targeted rape campaigns, prompted new understandings of "war crimes" and "crimes against humanity" on an international scale. Far less vicious but significant, the transition out of the Cold War left many women struggling economically and socially under the imposition of Western models, while postcolonial migrations generated racist and particularly anti-Muslim sentiment among white Western Europeans. These demographic shifts sparked debates about the merits of assimilation versus cultural relativism as well as notable movements in defense of a diverse Europe, such as Afro-feminism. Thus, while the 1990s were meant to be the beginning of a reunified Europe after decades of the Cold War, this unity was elusive amid new concerns around economics, immigration, health, and xenophobia, impacting European women in distinct ways.

"Thatcherism" and the Neoliberal Turn

In the lead up to the end of the Cold War in the 1980s, some Western European countries, such as Great Britain and West Germany, shifted away from social democracy and toward neoliberalism. The impetus for this shift was Britain's first female prime minister, Margaret Thatcher, and indeed, many scholars use "Thatcherism" to describe the political and economic revolution that Thatcher led from her election in 1979 to her reluctant resignation in 1990. Thatcherism's tenets were a revival of the free market, privatization of industries, and encouraging individuals to "help themselves" without aid from the state. Interestingly, Thatcher also emphasized domesticity and drew on the motif of the housewife in her campaigns, once commenting "perhaps it takes a housewife to see that Britain's national housekeeping is appalling."[1] Images of her preparing meals in a kitchen and famously waving her handbag at other European leaders were ubiquitous.[2] Thatcher's conservative social politics appealed to women and men who had felt out of step with the postwar social and sexual revolutions. Her ideas signaled a backlash against second-wave feminists and, more importantly, the social welfare programs that had characterized postwar Western Europe. The suffragette's dream of a female prime minister was bittersweet, as the quality of life for many British women deteriorated markedly under her leadership.

On the surface, Thatcher's government introduced legislation to benefit women, such as the 1975 Employment Protection Act, which prevented pregnant women from being fired and allowed women to work and be mothers. However, in 1980, Thatcher added new stipulations that greatly limited the law's impact. Under the new rules, women were required to have worked for the same employer for at least sixteen hours a week for two years to be eligible for job protection, in contrast to the original stipulation of having the same employer for just six months. Many working women, especially mothers and women of minority groups, worked fewer than sixteen hours a week or changed jobs more frequently. As a result, the Employment Protection Act predominantly benefited white-collar over poor and working-class women.[3] Overall, Thatcher's politics weakened women's employment rights.[4] She also decreased spending on social programs that many women relied on, such as funding for childcare and early childhood education—cuts that negatively impacted more women than men.[5]

Though Thatcher espoused traditional gender roles, her lived experience was quite different. Despite being a wife and mother of twins, she worked full time outside of the home in roles traditionally gendered male. She was often the only female politician at international summits and conferences and was hawkish on international policy. Thatcher frequently campaigned on the issue of defense policy, especially nuclear armament, as an aggressive sign of national strength against the Soviet Union. Her 1976 "Britain Awake" speech earned her the moniker "Iron Lady" in the Soviet press. She simultaneously sought to be a maternal figure and a warrior against communism and for the free market.[6]

Thatcher had a significant yet unintended effect on women organizing in the UK. Her policies prompted renewed, unified feminist opposition across movements, as organizations with distinct ideologies aligned in their efforts to fight back.[7] In 1987, Diane Abbott, the first Black woman elected to the British House of Commons, was motivated to run to counter Thatcher's economic policies and declared her win a victory for socialism. New activist alliances formed in the wake of harmful policies and legislation. For example, after Thatcher's extensive pit closures decimated mining communities, the groups Lesbians and Gays Support the Miners and Lesbians Against Pit Closures protested alongside the National Union of Mineworkers during the UK miners' strike of 1984 to 1985.[8]

In 1995, fifty-seven British women were interviewed about their opinions on Thatcher and her reign as prime minister. One interviewee said, "When she first got in, I thought, 'Oh great! A woman! A woman is in charge ... of the country!'"[9] Likewise, in response to the question of whether Thatcher changed how women were viewed, another subject believed Thatcher was a symbol of women's new opportunities and status: "She's fought her way to the top ... She's shown men she can do the job as well as they can, if not better."[10] However, many respondents said that while they initially thought her election marked an overall achievement for women, they became disappointed over time due to her gender politics. Moreover, Thatcher herself did not agree with sentiments of female empowerment. When asked about the gender significance of her election, she replied, "It is not a victory for Margaret Thatcher, it's not a victory for women—it's a victory for someone in politics."[11] Few women appreciated Thatcher's antifeminist statements or how little she did to address women's equality or gender issues.[12] Some noted that she had not promoted or encouraged women in politics, although she certainly had the power to do so; she did not even appoint any women to her cabinet.[13] Indeed, Thatcher's election was not necessarily a watershed moment for women. The Conservative Party was similarly uninterested in increasing women's political opportunities and many conservatives did not take Thatcher's candidacy seriously, despite her being a party member.[14] Thatcher's legacy remains that of an unsympathetic leader, especially for women, and her reign helped usher in a larger shift toward more conservative far right politics in the 1980s.

The HIV/AIDS Epidemic and Women's Healthcare

Alongside political and social shifts in the 1980s, including decreasing social welfare safety nets, the emergence of HIV/AIDS highlighted societal tensions around sexuality, public health, and government responsibility well into the 1990s. The discovery of HIV (the Human Immunodeficiency Virus) and its frequent development into the disease AIDS (Acquired Immune Deficiency Syndrome) caused an epidemic first noticeable among gay male communities in California in the early 1980s. Activism to raise awareness about the illness and promote effective public health responses to HIV/AIDS centered primarily in the United States followed by Western Europe and Australia in the 1980s and 1990s. In 1987, the World Health Organization (WHO) launched the Special Programme on AIDS, the first global initiative to address the epidemic, grounding their methods in public health, evidence-based conclusions, and a participatory rights-based approach, especially once the virus was seen as a heterosexual crisis devasting Africa.[15]

In many European countries, HIV/AIDS activism initially dovetailed with campaigns for homosexual rights and against homophobia with new urgency as death tolls rose most visibly among men who slept with men.[16] In the UK, activists developed informal coalitions with public health professionals and physicians to shape the policy and agenda of a reluctant government.[17] Within Western Europe, France was one of the countries most affected by AIDS and, correspondently, a site of great success in AIDS activism. In 1983, French gay rights activists founded the organization *Vaincre le Sida* (Defeat AIDS) and established ACT UP-Paris in 1989 as an openly gay and lesbian political action group rather than one solely providing health services.[18] Like its American namesake, AIDS Coalition to Unleash Power (ACT UP), ACT UP-Paris criticized what they viewed as political and medical indifference to HIV/AIDS, staging radical public demonstrations such as "die-ins" and enacting "zaps"—an onslaught of disruptive protests targeting individuals or organizations identified as enemies to the cause.[19] While homosexual men were among the most visible early HIV/AIDS activists in Europe as in the US, women—of all sexualities—as well as heterosexual men, also played significant roles.[20]

AIDS activism and responses prompted conversations across political, social, and cultural milieus, and created space for new alliances and broader social change. Before discussions of AIDS, in conservative Ireland, where 95 percent of the population was Catholic there had been no mandatory sex education in schools, and only married couples could obtain contraceptives by prescription, in accordance with church teachings.[21] Although access to condoms was limited, they could be ordered by mail without a prescription, and some women's health centers supplied them in defiance of the state and the Catholic Church. When Irish AIDS activism began in 1985, it emerged from a more radical, socialist, and nationalist wing of the gay rights movement that saw an opportunity for broader liberalizing reform.[22] The Dublin Lesbian and Gay Men's Collective—a group that campaigned on a variety of issues such as women's rights and reforming contraception laws, and advocated for access to abortion and divorce—launched Gay Health Action (GHA) to address the AIDS crisis. Although homosexual acts were criminalized in Ireland, the Irish state covertly supported health care for AIDS prevention, even if they did not support or fund GHA.[23]

The Dublin Collective was primarily a homogenous gay male organization, and indeed gay men were generally the public face of HIV/AIDS activism, especially early on. Some scholars maintain that women were less visible because they tended to work behind the scenes, while others argue that the media chose to focus primarily on gay men.[24] Although Lesbian Health Action, a GHA splinter group, did receive a small amount of press coverage in Ireland, many more European women took on invaluable roles in HIV/AIDS activism.[25] In her work on New York City's branch of ACT UP, Sarah Schulman argues that women, particularly lesbians, formed the group's institutional backbone due to both prior feminist organizing and experiences of gendered disenfranchisement within networks of power that white gay men rarely had to negotiate.[26] It is likely that similar dynamics permeated activist communities in Western Europe and contributed to women's invisibility in the movement.

The link between HIV/AIDS and male homosexuality impacted not only media coverage and scholarly analyses of activist women, but also medical and government responses to women with the virus.[27] Due to this gender imbalance, research into AIDS treatment has primarily focused on men without acknowledging physical differences that could influence outcomes for women. Likewise, drug treatment research has excluded women for fear it could affect their reproductive health. According to AIDS researcher Emily Scharf, writing in 1992, "A decade has passed since AIDS illnesses were first recognized, and yet women remain invisible."[28] By the end of the 1980s, young to middle-aged men still comprised the majority of reported cases, but the number of cases reported in women and children rose in this decade as well.[29] Moreover, women were often more susceptible to HIV, especially if they had worse access to healthcare, fewer opportunities for self-care as the expected caregivers of others, and had to compel sexual partners to wear condoms (unlike their control over oral contraceptives). In fact, a research report from 1990 noted that AIDS had become the leading cause of death for women aged twenty to forty in major cities in the Americas, Western Europe, and Sub-Saharan Africa.[30]

Women who were HIV positive took matters into their own hands and established support groups, such as Positively Women, a British self-help support group formed in 1987. The group's intent was to create a space to share common experiences, empower each other, advance education and research about women's health, and find community-centered advice and assistance.[31] One woman who found support in Positively Women had contracted HIV through intravenous drug use and described the isolation of her diagnosis: "[After] I was diagnosed HIV positive, I wandered about pretty aimlessly, trying to stay off drugs without much success. I couldn't cope alone ... At one drug rehab unit I was told to leave because I tried to talk about being positive—they didn't want to know."[32] Positively Women also published interviews and testimonies to provide information and comfort to other women living with the virus. Women who contracted HIV or passed it on faced the daunting task of informing their partners. This was the case with Kate, who noted: "The hardest bit about telling someone you love is dealing with their grief. Seeing the pain, fear and despair flash across their faces is the most terrible thing."[33] Another woman, Susan, sought an AIDS test after traveling to England from Central Africa, only to face a doctor steeped in the stereotypes of the age; he told her it was unlikely she could have contracted AIDS because her boyfriend was not bisexual and she was not a prostitute. However, she did test positive, likely from a medical injection she had received at home in Africa.[34] Writing about her experience, Susan noted the shame attached to the virus: "People here are prejudiced about AIDS; they think you are promiscuous ... I think safer sex information for different cultures is important."[35] Immigrant communities had additional stressors when addressing the AIDS crisis due to language, cultural, and socio-economic barriers and the general social exclusion many faced. These hurdles to accessing prevention and care made minority women especially vulnerable to contracting HIV and, in some cases, more prone to bias and xenophobia when seeking healthcare.

In Eastern Europe, HIV/AIDS was seen as a Western issue, largely because government censorship did not acknowledge that the virus could spread through intravenous drug use, and states did not typically address drug use in social and health services in general.[36] Low transmissions rates in East Germany were believed to be connected to the state's strict travel restrictions; indeed, the weekly West German news magazine *Der Spiegel* referred to the Berlin Wall as "East Germany's condom."[37] In addition, homosexuality was a criminal offense in many Eastern countries such as the Soviet Union, and data collection of HIV cases remained limited. As in Western nations, Eastern European lesbian and gay activism increased during the HIV/AIDS crisis, even if groups could not meet openly. Hungarian homosexual organizations convened privately in the early 1980s but by 1986, Hungary's first openly homosexual organization was founded to promote AIDS prevention and counseling among gay men as well as support and leisure activities. Hungarian activists also reached out to Western groups for support and solidarity. In 1987, the Viennese Homosexual Initiative in Austria organized a regional international meeting for gay activists in nearby Budapest. Since these groups worked across the Cold War divide, security forces watched them closely.[38]

Like environmental crises to come, the AIDS pandemic exposed Eastern Bloc states' inability or unwillingness to reassure their citizens. Plagued by a lack of vital medical supplies (i.e., syringes, protective clothing, rubber gloves, sterilization and disinfectant materials), Eastern European healthcare workers were vulnerable to contracting the virus themselves.[39] In Poland, the primary source of HIV/AIDS infection was contaminated needles from injection drug use, followed by male homosexual sex due to condoms' poor quality. The state response was inadequate and homophobic: increasing surveillance and repression of gay men.[40]

Finally, HIV/AIDS was not the only health crisis impacting European women in the 1980s and 1990s. Breast cancer was also prevalent and prompted women-specific health measures on an unprecedented scale. According to the World Health Organization, breast cancer survival rates began to improve in the 1980s due to increased early detection and new modes of treatment in high-income countries.[41] Research conducted from 1989 to 2006 concluded that deaths from breast cancer decreased by roughly a quarter in much of Northwestern Europe and Scandinavia.[42] In Sweden, mortality rates have steadily decreased since 1972, but the downward trend did not begin until 2006.[43] Despite similar healthcare services and risk factors across countries, the use of mammograms for detection varied.[44] In contrast to Western Europe, the USSR and the Soviet republics reported more cases of breast cancer in the 1980s and 1990s than in previous decades, primarily among women aged forty to sixty in rural and urban areas. The USSR Ministry of Health, which conducted the research, determined that their increase in cases matched those in Western Europe.[45] Growing awareness of breast cancer throughout the 1980s necessitated oncological services for women, including early detection, treatment, and rehabilitation measures in both Eastern and Western Europe. Cancer research is often connected to environmental contaminants, so it is unsurprising that ecological and other urgent activist movements also increased during this period.

Feminism Meets Environmental, Antinuclear, and Peace Movements

Environmental activism in the 1980s and 1990s—particularly against nuclear reactors and their biproducts, waste, and utility for dangerous weaponry—united women who had not previously worked together or necessarily been politically engaged.[46] In 1979, the same year Margaret Thatcher was elected prime minister in Britain, another European woman rose to prominence as the public face of these environmental issues: West Germany's Petra Karin Kelly. A cofounder of the German Green Party, Kelly worked at the European Commission in Belgium from 1971 to 1983 on international antinuclear, antiwar, and feminist measures, and was then one of twenty-six Green Party members elected to the West German parliament in 1983.[47] Kelly's interconnected pro-environment, pro-peace, and pro-woman stances could not have been more different from Thatcher's ideals.

Kelly critiqued the nuclear arms race as an attack on "feminine values" and on nature, and challenged conservative politicians and Thatcher directly, arguing, "Women in power such as Margaret Thatcher ... have only come into power ... because they have adapted themselves to male values and male ideologies."[48] The media was instantly drawn to Kelly's flashy political style and intelligent articulation of salient issues.

Kelly's rise to national and international prominence occurred as increasing numbers of women took part in local ecological movements. While they remained underrepresented in regional, national, and international politics, Kelly and other women broke this trend throughout the 1980s as European environmental activism reached new heights in response to nuclear weapons and the escalation of nuclear power. Kelly wrote about feminist and environmental solidarity in her 1984 book *Fighting for Hope*: "I have been with many women, whether I marched alongside them in ... Hiroshima ... or spoke to them at the UN Plaza ... Women all over the world are rising up, and infusing the anti-nuclear and peace movements with a vitality and creativity never seen before."[49] Kelly lectured and protested around the globe, for example, advocating for the release of women political prisoners in Moscow's Red Square. She took part in dramatic actions such as a September 1983 human blockade, where she was one of hundreds of thousands of people who encircled US military bases, forming a 100-kilometer human chain that stretched from across Southwest Germany.[50] She believed civil disobedience was a key protest measure, but noted that she also supported open dialogue with the police and armed forces to create "the opportunity to rethink" employing violence against protesters.[51] At the same time, Kelly was one of many activists who used her body to block the passage of heavy weapons transport, dramatizing both militarization and human vulnerability, and making abstract nuclear threats concrete.

Across Western Europe—in the Netherlands, West Germany, Scandinavia, Belgium, Spain, Greece, Italy, and Great Britain—women of different backgrounds led environmental and antinuclear movements in the 1980s.[52] As with Kelly's approach, these movements bridged gaps between contemporaneous causes, connecting ecological concerns, the need for regional authority, and women's rights.[53] These environmental activists believed they were fighting a specifically patriarchal drive to advance nuclear technologies and warfare. Demanding political action, they captured headlines by occupying military complexes and staging radical public protests, such as a "go-in" where fifty pregnant women and new mothers marched into the state parliament building in Stuttgart, West Germany.[54] Another protest in Gorleben, West Germany contested storing nuclear waste in the community, and launched the slogan "Women Fight for Life!" to call for an international women's meeting on the premises.[55] As the protest intensified, the West German newspaper *Die Zeit* reported on women's shifting roles amid a collective feminist environmental agenda: "Women who had never worried about anything aside from their husbands and children left their kitchens and stepped up to the speaker's platform."[56] Despite the paternalist tone, many of these activists did challenge age and gender biases, presenting a sharp contrast to students rioting in the streets in major cities. Older women threw rocks while those from farming communities knitted on tractors on illegally occupied land.[57] *Die Zeit* captured this aspect of ecofeminist protests by quoting fifty-year-old housewife Marianne von Alemann, who declared, "The arrogance of politicians who don't mind leaving the dangers of nuclear power to future generations is so shocking that it's simply beyond me."[58]

Greenham Common and Women's Peace Camps

The formation of women's "peace camps" exemplifies the combination of feminism, environmentalism, peace activism, and (in some cases) antiracism that characterized these movements against nuclear power.[59] Ecofeminism spread through an international network of women's peace initiatives, uniting far-flung activists and projects. A women's peace and nuclear disarmament camp in the small Sicilian town of Comiso, for example, became a global symbol of feminist peace action. The group ultimately connected with an operation in England known as the Greenham Common Women's Peace Camp.

Located 50 miles west of London, Greenham Common was the site of multiple protest camps that garnered international attention. Thousands of women from Britain and other countries lived at the camp from its founding in 1981 until 2000, organizing a variety of demonstrations to critique what they saw as a patriarchal and masculine nuclear arms race.[60] In December of 1982, on the third anniversary of NATO's decision to employ cruise missiles in Europe, 30,000 women joined hands around the 9-mile perimeter of the Greenham Common US Air Force base, entitling the action "Embrace the Base" (Figure 7.1). Soon after, on New Year's Day 1983, activists danced and sang atop partially built missile silos.[61] With such initiatives, Greenham became a model of women's direct-action protests that inspired other peace camps worldwide.

The Greenham protestors took a maternalist approach, arguing that as women and mothers, their activism was about protecting their children. While they may not have recognized the ways that this framework could be limiting, Greenham women did work to address race—a factor that environmental and peace movements (as well as broader feminist movements) often ignored. This was largely due to the influence of Wilmette Brown, a Black British woman who led the King's Cross Women's Centre in London. The Women's Centre fought for the rights of Black women,

FIGURE 7.1 *Women form a chain around Greenham Common US Air Force base, December 12, 1982. Getty Images.*

especially sex workers, to have clean and safe housing, fair wages, and labor protections, and sought an end to rape and violence against women. Like some of the activists at the Greenham peace camp, Brown and her organization promoted dismantling the US military-industrial complex as a means to address the racism, sexism, and class oppression they believed stemmed from capitalism and patriarchy. In 1985, the two groups formed a coalition.[62]

Greenham's connection to Wilmette Brown introduced white women at the peace camp to issues with which they had little prior experience. In an interview, activist Juliet Yelverton openly noted her limited exposure to racial injustice and new understanding of intersectional oppression: "Before the Occupation, ... I hadn't realized the depth of vulnerability that Black people, especially Black women, feel in regard to the police."[63] Listening to Brown and others changed Yelverton's perspective: "I began to put my own feelings and experience with the police together with Black women's."[64] In her 1982 essay "White Women Listen! Black Feminism and the Boundaries of Sisterhood," historian Hazel Carby articulated that primarily white feminist movements did not recognize the lives of Black women, racism in society, or how feminism had ignored racism within the movement.[65]

The interracial coalitions forged at Greenham and other partnerships among diverse women became more common during the 1980s and 1990s, as white feminists like Yelverton attempted to understand intersectional oppression and integrate it into their analyses. This period saw a significant evolution of feminist ideologies in the West, moving away from second-wave feminism into what scholars have identified as a third wave of the movement. Western European environmental and antinuclear activism were part of this shift toward a feminism that included a diversity of women and issues.

Women's Activism in Eastern Europe

In Eastern Europe, women's activism was also multifaceted but, as seen in earlier chapters, the political context was very different than in the West. Eastern European women had been participating in nationalist and antifascist movements since the nineteenth century, long before many Western women, and continued to do so throughout the twentieth. By the height of the Cold War, much of Eastern European women's activism was part of larger, ongoing opposition to Soviet-style communism. At the same time, many women's political participation was not through resistance to the state but through its communist system.

In this context, while Eastern European women were clearly politically engaged, the nature of communism complicates the question of feminism. Indeed, official party ideology endorsed women's equality as part of the overarching emancipation of the working class. Yet scholars debate if Eastern Bloc states had intentional feminist philosophies and organizations akin to those in the West. On the one hand, many worked within socialist state organizations to improve conditions for women with initiatives expanding education, childcare for working mothers, and social welfare for widows and divorcees. On the other hand, as representatives of the state and in service of state goals, it is unclear if these women were genuinely committed to these causes.[66] Central to the debate is the question of how much agency anyone has in a one-party state. But whether or not they were true believers in the communist project, working within the constraints of the state was still the primary means available to address women's equality. Furthermore, in both the East and the West, defining a movement as "feminist" is fuzzy, as few participants saw themselves primarily as feminist activists.

With women's issues infusing Western political discourse and global initiatives, such as the UN's declaration of 1975 as International Women's Year, feminism and its relevance in the Eastern Bloc was also of interest to communist states. In 1976, for example, Marxist centers in Croatia organized an event that debated feminism. Soon after, in 1978, a larger international conference in Belgrade, Serbia included women from Poland, Hungary, and Yugoslavia as well as from the Western nations of England, Italy, and France. In response, pro-regime Yugoslav media accused communist feminists of importing corrupt Western ideologies.[67]

Many communist countries had both de facto feminism and official feminism, especially if one defines as feminist any actions to improve women's lives, health, work, family, sexuality, society, culture, and the law. Consider, for example, Vida Tomšič—a Slovenian lawyer, Communist Party member, and socialist politician who drafted many state policies on women's issues in the Socialist Federal Republic of Yugoslavia. Tomšič held many prominent political positions, such as president of the Federal Council for Family Planning from 1971 to 1978 and participated in UN working groups (such as on social development, women's rights, childcare and family planning) and other international conferences and commissions on women's issues.[68] As a Marxist, Tomšič believed that class equality would end patriarchy, legally and culturally; if reproductive rights were considered human rights and maternity and childcare could be managed by the society as a whole, women and men could both participate fully in politics and the economy. Because her values aligned with the official policies, scholars consider Tomšič a feminist activist in her own right, not just a functionary of the state. Moreover, in addition to state-sanctioned women's organizations, Yugoslavia was one of the few countries within the Eastern Bloc where distinct feminist groups emerged in the 1970s, such as the organization Woman and Society in 1978.[69]

In truth, communist rhetoric of women's equality through working-class liberation did not translate into a reality for women in socialist states.[70] Though communism conceived of androgynous workers, women were expected to be both producers and reproducers for the state and thus endured the double burden discussed in the previous chapter. Amid this and other broken promises, by the 1970s many Eastern European women were calling for more democratic societies, and opposition movements much larger than feminist politics pervaded. Resistance to Soviet-style communism had become more pronounced after Stalin's death in 1953, with a revolution in Hungary in 1956 and the Prague Spring in 1968. Subsequent publishing bans in Czechoslovakia gave rise to the self-publishing resistance movement *samizdat* in the early 1970s as well as underground opposition groups, such as the counterculture band the Plastic People of the Universe. Though the band was not overtly political, the Czechoslovak state saw its representation of freedom of thought and expression as a threat and in 1976, arrested a band member and others associated with it.[71] In 1977, 242 people signed a document protesting the arrests known as Charter 77. The charter called for a more open society, citing government failure to abide by human rights and UN conventions they had signed, spanning from 1960 to the Helsinki Accords in 1975. Documents later added to the charter highlighted social and economic issues such as unequal pay for women.[72] Czech women believed Charter 77's call for universal human rights naturally included gender equality, and the document lay the groundwork for future Czech feminism.[73]

However, many women who signed the charter faced government reprisal, including accusing signatories of prostitution and forcing hospitalization, purportedly for fear they would spread venereal disease. The police forcibly hospitalized Zdena Erteltová, who did not sign the Charter but was a *samizdat* copyist, after she refused to report on the author of the work she was reproducing. She was hospitalized for fourteen days without contact with her family or a lawyer and, upon her release, was beaten in the street so badly she had a concussion.[74] Dissenting women were undeterred by such treatment and forty-nine women signed a letter of support for Erteltová.[75]

Beginning the in the 1980s, Eastern European peace, environmental, labor, and women's movements developed underground in increasing numbers and with new coalitions.[76] In East Germany, for example, churches served as important sites of activism, especially in East Berlin, where churches hosted the annual national Peace Workshop starting in 1982 that drew crowds of thousands. The East Berlin group "Women for Peace" penned a petition that 200 women signed in direct response to East German legislation requiring women to also complete compulsory military service.[77] This burgeoning peace movement demonstrated that many East Germans had overcome their fear of repression enough to meet more openly, rather than only in local circles of like-minded friends.[78] Dissident activists also utilized creative approaches to fight against authoritarian regimes. One tactic to evade government censorship was "mimetic resistance"—quoting legislation or state constitutions, which could not be considered illegal or inappropriate—or by using innocuous expressions in acts of protest. The only all-female Czechoslovak band in the alternative music scene, Zuby Nehty, got past censors, for example, with lyrics "Let us rejoice and let us make merry," but much to the government's dismay the lyrics were set to funereal music in a dark and minor key.[79]

In Poland, alongside underground *samizdat* distribution, women spoke out politically in the 1980s, starting a public opposition movement that challenged the government to its core.[80] A particular incident involving Anna Walentynowicz, a Second World War orphan, single mother, and crane operator for thirty years, sparked nationwide protests.[81] On August 7, 1980, Walentynowicz was fired from the shipyard where she worked, only fifty days from retirement, as punishment for her activism and outspoken support for trade unions. Outraged, Walentynowicz's coworkers went on strike and workers throughout the country followed suit. On August 31, 1980, protesters established the independent trade union Solidarity, and it quickly blossomed into a larger anti-Soviet grassroots movement that garnered widespread support.[82] In an attempt to retain control of the situation, the Polish communist government legally recognized the union, but Solidarity was not easy to keep in check. Activists sent reports of their actions to foreign media outlets, who publicized the escalating Polish movement. However, the Western press often excluded the female civic and community leaders organizing at the grassroots level; only Walentynowicz made the news, even though she was just one of many women among Solidarity's leadership.[83]

On December 12, 1981, sixteen months after Walentynowicz was fired, the Polish state declared martial law, outlawed Solidarity, and imprisoned around 9,000 male and 1,000 female activists—a clear gender imbalance.

With much of the organization's male leadership arrested or in hiding, a core group of women sustained Solidarity by maintaining connections with union's larger national network, protecting leaders in hiding, and smuggling funds and equipment into Poland.[84] Solidarity continued to support strikes and other anti-government actions, such as joining women in Łódź in a "hunger march" through the city to protest food shortages. Carrying their children, pushing strollers, and assisting women in wheelchairs, marchers' banners read, "Our Children are Hungry," "Down with Food Lines," and other messages, challenging perceptions of them as apolitical women.[85] Solidarity clearly needed women's support to succeed—and it did, outlasting the Cold War itself—and was just one of many ways women's activism contributed to the end of communism in Poland.

The Chernobyl Nuclear Disaster

Women throughout the Eastern and Western Blocs claimed public and political spaces for discourse on feminism, democracy, and peace, but their environmental organizing in response to the Chernobyl nuclear disaster sparked another kind of activism. On April 26, 1986, four large graphite reactors at the Chernobyl Nuclear Power Plant in Ukraine exploded and released more than 100 times the radioactive material of the bombs dropped on Hiroshima and Nagasaki combined. The explosion impacted around five million people across Northwestern Europe as well as plants, animals, science, and governments worldwide. The human cost was immeasurable; emergency workers died on the spot, an additional 30,000 died from radiation exposure, and at least 2,000 cases of thyroid cancer followed.[86] The sheer scale of the disaster forced Soviet leader Mikhail Gorbachev to make an official announcement that acknowledged the disaster and called for foreign support, ushering in a new period of state transparency, public openness, and debate in the USSR known by the Russian word *glasnost*.[87] By amplifying the layers of disfunction in the Soviet Union, the deadly tragedy undoubtedly contributed to the end of the Cold War; as one historian noted, Chernobyl's greatest victim was the Soviet state.[88]

After the explosion, those living within a 30-kilometer radius were evacuated from the area until high levels of radiation were discovered farther out, leading to additional evacuations. By the end of 1986, around 116,000 people from 188 towns had been evacuated. Evacuees were relocated to apartments in urban areas and newly constructed housing in rural areas throughout the USSR (Figure 7.2). Children between the ages of 5 and 15 were sent to summer camps, and pregnant women and mothers with young children and infants were sent to hotels, rest homes and sanatoria, dividing families and causing lasting effects.[89] Women played crucial roles as journalists and scientists working to understand and address Chernobyl's fallout, collecting much of the amassed information about how the disaster

FIGURE 7.2 *Chernobyl evacuees in a newly built village, Ternopilske, near Kiev. Public domain.*

impacted Soviet citizens. Journalist Svetlana Alexeivich interviewed hundreds of people in Chernobyl's aftermath, while another key journalist, Alla Yaroshinskaya, uncovered many of the state's lies and concealment efforts.[90]

Likewise, two female scientists exposed a cover-up of one of Chernobyl's most significant public health consequences. After the nuclear disaster, an alarming number of cases of thyroid cancer appeared among fieldworkers, tractor drivers, pregnant women, and, notably, children. In 1989, young pediatric endocrinologist Valentina Drozd discovered six cases of thyroid cancer, which rose to thirty-one cases by the following year. Since thyroid cancer was considered rare in children, Drozd reported the cases to her supervisor Larisa Astakhova as a significant medical event and encouraged her to present the troubling findings at an upcoming Soviet conference in Chernihiv on Chernobyl's public health effects. Astakhova was hesitant to do so. Scientific research was generally a male domain and in Soviet medicine, female researchers who broke ranks with established opinions or state views were easily shut down. Ultimately, Astakhova presented Drozd's findings at the 1991 conference, only to be met with grumbles from the largely male audience of scientists from Moscow, the World Health Organization, and the US National Cancer Institute. Humiliated and furious, Astakhova eventually left the stage in tears after a heckler called out, "Get off the stage, you little fool!" While the prevalence of thyroid cancer was no secret, prominent medical organizations dismissed Astakhova and her findings, regarding the disclosure from a female scientist as a threat.[91]

In the decades after Chernobyl, reactions and responses continued to have gendered impacts, not only on scientists like Astakhova and Drozd but also on women who had worked with nuclear waste since the 1950s. Natalia Manzurova, a scientist specializing in radioactive landscapes, believed the disaster exposed the corruption at the core of Soviet society, providing a tragic example of the harm and mistreatment involved in secretly harboring nuclear power.[92] In 2005, Manzurova established a nonprofit organization (NGO) to address environmental contamination from a plant in Ozersk, Russia, where she joined forces with Nadezhda Kutepova, who had founded a women's organization in the same town. The two made a powerful team. At the new nonprofit, local women shared their experiences with nuclear waste long before Chernobyl, revealing the ways that gender influenced state responses under the authoritarian regime. They reported being forced to clean up radiation in the 1950s and 1960s, including while pregnant, and since Soviet law forbade employing pregnant women, their work was not officially recorded.[93] Without such records, many women were ineligible for the special medical subsidies and pensions offered for those working with radiation cleanup. Their gendered status as pregnant women hurt them doubly: they risked their children's lives and received none of the special compensation for such dangerous work.[94] Manzurova and Kutepova's commitment to exposing these injustices should be not underestimated. As environmental historian Kate Brown underscores, "Two women—marginally employed, working out of their apartments, Manzurova fighting [her own] health problems, Kutepova raising small children—were the ones shouldering the massive detritus of the Soviet nuclear weapons complex."[95] Their and other women's crucial documentation and examination of the Chernobyl disaster and its effects, especially on women and children, were key to exposing the dysfunction of the Soviet state and ultimately ending the Cold War.

After the Wall Came Down

Meant to "protect" East German citizens from the corrupting influence of the capitalist West, the Berlin Wall separating East and West Germany became a concrete symbol of the two Cold War factions. When the Berlin Wall fell on November 9, 1989, it signaled an end to the Cold War. Almost immediately, on November 10 and 11, members of East German political parties as well as opposition and peace movements met to discuss and negotiate East Germany's future. Bärbel Bohley, an East German peace activist who had founded the groups Women for Peace and Peace and Human Rights Initiative, was arrested and expelled in 1988, but returned in 1989 and participated in the negotiations. They ultimately voted for unification, but many were disappointed that the move did not allow for more socialist compromises. Indeed, this was an issue for many of the activists and political leaders, like Bohley, who were considering what would become of former Eastern Bloc countries and their progressive social welfare policies. The future of socialist political parties, trade unions, women's leagues, and initiatives for peace and environmental justice remained uncertain. In Poland, discussions now known as the Polish Round Table Talks were conducted on February 6 and April 5, 1989, between representatives of the opposition movement (such as Solidarity) and political parties (such as the Polish United Workers Party). The talks centered on how to democratize the economy and political system, including questions of political pluralism, freedom of speech, and introducing economic competition. The prospect of a more progressive women's agenda, however, seemed bleak; of the Round Table's sixty participants, only one was a woman—a representative from Solidarity.[96]

The freedom of the individual, a key political tenant of the Western capitalist model, has operated on the false assumption of a level playing field wherein certain groups—particularly women and minorities—have not fared well. In the post-Cold War era, few women were able to find a third option or a compromise between the two Cold War models. Indeed, many women in former Eastern Bloc countries often bore the brunt of new structural changes, as the Western emphasis on male breadwinners led to more female unemployment, and the economic shock of joining Western and world markets and losing key social supports left them in precarious circumstances.[97] Government and economic reorganizing also caused many women to lose their jobs at the same time that prices were increasing, social services were decreasing, and access to nutrition, education, and training programs was shrinking.[98] Yet while these challenges were by no means insignificant, they pale in comparison to the horrors that unfolded in the region formerly known as Yugoslavia.

The Yugoslav Wars and the Battleground of Women's Bodies

At the end of the Cold War, the system that had held together the diverse Balkan states that made up Yugoslavia fractured, and ethnic tensions tore apart newly formed states, leading to brutal sectarian wars.[99] Serbia, led by Slobodan Milošević, was determined to create a large, dominant Serbian state by eliminating non-Serb minorities in ethnically diverse areas and preventing other states from seceding. When states such as Croatia, Slovenia and Bosnia–Herzegovina did secede, Serbian invasion followed. From 1991 to 1999, multiple conflicts, civil wars, and invasions plagued the region. Refugees fled and trapped civilians died by the tens of thousands. Most notably, brutalities such as rape, mutilation, castration, and the posthumous butchering and burning of bodies accompanied these military campaigns.[100] Some refer to the period as one of "ethnic cleansing" and others genocide.[101]

The gendered dimensions of these brutalities would come to the fore during later war crimes tribunals, revealing that women and girls were particularly terrorized during the Yugoslav Wars. Armed Serb forces invaded towns and villages and forced thousands of Muslim women into camps, motels, schools, and sports halls, where they were repeatedly raped by Serb soldiers.[102] Scholars estimate, conservatively, that between twenty and fifty thousand women were raped during the wars in Bosnia–Herzegovina and Kosovo.[103] While, as discussed previously, women's bodies served as a metaphorical battleground during the Cold War, the Yugoslav conflicts made them physical and strategic sites of attack. In their capacity to reproduce, women were seen as the biological boundaries of an ethnoreligious group.[104] The mass rape and impregnation of minority women mirrored the mass killing of men and boys with the specific goal of destroying an ethnic group and its lineage.[105] In what historian Mirko Grmek has termed "memorycide," in addition to killing and driving out populations, Serb forces also destroyed schools, churches, museums, libraries, birth and death records, and significant architectural structures to eliminate any reminders or remnants of a culture.[106] Serb leaders (and to a lesser degree Croats and Muslims) depended on fear and terror as well as the dehumanization, deportation, and destruction of a specific nationality, ethnicity, political, or religious group and its history as a primary tactic of war, intended to wholly destroy a people and cleanse society of its existence.[107]

On May 15, 1992, fifteen-year-old Edina fled her village of Bratunac (in eastern Bosnia–Herzegovina) with her mother, father, sister, and brother, where they hid in tents in the woods for ten rainy nights with other Muslims. During a trip to obtain food and necessities, one of their Serb neighbors captured and detained the group in a large building with forty other people—men and women, young and old. After a few days, Edina and two other girls were taken to a deserted house and instructed to undress. Edina refused and had her clothes torn from her body. "I began to scream," she reported in an interview. "He raped me … He kept going … into the night … I lost any sense of time. When he wanted to sleep, he stayed on top of me … He [hand]cuffed me [to the table] … [He] had a gun that he hid under the pillow."[108] Two days later, the neighbor who had caught her family repeatedly raped her as well.[109]

Amid ongoing atrocities, survivors often found responses from governments, the media, and the international community to be severely lacking. In addition to mass rape campaigns targeting women, men were killed en masse, leaving countless women mourning their sons, fathers, brothers, and husbands. One mother recounted how her son was pulled from her with no intervention from the UN Peacekeepers who had been deployed to the region: "[They] took my child from me, right in front of the eyes of the [Peacekeeper] Dutch soldiers."[110] Indeed, in one of the program's great failures, Peacekeepers often turned their backs on violence during the Yugoslav Wars, such as the 1995 massacre in the Bosnian town of Srebrenica. There, Bosnian Serbs attacked the non-Serb population with particular brutality, including starvation, shelling, and, finally, systematic mass murder. In the wake of the massacre, grieving women appeared on television and recounted how they saw their men taken away, but felt they had to fight for media attention.[111]

In the absence of official protections, NGOs took on much of the work of supporting women who were survivors of violence, displaced by the wars, or in need of humanitarian aid. In 1993, Bosnian Muslim Zejneba Sarajlic founded Women of Podrinje, a support group and source of humanitarian aid for displaced persons that later also collected and cataloged photos of those killed. Also in 1993, an organization of and for rape survivors called *Žena-Žrtva Rata* (Women Victims of War) formed to work with Islamic religious authorities for community acceptance of women who had survived rape in Bosnia.[112] Feminist organizations also fought against the war and for survivors. Starting in 1991, the Serb group Women in Black Against War demonstrated for seven years in front of the Belgrade National Assembly. In 1993, a women's therapy center called Medica opened in Zenica, Bosnia–Herzegovina with an all-female staff to provide medical and psychological aid. Notably, Medica provided services to all three ethnic groups in Bosnia–Herzegovina: Croatian, Serbian, and Muslim. As a spokeswoman from the group explained: "We decided to found Medica on our own initiative when we realized that none of the main international humanitarian organizations were able to provide concrete help for these women."[113] The organization also collected data from refugee camps to analyze violence against women in war and report their findings to the UN Tribunal that followed.

NATO finally conducted airstrikes in Bosnia–Herzegovina in 1995 and then in 1999 during the Kosovo War, in both cases too late to save many, especially women from horrific ends. Afterward, Serbia, Bosnia–Herzegovina, Croatia, Slovenia, and Macedonia became new independent republics, and the Serbian leader Milošević was arrested and tried in the International Court of Justice. He died in 2006, however, before the verdict was issued for his four-year trial.

The War Crimes Tribunal and Women's Testimonies

The history of these atrocities includes how survivors lived on with their trauma, with the injustice of seeing former attackers go free, and with attempts to rebuild society. In 1993, the United Nations established the International Criminal Tribunal for the former Yugoslavia (ICTY) as a judicial response to the large-scale war crimes and crimes against humanity that occurred during the Yugoslav Wars. As part of ICTY efforts, scholars conducted a series of interviews in which women recounted what they endured for prosecutorial purposes and the historical record. Their stories were traumatic to recount and are difficult to read.

The ICTY ran from 1993 to 2017 and instituted a special Victims and Witnesses Section (VWS)—the first of its kind in international criminal justice—to preserve the safety and dignity of vulnerable witnesses. Considering the wars' systematic rape campaigns, the tribunal needed distinct new procedures to protect sexual assault survivors and to collect evidence about their assaults, such as not requiring corroboration of their testimonies and the legal ability to infer the absence of consent when rape has occurred as part of an ongoing genocide campaign or detention of victims. The VWS also instituted safety measures such as withholding witnesses' names, allowing them to testify from behind screens, and aiding in relocation to another country when their lives were in danger. The new procedures demonstrated attempts to provide emotional sensitivity to the trauma of testifying about rape and sexual assault.[114]

Several landmark cases resulted from the ICTY's investigations, findings, and indictments. Perhaps most significantly, the tribunal expanded definitions of crimes against humanity and international human rights laws to include sexual violence as a war crime in violation of the Geneva Conventions of 1949; a crime against humanity and genocide; a tool of war to intimidate, persecute, and terrorize the enemy; and as a form of torture.[115] Additionally, more than seventy individuals were charged with crimes of sexual assault and by 2011, over thirty of them were convicted. While the ICTY emphasized the importance of achieving justice through a fair trial and impartial tribunal, its 1994 annual report also addressed the question of retribution, asking: "How could a woman who had been raped by servicemen from a different ethnic group or a civilian whose parents or children had been killed in cold blood quell their desire for vengeance if they knew that the authors of these crimes were left unpunished?"[116] Indeed, this question remains unanswered as survivors are still demanding explanations about neighbors and acquaintances who became killers and rapists, soldiers' inability to refuse orders, and international responses and policies of nonintervention. Some are also still waiting for news of lost family members, such as one mother who stayed in a refugee camp until 2004, when her son's body was finally dug up and identified: "When my oldest son was found, I lost my hope. I knew ... I still pray to God that I will hear that my other son is somewhere."[117]

After the wars, many surviving women lived in poverty in refugee camps, battling loneliness. By 2005, some received money to repair and return to their homes. But the taboo of rape remained strong, and thousands of survivors faced stigma and contempt when trying to address their trauma, including familial rejection of women who had been raped and infanticides of children born from rape.[118] In 2009, Amnesty International published the report *Bosnia and Herzegovina: "Whose justice?": The women of Bosnia and Herzegovina are still waiting*, noting national judicial systems' devastating inadequacy in addressing sexual violence.[119] For many survivors the war has not truly ended.

Immigration, Xenophobia, and the Rise of the Far Right

Immigration to Western Europe increased with the fall of the Cold War order and, after decades of postcolonial migrations, tensions around race, ethnicity, and religion came to the fore. Xenophobia rose alongside greater competition for jobs amid economic crises in the 1980s and 1990s, resulting, for example, in race riots in Great Britain in the 1980s and an upsurge in anti-immigrant and white nationalist organizations. In Western Europe, violence against Muslims and immigrants increased, most famously in the deadly attacks on both Turkish Germans who had lived in Germany for decades and newer asylum seekers in Solingen and Mölln. Indeed, another political revolution arose in the 1980s—far right nationalist groups that politicized immigration and ethnic demographic shifts, with lasting effects. In France, for example, new political parties made nationalism and anti-immigrant policies central to their platforms. Jean-Marie Le Pen served as the president of the far-right National Front political party from 1972 to 2011, and he gained popularity with his focus on "traditional culture and values." The National Front had its first electoral success in 1984, when Le Pen won a seat in the European Parliament. Although he was never elected president of France, Le Pen's political rhetoric fired up both the Left and the Right and could not be ignored.

A key feature of this rise of the far right was its political and at times physically violent attacks on Muslim minorities, many of whom were in Europe due to its legacy of colonialism or guest worker programs—both initiated by the host states now rejecting them. These attacks often addressed women's bodies specifically, the most visible dispute being the headscarf debate, which asked: should Muslims be allowed to wear headscarves in public schools in a secular country?

Since the French Revolution, French republicanism was based on individual rights that freed citizens from religious identifications and considered all equal (except colonial subjects) as secular citizens. Under this republican logic, some interpreted Muslim women's headscarves as imposing religion on a secular nation. Many ethnic French citizens (as well as British and Germans) saw the immigration of a different religious and ethnic group as a threat to what they saw as their national cohesiveness; their "Frenchness." The ensuing debate was essentially one of assimilation versus cultural relativism, and girls and women's bodies were central.

On October 3, 1989, three Muslim French girls were expelled from school, despite good academic and disciplinary records, for refusing to remove their headscarves (Figure 7.3). The town was brewing with class, religious, and cultural tensions, and some viewed this piece of fabric as a symbol of "oppressive Islam" or at the very least the incompatibility of Islam and French identity. Public demonstrations also erupted in support of the girls' right to cover their hair in school. Public school was seen as a place to instill French nationalism and values, and the headscarves were seen as political emblems that could threaten the state's proclaimed secularism. As historian Joan Scott has argued, excluding girls with (Muslim) religious dress from public schools would thwart their participation in secular French democracy and culture. Moreover, since prohibiting headscarves forced girls to choose between their education and their religion, Scott suggests that perhaps the French government was less interested in these girls' opportunities and more interested in their own opinions about what was acceptable in French society.[120]

The debate over full visual access to girls' and women's hair led to disagreement regarding how much of the female body should be revealed.[121] Notably, many ethnic French feminists asserted that headscarves were a symbol of Muslim women's religious oppression from which they had a responsibility to free them. This perspective provided an interesting

FIGURE 7.3 *Fatima Achaboun (center), a young French-Tunisian girl, is surrounded by friends on October 9, 1989, in the school courtyard, after having been authorized to return to school on the condition that she does not wear her Islamic headscarf in the classroom. Getty Images.*

juxtaposition with feminists' longstanding battles for women to have full legal control over their bodies and the ability to make their own choices about it. Similarly in the Netherlands, political activist Ayan Hirsi Ali saw Islam solely as patriarchal and antiassimilationist, chastising Amsterdam's mayor for championing multiculturalism and having an "unreflective, unexamined tolerance of Islamic communities and their activities."[122] This critique from a "secular Muslim women" delighted the political right by providing a champion of their own critiques of immigrant communities. Hirsi Ali was a Somali-born political refugee, who arrived in the Netherlands in 1992 after being subjected to genital mutilation at five years of age. She worked with Somali women asylum seekers and in hostels for abused women from 1995 to 2001, her life experiences inseparable from her politics. Women and girls' hair and whether they should be permitted to cover it was the touchpoint for a larger discussion on Muslim minorities in Europe and would persist as an issue into the twenty-first century. Indeed, in 1994 and 2003, debates again emerged over whether girls could wear Islamic hair and face coverings in French public schools.[123]

Afro-Feminism in the 1980s and 1990s

In some areas, the 1980s and 1990s was also a period of increased awareness and discussion of the experience of Black European women. This era saw a reckoning with feminist theory and politics that did not adequately consider race and class, as seen in the testimonies from Greenham Common. Concurrent with other Western European Black feminist activists such as Wilmette Brown, Black German feminists and lesbians established the organization Afro-German Women (ADEFRA) in multiple cities across West Germany.[124] Cofounded by Katja Kinder and Katharine Oguntoya, the organization was intended to fight racism and provide a sense of community to Afro-Germans.[125] In an evolution of Black feminist movements from the 1960s and 1970s, such as Brown's Wages for Housework campaign, ADEFRA practiced "Black women's internationalism," fusing transnational feminism, antiracist African-diasporic politics, and gay rights. The organization not only forged feminist coalitions with other grassroots movements in West Germany, such as the Initiative of Black Germans, but also served as a practical form of resistance and survival in predominantly white West Germany where many Afro-Germans had little contact with one another.[126]

The Caribbean American poet and prominent feminist and lesbian activist Audre Lorde was heavily involved in Black women's internationalism. Lorde lived in Berlin as a visiting professor, performing her poetry, giving speeches, and building community with Black German women. White German feminists—who did not generally acknowledge that there were Black women in Germany, let alone Black feminist theorists—attended Lorde's lectures as well, leading to long overdue discussions of the intersections of race, class, sexuality, and gender.[127] Lorde's literary prowess proved inspirational. In 1988, ADEFRA published the first issues of *Afrekete: Magazine for Afro-German and Black Women*, which featured artwork, poetry, letters, historical articles, and conference reports, providing a literary and political outlet to far-flung Black lesbians and feminists.[128] The pivotal *Showing our Colors: Afro-German Women Speak*—considered the first book published by Afro-Germans and the first written use of the term "Afro-German"—was published soon after in 1991 and cemented the place of Afro-feminism in Germany specifically, and Europe broadly.[129]

Conclusion

Waves of change in the last two decades of the twentieth century brought both radical shifts and frustrating continuities for many European women. Riding the second-wave of feminism, women's rights drew new attention nationally and internationally, especially within the United Nations and the European Union, and women's education and employment access increased accordingly. However, the 1980s ended the postwar coalition among many Western governments and ushered in a new era of neoliberalism that disproportionally impacted women with cuts to social services and a move away from the welfare state. Thus, the cultural shift to two-income households did little to alleviate women's age-old double burden.

Intersectional movements for peace, ecology, an end to nuclear armament, women's rights, and more democracy influenced how the Cold War ended between 1989 and 1991. Historians often refer to the end of the Cold War as an era of revolutions, marked by a peaceful transfer of power rather than the feared nuclear war. As this chapter has demonstrated, though, the post-Cold War period was traumatic for many European women. Violent ethnic cleansing campaigns in the former Yugoslavia were carried out on women's bodies, leaving many survivors alone, in poverty, and unable to tell their stories. International war crimes tribunals brought landmark decisions, however, in the legal categorization of violence against women, such as classifying rape during warfare as illegal torture and a crime against humanity. In addition, the AIDS pandemic and other health crises recognized no borders and states struggled to research, prevent, and fight the disease, all while facing cultural and legal biases against homosexual communities.

Europe continued to redefine itself in the post-postwar era. Immigration, especially of Muslims, changed the demographic landscape of Western Europe, and Muslim women became symbols of either not belonging or of multiculturalism. This and many other issues discussed in this chapter, including gendered violence, environmental activism, and evolutions of feminist politics, would persist into the twenty-first century. As the next and final chapter will show, the new millennium continued to bring revolutionary change alongside stubborn continuities.

8

The New Millennium

Introduction

The turn of the twenty-first century witnessed multiple catalysts for change, with broad implications for European women. Industrialization, mass education, and new social and civil rights legislation coupled with sophisticated technology, communication, and travel created unprecedented contexts that impacted women in ways not previously possible.[1] Globalization, or the linking of people, economies, cultures, and politics, was a marked change in the early 2000s, making national boundaries less significant than ever before. Free trade, outsourcing, supranational security, environmental and health organizing, and especially migration impacted women and men's lives in new ways across the globe. Humans and activity flowed more fluidly. The growth of the European Union (EU) and the introduction of a common currency, the Euro, emphasized the decline of the nation-state. The expansion of suffrage, access and information about contraception, and a global agenda for women's rights in the twentieth century worked to lessen the differences between the global North, South, East, and West in the twenty-first. And with the development of the world wide web and digital access—prompting the era's designation as the "Digital Age"—some researchers concluded that new digital technologies could alleviate the gender gap by increasing opportunities for participation in labor and financial markets.[2]

In 2004, UN Foundation senior fellow Geeta Rao Gupta commented on globalization's impacts on women, writing that it was "inevitable, transformative, and for better or for worse." Gupta continued, "And like marriage ... societal constructions of gender [mean that] globalization affects women differently than men."[3] In some cases, globalization increased women's income and employment opportunities with a freer flow of goods and capital. At the same time, women bore the brunt of capitalism's endless search for the cheapest labor, as outsourcing fell heavily on young women in the developing world, especially in informal and semiformal sections of the economy that included low-paying, seasonal, and insecure jobs.[4] In this and many other ways, early-twenty-first-century globalization was gendered, intertwined, and disproportionately affected women, with varied outcomes for their well-being.[5]

This final chapter takes stock of how these more recent trends relate to the history recounted in previous chapters. It highlights how industrialization, globalization, democratization, and activism continue to influence European women's lives. It also explores how sex, gender, and power intersect with the impacts of decolonization and immigration, and how evolving environmental activism combined with calls for sustainable development have far-reaching effects on women's economic development and well-being. Finally, it emphasizes European women's leadership in the issues, crises, and shifts that shaped the early 2000s.

Sex Trafficking and Gendered Exploitation

Europe in general, and Northwestern Europe specifically, has long been a migration destination for women looking for work.[6] While migrants have always sought various employment opportunities, the economic collapse of Eastern Europe after the end of the Cold War in the early 1990s was the impetus for much sex work migration—and exploitation within it. The swift return to market-driven economies was devastating for citizens caught in the middle of two competing systems, and many young women from economically ravaged Eastern Europe moved across borders that were made softer by the war's end. As a result, the "Eastern European prostitute" became a potent symbol for post-Cold War Eastern Europe in general—destitute and prostrate to the world economic market.[7] The expansion of the Eastern European legal and illegal sex trade highlights the economic and gender disparities of post-Cold War Europe. Moreover, it exhibits the interconnected and exploitative realities of globalization, and how they played out on women's bodies.

Sex work migration increased dramatically alongside changing European labor and immigration laws. European integration after the Cold War brought about denationalization, as the expanding EU eliminated many travel restrictions, border stops, and visa requirements. For migrants from former Soviet satellite countries or regions, however, journeying to and within the EU was not free; traveling without a visa made one an illegal immigrant, including those from Ukraine, Belarus, and Russia. Many Eastern European women were "trafficked" into Western Europe or exploited sexually in exchange for being smuggled across a border, often with false promises of finding work not in the sex trade. Researchers have had trouble tracking the numbers of trafficked individuals but found that the majority came from former Soviet countries.[8]

In interviews, trafficked women recounted how they got to Western Europe and what they endured. "Anna" recalled that she was approached at age seventeen and promised work as a photo model in Italy. Upon her arrival, she was sold to a "protector" who controlled her for seven years.[9] A Ukrainian woman explained how at the time of national independence, all bank deposits were transferred to Russia's central bank, wiping out hundreds of thousands of Ukrainians' life savings. Desperate to support her bankrupt family, she agreed to go to Italy to work as a waitress but was sold into the sex trade instead.[10] Another Ukrainian woman described the horrific conditions she endured to be able to send small amounts of money to her family: "The street is hell. The street completely destroyed me. I was always drunk, always not well covered in the winter. The protector beat me constantly. The clients also beat me. I hated myself"[11] Volunteers from the NGO TAMPEP—a network led by migrant sex workers—found her years later, passed out, bloody, naked, infected with several sexually transmitted infections, and with critical psychological trauma.[12]

The narrative of the trafficked woman is complicated, however, by studies of women who knowingly traveled to enter the sex trade and worked independently of organized crime and traffickers. "Sex Workers," the term used in scholarship, highlights the production and labor of sex and includes sexual labor in broader labor histories. Some sex workers have pushed for decriminalization. Others contend that sexual labor is just one part of a larger study of human trafficking as a reason to restrict border crossings. The intersections of migration, sex, commerce, and coercion are muddy, and many states have chosen to turn a blind eye—for example, not making arrests even when the actions are illegal.[13] In other states, such as the Netherlands, the process of decriminalizing sex work has not necessarily helped to curb trafficking and criminality.[14] Most sex workers remain in danger and in a legal no-man's-land, even as sex trafficking has become a central concern among Eastern European feminists in the twenty-first century.

Twenty-first Century Feminisms

The Ukrainian feminist group FEMEN grabbed media attention in 2008 with public protests against sex trafficking, as well as sexual harassment at universities and women's oppression in Ukrainian society in general.[15] As with generations of feminists before—such as the nineteenth-century suffragettes and the Dutch feminists Dolle Mina—they engaged in street action. And like the turn of the century futurists seen in chapter two, FEMEN also turned many heads when they appeared topless with the slogan "My body is my weapon!" painted on their bare chests. Protesting heavily against the sex trade and against Ukraine as a destination for sex tourism, FEMEN garnered global media attention, support, and critique with their feminist use of sexual exhibitionism.

The new millennium would continue to see similarly brazen approaches to feminist activism. In 2012, the Russian feminist guerilla activist punk band Pussy Riot prayed in Moscow's main cathedral for the Virgin Mary to be a feminist and "chase Putin away." The punk group drew on religious symbolism by singing traditional church music with modified lyrics and interspersed with punk petitions, blurring the lines between the sacred and the profane to great effect. The video of their performance went viral on YouTube, as did news of their arrest and two-year imprisonment in Siberia for "hooliganism." The performance sparked a debate engaging the Russian Orthodox Church, politics, feminism, and intellectual freedom. One side found the protest offensive and inappropriate, and the other side declared it necessary and effective. The band itself has described Pussy Riot's performances as sharp political critiques meant to mock the church, which they see as a historical leader of patriarchy.[16] In figure 8.1, the group performs in Houston, TX under the banner, "Virgin Mary please get rid of Putin." Three members of the group have their palms touching evenly and raised in the symbol of prayer. They wear knitted head and face coverings, a play on women's traditional domestic craft work merged with activist performance art.

Western audiences in particular seized on the Russian feminists and their critique of the Russian government, as journalists and celebrities—such as the American Madonna and the Icelandic singer-songwriter Björk—sang, wrote, and tweeted about them.[17] In Russia, however, many did not comprehend their vision and, according to public opinion polls, seemed uncomfortable with activist women in general.[18]

FIGURE 8.1 *Pussy Riot performs at the Day for Night festival in Houston, Texas, December 16, 2017, in front of the message, "Virgin Mary please get rid of Putin." Photo by Rick Kern / WireImage courtesy of Getty Images.*

Both FEMEN and Pussy Riot used sexual language and imagery in protest against their governments, harnessing sexuality and gender for radical feminism and antigovernment action.[19] Scholars and activists have used the term "sextremism" to describe this innovative feminist mobilization of sexuality, gender, and the body, even though gendered bodies have long occupied protest spaces.[20] Some, however, question the usefulness of sextremism and argue that topless and otherwise sexualized protests reproduce patriarchal norms and undermine the actions' effectiveness.[21] While FEMEN protesters are overwhelmingly thin, white, and play on sexuality, the protesters counter that the media has seized on those most fitting this description. Indeed, FEMEN claim they are beating the media at their own game.[22] Although sextremism offers a new idiom for radical or extreme feminist action, FEMEN and Pussy Riot followed historical patterns of public activism but, like many in the Digital Age, they harnessed media and technology to promote their messages.

In addition, both groups represent the fluid and expansive nature of feminism's evolution in the early 2000s, as the "third wave" transitioned into the "fourth" alongside the emergence of "post-feminism." Characterized by intersectionality, these iterations extended well beyond gender alone as a framework of oppression. For example, FEMEN's main objective is women's rights but, like Pussy Riot, also took a politicized antireligious stance (among others). On the other hand, Pussy Riot identifies more as antigovernment than as committed to women's rights specifically, which according to anthropologist Emily Channell, makes their feminism "more powerful and therefore more dangerous."[23]

However, a more expansive analysis of women's oppression did not prevent divisions among early-twenty-first-century feminists. FEMEN also garnered media attention for their attacks on Islamic fundamentalism's relationship to women, offending many Muslim feminists.[24] A student editorial responded by calling the group "topless imperialists" for imposing Western views and casting Muslim women solely as victims.[25] FEMEN defended their position on their official blog, stating that they had not intended to undermine Islamic feminists but were acting in accordance with their mission against "all the plagues of patriarchy."[26] Like earlier feminist movements, those that emerged in the new millennium did not always agree on the path forward.

Islamic Women in Europe

As discussed in previous chapters, postcolonial and postwar immigration changed the face of Europe, and FEMEN's commentary reflected a wider discussion about Muslim women in the early 2000s. Since many European countries identify culturally or officially as Christian nations, Muslim immigrants became the subject of debate—and in many cases misconceptions—regarding topics both public (such as education) and private (such as marriage). While debates around circumcision for boys also pitted supposedly secular European medical opinions against the religious and cultural customs of Muslim (and Jewish) communities, most of the criticism was directed toward the treatment of Muslim women and girls. Europeans grappled with the model of individual rights versus a desire to "protect" women and girls from practices they found oppressive. Often citing unfamiliar customs such as arranged marriages as well as reports of violence such as "honor killings," many viewed Muslims as decidedly not European.[27]

The September 11, 2001, terrorist attacks on the US World Trade Center created an entirely new context for these debates. By 2003, a "War on Terror" launched primarily by the US and the North Atlantic Treaty Organization (NATO) was in full effect, leading many European leaders to view Islamic communities in their countries in a different light. After September 11th, some states considered Muslim immigrants to be outsiders for a new reason—the threat of international terrorism, not just for domestic cultural differences. According to immigration historian Rita Chin, "It was not just that Muslim immigrants seemed potentially incompatible with Western society; now they posed a security threat to the very existence of Europe itself."[28] This essentialization of Islamic communities—as not just incompatible with "European values" but also as dangerous—again placed women's bodies and access to them at the center of the debate. Secularizing and sexualizing Muslim European girls and women—banning burkinis at French beaches, for example—was folded into the cultural War on Terror with a new urgency.

The debates about women and girls in immigrant communities, especially in Islamic communities, came to a head in the early 2000s with the "headscarf debate." The Islamic hair covering became the grounds for a fight between notions of cultural relativity and assimilation that sought to define who could be "European." The idea that European citizens had to be secular in culturally Christian communities (ones with long histories of antisemitism, no less) was seen as hypocritical and disrespectful. The longer history of colonialism and—in the French case, especially—of violent and bloody decolonization was a dark historical backdrop of policing postcolonial immigrants.[29]

Muslim activists formed their own organizations to protest both the policing of women within their communities and European states' opinions on how Muslim women should live. In France, Fadela Amara, a second-generation Algerian immigrant, founded the group Ni Putes ni Soumises (Neither Whores nor Submissives) in March 2002 to encourage Muslim women to speak out against violence against women perpetrated by men who saw themselves as the guardians of family honor.[30] This violence occurred within the larger context of worsening living conditions, decreasing employment opportunities, and further segregation from mainstream French society. Ni Putes ni Soumises also denounced French society's tendency to only recognize Muslim women as passive and voiceless and do little to intervene to secure their freedom of movement and physical security.[31]

At this time, France also instituted a law banning religious symbols in schools, reflecting an attitude that stretched back to 1989, as discussed in the last chapter. Critics found that the ban disproportionately impacted Muslim girls and prevented many from attending public schools—the very places where states instill secular, national values. In October 2004, Cennet Doganay, a fifteen-year-old French Muslim girl, shaved her head in protest. This act enabled her to follow French law and, in alignment with her religious beliefs, not show her hair in public. Even so, Doganay clarified that the move was an act of rebellion, telling the press, "I respect the law but the law doesn't respect me."[32] Her mother explained that Doganay had also tried to enter class with a traditional French beret but was made to leave nonetheless, implying the ban was aimed at more than just the cloth. She reported that the experience had a negative impact on her daughter: "She has been traumatised [sic] since the start of the term. ... All she wanted ... was to go to school like everyone else."[33] At the heart of the controversy was the question of who controlled girls and women: Was it their families that required the head covering or the state that required its removal? What were the motivations on each side and did girls and women have a say in the matter? Disparate groups could not agree on the answers to these questions, even in more serious cases of violence against women.

On February 7, 2005, a Kurdish German shot his 23-year-old sister, Hatun Sürücü, at a Berlin bus stop, declaring that she had compromised the family's "honor" by "living like a German." She had fled an abusive marriage and moved with her son to a home for single mothers while trying to finish her education. The German media seized on the event as a horrifying example of the failure of immigrant and German "parallel worlds," citing "misguided tolerance" and calling for new investigations of patriarchal family structures and "integration problems."[34] Scholars argue that this media coverage both created and strengthened boundaries between immigrants and majority societies in Western Europe—boundaries that interlace ethnicity, national origin, religion and gender.[35] In an escalation of the headscarf debate, such coverage employed violence against women as a marker of immutable difference between immigrant and majority communities.[36] In Britain, the Netherlands, and Germany, for example, government publications, scholars, and the media have reported that rates of domestic violence against women was higher in immigrant communities.[37] However, the issue exists for all women and patriarchy is a cultural phenomenon separate from Islam. Activists from within Muslim and immigrant communities argued that the Western ideal of female emancipation ignored alternative forms of female agency, as was the case with the critique of FEMEN.

European women who converted to Islam also evoked strong emotional responses when seen in traditional Islamic dress or with men whom onlookers perceived as Muslim. Some of these women faced discrimination, such as losing their jobs after adopting traditional Islamic dress, and also violence, such as a German woman who had her car torched in her East Berlin neighborhood.[38] German convert to Islam, Kathrin Klausing, and her Kuwaiti-German husband Omar Abo-Namous's disrupted honeymoon is a case in point. During their honeymoon in 2007, the newlyweds arrived by taxi late at night at their rented cabin in in the small village of Hamwiede, Germany, on the outskirts of Hannover. The next morning, locals called the police, stating that the couple looked suspicious based on their appearance and dress—apparently the man looked "Middle Eastern," and the woman spoke perfect German yet wore a headscarf.[39] The police arrived at around ten o'clock that night, armed with pistols and automatic weapons, and pounded on the door, demanding they open it.[40] As Abo-Namous did so, they stormed the cabin and searched it while the couple was made to wait on the couch. Klausing and Abo-Namous tried unsuccessfully to sue, incurring 2,000 euros in legal fees. The court judgement noted that the police acted appropriately because they feared the couple had a "terrorist background." Klausing responded to the judgment by pointing out the open discrimination: "Whenever I wear Muslim clothing, is it really a reason for the police to storm my house?"[41] Appearances were not the only cultural difference anti-immigrant campaigners seized on.

Interestingly, some anti-Muslim and anti-immigrant arguments also claimed that the homophobic views often associated with strict religious communities—unlike "European" ones—were part of what made these groups inassimilable. Some governments and organizations insisted that Islam was inherently homophobic and therefore inherently incompatible with European values. Although these same "Christian" nations had condemned homosexuality for centuries, by the new millennium gay rights were ironically seen as a defining feature of European laws and culture.

Decriminalizing Homosexuality and LGBTQ+ Communities

In the late twentieth century, gay and lesbian movements along with the EU, Council of Europe, and other supranational courts drove the decriminalization of homosexuality, marking a crucial shift. By 2001, most European countries had decriminalized same-sex relations.[42] Civil unions and marriage equality followed, starting with legal civil unions in Denmark in 1989 and same-sex marriage in the Netherlands in 2001. Southern European LGBTQ+ groups organized to overcome religious objections and normalize homosexual relations, while EU policy has "mainstreamed" gay and lesbian rights as well as prohibiting discrimination based on sex.[43] In fact, a Council of the European Union resolution requires EU representatives to monitor the human rights of LGBTQ+ persons and report violations publicly.[44]

These legislative changes accompanied cultural shifts in LGBTQ+ acceptance. This included increased recognition of nontraditional families. In 2007, the Lesbian and Gay Association of Berlin–Brandenburg launched a campaign to promote LGBTQ+ families. In keeping with the conflict between culturally Christian and culturally Muslim communities, the campaign's posters declared, "A family is where the Children are!" and were printed in German and Turkish. Public opinion crossed cultural lines, however, as many were divided on "rainbow families" with same sex parents.

European LGBTQ+ communities grew in size and visibility during this period. International events, such as the Berlin Love Parade—an annual gay pride event—and the upbeat Eurovision Song Contest—a live competition of one song per nation—have particular and special significance to European LGBTQ+ communities, promoting pride and positive queer identities. Supranational European organizations also began to support gay communities, such as the European Commission's funding for LGBTQ+ NGOs and for the European International Gay and Lesbian Association.

Equality and Gender Roles

Alongside greater acceptance toward LGBTQ+ communities in the early twenty-first century, the idea of a "European" gender system was more elusive than ever. Concepts of women's or men's roles had evolved, and even as national borders weakened in the expanding and strengthening European Union there were no universal gendered experiences. However, the last three decades had shown that while trends toward more quality existed, they were neither guaranteed nor necessarily permanent. Within the EU, pockets of traditional lifestyles and patriarchal cultures challenged equitable family models.

In addition, much European policy still relies on a gender-neutral "adult worker" model that does not acknowledge that women continue to do most unpaid care work. Even in progressive Scandinavian countries, the ever-present "double burden" persists.[45] For migrant families, the 2003 EU Family Reunification Directive has inadvertently upheld a single breadwinner model by requiring migrants to prove they could support their family members and provide sufficient housing. While guest worker programs allowed European women to "return to the home" in a pronatalist drive, it is increasingly foreign-born women who provide the care work—as maids and nannies—that enables many European women to now work full-time and pursue careers.[46]

The birth of a child cements gendered parental roles, and more European fathers are taking paternity leave than ever before. According to a 2014 study, more European fathers are concerned about their domestic role and worrying that their paid labor prevents them from fulfilling their family duties.⁴⁷ Paternity leave policies vary across Europe's more than twenty states, with Spain offering new fathers 100 percent of their salary and Germany offering 67 percent, for example. Mothers take the majority of transferable leave, which can be used by either parent. Iceland's paternity leave does the most to advance gender equity as the only country were men and women get the same amount nontransferable leave, but no country yet offers equal, nontransferable, well-paid leave for each parent.⁴⁸ "The aim of this Act is to ensure a child's access to both her/his parents," reads a line from the Icelandic Act no. 95/2000 that made parental leave a gender neutral entitlement.⁴⁹ One Icelandic father, Örn, recalled why it was important for him to take his leave to bond with his son: "It creates a closer bond between the father and child to be alone [together]."⁵⁰ At the same time, an Icelandic mother commented on returning to work with ease, because she could leave her baby with the child's father: "[It's] so comfortable, the idea of being able to start work without sending her to a babysitter or day care."⁵¹

In 2009, the European Union experienced a currency crisis known as the eurozone crisis or European debt crisis, when multiple eurozone states were unable to either repay or refinance their government debt.⁵² A lack of coordination and regulation between these interconnected economies created imbalances that affected the whole eurozone, as some countries provided bailouts and others enacted extreme austerity measures. Political scientists Roberta Guerrina and Annick Masselot noted in 2018 that women's economic equality was a casualty of the crisis, as higher political and economic priorities sidelined gender equity efforts.⁵³ The European Union had previously developed a range of policies designed to foster equality within and among (very diverse) member states. Additionally, the austerity measures and subsequent cuts to services and programs disproportionately impacted women and minorities—the largest cohort of the unskilled secondary job market.⁵⁴ Cuts to public sector services and benefits were unfortunate as policymakers and scholars agreed that gender equality should be a consistent EU goal, not just in "the good times."⁵⁵ A working document of the Gender Committee of the Platform for the Citizen Audit of Spain's Debt emphasized that women deserved recognition for their contributions to the economy: "One of these invisible debts is the gender debt, the debt society has with regard to women. Women are the creditors ... as they perform the care work that enables the production of workers. ... [Many] women have a double workload, [and] only one part is recognized."⁵⁶

Women in the UN and the Military

Despite such setbacks, European women made major strides in international activism and influence in the second decade of the twenty-first century, including continuing challenges of European reunification. Twenty years after the fall of the Soviet Union, the continued distinction between Eastern and Western Europe demonstrates the lasting gendered impacts of the Cold War. In 2000, two UN publications—UNIFEM's *Progress of the World's Women* investigative report and the UN Department of Economics and Social Affair's *World's Women: Trends and Statistics* report—noted that, despite improvements in women's employment opportunities, women in Eastern Europe faced many obstacles: lower rates of schooling for girls, household income inequality, and higher rates of unemployment and poverty among women.[57] Women in these areas saw worsening economic conditions and few benefits of recent progress.

The UN and other international organizations have taken measures to address lingering inequalities. In 2010, the United Nations Entity for Gender Equality and the Empowerment of Women (known as UN Women) was established to focus on, among other issues, gender equality; women's empowerment; stopping violence against women and girls; and sustainable development; and, in 2013, the United Nations Human Rights Office launched the Free and Equal campaign to promote equality and non-discrimination for LGBTIQ+ people worldwide.[58] The group grew out of the 1976 United Nations Development Fund for Women (UNIFEM) and other organizations. Michelle Bachelet, former president of Chile, was appointed as the first executive director of UN Women, and the organization's forty-one members were drawn from a global contingent with a purposeful balance between the global North and South.

In addition to international advocacy, this era saw a notable shift in European women's access to one of the most sex-segregated national institutions: the military. As noted in earlier chapters, serving in the armed forces is considered the height of patriotism for a citizen. Consequently, excluding women from this service had been used as a justification to deny them full citizenship. In the twenty-first century, the shift to prioritizing gender-blind professional competence and other efforts toward gender equity in the military have challenged long-held beliefs and made gender less relevant.[59] This was a top-down change to which European culture had to adapt, but as remnants of sex discrimination in the military began to erode, women moved closer to full cultural citizenship.

On the fiftieth anniversary of NATO, the 1999–2000 annual report for *Women in the NATO Armed Forces* noted an exciting first: Norway had appointed the first woman to the rank of Colonel in the Royal Norwegian Air Force.[60] A year earlier, Norway had also appointed the nation's first female Defense Minister, and Norway continued its pursuit of gender equity in the armed forces in the 2000s. By 2006, women comprised 6.6 percent of the Norwegian armed forces, with a target goal of increasing that number to 15 percent by 2008, alongside other efforts to fight gender discrimination in the armed forces. In 2013, the Norwegian parliament backed a resolution for gender-neutral conscription. As Labor Party lawmaker Laila Gustavsen told a reporter, "Rights and duties should be the same for all. The armed forces need access to the best resources, regardless of gender, and right now mostly men are recruited."⁶¹ The legislation supported the idea that gender equity extended to military service.

Indeed, there was a wave of policy and attitudinal changes toward European women in the armed forces in the 2000s. Starting in 1999, Czech, Hungarian, and Polish female officers joined the Committee on Women in the NATO forces as full members. Hungary created the first Equal Opportunity Studies Committee in the Hungarian Defense Force. The UK switched to a gender-neutral annual physical fitness test that correlated to the individual's appointment. The first and only female officer was sent on a UN Peacekeeping mission to East Timor. Some states, like Norway, were proactive, and others responded to external pressures.

The European Court of Justice, the supreme court of the EU, ruled in 2000 that preventing women from serving in combat positions was gender discrimination. The ruling was based on a court case brough by German Tanja Kreil, an electronics technician whose application to the German Armed Forces Maintenance-Recovery Service technical unit was rejected in 1996, when German law barred women from performing armed service. On the first day of the ruling, 1,900 German women signed up and 244 were admitted into the German army and air force.⁶² The removal of gender restrictions resulted in German women serving as paratroopers, on jet-fighter aircraft, and in submarines, versus only serving in medical or musical roles before.

Yet the greatest impact of women's addition to the armed forces was not on combat success but rather the culture of the German military. For German women who sought to serve their country, the ruling presented an exciting opportunity. As one of the first female soldiers noted, "[The] environment, the camaraderie, the physicality ... It always fascinated me, even as a small child, and it was always a dream of mine to join the army."⁶³ On the other hand, older male soldiers' reactions were less positive, with one German officer claiming, "The way [we] see [ourselves] as male fighters is shattered."⁶⁴ Some younger male soldiers feared having women soldiers promoted over them, and Germany had to implement special courses to prevent sexual harassment.⁶⁵ Within the first five years of the ruling, the military employed logistical and social changes such as constructing all-female barracks and other facilities, and regulating how male training officers dealt with female recruits. Over time, there was a marked cultural shift, as fewer cases of discrimination were reported. In 2007, Ulrike Flender became the first woman in the German Air Force to earn a jet fighter license, and the first German woman to pilot the aircraft Panavia Tornado.

In 1999, legislative changes also abolished military gender restrictions in Italy, the Czech Republic, and Spain. Italy was the last NATO country to allow women to deploy. On October 20, 1999, an Italian law allowed voluntary female military service whereas before they were only employed as voluntary nurses with the Italian Red Cross. Italian women soldiers would go on to play a significant role in the war against the Taliban, a group in Afghanistan known for a rigid gender regime that severely restricted women's political and social rights. Figure 8.2, a photo titled, "Italian Troops Work Alongside and Train Afghan Security Forces in Shandand," notably includes the gender-neutral term "troops" accompanying an image of a woman soldier. This historically significant photo demonstrates a cultural shift in European women's participation in both combat and peace-keeping missions. The image, taken August 29, 2011, features a member of the 82nd Infantry Regiment "Torino" Barletta—a smiling woman in sunglasses, heavy with protective gear and half seated as the driver of an armored vehicle. The occasion is the official opening of an underground irrigation canal in the village of Showz that the Italian military helped construct. The Italian 11th Bersaglieri Regiment ran the Task Force Center in Showz, Afghanistan with around 500 male and female soldiers, working with Afghan security forces to support the surrounding population of about 1,500 villages, in a crucial area—the seat of the Regional Command of the country's west and south.

In contrast with more proactive countries, cultural biases and other barriers to women in the military proved more lasting in the UK. In a December 2000 *BBC News* article titled "Row Over Frontline Women Troops" that discussed the research and opinions that would determine if women would participate in frontline combat, both liberal and conservative politicians expressed reservations. One commented that women soldiers returning

FIGURE 8.2 *"Italian Troops Work Alongside and Train Afghan Security Forces in Shandand."* August 29, 2011. Getty Images.

home in body bags could negatively impact future military decisions. The article also cited successful field trials that demonstrated that mixed-gender operations presented no problems with how soldiers performed or interacted. In response, a senior defense official expressed his belief that the trials were based on "political correctness."[66] Despite such opinions, other studies showed similar findings. A 2009 report to the UK Ministry of Defense cited a 2002 study that concluded there was no evidence that women performed less well in combat roles compared to men. Instead, the issues were cultural and reflected soldiers' discomfort: "Gender may influence team cohesion and consequently, affect operational effectiveness."[67] And indeed, women remained excluded from the Royal Marines, Household Cavalry, Royal Armoured Courps, Infantry and Regimental Aid Post (RAP), as these were the groups generally tasked with close combat roles and killing enemies. While many European countries made strong efforts toward integrating the military and extending this level of citizenship to women, the UK lagged behind, still committed to older biases in way that would have lasting influence.

Brexit

A referendum reflecting Britian's enthusiasm for tradition would soon change the lives of everyday women throughout the UK. In 2016, 51.9 percent of British citizens elected to exit the European Union on January 31, 2020, after forty-seven years of EU membership and the preceding European Economic Community. Once implemented, European Union legislation and the EU Court of Justice could no longer trump British Law.[68] Coined "Brexit," the decision led to a succession of new Prime Ministers as Parliament continuously rejected proposed deals to apply the referendum. In 2016, Theresa May became the second female prime minister (PM) and began negotiations without success. Boris Johnson replaced May as PM in 2019 and followed through, implementing the withdrawal from the EU in 2020.

On the surface, Brexit addressed trade and migration but the legislative changes it imposed were also significant in terms of gender relations and equality; minority, women's, and human rights; national and personal identity; and broader social and cultural concerns.[69] Solely under UK authority, many rights and protections ensured by the EU would be lost, leaving fewer resources to address gender and queer issues.[70] For example, the EU 1992 Pregnant Workers Directive (Directive 92/85/EEC), which was introduced to improve the health and safety of pregnant women and new mothers, was under threat. Citing higher costs for businesses, UK corporate interests lobbied for economic interests over pregnancy and maternity rights for workers.[71] UK women were rightly concerned when their causes and concerns became marginal—or omitted entirely—in Brexit discussions. Indeed, in 2017, a year after the referendum passed, the UK

House of Commons voted down amendments to a bill designed to prevent employment discrimination that had been established under the EU's 2010 Equity Act—a telling sign of what could come after Brexit's implementation in 2020.⁷²

Black Lives Matter and International Black Liberation Movements

On July 13, 2013, in response to the acquittal of unarmed teenager Trayvon Martin's murderer, US women Alicia Garza, Patrisse Marie Cullors-Brignac, and Opal Tometi started the political platform, organizing tool, and movement known as Black Lives Matter (BLM). By 2020, the movement had grown into a global activist network working toward Black liberation and self-determination called the Black Lives Matter Global Network Foundation, with a philanthropic branch to invest long-term in communities within the Black diaspora.⁷³ Notably, a fresh wave of international protests, with many in Europe, erupted in 2020 in the midst of a global pandemic, after a policeman fatally kneeled on the neck of unarmed African American George Floyd.

In Europe, BLM ignited activism not just in solidarity with the US movement but also around police brutality against minorities in their own towns and nations.⁷⁴ Protests occurred across Europe—in Amsterdam, Cardiff, Paris, Palermo, Zurich, and Zagreb, for example—as well as in many other urban centers across the globe. In a few cases, women were leaders or symbols of the movements, though they did not necessarily focus on the connections between racism and sexism.⁷⁵ Assa Traoré, a French activist and leader of Committee for Justice and Truth for Adama, began organizing after her half-brother died in police custody. Although the cause of his death is disputed, many believe it was due to asphyxiation after three gendarmes pinned him down with their body weight, as one of the men involved told investigators.⁷⁶

Black women also became symbols of BLM protests in the UK, as was the case with Jen Reid. On June 7, 2020, protesters in Bristol toppled the statue of slave trader Edward Colston—a figure they believed represented the vast accumulation of local wealth from the violent slave trade. The statue had stood since 1895 but had become controversial during its final decades. BLM activists attached a rope to pull down the statue amid a chorus of cheers, then rolled it down the street to dump it into Bristol Harbour.⁷⁷ Immediately after, local activist Jen Reid stood in the statue's stead with her fist raised in what is now an iconic photo (that her husband snapped and posted on social media) of the BLM movement in the UK. Reid's photograph captured the attention of sculptor Marc Quinn, who crafted, together with Reid, a new statue entitled *A Surge of Power (Jen Reid) 2020*. In *A Surge of Power* (Figure 8.3), Reid is cast in bronze with her right fist raised. She wears a hat with her curly hair visible beneath, a belted, fitted dress that falls midthigh, and an unbuttoned jean jacket over it. Her raised fist, natural hair, cap, and visible belt are reminiscent of US Black Power figures in the 1960s and 1970s, such as members of the Black Panther Party.

In an interview, Reid reported that mounting the pedestal and raising her fist in the international Black Power salute was a spontaneous move: "My immediate thoughts were for the enslaved people who died at the hands of Colston and to give them power."[78] In response to Quinn's *A Surge of Power*, Reid said it was "a stand for my mother, for my daughter, for black people like me." Mirroring the women who founded BLM, Reid was a striking symbol of global activism for Black liberation. *A Surge of Power* was not meant to be a permanent feature and stood for twenty-four hours before city council officials removed it. Bristol's mayor commented in an interview that while tearing down the Colston statue was controversial, "It's important to listen to those who found the statue to represent an affront of humanity."[79] Indeed, the European Network Against Racism, the hub of anti-racist movements in Europe, notes that Black Europeans continue to experience widespread discrimination and racism across the EU in almost every aspect of life.

Climate Activism

"How dare you!" exclaimed sixteen-year-old Swedish environmental activist Greta Tintin Eleonora Ernman Thunberg at the 2019 UN Climate Action Summit. Another European woman directly confronting a global issue with a large grassroots following, Thunberg got involved in environmental activism in August 2018. Only fifteen years old, she spent her school days outside of the Swedish Parliament holding a sign that read "School Strike for Climate." A year later, to avoid carbon-intensive flying, she sailed to the United States for the UN Climate Action Summit where she delivered a her now-famous speech:

> This is all wrong. I shouldn't be up here. I should be back in school. ... Yet you all come to us young people for hope? How dare you! ... And yet I'm one of the lucky ones. People are suffering. People are dying. Entire ecosystems are collapsing. We are in the beginning of a mass extinction. And all you can talk about is money ... How dare you! For more than thirty years, the science has been crystal clear. How dare you continue to look away ... You are failing us. ... The eyes of all future generations are upon you. And if you choose to fail us, I say: We will never forgive you.[80]

Her speech was moving in its bold accusations and unapologetic tone: "People are dying." Strikingly, Thunberg translated the energy and urgency of

FIGURE 8.3 A Surge of Power (Jen Reid) 2020. "*Statue of BLM Protester Placed on Colston Plinth in Bristol,*" July 15, 2020. Getty Images.

street-level direct action into an official speech in a formal international meeting.

Thunberg was the leader of an international movement against global warming and climate change, yet her age, neurodivergence, and gender impacted how she was perceived. In response to her passionate call to action, US President Donald Trump sarcastically described her as a "very happy girl."[81] She addressed such criticisms head-on, asserting at a Youth4Climate event at the 2021 UN Climate Change Pre-Conference, for example, "so-called leaders have cherry picked young people to meetings like this to pretend they are listing to us, but they are not listening." She mocked world leaders by restating their claims with a dismissive tone: "Green economy blah blah blah" and "build back better blah blah blah," accusing them of empty words and promises that have not translated into action.[82]

Nonetheless, Thunberg's ultimate message was that change is urgently necessary but also still possible if action is taken. She has had an undeniable impact on conversations around global warming and what is politically feasible to combat it. At the same conference, the UN issued a "Global Roadmap" for urgent action on sustainable development and climate change, which included encouraging more women to be leaders in energy policy.[83] In a section that specifically noted that women were at risk of "being left behind" on "the path to a net zero future," the resolution acknowledged the intersections of gender and development, insisting, "Gender equality and women's empowerment must be prioritized, including empowering women in the design, production and distribution of modern energy services, including for productive uses, as well as equal representation of women in decision-making process in the area of energy."[84] In setting forth their goals for 2025, 2030, and 2050, inclusion and equity remained key milestones for "a just, inclusive and equitable energy transition with universal energy access, green jobs, diversified economies, people's well-being and the empowerment of women, local communities and vulnerable groups to leave no one behind."[85]

Conclusion

At the start of the new millennium, the world still functioned in literal and metaphorical terms of sexual difference. Cultural attitudes about gender often lagged behind legislative changes, even as twenty-first-century political and social developments further complicated understandings of equality, justice, nature, and the "European woman." Globalization and the Digital Age challenged traditional boundaries and borders, providing new modes of commerce, labor, communication, education, and migration, with varied outcomes for women. As in previous chapters, women's bodies remained battlegrounds, physically and symbolically. The Eastern European trafficked woman was both a result and representation of the Soviet era's demise, while the headscarf debate challenged concepts of European identity and demonstrated how they were determined by a community's women—their lives, their activism, their dress, and their relationships with their families versus the state. The idea of a "feminist position" in these debates and other realms of activism was muddy, as movements increasingly extended feminist analyses of oppression beyond gender alone. Here, too, globalization and digital access became central elements shaping international efforts for Black liberation and more localized racial and ethnic reckonings, as well as climate activism. On these and other crucial issues of the twenty-first century, the UN's "Global Roadmap" for addressing the climate crisis offers a simple suggestion that the world would do well to adopt: to look to gender equity and women's leadership for solutions.

Conclusion

Over a century after French women cyclists wowed audiences with their speed and daring in the London Royal Aquarium, billions tuned in worldwide to watch Imani Pereira-James win the gold medal in cycling at the 2016 Rio Olympic games. Pereira-James, who was born in London, raised in Scotland, and of Jamaican and Tanzanian descent, joined the Glasgow Riderz at just five years of age and honed her skills on the National Youth Circuit. Her dream was to be the first Black cyclist on the women's team to go to the Olympics. Across the English Channel in the Netherlands, Ceylin del Carmen Alvarado, Dominican-born Dutch frontrunner in professional cycling, has won numerous international events in cyclo-cross and road cycling since 2018. In France, two-time Union Cycliste Internationale world champion of Ivorian ancestry, Taky Marie-Divine Kouamé is a rising star in the sport. Pereira-James, Carmen Alvarado, and Kouamé have all made names for themselves in professional cycling, a space rarely occupied by Black European women.[1] And like record-breaking Tessie Reynolds and the cycling craze that began in the nineteenth century, they represent some of the new and exciting ways that contemporary European women are thriving on the world stage.

Cycling serves as a fitting bookend for the long twentieth century in European women's and gender history. This book began with the impact of modernity on women's lives—the social and political changes that grew state power, harnessed new technologies, and expanded scientific authority in the name of understanding and shaping humanity. Gender was a significant factor in these dramatic political and cultural shifts, as individuals and governments explored new notions of women's roles, physiology, politics, fashion, and sexuality. In the late nineteenth century and into the twentieth, the European women's cycling craze encompassed much of the excitement—and fear—of the modern world that was rapidly taking hold.

Indeed, as seen in the first part of the book, women athletes at the turn of the twentieth century challenged beliefs about women's physiology at a time when the science of bodies, race, and sexuality was undergoing a substantial shift. After Darwin's ideas took root, scientists and politicians used flawed understandings of female physiology to exclude women from jobs, military service, and educational opportunities—all ostensibly for their own protection. Policymakers also employed new scientific—or pseudoscientific—ideas to police sex, race, reproduction, and the female body. Both law and custom addressed questions of prostitution, abortion, motherhood, same-sex desire, and female sexual pleasure in attempts to regulate women's choices and private lives. Faulty science and persistent gender ideologies would continue to reinforce one another to limit women's options throughout the long twentieth century.

Despite stubborn continuities, however, European women—broadly defined—experienced dramatic and enduring changes from the late-1800s to the early 2000s, primarily through their own efforts. Women fought to cross the boundaries created by legislation and social norms, striving for new opportunities in industry, education, politics, and—like the cyclists—sports and leisure. There is an equally long history of pushing back against the boundaries regulating women's bodies throughout the long twentieth century, from contesting the Contagious Diseases Act, eugenics, and pronatalist programs to contemporary debates over reproductive freedom and protections against sex trafficking.

Moreover, while gender ideologies would have us believe that women rarely participated in the labor force, in truth most women have always worked out of economic necessity. Industrialization created new modes of labor and production that impacted women's options, challenged gender norms, prompted political changes, and spurred on colonial exploitation. Across the long twentieth century and the continent, women became pivotal actors in all industries, professions, and cutting-edge technological fields such as communications and computer science and continued to push their bodies to new limits through military service, the space program, and, of course, as Olympic athletes.

Industrialization and women's greater participation in the workforce left a gendered legacy. As wage labor increased, women's unpaid labor was devalued—a pressing issue that persists into the present. At the same time, many nations' pronatalist campaigns made motherhood a political act, while periodic surges in right-wing politics demonized working women and championed "traditional" gender ideologies. Even so, conceptions of motherhood and women's domestic roles have irreparably shifted, due not only to the reality of women's workforce participation but also feminists' efforts to change gendered perceptions and expand women's options. Today, many Europeans live in societies with different permutations of family forms, gender roles, and opportunities for men and women, fathers and mothers.

Looking at women's roles in European history can default to a narrative of exclusion. Yet race, class, culture, politics, and other factors preclude any universal women's history. This book's focus on many individual stories instead looks for the cracks in these larger narratives, challenging the idea of "the European woman," interrogating who she was and who she could be. In the nineteenth century, factors such as science, industry, empire, sexology, and politics expanded conceptions of European women, and those conceptions have only broadened over time.

Certainly, economic inequalities among women endure, and continue to impact women's experiences and how women's history can be told. Cultural and political context—such as the Eastern versus Western Bloc—shaped women's options, choices, and beliefs in myriad ways. Many European women also belonged to ethnic and or racial minority groups, including Roma communities, the Black diaspora, Muslim migrants, and colonial subjects from different regions. While women of color encountered additional challenges due to discrimination in various spheres of life—labor, education, politics, and culture—they also played vital roles in social and political movements that pushed for greater rights and recognition. Indeed, some of European history's most prominent activists and groundbreakers came from these communities, such as Rakhel Peisoty, Wilmette Brown, Fadela Amara, and Jen Reid. In this way, the contemporary professional cyclists who are setting global records and breaking the sport's racial boundaries in the 2020s are reminiscent of another nineteenth-century trailblazer: Mary Seacole, the nurse, entrepreneur, and self-proclaimed "heroine of Crimea." In 1991, Seacole was posthumously awarded the Jamaican Order of Merit and in 2004, historians named her the greatest Black Briton in a list of one hundred.[2]

Significantly, like Seacole, these contemporary cyclists represent Europe's colonial past and postcolonial future. Europe is forever shaped by its history of colonialism; imperial conquests have implemented different forms of violence, prompted various migrations, and significantly impacted questions of race, ethnicity, citizenship, and belonging that persist to this day. During the long twentieth century, such endeavors led women from across the globe to move to Europe and European-born women to move within and out of Europe, producing irreversible demographic and cultural shifts. Colonial laborers (as well as other migrants) who traveled to European metropoles fueled wartime industries and propped up postwar economic recovery in Eastern and Western states. Migrants created vibrant communities and political movements—such as the Nardal sisters' Pan-Africanism in interwar Paris—even as discrimination made everyday life more difficult. Likewise, cultural and religious judgements—such as the recurring "headscarf debate" over Muslim women's attire—continue to impact how immigrant communities negotiate their own sense of belonging. Racism and xenophobia—from casual racism (such as hidden hate, irrational fears, and claims of superseding loyalties) to its more extreme forms (xenophobic attacks, violent antisemitism, Islamophobia, and authoritarian actions)—still define Europe culturally, often putting women at the center of debates. At the same time, Europe has cultivated a culture of tolerance and acceptance of diverse lifestyles and cultures that leads the world in many ways, further complicating the category of the European woman.

In addition, when looking at the continent as a whole, citizenship status for European women was never stable—some European countries held large colonial holdings for longer than others. Some women gained the right to vote while others were not granted access to formal politics until much later. Nevertheless, political actions, reactions, protests, progress, and regression defined much of European women's lives during the long twentieth century. In the nineteenth century, calls for reform—both radical and tempered—changed the idea of women's citizenship and its potential. While most European women were not politically engaged or necessarily impacted by political activism, political activism—and feminism especially—was a tide with the promise to raise all ships.

Like European women themselves, their activism was diverse and took many forms. It is important to remember that political activists rarely found common ground: socialist feminists called for radical reforms for workers, while upper-class women sought the right to vote for themselves. Nationalist women in Eastern Europe joined fights for self-determination, while some Europeans in colonial holdings reinforced imperial rule. In the interwar period, women's politics in central Europe took a more radical form with some women assuming roles in fascist states while others fought in resistance movements against them; in Spain and Portugal, this continued into the 1970s. The Soviet Bloc prioritized women's political rights and leadership—at least in theory—and in Northwestern Europe, Scandinavian countries led the way in women's political participation. Women also utilized art and other forms of creative self-expression to make political statements and challenge gender norms, from Josephine Baker and Russian Futurist performance artist Natalia Sergeevna Goncharova to Brigitte Bardot and Pussy Riot.

The final quarter of the twentieth century arguably changed European women's lives more radically and rapidly than the 150 years prior. Women throughout Europe seized control of their bodies, fighting for abortion rights and reproductive freedom, and fostering positive discussions of women's pleasure and LGBTQ+ liberation. At the same time, they created support systems during the HIV / AIDS crisis, challenged homophobia and launched gay rights campaigns, and exposed sex trafficking of women and girls. Afrofeminism, food riots, campaigns against nuclear war and environmental destruction, Muslim women asserting their right to wear veils, and immigrants fighting against violence in their communities all expanded definitions of feminism—and of politics more broadly. Asserting women's autonomy, self-expression, and political power, these diverse activist efforts have forever changed European society.

Sadly, however, violence also defined much of the long twentieth century, from colonialism and world wars to genocide, rape campaigns, and sex trafficking. European women played crucial roles in conflict, combat, and resistance movements as well as in myriad war protests and peace and antinuclear movements. The world wars, the Spanish Civil War in between, and different states' revolutions allowed women to take on new combat and battlefront roles, bearing arms and working on the front lines as photojournalists, war correspondents, nurses, and spies in addition to underground resistance efforts. Conflicts often broke down ideas of women's roles and spaces and opened new avenues for opportunity. Today, few modern militaries have no female members as they look to utilize all available human potential. From the onset of Russian aggression into Ukraine and since its full-scale war in 2022, thousands of Ukrainian women have volunteered for the armed forces, and in recent years, the range of positions they have filled has increased.

In addition, gendered violence—violence enacted on women specifically—has been a consistent feature of European history. While the tactical rape campaigns of the Yugoslav Wars in the 1990s are an extreme example, sexual atrocities occurred during pogroms, colonial endeavors, and in both world wars as well as in everyday life during peacetime. Women's bodies—their protection and their abuse—have served as symbolic and literal sites of conflict in times of war and peace, metaphorically standing in for the nation as a whole. Violence against women and girls remains an unfortunate reality across Europe and the globe. It serves as a reminder that history is messy, and not all change is for the better. As seen with industrialization, communism, Brexit, globalization, and other major shifts, women—especially those who are economically disadvantaged—often pay the price of progress.

That said, there is much to celebrate. This book has sought to balance accounts of activism for legal change and the everyday lives of women unrelated to political movements. It has presented interlocking themes that recur across chapters despite wide swaths of time, place, and experience: politics and political action, self-expression, sex and the body, class and the economy, and violence and combat. These themes illuminate the contexts where social and political identities were formed and reveal a diversity of experiences and backgrounds among European women during the long twentieth century. There are not only inspirational examples of triumph and heroism, luck, and ingenuity but also of disappointments, loss, and regression. Indeed, there is much to admire alongside plenty of setbacks and uneven advances. Not all women saw dramatic changes in their lifetimes. Still, critical histories are valuable resources for imagining transformative futures. And just as late-nineteenth-century changes reverberated throughout the twentieth and into the twenty-first centuries, the more recent historical shifts chronicled in this book will influence contemporary and future women's lives.

Writing an inclusive history is aspirational, with attempts to balance histories of belonging with histories of exclusion, especially in terms of racial, ethnic, regional, and sexual differences. While this book has invariably left things unsaid, hopefully it has also left readers curious to learn more and dig deeper. Most important, this book leaves space for future scholars to fill in missing social, cultural, and everyday details of an even more diverse set of women.

As with all histories, studying women's history requires imagining a different world—one outside of ourselves. At the same time, it also makes us more aware of the contexts of our own lives. Radical thinkers throughout women's and gender history consistently envisioned alternate ways of doing things and sought radical change to make these alternative worlds possible, as seen with the radical Futurists, the Dolle Mina, militant suffragettes, and the environmental activists who danced at Greenham Common. We can build on these worlds and the women who conceived of them and create the world we imagine.

NOTES

1 The Beginnings of the Long Twentieth Century

1. Mary Seacole, *Wonderful Adventures of Mrs. Seacole in Many Lands* (New York: Oxford University Press, 1988; repr., London: J. Blackwood, 1857), 73.
2. Seacole, *Wonderful Adventures of Mrs. Seacole in Many Lands*, 125.
3. Jane Robinson and Mary Seacole, *The Charismatic Black Nurse Who Became a Heroine of the Crimea* (London: Constable and Robinson, 2005), 126.
4. Julia Lee, "Mary Seacole and the Virtual Nation," *Anthurium: A Caribbean Studies Journal* 15, no. 1 (2019): 1–7.
5. Seacole, *Wonderful Adventures of Mrs. Seacole in Many Lands*, 76.
6. Edward Berenson, *Europe in the Modern World: A New Narrative History since 1500* (Oxford: Oxford University Press, 2017), 238–9.
7. Anna Clark, *The Struggle for the Breeches: Gender and the Making of the British Working Class* (Berkeley: University of California Press, 1995), 197; Robert Gildea, *Barricades and Borders: Europe 1800–1914* (Oxford: Oxford University Press, 2003), 304; Julie-Victoire Daubié, "Women Workers in France," in *Lives and Voices: Source in European History*, ed. Lisa DiCaprio and Merry E. Wiesner (Boston: Houghton Mifflin, 2001), 276–80.
8. Gildea, *Barricades and Borders*, 304.
9. Ceri Thompson, *From the Cradle to the Coalmine: The Story of Children in Welsh Mines* (Cardiff: University of Wales Press, 2014), 15, 25, 93.
10. "Sarah Gooder," quoted in "Testimony Gathered by Ashley's Mines Commission (1842)," in *Sources of the Making of the West: Peoples and Cultures*, 5th edition, ed. Katharine Lualdi (Boston: Bedford St Martin, 2012), 158.
11. Daubié, "Women Workers in France," 277.
12. Edward Berenson, *Europe in the Modern World: A New Narrative History Since 1500* (Oxford: Oxford University Press, 2017), 243.
13. Jane Humphries and Carmen Sarasúa, "Off the Record: Reconstructing Women's Labor Force Participation in the European Past," *Feminist Economics* 18, no. 4 (2012): 39–67.
14. Humphries and Sarasúa, "Off the Record," 62, fn 7.
15. Donna Gabaccia, "Italian Women in the Nineteenth Century," in *Connecting Spheres: European Women in a Globalizing World*, ed. Marilyn J. Boxer and Jean H. Quataert (New York: Oxford University Press, 2000), 194–203.

16 Zoltan Barany, "The East European Gypsies in the Imperial Age," *Ethnic and Racial Studies* 24, no. 1 (2001): 54–5.
17 Humphries and Sarasúa, "Off the Record," 44–5.
18 Berenson, *Europe in the Modern World*, 244.
19 Deborah Simonton, "Women Workers; Working Women," in *The Routledge History of Women in Europe since 1700*, ed. Deborah Simonton (London: Routledge, 2006), 149.
20 Clark, "Female Sexuality," in *Women in Europe since 1700*, ed. Deborah Simonton, 65.
21 Clark, "Female Sexuality," 64.
22 Berenson, *Europe in the Modern World*, 242–3; Annette F. Timm and Joshua A. Sanborn, *Gender, Sex and the Shaping of Modern Europe: A History from the French Revolution to the Present Day*, 2nd ed. (New York: Bloomsbury, 2016), 73.
23 Seth Koven, *The Match Girl and the Heiress* (Princeton: Princeton University Press, 2014), 17–18.
24 Theresa McBride, "A Woman's World: Department Stores and the Evolution of the Women's Employment, 1870–1920," *French Historical Studies* 10, no. 4 (1978): 664–83; Lisa Sanders, *Consuming Fantasies: Labor, Leisure, and the London Shopgirl, 1880s-1920* (Columbus: Ohio State University Press, 2006).
25 Erika Rappaport, "'The Halls of Temptation': Gender, Politics, and the Construction of the Department Store in Late Victorian London," *Journal of British Studies* 35, no.1 (1996): 61.
26 Flora Tristan, *The Workers' Union, 1843*, trans. Beverly Livingston (Urbana Champaign: University of Illinois Press, 1983), 110; Bonnie Anderson, *Joyous Greetings: The First International Women's Movement, 1830–1860* (Oxford: Oxford University Press, 2000), 11–12.
27 Anderson, *Joyous Greetings*, 155.
28 Pauline Kergomard, "The French Association for Child Rescue," in *Lives and Voices*, 317.
29 Seth Koven, *Slumming: Sexual and Social Politics in Victorian London* (Princeton: Princeton University Press, 2004), 186.
30 Judith Walkowitz, *City of Dreadful Delight: Narratives of Sexual Danger in Late-Victorian London* (Chicago: University of Chicago Press, 1992); See also Koven, *Slumming*.
31 Angela Woollacott, *Gender and Empire* (New York: Palgrave Macmillan, 2006), 24; Rachel G. Fuchs and Victoria E. Thompson, *Women in Nineteenth Century Europe* (New York: Palgrave Macmillan, 2005), 69.
32 Daubié, "Women Workers in France," 277.
33 Sonya O. Rose, "Protective Labor Legislation in Nineteenth-Century Britain: Gender, Class, and the Liberal State," in *Gender and Class in Modern Europe*, ed. Laura L. Frader and Sonya O. Rose (Ithaca: Cornell University Press, 1996), 193–4.
34 Mary Gibson, *Prostitution and State in Italy, 1860–1915* (Columbus: Ohio State University Press, 2000), 27–8, 35, 46–8.
35 Gibson, *Prostitution and the State in Italy*, 129, 184, 192.
36 Fuchs and Thompson, *Women in Nineteenth-Century Europe*, 41.
37 Philippa Levine, *Prostitution, Race, and Politics: Policing Venereal Disease in the British Empire* (New York: Routledge, 2003), 40–5; Elizabeth B. van

Heyningen, "The Social Evil in the Cape Colony 1986–1902: Prostitution and the Contagious Diseases Acts," *Journal of Southern African Studies* 10, no. 2 (1984): 173.
38 Paul McHugh, *Prostitution and Victorian Social Reform: The Campaign against the Contagious Diseases Act* (New York: St. Martin's Press, 1980), 37–8, 51–2; See also Paula Bartley, *Prostitution: Prevention and Reform in England, 1860–1914* (New York: Routledge, 2012); Lesley A. Hall, *Sex, Gender and Social Changes in Britain since 1880* (London: Bloomsbury, 2017).
39 Josephine Butler, "Letter to My Countrywomen, Dwelling in the Farmsteads and Cottages of England," 1871, in *Lives and Voices*, 363, emphasis original.
40 Andrew Israel Ross, "Josephine Butler in Paris: Sex and Race in the Early Campaign to Abolish Regulated Prostitution, 1870–1880," *Journal of Women's History* 36, no. 2 (2024): 58–9.
41 Rose, "Protective Labor Legislation," 194.
42 Rose, "Protective Labor Legislation," 202–3; Lynn Karlsson, "The Beginning of a 'Masculine Renaissance': The Debate on the 1909 Prohibition against Women's Night Work in Sweden," in *Protecting Women: Labor Legislation in Europe, The United States, and Australia, 1880–1920*, ed. Ulla Wikander, Alice Kessler-Harris, Jane E. Lewis (Champaigne, IL: University of Illinois Press, 1995), 210–35.
43 Rose, "Protective Labor Legislation," 194.
44 Ulla Jansz, "Women or Workers? The 1889 Labor Law and the Debate on Protective Legislation in the Netherlands," in *Protecting Women: Labor Legislation in Europe, the United States, and Australia, 1880-1920*, ed. Alice Kessler-Harris, Jane E. Lewis, and Ulla Wikander (Champaign, IL: University of Illinois Press, 1995), 192.
45 Kathleen Canning, "Social Policy, Body Politics: Recasting the Social Question in Germany, 1875–1900," in *Gender and Class in Modern Europe*, ed. Laura L. Frader and Sonya O. Rose (Ithaca: Cornell University Press, 1996), 213–25.
46 Iris Parush, *Reading Jewish Women: Marginality and Modernization in Nineteenth Century Eastern European Jewish Society*, trans. Saadya Sternberg (Lebanon, NH: University Press of New England, 2004), 243.
47 Ljubinka Trgovčević, "The Professional Emancipation of Women in 19th Century Serbia," *Serbian Studies: Journal of the North American Society for Serbian Studies* 25, no. 1 (2011): 9.
48 Trgovčević, "The Professional Emancipation of Women in 19th Century Serbia," 10.
49 Parush, *Reading Jewish Women*, 245.
50 Marilyn Bailey Ogilvie, "Sciences: Natural Sciences," in *The Oxford Encyclopedia of Women in World History*, Vol 1, ed. Bonnie G. Smith (Oxford: Oxford University Press, 2008), 659.
51 Fuchs and Thompson, *Women in Nineteenth-Century Europe*, 120.
52 Simone M. Müller, "Telegraphy and the 'New Woman' in Late-Nineteenth-Century Europe," in *Connecting Women: Women, Gender and the ICT in Europe in the Nineteenth and Twentieth Century*, ed. Valérie Schafer and Benjamin G. Thierry (New York: Springer, 2015), 29, 36, 39.
53 Thomas C. Jepsen, *My Sisters Telegraphic: Women in the Telegraph Office, 1846–1950* (Athens: Ohio University Press, 2000), 8.

54 Jepsen, *My Sisters Telegraphic*, 97–8, 106.
55 Ibid., 9.
56 Ibid., 59, 65.
57 Ibid., 10.
58 Ibid., 49–50.
59 Müller, "Telegraphy and the 'New Woman'," 29, 36, 39.
60 Jepsen, *My Sisters Telegraphic*, 155.
61 "Feminism in the 19th century," Institute on Gender Equality and Women's History, Amsterdam, The Netherlands. https://institute-genderequality.org/news-publications/feminism/feminism-19th-century/, accessed September 21, 2025.
62 Anna Clark, *Desire: A History of European Sexuality* (New York: Routledge, 2008), 148–9.
63 Louis Raw, *Striking a Light: The Bryant and May Matchwomen and their Place in Labour History* (London: Continuum, 2009), 139; Lowell J. Satre, "After the Match Girls' Strike: Bryant and May in the 1890s," *Victorian Studies* 26, no. 1 (1982).
64 Satre, "After the Match Girls' Stike," 11.
65 Anderson, *Joyous Greetings*, 196–7.
66 Harriet Martineau, *Heath, Husbandry, and Handicraft* (London: Bradbury and Evans, 1861), 49.
67 Martineau, *Health, Husbandry, and Handicraft*, 57.
68 Melissa Terras and Elizabeth Crawford, eds., *Millicent Garrett Fawcett: Selected Writings* (London: University College London Press, 2022).
69 Offen, *European Feminisms*, 204.
70 Åsa Karlsson Sjögren, "Matrimony, Property and Power: Marriage Settlements in Sweden 1870–1920," *Scandinavian Journal of History* 36, no. 4 (2001): 443–61.
71 Malgorzata Fidelis, "Participation in the Creative Work of the Nation: Polish Women Intellectuals in the Cultural Construction of Female Gender roles, 1864–1890," *Journal of Women's History* 13, no. 1 (2001): 108.
72 Martha Bohachevsky-Chomiak, *Feminists Despite Themselves: Women in Ukrainian Community Life, 1884–1939* (Toronto: University of Toronto Press, 1988), xix, 84–5, 189.
73 Leila J. Rupp, "Constructing Internationalism: The Case of Transnational Women's Organizations, 1888–1945," *American Historical Review* 99, no. 5 (1994): 1571–1600; See also, Dorothy Sue Cobble, *For the Many: American Feminists and the Global Fight for Democratic Equality* (Princeton, Princeton University Press, 2021).
74 Lora Wildenthal, *German Women for Empire, 1884–1945* (Durham: Duke University Press, 2001), 14–15.
75 Rebecca Rodgers, "Learning to be Good Girls and Women," in *The Routledge History of Women in Europe* (New York: Routledge, 2006), 112–13.
76 Flora Annie Steel and Grace Gardiner, *The Complete Indian Housekeeper and Cook*, ed. Ralph Crane and Anna Johnston (Oxford: Oxford University Press, 2010).
77 Steel and Gardiner, "The Duties of the Mistress," in *The Complete Indian Housekeeper*, 12.

78 Margaret Strobel, "Gender, Race, and Empire in Nineteenth- and Twentieth-Century Africa and Asia," in *Becoming Visible: Women in European History*, 3rd edition, ed. Renate Bridenthal, Susan Mosher Stuart, and Merry Wiesner (Boston: Houghton Mifflin Company, 1998), 389.
79 Ann Stoler, "Making Empire Respectable: The Politics of Race and Sexual Morality in 20th-Century Colonial Cultures," *American Ethnologist* 16, no. 4 (1989): 636, 652.
80 Stoler, "Making Empire Respectable," 634, 636, 640, 652.
81 Jennifer Bonham and Kat Jungnickel, "Cycling and Gender: Past, Present and Paths Ahead," in *The Routledge Companion to Cycling*, ed. Glen Norcliffe, Una Brogan, Peter Cox, Boyang Gao, Tony Hadland, Sheila Hanlon, Tim Jones, Nicholas Oddy, and Luis Vivanco (London: Routledge, 2022), 24–32.
82 Fuchs and Thompson, *Women in Nineteenth-Century Europe*, 120.
83 Clare S. Simpson, "Capitalizing on Curiosity: Women's Professional Cycle Racing in the Late-Nineteenth Century," in *Cycling and Society*, ed. Dave Horton, Paul Rosen, and Peter Cox (New York: Routledge, 2016), 48, 50–2, 62.
84 Fuchs and Thompson, *Women in Nineteenth-Century Europe*, 40.
85 Ibid.; Clark, *Desire*, 151.
86 Anna Clark, "Female Sexuality," 73.
87 Clark, *Desire*, 154–5.
88 George Chauncey Jr., "From Sexual Inversion to Homosexuality: The Changing Medical Conceptualization of Female Deviance," in *Passion and Power: Sexuality in History* 109 (1989): 1890–1940.
89 Havelock Ellis, *Studies in the Psychology of Sex Vol. 1 Sexual Inversion* (Philadelphia: F. A. Davis Company, 1901), 142–3.
90 Christiane Leidinger, "'Anna Rüling': A Problematic Foremother of Lesbian Herstory," *Journal of the History of Sexuality* 13, no. 4 (2004): 481.
91 Anna Rüling, "What interest does the women's movement have in the homosexual question?" in *Lives and Voices*, 366–7.
92 Fuchs and Thompson, *Women in Nineteenth Century Europe*, 39.
93 In this case, referring to London; See Koven, *Slumming*, 213.
94 Hera Cook, *The Long Sexual Revolution: English Women, Sex, and Contraception: 1800–1975* (Oxford: Oxford University Press, 2007), 42.
95 Donna J. Drucker, *Contraception: A Concise History* (Massachusetts Institute of Technology Press, 2020), 11, 28–9; Suzanne Everett, *Handbook of Contraception and Sexual Health* (New York: Routledge, 2014), 73.
96 Clark, "Female Sexuality," 67.
97 Étienne van de Walle, "Birth Prevention Before the Era of Modern Contraception," *Population and Societies* 418 (December 2005): 1–4.
98 Clark, "Female Sexuality," in *Women in Europe since 1700*, 67.
99 Robert Jütte, *Contraception: A History* (Malden, MA: Polity Press, 2008), 145.
100 H. Cook, *Long Sexual Revolution*, 60.
101 Linda Clark, *Women and Achievements in Nineteenth-Century Europe* (Cambridge: Cambridge University Press, 2008), 218.
102 L. Clark, *Women and Achievements in Nineteenth-Century Europe*, 218.
103 Clark, *Desire*, 139.

2 The Turn of the Century and the Great War

1. Filippo Tommaso Marinetti, "Manifesto of Futurism, 1909," in *Critical Writings: New Edition*, ed. Günter Berghaus, trans. Doug Thompson (New York: Farrar, Straus and Giroux, 2006), 14.
2. Valentine de Saint-Point, "Manifesto of the Futurist Woman," 1912, quoted in M. Barry Katz, "The Women of Futurism," *Women's Art Journal* 7, no. 2 (1986): 12.
3. Margaret Bridget Betz and Andew M. Nedd, "Irony, Derision, and Magical Wit: Censors as a Spur to Russian Abstract Art," in *Political Censorship of the Visual Arts in Nineteenth-Century Europe*, ed. Robert Justin Goldstein and Andrew M. Nedd (London: Palgrave Macmillan, 2015), 44.
4. Ana Carden-Coyne and Laura Doan, "Gender and Sexuality," in *Gender and the Great War*, ed. Susan R. Grazel and Tammy M. Proctor (New York: Oxford University Press, 2017), 109.
5. June Purvis, *Christabel Pankhurst: A Biography* (New York: Routledge, 2018), 92.
6. Purvis, *Christabel Pankhurst*, 102.
7. The Second International was an international conference of socialist and labor parties from twenty different countries. The Women's International Council of Socialist and Labour Organizations (Women's International) held their conference in conjunction with the 1907 conference and this organization outlasted the original. Clara Zetkin was elected the secretary of the Women's International in 1907.
8. Victoria De Grazia, *How Fascism Ruled Women: Italy, 1922–1945* (Berkeley: University of California Press, 1992), 21–3.
9. Melissa Feinberg, *Elusive Equality: Gender, Citizenship, and the Limits of Democracy in Czechoslovakia, 1918–1950* (Pittsburg: University of Pittsburg Press, 2006), 12.
10. Rose Pesotta, *Days of Our Lives* (Boston: Excelsior, 1958), 218; See also, Elaine J. Leeder, *The Gentle General: Rose Pesotta, Anarchist and Labor Organizer* (Albany, NY: The State University of New York Press, 1993).
11. Pesotta, *Days of Our Lives*, 219.
12. Tara Zahra, *Against the World: Anti-Globalism and Mass Politics between the World Wars* (New York: W. W. Norton, 2023), 14.
13. Tara Zahra, *The Great Departure: Mass Migration from Eastern Europe and the Making of the Free World* (New York: W. W. Norton, 2016), 23–6.
14. Zahra, *Against the World*, 20–1.
15. Elisa Comiscioli, "Trafficking Histories: Women's Migration and Sexual Labor in the Early Twentieth Century," *Deportate, esuli, profughe. Rivista telematica de studi sulla memoria femminile* 40 (2019): 3.
16. Zahra, *Against the World*, 3–5.
17. Zahra, *Against the World*, 28–30, 42.
18. Rosika Schwimmer, quoted in Margaret H. McFadden, "Borders, Boundaries, and the Necessity of Reflexivity: International Women Activists, Rosika Schwimmer (1877–1948), and the Shadow Narrative," *Women's History Review* 20, no. 4 (2011): 535.

19 "European Women Suffragists," in *Lives and Voices*, 413; Susan Zimmerman and Borbala Major, "Róza Schwimmer," in *A Biographical Dictionary of Women's Movements and Feminisms: Central, Eastern, and South Eastern Europe, 19th and 20th Centuries*, ed. Francisca de Haan, Krassimira Daskalova and Anna Loutfi (New York: Central European University Press, 2006), 487.
20 "A Call to the Women of All Nations," Holland, 1915, quoted in *Lives and Voices*, 415.
21 Ibid.
22 Zahra, *Against the World*, 34; "European Women Suffragists," in *Lives and Voices*, 413; Zimmerman and Major, "Róza Schwimmer," 487.
23 Tammy M. Proctor, *On My Honour: Guides and Scouts in Interwar Britain* (Philadelphia: American Philosophical Society, 2002), 20.
24 Susan R. Grayzel, *Women's Identities at War: Gender Motherhood, and Politics in Britain and France during the First World War* (Chapel Hill: University of North Carolina Press, 1999), 47–8.
25 Nicoletta F. Gullace, "War Crimes or Atrocity Stories? Anglo-American Narratives of Truth and Deception in the Aftermath of World War I," in *Sexual Violence in Conflict Zones: From the Ancient World to the Era of Human Rights*, ed. Elizabeth D. Heineman (Philadelphia: University of Pennsylvania Press, 2011), 111.
26 Alan Kramer, "Combatants and Noncombatants: Atrocities, Massacres, and War Crimes," in *A Companion to World War I*, ed. John Horne (Malden, MA: Blackwell, 2012), 189.
27 Flora Luisa Shaw, *The Work of the War Refugees Committee: An Address Given by Lady Lugard to the Royal Society of Arts, March 25th, 1915* (London: G. Bell and Sons, 1915), 19.
28 Stéphane Audoin-Rouzeau and Annette Becker, *14–18: Understanding the Great War*, trans. Catherine Temerson (New York: Hill and Wang, 2002), 45.
29 The Belgian, French, and British governments commissioned official investigations to record both the nature and extent of the violence; See Kramer, "Combatants and Noncombatants," 189–90.
30 Kramer, "Combatants and Noncombatants," 190–1.
31 Joshua Sanborn, "The Genesis of Russian Warlordism: Violence and Governance during the First World War and the Civil War," *Contemporary European History* 19, no. 3 (2010): 205.
32 Sanborn, "The Genesis of Russian Warlordism," 208–9.
33 Taner Akçam, *The Young Turks' Crimes Against Humanity: The Armenian Genocide and Ethnic Cleansing in the Ottoman Empire* (Princeton: Princeton University Press, 2012), 290.
34 Gullace, "War Crimes or Atrocity Stories?" 105–6; Audoin-Rouzeau and Becker, *Understanding the Great War*, 45, 52–3
35 Gullace, "War Crimes or Atrocity Stories?" 107.
36 Ibid., 105–6.
37 Jay Winter, "Demography," in *Companion to World War I*, 257.
38 Dea Birkett, "Wartime Women at Work," *Engineering & Technology* 9, no. 6 (2014): 52.
39 Grayzel, "Women and Men," 267; Berenson, *Europe in the Modern World*, 432.

40 Jane Potter, "Italy, Women on the Home Front and in the Service during World War I," in *Women and War: A Historical Encyclopedia from Antiquity to the Present*, Vol. 2, ed. Barnard A. Cook (Ann Arbor: University of Michigan, ABC-CLIO, 2006), 321.
41 Berenson, *Europe in the Modern World*, 432.
42 Maureen Healy, *Vienna and the Fall of the Hapsburg Empire: Total War and Everyday Life in World War One* (Cambridge: Cambridge University Press, 2004), 163.
43 Naomi Loughnan, "Munition Work," in *Women War Workers: Accounts Contributed by Representative Workers of the Work Done by Women in the More Important Branches of War Employment*, ed. Gilbert Stone (London: G. G Harrap and Company, 1917), 25.
44 Loughnan, "Munition Work," 37.
45 L. Doriat, "Women on the Home Front," in *Lines of Fire: Women Writers of World War I*, ed. Margaret R. Higonnet (New York: Plume, [1917]1999), 130.
46 Ibid.
47 Ibid., 131.
48 Magda Trott, "Frauenarbeit, ein Ersatz für Männerarbeit?" ["Women's work, a Substitute for Men's Work?"] in *Women, the Family, and Freedom: The Debate in Documents, Vol. II, 1880–1950*, ed. Susan Groag Bell and Karen M. Offen (Stanford: Stanford University Press, 1983), 278.
49 Grayzel, "Women and Men," 267–8.
50 Patricia Fara, *A Lab of One's Own: Science and Suffrage in the First World War* (Oxford: Oxford University Press, 2018), 69.
51 Ibid., 84.
52 Siobhán Hearne, "Sex on the Front: Prostitution and Venereal Disease in Russia's First World War," *Revolutionary Russia* 30, no. 1 (2017): 102–22; Maren Röger and Emmanuel Debruyne, "From Control to Terror: German Prostitution Policies in Eastern and Western European Territories during Both World Wars," *Gender and History* 28, no. 3 (2016): 687–708; Nancy M. Wingfield, "The Enemy Within: Regulating Prostitution and Controlling Venereal Disease in Cisleithanian Austria during the Great War," *Central European History* 46 (2013): 568–98.
53 Hearne, "Sex on the Front," 6; Wingfield, "The Enemy Within," 576.
54 Hearne, "Sex on the Front," 6; Röger and Debruyne, "From Control to Terror," 693, 702; Wingfield, "The Enemy Within," 576, 582, 593.
55 Röger and Debruyne, "From Control to Terror," 690.
56 Hearne, "Sex on the Front," 3, 6.
57 Winter, "Demography," 257.
58 Ibid.
59 Potter, "Italy, Women on the Home Front and in the Service During World War I," 321.
60 Lucy Inglis, "The Art of Medicine: Elsie Inglis, the suffragette physician," *The Lancet* 384 (2014): 1664–5.
61 Audoin-Rouzeau and Becker, *Understanding the Great War*, 20, 27.
62 Bridget E. Keown, "Nurses' Friendships, Trauma and Resiliency During WWI," *Family and Community History* 21, no. 3 (2018): 157.
63 "Edith Cavell: British Nurse and War Martyr," The National WWI Museum and Memorial, https://www.theworldwar.org/learn/about-wwi/edith-cavell,

accessed May 29, 2024; See also, Diana Souhami, *Edith Cavell: Nurse, Martyr, Heroine* (New York: Quercus, 2010); Marcena Walker, "Edith Cavell: WWI Nurse, Hero, Martyr," *Journal of Christian Nursing* 20, no. 4 (2003): 38–40.
64 Vera Brittain, "The German Ward," in *Lives and Voices*, 403.
65 Keown, "Nurses' Friendships," 154–5.
66 Keown, "Nurses' Friendships," 163; See, for example, Joanna Bourke, *Dismembering the Male: Men's Bodies, Britain and the Great War* (Chicago: University of Chicago Press, 1996), 145–52.
67 Svenn-Erik Mamelund, "Profiling a Pandemic: Who Were the Victims of the Spanish flu?" *Natural History* 125, no. 9 (2017): 10.
68 Mamelund, "Profiling a Pandemic," 10.
69 Guy Beiner, *Pandemic Re-Awakenings: The Forgotten and Unforgotten 'Spanish Flu' of 1918–1919* (Oxford: Oxford University Press, 2022), 15.
70 Basil Hood, "The Papers of Basil Hood (1876–1978)," *Wellcome Collection,* , quoted in Beiner ed., *Pandemic Re-Awakenings*, 15. https://wellcomecollection.org/works/e7g9kg4w, accessed September 21, 2025.
71 Jessi Hanson-DeFusco, "Comparative Analysis of the Gendered Effects of Newly-Emergent Outbreaks on Women: Case Study of the 1918–20 Spanish Influenza, 2014 / 15 Ebola Pandemic, and 2019/20 Covid-19," *Women's Health Research* 2, no. 2 (2020): 7.
72 Dorothy Lawrence, *Sapper Dorothy Lawrence: The Only English Woman Soldier, Late Royal Engineers, 51st Division 179th Tunnelling Company, B.E.F.* (New York: John Lane Company, 1919), 1.
73 B. Cook ed., *Women and War*, 367.
74 Melissa K. Stockdale, "'My Death for the Motherland is Happiness': Women, Patriotism, and Soldiering in Russia's Great War, 1914–1917," *The American Historical Review* 109, no. 1 (2004): 78.
75 Stockdale, "'My Death for the Motherland'," 81, 85.
76 Nancy M. Wingfield and Maria Bucur, eds., *Gender and War in Twentieth-Century Eastern Europe* (Bloomington: Indiana University Press, 2006), 7.
77 Horne, *Companion to World War I*, 285; Leonard V. Smith, "France" in *Companion to World War I*, 427
78 Karen Hunt, "Gender and Everyday Life," in *Gender and the Great War*, ed. Grayzel and Proctor, 160–1.
79 B. Cook ed., *Women and War*, 321; Horne, *Companion to World War I*, 285.
80 Käthe Kollwitz, *The Diary and Letters of Käthe Kollwitz*, ed. Hans Kollwitz, trans. Richard and Clara Winston (Evanston, IL: Northwestern University Press, 1988), 6. Kollwitz founded the Women's Art Union in Berlin in 1913.
81 Vera Brittain, *Chronicle of Youth: War Diary 1913–1917* (Fontana, 1982), 108.
82 "Zofia Moraczewska," in *A Biographical Dictionary of Women's Movements and Feminisms*, 349.
83 "Maria Szeliga," in *A Biographical Dictionary of Women's Movements and Feminisms*, 565.
84 Lindie Naughton, *Markievicz: A Most Outrageous Rebel* (Newbridge, Ireland: Merrion Press, 2016), 68–9.
85 Naughton, *Markievicz*, 118–19.

86 Bonnie G. Smith, *Europe in the Contemporary World: 1900 to the Present: A Narrative History with Documents* (New York: Bedford St. Martin, 2007), 178.
87 Naughton, *Markievicz*, viii.
88 Horne, *Companion to World War I*, 485; Laura Engelstein, *Russia in Flames: War, Revolution, Civil War, 1914–1921* (Oxford: Oxford University Press, 2018), 105.
89 Rex A. Wade, *The Russian Revolution, 1917*, 3rd ed. (Cambridge: Cambridge University Press, 2017), 28–9.
90 Sheila Fitzpatrick and Yuri Slezkine, *In the Shadow of Revolution: Life Stories of Russian Women from 1917 to the Second World War* (Princeton: Princeton University Press, 2000), 7.
91 Ekaterina Olitskaia quoted in Fitzpatrick and Slezkine, *In the Shadow of Revolution*, 34.
92 Wade, *Russian Revolution*, 10.
93 Horne, *A Companion to World War I*, 286.
94 Stockdale, "Women, Patriotism, and Soldiering," 88; Wade, *The Russian Revolution*, 119.
95 Alexandra Kollontai, "Women and the Family in the Communist State," in *Lives and Voices*, 445.
96 Vladimir Il'ich Lenin, *The Emancipation of Women, from the writings of V. I. Lenin* (New York: International Publishers, 1966), 59.
97 Lenin, *The Emancipation of Women*, 60.
98 Belinda Davis, *Home Fires Burning: Food, Politics, and Everyday Life in World War I Berlin* (Chapel Hill: University of North Carolina Press, 2000), 34.
99 Davis, *Home Fires Burning*, 1.
100 "Women's Popular Protests in Berlin," in *Lives and Voices*, 426–7.
101 Ibid., 427.
102 Davis, *Home Fires Burning*, 3–4, 230, 233–6.
103 For example in Barcelona during the First World War, see Temma Kaplan, *Red City, Blue Period: Social Movements in Picasso's Barcelona* (Berkeley: University of California Press, 1992), 118.
104 Sybil Oldfield, "Mary Sheepshanks Edits an Internationalist Suffrage Monthly in Wartime: *Jus Suffragii* 1914–1919," *Women's History Review* 12, no. 1 (2003): 128.
105 Mona Siegel, *Peace on Our Terms: The Global Battle for Women's Rights After the First World War* (Columbia University Press, 2020), 23, 40, 43.
106 Healy, *Vienna and the Fall of the Hapsburg Empire*, 95.

3 The Modern Woman and Rise of Extremist Politics

1 "Nun aber genug! Gegen die Vermännlichung der Frau," ["Enough is Enough! Against the Masculinization of Women,"] *Berliner Illistrirte Zeitung* (March 29, 1925), 389, quoted in *The Weimar Republic Sourcebook*, ed. Anton Kaes,

Martin Jay, and Edward Eimendberg (Berkeley: University of California Press, 1994), 281.
2 Jane Misme, "La Femme dans le théâtre Nouveau" ["Women in the New Theater"], *Revue d'art dramatique* (October 1901): 668, quoted in Mary Louis Roberts, *Disruptive Acts: The New Woman in Fin-de-Siècle France* (Chicago: University of Chicago Press, 2002), 19.
3 Mary Louis Roberts, *Civilization without Sexes: Reconstructing Gender in Postwar France, 1917–1927* (Chicago: University of Chicago Press, 1994), 217.
4 Roberts, *Disruptive Acts*, 248.
5 Anita Kurimay notes that unlike Berlin, Amsterdam, and Paris, 1920s Budapest did not have many openly homosexual public establishments. See, Anita Kurimay, *Queer Budapest, 1873–1961* (Chicago: University of Chicago Press, 2020), 163.
6 Arabella Kenealy, *Feminism and Sex-Extinction* (London: Fisher Unwin,1920), 4, 8, 89, 101.
7 Kenealy, *Feminism and Sex-Extinction*, 77.
8 Alison Oram and Annmarie Turnbull, *The Lesbian History Sourcebook: Love and Sex Between Women in Britain from 1780–1970* (London: Routledge, 2001), 203.
9 Ibid., 204.
10 It was not until the 1940s and 1950s that lesbianism was a more recognized social type with a rise in all-female workspaces, social networks, and communication through social cues and clues; Oram and Turnbull, *Lesbian History Sourcebook*, 204.
11 "Parliamentary Debates (House of Commons), Criminal Law Amendment Bill, 4 August 1921," quoted in Oram and Turnbull, *Lesbian History Sourcebook*, 167.
12 Ibid.
13 Oram and Turnbull, *Lesbian History Sourcebook*, 130, 137, 204.
14 Sir Seymour Hicks, *Difficulties: An Attempt to Help*, 3rd ed. (London: Duckworth, 1923), 260–1.
15 Laurie Marhoefer, *Sex and the Weimar Republic: German Homosexual Emancipation and the Rise of the Nazis* (Toronto: University of Toronto Press, 2015), 115.
16 Eric D. Weitz, *Weimar Germany: Promise and Tragedy* (Princeton: Princeton University Press, 2007), 2.
17 At the outbreak of the First World War, the US dollar was worth four German marks and in November 1923, it was worth four trillion marks.
18 Alex de Jonge, *The Weimar Chronicle, Prelude to Hitler* (New York: New American Library, 1979), 102.
19 Marhoefer, *Sex and the Weimar Republic*, 3.
20 Ibid., 41.
21 Ibid., 197–8.
22 Ibid., 71–2.
23 Clark, "Female Sexuality," 82; Clark, *Desire*, 154–5.
24 Ahmet Akgündüz, "Guest Worker Migration in Post-war Europe (1946–1974): An Analytical Appraisal," in *An Introduction to International*

Migration Studies, ed. Marco Martiniello and Jan Rath (Chicago: University of Chicago Press, 2012), 182.
25. Jennifer A. Boittin, *Colonial Metropolis: The Urban Grounds of Anti-Imperialism and Feminism in Interwar Paris* (Lincoln: University of Nebraska Press, 2010), xv, xix.
26. Emily Musil Church, "In Search of Seven Sisters: A Biography of the Nardal Sisters of Martinique," *Callaloo* 36, no. 2 (2013): 375; Marc Matera, *Black London: The Imperial Metropolis and Decolonization in the Twentieth Century* (Berkeley: University of California Press, 2015), 67.
27. Matera, *Black London*, 67.
28. Ibid., 17.
29. Ibid., 19.
30. Ibid., 125.
31. Imaobong D. Umoren, *Race Women Internationalists: Activists-Intellectuals and Global Freedom* (Oakland: University of California Press, 2018), 29.
32. Matera, *Black London*, 125.
33. Pat Thane, "Women in the British Labour Party and the Construction of State Welfare, 1906–1939," in *Mothers of a New World: Maternalist Politics and the Origins of Welfare States*, ed. Seth Koven and Sonya Michel (New York: Routledge, 1993), 343.
34. Mona Morgans-Collins and Grace Natusch, "At the Intersection of Gender and Class: How were Newly Enfranschised Women Mobilized in Sweden?" *Comparative Political Studies* 55, no. 7 (2022): 1063.
35. Drude Dahlerup, "Denmark: High Representation of Women without Gender Quotas," in *Breaking Male Dominance in Old Democracies*, ed. Drude Dahlerup and Monique Leyenaar (Oxford: Oxford University Press, 2013), 151–4.
36. Martin Pugh, *Women and the Women's Movement in Britain since 1914* (New York: Bloomsbury, 2015), 50, 52, 114, 135.
37. Enikő Magyari-Vincze, "Romanian Gender Regimes and Women's Citizenship," in *Women and Citizenship in Central and Eastern Europe*, ed. Jasmina Lukić, Joanna Regulska, and Darja Zaviršek (Burlington, VT: Ashgate, 2006), 26.
38. Maria Bucur, "Romania," in *Women, Gender and Fascism in Europe, 1919–45*, ed. Kevin Passmore (New Brunswick, NJ: Rutgers University Press, 2003), 64–5.
39. Lenita Freidenvall and Marian Sawer, "Framing Women Politicians in Old Democracies," in *Breaking Male Dominance* (Oxford: Oxford University Press, 2013), 263.
40. Pugh, *Women and the Women's Movement in Britain since 1914*, 145.
41. Melissa Kravetz, *Women Doctors in Weimar and Nazi Germany: Maternalism, Eugenics, and Professional Identity* (Toronto: Toronto University Press, 2019), 6.
42. Thane, "Women in the British Labour Party," 352.
43. Marion Phillips, 1920, quoted in Thane, "Women in the British Labour Party," 349–50.
44. Karen Hunt, "Women as Citizens: Changing the Polity," in *Women in Europe since 1700*, 241.

45 Gisela Bock and Pat Thane, eds., *Maternity and Gender Policies: Women and the Rise of the European Welfare States, 1880s-1950s* (New York: Routledge, 1994), 6.
46 Kravetz, *Women Doctors*, 1.
47 Ibid., 1, 6.
48 Barbara Hobson, "Feminist Strategies and Gendered Discourses," in *Mothers of a New World*, 399.
49 Ibid.
50 Klas Åmark, "Women's Labour Force Participation in the Nordic Countries During the Twentieth Century," in *The Nordic Model of Welfare: A Historical Reappraisal*, ed. Niels Finn Christiansen, Klaus Petersen, Nils Edling, and Per Haave (Copenhagen: Museum Tusculanum Press, 2005), 312.
51 Hobson, "Feminist Strategies," in *Mothers of a New World*, 408.
52 Jochen Hellbeck, *Revolution on my Mind: Writing a Diary under Stalin* (Cambridge, MA: Harvard University Press, 2006), 125.
53 Hellbeck, *Revolution on my Mind*, 126.
54 William J. Chase, *Workers, Society, and the Soviet State: Labor and Life in Moscow* (Urbana, IL: University of Illinois Press, 1987), 109–10.
55 Engelstein, *Russia in Flames*, 111, 265, 398, 525
56 Barbara Alpern Engel, *Women in Russia, 1700–2000* (Cambridge: Cambridge University Press, 2004), 178.
57 Hellbeck, *Revolution on My Mind*, 75.
58 Fitzpatrick and Slezkine, *In the Shadow of Revolution*, 235.
59 Ibid., 237.
60 Berenson, *Europe in the Modern World*, 484, 495.
61 Lauren E. Forcucci, "Battle for Births: The Fascist Pronatalist Campaign in Italy 1925–1938," *Journal for the Society for the Anthropology of Europe* 10, no. 1 (2010): 4–13.
62 Forcucci, "Battle for Births," 11.
63 Willson, "Italy," in *Women, Gender and Fascism in Europe*, 22.
64 Ibid., 20–1.
65 Ibid., 21.
66 Ibid., 15.
67 Cheryl Koos and Daniella Sarnoff, "France," in *Women, Gender and Fascism in Europe*, 179–80.
68 Lucienne Blondel, "La Solidarité Française" ["French Solidarity"], quoted in *Lives and Voices*, 492.
69 Sandi E. Cooper, "Women in War and Peace, 1914–1945," in *Becoming Visible*, 448.
70 Blondel, "La Solidarité Française," 492.
71 Cooper, "Women in War and Peace, 1914–1945," 448.
72 Kirsten Heinsohn, "Germany," in *Women, Gender and Fascism in Europe*, 52.
73 See, Claudia Koonz, *Mothers in the Fatherland: Women, the Family and Nazi Politics* (New York: St. Martin's Press, 1987), 71, 75, 140–8; Gisela Bock, "Ein Historikerinnenstreit?" ["Quarrel among historians of women"], *Geschichte und Gesellschaft* 18 (1992): 400–4.
74 Doris L. Bergen, *War and Genocide: A Concise History of the Holocaust*, 3rd ed. (New York: Rowman and Littlefield, 2016), 56.

75　Gisela Bock, "Racism and Sexism in Nazi Germany: Motherhood, Compulsory Sterilization, and the State," in *When Biology Becomes Destiny: Women in Weimar and Nazi Germany*, ed. Renate Bridenthal, Atina Grossmann, and Marion Kaplan (New York: Monthly Review Press, 1984), 271–96.
76　"The Mass Sterilization Program," *United States Holocaust Memorial Museum*. https://encyclopedia.ushmm.org/content/en/article/the-biological-state-nazi-racial-hygiene-1933-1939, accessed July 1, 2024.
77　Henry Friedlander, *The Origins of Nazi Genocide: From Euthanasia to the Final Solution* (Chapel Hill: University of North Carolina Press, 1995), 17.
78　Bock, "Racism and Sexism in Nazi Germany," 274.
79　Mark Mazower, *Dark Continent: Europe's Twentieth Century* (New York: Vintage, 1998), 91.
80　Mazower, *Dark Continent*, 92.
81　Bock, "Racism and Sexism in Nazi Germany," in *When Biology Becomes Destiny*, 272.
82　Bucur, "Romania," 62.
83　Ibid., 65.
84　Bock, "Racism and Sexism in Nazi Germany," 276–82.
85　Robert Gellately, *Backing Hitler: Consent and Coercion in Nazi Germany* (Oxford: Oxford University Press, 2001), 52.
86　Marion A. Kaplan, *Between Dignity and Despair: Jewish Life in Nazi Germany* (New York: Oxford University Press, 1998), 150–1.
87　Bock, "Racism and Sexism in Nazi Germany," 274
88　"The Biological State: Nazi Racial Hygiene, 1933–1939," *United States Holocaust Memorial Museum*. https://encyclopedia.ushmm.org/content/en/article/the-biological-state-nazi-racial-hygiene-1933-1939, accessed September 21, 2025.
89　Bergen, *War and Genocide*, 82–3.
90　M. Kaplan, *Between Dignity and Despair*, 150–1.

4　The Second World War and the Holocaust

1　Eleanor Beardsley, "Josephine Baker is the first Black woman to be inducted into France's Pantheon," *NPR*, November 30, 2021. https://www.npr.org/2021/11/30/1059776777/josephine-baker-france-pantheon, accessed June 21, 2022.
2　Hallie Murray, *The Role of Female Spies in World War II* (New York: Cavendish Square Publishing, 2019), 67; Pedro Cravinho, "The 'Black Angel' in Lisbon: Josephine Baker challenges Salazar, live on television," *EU-topias: EU-topias: revista de interculturalidad, comunicación y estudios europeos* 18 (2019): 124.
3　Cravinho, "The 'Black Angel' in Lisbon," 124.
4　Peggy Caravantes, *The Many Faces of Josephine Baker Dancer, Singer, Activist, Spy* (Chicago: Chicago Review Press, 2015), 84.
5　Murray, *The Role of Female Spies*, 66.
6　Caravantes, *The Many Faces of Josephine Baker*, 89

7   Murry, *The Role of Female Spies*, 66; Cravinho, "The 'Black Angel' in Lisbon," 125.
8   Beardsley, "Josephine Baker," 2021.
9   Margaret Higonnet and Patrice Higonnet, "The Double Helix," in *Behind the Lines: Gender and the Two World Wars*, ed. Margaret Randolph Higonnet, Jane Jenson, Sonya Michel, and Margaret Collins Weitz (New Haven: Yale University Press, 1987), 31–48; Melissa Feinberg, "Dumplings and Domesticity: Women, Collaboration, and Resistance in the Protectorate of Bohemia and Moravia," in *Gender and War in Twentieth-Century Eastern Europe*, ed. Nancy W. Wingfield and Maria Bucur-Deckard (Bloomington: University of Indiana Press, 2006), 95–6.
10 Wingfield and Bucur-Deckard, *Gender and War in Twentieth-Century Eastern Europe*, 6.
11 Feinberg, "Dumplings and Domesticity," 103–4.
12 Richard Overy, *The Battle of Britain: The Myth and the Reality* (New York: W.W. Norton and Company, 2002), 13.
13 Jane Potter, "Valiant Heroines or Pacific Ladies? Women in War and Peace," in *History of Women in Europe since 1700*, ed. Deborah Simonton (New York: Routledge, 2006), 259; "The Women of the Second World War," Prime Minister's Office and Ministry of Defense, April 16, 2015, https://www.gov.uk/government/news/the-women-of-the-second-world-war.
14 Annemarie Tröger, "A Female Assembly-Line Proletariat," in *When Biology Becomes Destiny: Women in Weimar and Nazi Germany*, ed. Renate Bridenthal, Atina Grossmann, and Marion Kaplan (New York: Monthly Review Press, 1984), 245–6.
15 Leila J. Rupp, *Mobilizing Women for War: German and American Propaganda, 1939–1945* (Princeton: Princeton University Press, 1978), 82.
16 Field Marshal Walter von Reichnau, "'Conduct of Troops in Eastern Territories,' Oct 10, 1941, doc. UK-81 in Office of the United States Chief of Counsel for Prosecution of Axis Criminality," *Nazi Conspiracy and Aggression* (Washington, DC: US Government Printing Office, 1946), 8:585–7, quoted in *The Nazi State and German Society: A Brief History with Documents*, ed. Robert G. Moeller (Boston: Bedford St. Martins, 2010), 116–17.
17 Tony Judt, *Postwar: A History of Europe Since 1945* (New York: Penguin Press, 2005), 16–17.
18 Käthe Ricken, diary, 1943, in *War Wives: A Second World War Anthology*, ed. Colin Townsend and Eileen Townsend (London: Grafton Books, 1989), 274–76.
19 Ricken, diary, 1943, quoted in *The Nazi State and German Society*, 127.
20 Joshua Levine, *Forgotten Voices of the Blitz and the Battle for Britain: A New History in the Words of Men and Women on Both Sides* (New York: Random House, 2007), 251.
21 "Virtual Exhibition: West Indian Soldier," *National Army Museum*. https://www.nam.ac.uk/sites/default/files/learning-resource-files/2021-08/West%20Indian%20Soldier%20Learning%20Exhibition%20Tour%20Film%20-%20Teacher%20Notes.pdf, accessed July 1, 2024.
22 "Ena Collymore-Woodstock interviewed alongside her daughter," National Army Museum, "Virtual Exhibition: West Indian Soldier."
23 Alan Harfield, "The Women's Auxiliary Corps (India)," *Journal of the Society for Army Historical Research* 83 (2005): 250.

24 Yasmin Khan, "Women and War in the British Empire," *War and Society* 39, no. 3 (2020): 229.
25 Smith, "Postimperial Europe c 1947–1980," in *Europe in the Contemporary World*, 499.
26 Michael Paterson, *Voices of the Codebreakers: Personal Accounts of the Secret Heroes of World War II* (Barnsley, S. Yorkshire: Greenhill Books, 2018), 11.
27 Paterson, "Bletchley Park," in *Voices of the Codebreakers*, 61–2.
28 Ralph Erskine, "The First Naval Enigma Decrypts of World War II," *Cryptologia* 21, no. 1 (1997): 43.
29 Paterson, *Voices of the Codebreakers*, 63.
30 Eleanor Ireland, quoted in Janet Abbate, *Recoding Gender: Women's Changing Participation in Computing* (Cambridge, MA: The MIT Press, 2012), 21.
31 Abbate, *Recoding Gender*, 22.
32 Svetlana Alexievich, *The Unwomanly Face of War: An Oral History of Women in World War II*, trans. Richard Pevear and Larissa Volokhonsky (New York: Random House, 2017), xii.
33 Potter, "Women in War and Peace," in *The Routledge History of Women in Europe*, 284.
34 Alexievich, *The Unwomanly Face of War*, xii.
35 Ann Taylor Allen, *Women in Twentieth-Century Europe* (New York: Palgrave Macmillan, 2008), 61–2.
36 Anna Krylova, *Soviet Women in Combat: A History of Violence on the Eastern Front* (Cambridge: Cambridge University Press, 2010), 11–13, 16–18, 80–2, 100.
37 Krylova, *Soviet Women in Combat*, 105.
38 Ibid., 106.
39 Ibid., 105.
40 Ibid.
41 Ibid., 35.
42 Ibid., 291.
43 Juliette Pattinson, *Behind Enemy Lines: Gender, Passing and the Special Operations Executive in the Second World War* (Manchester: Manchester University Press, 2007), 81, 136–43, 148–9.
44 Claire Hubbard-Hall and Adrian O'Sullivan, "Wives of Secret Agents: Skyscapes of the Second World War and Female Agency," *International Journal of Military History and Historiography* 39 (2019): 181–3.
45 Pattinson, *Behind Enemy Lines*, 136.
46 Ibid.
47 Ibid., 1.
48 Zoë Waxman, *Women in the Holocaust: A Feminist History* (Oxford: Oxford University Press, 2017), 1–2.
49 Joan Ringelheim, "The Split between Gender and the Holocaust," in *Women in the Holocaust*, ed. Dalia Ofer and Lenore Weitzman (New Haven: Yale University Press, 1998), 348–9.
50 Joan Ringelheim, "Women and the Holocaust: A Reconsideration of Research," *Signs* 10, no. 4 (Summer 1985): 741–2; Vera Laska ed., *Women in the Resistance and the Holocaust: The Voices of Eyewitnesses* (Westport, CT: Greenwood Press, 1983), 14–18; Marion A. Kaplan, *Between Dignity and*

Despair: Jewish Life in Nazi Germany (New York: Oxford University Press, 1998); Waxman, *Women in the Holocaust*, 2.
51 M. Kaplan, *Between Dignity and Despair*, 203.
52 Ibid., 8.
53 Waxman, *Women in the Holocaust*, 42.
54 Ibid.
55 Doris L. Bergen, *War and Genocide: A Concise History of the Holocaust*, 3rd ed. (New York: Rowman and Littlefield, 2016), 141, 215, 247; M. Kaplan, *Between Dignity and Despair*, 154.
56 M. Kaplan, *Between Dignity and Despair*, 208.
57 Waxman, *Women in the Holocaust*, 23.
58 Ibid., 29.
59 Yehuda Bauer, *Rethinking the Holocaust* (New Haven: Yale University Press, 2002), 165; Waxman, *Women in the Holocaust*, 47.
60 Bradley F. Smith and Agnes F. Peterson, eds. *Heinrich Himmler Geheimreden 1933 bis 1945* (Frankfurt Main: Propylaen, 1972), 162–183.
61 Ibid.
62 Bergen, *War and Genocide*, 195.
63 Alexandra Richie, *Warsaw 1944: Hitler, Himmler, and the Warsaw Uprising* (New York: Farrar, Straus and Giroux, 2013), 33–4.
64 M. Kaplan, *Between Dignity and Despair*, 203, 208.
65 Ibid., 19.
66 Bergen, *War and Genocide*, 141.
67 Bauer, *Rethinking the Holocaust*, 165.
68 Ria Bröring, diary, in *War Wives: A Second World War Anthology*, ed. Colin Townsend and Eileen Townsend (London: Grafton Books, 1989), 87–8.
69 Suzanne Vromen, *Hidden Children of the Holocaust: Belgian Nuns and their Daring Rescue* (New York: Oxford University Press, 2008), 11, 76, 145.
70 Vromen, *Hidden Children of the Holocaust*, 3.
71 Frank McDonough, *Sophie Scholl: The Real Story of the Women Who Defied Hitler* (Stroud, Gloucestershire: History Press, 2009), 150; Inge Scholl, *The White Rose: Munich 1942–1943*, 3rd ed., trans. Arthur R. Schultz (Middletown, CT: Wesleyan University Press, 2012), 114.
72 Ivana Pantelić, "Yugoslav female partisans in World War II," *Cahiets Balkaniques* 41 (2013): 239–50.
73 Jelena Batinić, *Women and Yugoslav Partisans: A History of World War II Resistance* (Cambridge: Cambridge University Press, 2015), 2.
74 Batinić, *Women and Yugoslav Partisans*, 2.
75 Lieutenant Peter Geissler, letter, 1942, quoted in Ben Shepherd, *Terror in the Balkans: German Armies and Partisan Warfare* (Cambridge, MA: Harvard University Press, 2012), 209. Emphasis original.
76 Batinić, *Women and the Yugoslav Partisans*, 3.
77 Bauer, *Rethinking the Holocaust*, 174–5.
78 Ibid., 182.
79 Bergen, *War and Genocide*, 265–9.
80 Hanna Lévy-Hass, *Diary of Bergen-Belsen*, trans. Sophie Hand (Chicago: Haymarket Books, 2009), 15.
81 Lévy-Hass, *Diary of Bergen-Belsen*, 74.

82 Ibid., 74, 78.
83 Bergen, *War and Genocide*, 269.
84 Pawel Wieczorek, "Women in the Context of the Warsaw Ghetto Uprising," *Warsaw Ghetto Museum*, May 7, 2020. http://1943.pl/en/artykul/women-in-the-context-of-the-warsaw-ghetto-uprising/, accessed September 21, 2025.
85 Emanuel Ringelblum, *Stosunki polsko – żydowskie w czasie II wojny światowej* ["Polish-Jewish relations during the Second World War'] (Warsaw, 1988), 126, quoted in Pawel Wieczorek, "Women in the Context of the Warsaw Ghetto Uprising," May 7, 2020.
86 Wieczorek, "Women in the Context of the Warsaw Ghetto Uprising," May 7, 2020.
87 Ibid.
88 "Es gibt keinen jüdischen Wohnbezirk in Warschau mehr!" ["The Jewish quarter of Warsaw is no more!"] National Archives, Record Group 238, National Archives Collection of World War II War Crimes Records, 1933–1949. https://catalog.archives.gov/id/6003996. Translated by the author.
89 Ibid.
90 Stefania Szochur Staszewska, *Pamiętniki z getta warszawskiego. Fragmenty i regesty*, ["Diaries from the Warsaw Ghetto. Excerpts and Registers"] compiled by M. Grynberg, (Warsaw, 1988), 177–8, quoted in Pawel Wieczorek, "Women in the Context of the Warsaw Ghetto Uprising," *Warsaw Ghetto Museum*, May 7, 2020. http://1943.pl/en/artykul/women-in-the-context-of-the-warsaw-ghetto-uprising/, accessed September 21, 2025.
91 Jennifer Popwycz, curator, "The People's War: Women, Children, and Civilians in the 1944 Warsaw Uprising," *The National WWII Museum*, Dec 15, 2021, https://www.nationalww2museum.org/war/articles/women-and-children-1944-warsaw-uprising, accessed September 21, 2025; Richie, *Warsaw 1944*, 221.
92 Popwycz, curator, "The People's War: Women, Children, and Civilians in the 1944 Warsaw Uprising."
93 Halik Kochanski, *The Eagle Unbowed: Poland and the Poles in the Second World War* (Cambridge, MA: Harvard University Press, 2012).
94 Richie, *Warsaw 1944*, 283, 306, 325, 334.
95 Barbara Drapikowska, "The Military Participation of Women in the Polish Armed Forces," *National Defence University Scientific Quarterly* 91, no. 2 (2013): 129.
96 Bergen, *War and Genocide*, 218.
97 Ibid., 219.
98 Felicia Morris, "Beautiful Monsters," *Legacy* 11, no. 1 (2011), 64–5; Olga Lengyel, *Five Chimneys: A Woman Survivor's True Story of Auschwitz* (Chicago: Academy Chicago Publishers, 1995).
99 Morris, "Beautiful Monsters," 63.
100 Wendy Lower, *Hitler's Furies: German Women in the Nazi Killing Fields* (New York: Mariner, 2013), 3, 7.
101 Lower, *Hitler's Furies*, 6–7.
102 Ibid., 103.
103 Ibid., 4.
104 Ibid., 4.
105 Ibid., 126–7.

106 Ibid., 2–3.
107 Ibid., 166.
108 Judt, *Postwar*, 13.
109 Richard Bessel, "The Shadow of Death in Germany at the End of the Second World War," in *Between Mass Death and Individual Loss: The Place of the Dead in Twentieth-Century Germany*, ed. Alon Confino, Paul Betts, and Dirk Schumann (New York: Berghahn Book, 2008), 59; See also Monica Black, *Death in Berlin: From Weimar to Divided Germany* (New York: Cambridge University Press, 2010).
110 In the postwar period, US military and popular publications both consistently used the German term *Fraulein* to stand in for "young lady" or unmarried woman and, colloquially, "miss" when referring to American GIs German girlfriends.
111 Elizabeth Heineman, "The Hour of the Woman: Memories of Germany's 'Crisis Years' and West German National Identity," *The American Historical Review* 10, no. 2 (1996): 354–95.
112 Frank Biess, *Homecomings: Returning POWS and the Legacies of Defeat in Postwar Germany* (Princeton: Princeton University Press, 2006), 65, 102, 121–2; Höhn, *GIs and Fräuleins*, 26, 103, 129.
113 Moeller, *Protecting Motherhood*, 11; Sibylle Meyer and Eva Schultz, *Wie wir das Alles geschafft haben: Alleinstehende Frauen berichten über ihr Leben nach 1945* (Munich: Beck, 1985), 92.
114 Scholars debate the final numbers in these campaigns, as eyewitnesses and survivors note that repeated attacks make estimating even more difficult.
115 Michael Marrus, *The Unwanted: European Refugees in the Twentieth Century* (New York: Oxford University Press, 1985), 325.
116 Judt, *Postwar*, 20.
117 Melissa Feinberg, *Communism in Eastern Europe* (New York: Routledge, 2022), 19.
118 Mary Louise Roberts, *What Soldiers Do: Sex and the American GI in World War II France* (Chicago: University of Chicago Press, 2013), 4.
119 M. Kaplan, *Between Dignity*, 203, 208; Joshua S. Goldstein, *War and Gender: How Gender Shapes the War System and Vice Versa* (Cambridge: Cambridge University Press, 2003), 337.
120 Roberts, *What Soldiers Do*, 133.
121 Maria Höhn, *GIs and Fräuleins*, 71–7, 91.
122 Atina Grossman, *Jews, German, and Allies: Close Encounters in Occupied Germany* (Princeton: Princeton University Press, 2007), 10.
123 Grossmann, *Jews, Germans, and Allies*, 184.
124 Ibid., 266.

5 Women in Divided Europe

1 Paula A. Michaels, "Comrades in the Labor Room: The Lamaze Method of Childbirth Preparation and France's Cold War Home Front, 1951–1957," *The American Historical Review* 115, no. 4 (2014): 1031–2.
2 Michaels, "Comrades in the Labor Room," 1033.

3 "Eastern Europe" in this period refers to countries with communist governments after the Second World War that were militarily and economically aligned with but not formally part of the Soviet Union.
4 See, for example, Susan Pedersen, *Family, Dependence, and the Origins of the Welfare State: Britain and France 1914–1945* (New York: Cambridge University Press, 1995), 419.
5 Harriet Jones, "The State and Social Policy," in *Women in Twentieth Century Britain: Social, Cultural and Political Change*, ed. Ina Zweiniger-Bargielowska (New York: Routledge, 2014), 328–30; Tony Judt, *Postwar: A History of Europe Since 1945* (New York: Penguin Press, 2005), 332.
6 Judt, *Postwar*, 72–5; 365–7.
7 Ibid., 73; See also, Peter Hennessy, *Having it So Good: Britain in the Fifties* (New York: Penguin Books, 2007), 22–8.
8 Bonnie G. Smith, "Introduction," in *Women and Gender in Postwar Europe: From Cold War to European Union*, ed. Joanna Regulska and Bonnie G. Smith (New York: Routledge, 2012), 3.
9 Beveridge Report (Social Insurance and Allied Services (Cmd 6404), 1942 paragraph 114, 117.
10 Smith, *Europe in the Contemporary World*, 568.
11 Regulska and Smith eds., *Women in Postwar Europe*, 2.
12 Smith, *Europe in the Contemporary World*, 449.
13 Ann Orloff, "Gender and the Welfare State," *Annual Review of Sociology* 22 (1996): 59–60; See also Pedersen, *Family, Dependence, and the Origins of the Welfare State*, 267–70, 397, 409–10.
14 Smith, *Europe in the Contemporary World*, 449.
15 Judt, *Postwar*, 487.
16 See, https://stats.bls.gov/opub/mlr/1983/02/art3full.pdf.
17 Kathleen Barry, *Femininity in Flight: A History of Flight Attendants* (Durham: Duke University Press, 2007), 180.
18 Wendy Webster, "'Race', Ethnicity and National Identity," in *Women in Twentieth Century Britain*, ed. Ina Zweiniger-Bargielowska (New York: Routledge, 2001), 297.
19 Marina Kiblitskaya, "Russia's Female Breadwinners," in *Gender, State, and Society in Soviet and Post-Soviet Russia*, ed. Sarah Ashwin (New York: Routledge, 2000), 56.
20 Susan Zimmerman, "The Changing Politics of Women's Work and the Making of Extended Childcare Leave in State-Socialist Hungary, Europe, and Internationally: Shifting the Scene," in *Life Course, Work, and Labour in Global History*, ed. Josef Ehmer and Carola Lentz (Boston: Walter de Gruyter, 2023), 228.
21 Kiblitskaya, "Russia's Female Breadwinners," 56.
22 Maria Adamson and Erika Kispeter, "Gender and Professional Work in Russia and Hungary," in *Gender in Twentieth-Century Eastern Europe and the USSR*, ed. Catherine Baker (New York: Palgrave Macmillan, 2017), 214, 216–17.
23 Ivan Simić, "Gender and Youth Work Actions in Post-War Yugoslavia," in *Gender in Twentieth-Century Eastern Europe and the USSR*, ed. Catherine Baker (New York, Palgrave Macmillan, 2017), 150.
24 Salvatore A. Engel-Di Mauro, "Citizenship, Systemic Change, and the Gender Division of Labor," in *Women and Citizenship in Central and Eastern*

Europe, ed. Jasmina Lukić, Joanna Regulska, and Darja Zaviršek (Burlington, VT: Ashgate, 2006), 63.
25 Zimmerman, "The Changing Politics of Women's Work," 228.
26 Ibid., 229, 231.
27 Dagmar Herzog, *Sexuality in Europe: A Twentieth-Century History* (Cambridge: Cambridge University Press, 2012), 192.
28 Ibid., 100.
29 Adamson and Kispeter, "Gender and Professional Work," 219.
30 Barbara Einhorn, *Cinderella Goes to Market: Citizenship, Gender and Women's Movements in East Central Europe* (New York: Verso, 1993), 44.
31 Simić, "Gender and Youth Work Actions in Post-war Yugoslavia," 149.
32 Colin Burgess and Rex Hall, *The First Soviet Cosmonaut Team: Their Lives, Legacy, and Historical Impact* (New York: Springer, 2009), 229.
33 Ibid., 230.
34 Ibid.
35 The Treaty of Rome, effective January 1, 1958, helped facilitate this movement by launching the European Economic Community (EEC), which eased trade between Belgium, France, Italy, Luxembourg, the Netherlands, and West Germany. Other supranational organizations, such as the International Labor Organization, Organization for Economic Cooperation and Development, and the Council of Europe, also helped organize bilateral and multilateral agreements that resulted in a free exchange of labor among nations.
36 Giovanna Campani, "Immigrant Women in Southern Europe: Social Exclusion, Domestic Work and Prostitution in Italy," in *Eldorado or Fortress? Migration in Southern Europe*, ed. Russell King, Gabriella Lazaridis, and Charalambos Tsardanidis (London: Palgrave Macmillan, 2000), 147–8.
37 Nermin Abandan-Unat, *Turks in Europe: From Guest Worker to Transnational Citizen*, trans. Caterine Campion (New York: Berghahn, 2011), 91.
38 Georges Photios Tapinos, "Female Migration and the Status of Foreign Women in France," in *International Migration Policies and the Status of Female Migrants: Proceedings of the United Nations Expert Group Meeting on International Migration Policies and the Status of Female Migrants San Miniato, Italy, 28–31 March 1990* (New York: United Nations, 1995), 104.
39 Jozefien De Bock, *Parallel Lives Revisited: Mediterranean Guest Workers and Their Families at Work and in the Neighbourhood, 1960–1980* (New York: Berghahn, 2018), 41–2.
40 Berenson, *Europe in the Modern World*, 718.
41 Interview with the author, Berlin, 2003.
42 See, for example, Lauren Stokes, *Fear of the Family: Guest Workers and Family Migration in the Federal Republic of Germany* (New York: Oxford University Press, 2022).
43 Johannes Velling, "Determinants of Family Reunification Among German Guest-Workers," *Vierteljahrshefts zur Wirtschaftsforschung* 63, no. 1(1994): 126–32.
44 "Gemeine Lumpen, Sauigels—rauswerfen" ["Vile scoundrels, swine—throw them out!"], *Der Spiegel* 53 (1977), https://www.spiegel.de/politik/gemeine-lumpen-sauigels-rauswerfen-a-7801dd78-0002-0001-0000-000040680181, accessed May 13, 2021.

45 Gabriella Lazaridis, "Filipino and Albanian Women Migrant Workers in Greece: Multiple Layers of Oppression," in *Gender and Migration in Southern Europe: Women on the Move*, ed. Flora Anthias and Gabriella Lazaridis (New York: Berg, 2000), 57.
46 "Aygül," Interview, Documentation Center and Museum of Migration in Germany (DOMiD) Interview 8, Frankfurt am Main, 22 May 1995. She ended up joining her parents in West Germany a few years later.
47 Christina Schwenkel, "Rethinking Asian Mobilities," *Critical Asian Studies* 46, no. 2 (2014): 235–58.
48 Mark Siemons, "Smuggling Discerned—Fingers Burned," *Frankfurter Allgemeine Zeitung* (February 25, 1995) in *Germany in Transit: Nation and Migration, 1955–2005*, ed. Deniz Göktürk, David Gramling, and Anton Kaes (Berkeley: University of California Press, 2007), 96.
49 "Agreement on the Procedures Concerning Pregnancy Among Vietnamese Women Laborers in the GDR," in *Germany in Transit*, 88.
50 Schwenkel, "Rethinking Asian Mobilities," 245.
51 Ibid.
52 Ibid., 248.
53 Bonnie G. Smith, *Women in World History: 1450 to the Present* (New York: Bloomsbury, 2020), 264–5.
54 "The Case of Djamila Boupacha," in *Lives and Voices*, 553–8.
55 Joan W. Scott, *The Politics of the Veil* (Princeton: Princeton University Press, 2007), 63.
56 Between 1945 and 1960, 300,000 people from the Dutch East Indies (now Indonesia) and, after 1965, large groups of workers from the former Dutch colony Surinam had moved to the Netherlands. By 1961, 541,000 migrants had arrived in Britain from the Caribbean, the Indian subcontinent, Africa, and Asia; and, by 1970, 800,000 former colonials had moved to France. See Rita Chin, *The Guest Worker Question in Germany* (Cambridge: Cambridge University Press, 2007), 26.
57 Karen Fog Olwig, "The Timescape of Post-WWII Caribbean Migration to Britain: Historical Heterogeneity as Challenge and Opportunity," in *Migration, Temporality, and Capitalism*, ed. Pauline Gardiner Barber and Winnie Lem (New York: Palgrave Macmillan, 2018), 43–4.
58 UN Population Division, "Measuring the Extent of Female International Migration," in *International Migration Policies and the Status of Female Migrants* (New York: UN, 1995), 66. https://digitallibrary.un.org/record/190600?ln=en
59 John Salt and James Clarke, "Europe's Migrant Groups," in *The Demographic Characteristics of Immigrant Populations*, ed. Werner Haug, Paul Compton, and Youssef Courbage (Strasbourg, France: Council of Europe Publishing, 2002), 44.
60 Smith, *Europe in the Contemporary World*, 523.
61 Justin Nordstrom, "The 'Kitchen Debate' Revisited: Abundance and Anti-domesticity in Cold War America," *Global Food History* 10, no. 3 (2024): 375–7.
62 "The Kitchen Debate Transcript," Central Intelligence Agency, 24 July 1959, https://www.cia.gov/readingroom/docs/1959-07-24.pdf.

63 M. Jane Slaughter, "'What's New' and is it Good for You? Gender and Consumerism in Postwar Europe," in *Women and Gender in Postwar Europe: From Cold War to European Union*, ed. Joanna Regulska and Bonnie G. Smith (New York: Routledge, 2012), 104–121.
64 Tammy M. Proctor, "Women, Popular Culture and Leisure," in *The Routledge History of Women in Europe Since 1700*, ed. Deborah Simonton (New York: Routledge, 2006), 331.
65 Stephanie M. Amerian, "The Fashion Gap: The Cold War Politics of American and Soviet fashion, 1945–1959," *Journal of Historical Research in Marketing* 8, no. 1 (2016): 65–82.
66 Ginette Vincendeau, *Brigitte Bardot* (New York: Palgrave Macmillan, 2013), 5.
67 Susan E. Reid, "Cold War in the Kitchen: Gender and the De-Stalinization of Consumer Taste in the Soviet Union under Khrushchev," *Slavic Review* 61, no. 2 (2002): 214.
68 Reid, "Cold War in the Kitchen," 219.
69 Ibid., 220–1.
70 Simone de Beauvoir, *The Second Sex*, trans. H. M. Parshley (New York: Vintage Books, 1989), xxi.
71 Pilar Godayal, "Feminism and Translation in the 1960s: The reception in Catalunya of Betty Friedan's The Feminine Mystique," trans. Sheila Waldeck, *Translation Studies* 7, no. 3 (2014): 268.
72 Godayal, "Feminism and Translation," 274.
73 Juliet Mitchell, *The Longest Revolution* (New York: Pantheon Books, 1984), 18.
74 Ute Frevert, *Women in German History: From Bourgeois Emancipation to Sexual Liberation*, trans. Stuart McKinnon-Evans, Terry Bond, and Barbara Norden (Washington, DC: Berg, 1990), 273.
75 Matera, *Black London*, 326.
76 Matera, *Black London*, 118.
77 Matera, *Black London*, 110.
78 Donald Hinds, "The West Indian Gazette: Claudia Jones and the Black Press in Britain," *Race and Class* 50, no. 1 (2008): 92.

6 Fighting for Expanded Rights

1 Simone de Beauvoir, "I am a Feminist," in *Lives and Voices*, 574.
2 Karen Hagemann and Sonya Michel, eds., *Gender and the Long Postwar: The United States and the Two Germanies, 1945–1989* (Baltimore: Johns Hopkins University Press, 2014), 20.
3 Jeffery Weeks, *Sex, Politics and Society: The Regulation of Sexuality since 1880*, 3rd ed. (New York: Routledge, 2012), 368.
4 Louise Tyrer, "Introduction of the Pill and Its Impact," *Contraception* 59, no. 1, Supplement 1 (1999): 12S.
5 Yuliya Hilevych and Chizu Sato, "Popular Medical Discourses on Birth Control in the Soviet Union during the Cold War: Shifting Responsibilities and Relational Values," in *Children by Choice? Changing Values, Reproduction, and Family Planning in the 20th Century*, ed. Ann-Katrin

Gembries, Theresia Theuke, and Isabel Heinemann (Boston: De Gruyter Oldenbourg, 2018), 110.
6. Tyrer, "Introduction of the Pill," 13S–15S.
7. Rachel M. Pierce and Griselda Rowntree, "Birth Control in Britain, Part II: Contraceptive Methods Used by Couples Married in the Last Thirty Years," *Population Studies* 15, no. 2 (1961): 128.
8. Elizabeth Draper, *Birth Control in the Modern World: The Role of the Individual in Population Control*, 2nd ed. (New York: Penguin, 1972), 151.
9. Herzog, *Sexuality in Europe*, 3.
10. Silvia De Zordo, Joanna Mishtal, and Lorena Anton, eds., *A Fragmented Landscape: Abortion Governance and Protest Logics in Europe* (New York: Berghahn Press, 2018).
11. Regulska and Smith ed., *Women and Gender in Postwar Europe*, 3.
12. Smith, *Women in World History*, 286–7.
13. "Jean Purdy, IVF pioneer and co-founder of Bourn Hall," *Bourn Hall Fertility Clinic*, March 25, 2024. https://www.bournhall.co.uk/fertilityblog/jean-purdy-ivf-pioneer/, accessed December 8, 2024; See also, Jacques Cohen, Robert Edwards, Carole Fehilly, Simon Fishel, Jonathan Hewitt, Jean Purdy, George Rowland, Patrick Steptoe, and John Webster, "In Vitro Fertilization: A Treatment for Male Infertility," *Fertility and Sterility* 43, no. 3 (1985): 422–32.
14. Duncan Wilson, "In Vitro Fertilization, Infertility, and the 'Right to a Child' in 1970s and 1980s Britain," in *The Palgrave Handbook of Infertility History: Approaches, Contexts and Perspectives*, ed. Gayle Davis and Tracey Loughran (London: Palgrave Macmillan, 2017), 567.
15. Wilson, "In Vitro Fertilization, Infertility, and the 'Right to a Child'," 569–70, 565.
16. Jean Cohen, Alan Trounson, Karen Dawson, Howard Jones, Johan Hazekamp, Karl Gösta Nygren and Lars Hamberger, "The Early Days of IVF Outside the UK," *Human Reproduction Update* 11, no. 5 (2005): 456.
17. Heineman, *Before Porn was Legal*, 127; Eva-Maria Silies, "Taking the Pill after the 'Sexual Revolution': Female Contraceptive Decisions in England and West Germany in the 1970s," *European Review of History—Revue européenne d'histoire* 22, no. 1 (2015): 41–59.
18. Heineman, *Before Porn was Legal*, 101.
19. Ibid., 127.
20. Judt, *Postwar*, 396.
21. Heineman, *Before Porn was Legal*, 101, 105–7.
22. Josie McLellan, "'Even Under Socialism, We Don't Want to Do Without Love': East German Erotica," in *Pleasures in Socialism: Leisure and Luxury in the Eastern Bloc*, ed. David Crowley and Susan E. Reid (Chicago: Northwestern University Press, 2010), 221.
23. Ibid.
24. Ibid., 222; see also Josie McLellan, "Visual Dangers and Delights: Nude Photography in East Germany," *Past and Present* 205, no. 1 (2009): 143–74.
25. Peter C. Caldwell and Karrin Hanshew, *Germany Since 1945: Politics, Culture, and Society* (New York: Bloomsbury, 2018), 110.
26. Regulska and Smith, *Women and Gender in Postwar Europe*, 4; Clark, *Desire*, 200.

27 Rebecca Jennings, *Tomboys and Bachelor Girls: A Lesbian History of Post-war Britain 1945–71* (Manchester: Manchester University Press, 2007), 7, 40, 85, 175.
28 Robert G. Moeller, "The Homosexual is a 'Man,' the Homosexual Woman is a 'Woman': Sex, Society, and the Law in Postwar West Germany," *Journal of the History of Sexuality* 4, no. 3 (1994): 420.
29 Judit Takács, "Listing Homosexuals since the 1920s and under State Socialism in Hungary," in *Gender in Twentieth-Century Eastern Europe and the USSR*, ed. Catherine Baker (New York: Palgrave Macmillan, 2017), 165.
30 Jennings, *Tomboys and Bachelor Girls,* 134, 175.
31 Cynthia Kreisel, "Happy Motherhood and Lesbian Spaces," in *Women and Gender in Postwar Europe*, 130.
32 Jennings, *Tomboys and Bachelor Girls,* 107.
33 Ibid., 112.
34 Kreisel, "Happy Motherhood and Lesbian Spaces," 130.
35 Anna Borgos, "Secret Years: Hungarian Lesbian Herstory, 1950s–2000s," *Aspasia* 9, no. 1 (2015): 88; See also Kurimay, *Queer Budapest, 1873–1961*.
36 Emily Hamer, *Britannia's Glory: A History of Twentieth-Century Lesbians* (Bloomsbury, 2016), 183; Oram and Turnbull, *Lesbian History Sourcebook*, 240.
37 Mary L., "Petersfield," *Arena Three* 2, no. 2 (February 1965): 13, quoted in Oram and Turnbull, *Lesbian History Sourcebook*, 257.
38 "Miss A. M. A. J., Miss T. H," Ibid., 257–8.
39 Jennings, *Tomboys and Bachelor Girls,* 107.
40 Rachel Parker, Jonathan Garcia, and Robert M. Buffington, "Sexuality in the Contemporary World," in *A Global History of Sexuality: The Modern Era*, ed. Robert M. Buffington, Eithne Luibhéid, and Donna J. Guy (Malden, MA: Wiley Blackwell, 2014), 231.
41 Thorgerdur Einarsdóttier, "Women in Iceland: Strong Women—Myths and Contradictions," in *Female Well-Being: Toward a Global Theory of Social Change*, ed. Janet Mancini Billson and Carolyn Fluehr-Lobban (New York: Zed Books, 2005), 85.
42 Allen, *Women in Twentieth Century Europe*, 82.
43 Joyce Gelb, *Feminism and Politics: A Comparative Perspective* (Berkeley: University of California Press, 1989), 146.
44 Meike S. Baader, "Childhood and Happiness in German Romanticism, Progressive Education and in the West German Anti-authoritarian *Kinderläden* Movement in the Context of 1968," *Paedagogica Historica* 48, no. 3 (June 2012): 491.
45 Katharine Karcher, *Sisters in Arms: Militant Feminisms in the Federal Republic of Germany since 1968* (New York: Berghahn, 2017), 21.
46 Karcher, *Sisters in Arms*, 6.
47 Gisela Notz, *Warum flog die Tomate? Die autonomen Frauenbewegungen der Siebzigerjahr* (New Ulm: AG SPAK Bücher, 2018), 17.
48 Alex J. Todd, "The Protestor's Playground: Throughout the 1970s, the Feminist Group Dolle Mina Combined Radical Protests with Conceptual Art," *History Today* 69, no. 6 (June 2019): 15.
49 Ibid.
50 Gisela Kaplan, "France and the Netherlands," in *Contemporary Western European Feminism*, ed. Gisela Kaplan (New York: Routledge, 2014), 155.

51 Ibid.
52 Todd, "The Protestor's Playground," 15.
53 Karcher, *Sisters in Arms*, 13, 55.
54 Ibid., 61.
55 Ibid., 107, 136, 77.
56 Ibid., 121.
57 Libor Stloukal, "Understanding the 'Abortion Culture' in Central and Eastern Europe," in *From Abortion to Contraception: A Resource to Public Policies and Reproductive Behavior in Central and Eastern Europe 1917 to the Present*, ed. Henry P. David and Joanna Skilogianis (Westport, CT: Greenwood Press, 1999), 36.
58 Mary Ingham, *We are Now Thirty: Women of the Breakthrough Generation* (London: Eyre Methuen, 1981), 113.
59 The 1912 Infant's Life (Preservation) Act 1929 allowed the termination of pregnancy in cases where the mother's health was at risk.
60 Donna Harsh, "Society, the State, and Abortion in East Germany, 1950–1972," *The American Historical Review*, 102, no. 1 (1997): 53, fn 1.
61 Ana Prata, "Finding a Voice: Abortion Claim-making during Portuguese Democratization," *Women's Studies International Forum* 33, no. 6 (2010): 579–88.
62 Ibid., 583.
63 Ibid., 579–88.
64 Amy E. Randall, "'Abortion will Deprive You of Happiness!' Soviet Reproductive Politics in the Post-Stalin Era," *Journal of Women's History* 23, no. 3 (2014): 13–38.
65 Timm and Sanborn, *Gender, Sex, and the Shaping of Modern Europe*, 249.
66 Ibid.
67 Amilda Dymi and Pamela Pine, "Albania," in *From Abortion to Contraception*, 58–9.
68 Ibid., 61.
69 Ibid., 62.
70 Ibid., 63.
71 Lorena Anton, "On Memory Work in Post-communist Europe: A Case Study on Romania's Ways of Remembering its Pronatalist Past," *Anthropological Journal of European Cultures* 18, no. 2 (2006): 106–22; Henry P. David and Adriana Baban, "Women's Heath and Reproductive Rights: Romanian Experience," *Patient Education and Counseling* 28, no. 3 (1996): 237.
72 Anton, "On Memory Work in Post-communist Europe," 106–22.
73 David and Baban, "Women's Heath and Reproductive Rights," 238.
74 "Sonst prüde: Die 22 Millionen Rumänen sollen sich drastisch vermehren. Führer Ceaușescu will es so" ["Otherwise prudish: The 22 million Romanians are to increase their population drastically. Leader Ceaușescu wants it that way."] *Der Spiegel* 43 (1986). https://www.spiegel.de/politik/sonst-pruede-a-402dda5d-0002-0001-0000-000013521142, accessed October 18, 2021.
75 Ibid.; Lynn Morrison, "Ceaușescu Legacy: Family Struggles and Institutionalization of Children in Romania," *Journal of Family History* 29, no. 3 (2004): 170.
76 "Sonst prüde," *Der Spiegel* 43 (1986).

77 Ibid.
78 Henry P. David and Adriana Baban, "Women's Health and Reproductive Rights: Romanian Experience," *Patient Education and Counseling* 28, no. 3 (1996): 235–45.
79 Christina A. Pop, "Winners of Socialism: Fighting Infertility in Pronatalist Romania," *Medical Anthropology* 43 (2018): 4.
80 Pop, "Winners of Socialism," 3.
81 Vlad Odobescu, "Half a Million Kids Survived Romania's 'Slaughterhouses of Souls.' Now They Want Justice," *The World Global Post, Public Radio International*, December 28, 2015. https://www.pri.org/stories/2015-12-28/half-million-kids-survived-romanias-slaughterhouses-souls-now-they-want-justice, accessed October 18, 2021.
82 Sara M. Evans, "Sons, Daughters, and Patriarchy: Gender and the 1968 Generation," *The American Historical Review* 114, no. 2 (2009): 334.
83 Judt, *Postwar*, 406.
84 Keith A. Reader and Khursheed Wadia, "Women and the Events of May 1968," in *The May 1968 Events in France: Reproductions and Interpretations*, ed. Keith A. Reader and Khursheed Wadia (London: Palgrave Macmillan, 1993), 148–9.
85 Frevert, *Women in German History*, 296.
86 Reader and Wadia, *The May 1968 Events*, 151.
87 Ibid.
88 Paulina Bren, "1968 East and West: Visions of Political Change and Student Protests from across the Iron Curtain," in *Transnational Moments of Change: Europe 1945, 1968, 1989*, ed. Gerd-Rainer Horn and Padraic Kenney (New York: Rowan and Littlefield Publishers, 2004), 119.
89 Jan Pauer, "Czechoslovakia," in *1968 Europe: A History of Protest and Activism, 1956–1977*, ed. Martin Klimke and Joachim Scharloth (New York: Palgrave Macmillan, 2008), 169.
90 Heda Margolius Kovály, *Under A Cruel Star: A Life in Prague 1941–1968*, trans. Franci Epstein and Helen Epstein (New York: Homes and Meier, 1986), 181.
91 Kristyna Foltynova, "The Invasion of Czechoslovakia Through Women's Eyes," *Radio Free Europe / Radio Liberty*, August 20, 2018. https://www.rferl.org/a/invasion-of-czechoslovakia-through-womens-eyes/29442053.html, accessed Dec 10, 2024.
92 Megan R. Martin, "The Growth of Czech Feminism: Analyzing Resistance Activities Through a Gendered Lens, 1968 to 1993," *Gender, Equal Opportunities, Research* 10, no. 1 (2009): 39.
93 Harry Blutstein, "The Forgotten Protest," *Wilson Center*, July 15, 2021, https://www.wilsoncenter.org/blog-post/forgotten-protest, accessed September 20, 2021; Nick Nocita, "Politics and the Olympics," *Harvard International Review* 41, no. 2 (2020): 27.
94 Nocita, "Politics and the Olympics," 27.
95 Daniel Weissbort, "The Ordeal of Natalya Gorbanevskaya," *Index of Censorship* 1, no. 1 (1972): 120; "5 September 1968 (2102-A) Red Square," trans. John Crowfoot, https://bukovsky-archive.com/2020/08/25/5-september-1968-2102-a-red-square/, accessed September 20, 2021.
96 Ibid.

97 Bolton, *Worlds of Dissent*, 99.
98 Penn, *Solidarity's Secret*, 8.
99 Natalya Gorbanevskaya, "Writing for 'Samizdat'," *Index on Censorship* 6, no. 1 (1977): 34–5.
100 Régis Schlagdenhauffen, "Gay Rights and LGBTQI Movements in Europe," *Digital Encyclopedia of European History*. https://ehne.fr/en/node/12402, accessed November 15, 2024.
101 Karcher, *Sisters in Arms*, 36.
102 "Introduction," in *Sexualities in World Politics: How LGBTQ claims shape International Relations*, ed. Manuela Lavinas Picq and Markus Thiel (New York: Routledge, 2015).
103 Schlagdenhauffen, "Gay rights and LGBTQI movements in Europe."
104 Jennifer A. Miller, *Turkish Guest Workers in Germany: Hidden Lives and Contested Borders* (Toronto: University of Toronto Press, 2018), 143.
105 Ibid., 134–5.
106 Ibid., 140.
107 Eckart Hildebrandt, Werner Olle, Hildebrandt, Eckart, and Werner Olle. *Ihr Kampf ist unser Kampf: Ursachen, Verlauf u. Perspektiven d. Ausländerstreiks 1973 in der BRD* (Verlag 2000 [1975]).
108 Miller, *Turkish Guestworkers*, 146.
109 Reader and Wadia, *Women and the Events of May 1968*, 157.
110 Harold L. Smith, "The Women's Movements, Politics and Citizenship: 1960s–2000," in *Women in Twentieth Century Britain: Social, Cultural and Political Change*, 1st edition, ed. Ina Zweiniger-Bargielowska (New York: Routledge, 2001), 283; See also, Caitríona Beaumont, "The 'Silver Thread': Hazel Hunkins-Hallinan (1890–1982), the Six Point Group, and New Understandings of Intergenerational Female Activism in England, 1960s to 1980," *Women's History Review* (2024): 1–17.
111 Tara Martin, "The Beginning of Labor's End? Britain's 'Winter of Discontent' and Working-Class Women's Activism," *International and Labor and Working-Class History* 75 (2009): 52.
112 Sundari Anitha, Ruth Pearson, and Linda McDowell, "Striking Lives: Multiple Narratives of South Asian Women's Employment, Identity and Protest in the UK," *Ethnicities* 12, no. 6 (2012): 754–75.
113 Paweł Perzyna, "Strike in the City of Textile Workers in February 1971," *Institute of National Remembrance*, February 12, 2021. https://ipn.gov.pl/en/news/7070,Strike-in-the-city-of-textile-workers-in-February-1971.html, accessed March 18, 2022.
114 Padraic Kenney, "The Gender Resistance in Communist Poland," *American Historical Review* 104, no. 1 (1999): 410–11.
115 Kenney, "Gender Resistance," 411.
116 Ibid., 410.
117 Penn, *Solidarity's Secret*, 34.
118 Kenney, "Gender Resistance," 401.
119 Frances Doughty, "Lesbians and International Women's Year: A Report on Three Conferences," in *Our Right to Love: A Lesbian History Resource Book*, ed. Ginny Vida (Prentice Hall, 1978), 148.
120 Einarsdóttier, "Women in Iceland," 189.

121 "Icelandic Women Strike for Economic and Social Equality, 1975," *Global Nonviolent Action Database*. https://nvdatabase.swarthmore.edu/content/icelandic-women-strike-economic-and-social-equality-1975, accessed July 21, 2021.
122 "The 1975 Women's Strike: When 90% of Icelandic Women Went on Strike to Protest Gender Inequality," *Iceland Magazine*, October 24, 2018. https://icelandmag.is/tags/womens-strike, accessed December 10, 2024.
123 "Iceland: Women Stike," *New York Times*, October 25, 1976.
124 Anna Wojtyńska, "Black Protesters in Iceland: Transnational Flows and Entanglements," in *Mobility and Transnational Iceland: Current Transformations and Global Entanglements*, ed. Kristín Loftsdóttir, Unnur Dís Skaptadóttir, and Sigurjón Baldur Hafsteinsson (Reykjavik: University of Iceland Press, 2020), 248; Iceland has perhaps the only feminist political party in the world to enter parliamentary politics. See, Sogrõur Porgeirsdóttir, "Feminist Ethics and Feminist Politics," in *Law and Justice and the State in Nordic Perspective* 61 (1995): 35.
125 Einarsdóttier, "Women in Iceland," 192.
126 Selma James, *Sex, Race and Class, the Perspective of Winning: A Selection of Writings, 1952–2011* (Oakland, CA: PM Press, 2012).
127 Maud Anne Brack, "Between the Transnational and the Local: mapping trajectories and contexts of the Wages for Housework Campaign in 1970s Italian Feminism," *Women's History Review* 22, no. 4 (2013): 607–24.
128 "Housework – Unpaid Work," Flyer, Wages for Housework Committee, New York, NY, USA. *Barnard College Archives*, undated. http://bcrw.barnard.edu/archive/workforce/Wages_for_Housework.pdf, accessed November 1, 2021.
129 "Wages for Housework," Barnard Archive.
130 "Every Mother is a Working Mother," *Safire: Black Women for Wages for Housework (USA)* 1, no. 1 (Fall 1977): 3. https://globalwomenstrike.net/black-women-for-wages-for-housework-bulletin-autumn-1977/.
131 Carrie Hamilton, *Women and the ETA: The Gender politics of radical Basque nationalism* (New York: Manchester University Press, 2007), 82.
132 Tiago Fernandes, "Rethinking pathways to democracy: civil society in Portugal and Spain, 1960s–2000s," *Democratization* 22, no. 6 (2015): 1083; Prata, "Finding a voice," 579–88.
133 Hamilton, *Women and the ETA*, 2–3, 49.
134 Ibid., 82, 150–1.
135 Ibid., 136, 175.
136 Ibid., 20.
137 Ibid., 110.
138 "13 Killed as Paratroops Break Riot," *The Guardian*, January 31, 1972.
139 Theresa O'Keefe, "Policing Unruly Women: The State and Sexual Violence during the Northern Irish Troubles," *Women's Studies International Forum* 62 (2017): 70.
140 O'Keefe, "Policing Unruly Women," 70–1.
141 Lynne Shivers, "There is SOME Nonviolent Action in Northern Ireland," *Fellowship of Reconciliation NY* 39, no. 13 (1973): 4–5; Marie Hammond Callaghan, "Women's Responses to State Violence: Peace Women and

Peacebuilding in Northern Ireland," *Canadian Women's Studies / Les Cahiers de la Femme* 22, no. 2 (2003): 28–35.
142 Callaghan, "Women's Responses to 'Peace Women'," 28.
143 Shivers, "There is SOME Nonviolent Action," 4–5.
144 Jörg Neuheiser and Stefan Wolff, *Peace at Last? The Impact of the Good Friday Agreement on Northern Ireland* (New York: Berghahn Books, 2004), 157.
145 Callaghan, "Women's Responses to 'Peace Women'," 29.
146 Patricia Melzer, *Death in the Shape of a Young Girl: Women's Political Violence in the Red Army Faction* (New York: New York University Press, 2015), 2.
147 Melzer, *Death in the Shape of a Young Girl*, 46.
148 Ibid., Hamilton, *Women and the ETA*.
149 H. Cook, *The Long Sexual Revolution*, 1–3.

7 Revolutions and Rebirth

1 Jane Pilcher, "The Gender Significance of Women in Power: British Women Talking about Margaret Thatcher," *The European Journal of Women's Studies* 2, no. 4 (1995): 494; Wendy Webster, *Not a Man to Match Her: Feminist View of Britain's First Woman Prime Minister* (London: The Women's Press, 1990), 50.
2 Judt, *Postwar*, 541; Pilcher, "The Gender Significance," 494.
3 Heather Nunn, *Thatcher, Politics and Fantasy: The Political Culture of Gender and Nation* (London: Lawrence and Wishart, 2002), 23, 97–100, 102; Pilcher, "The Gender Significance," 494.
4 Ibid.
5 Zweiniger-Bargielowska, *Women in Twentieth Century Britain*, 285.
6 Nunn, *Thatcher*, 22.
7 Zweiniger-Bargielowska, *Women in Twentieth Century Britain*, 285–7.
8 Lucy Robinson, *Gay Men and the Left in Post-War Britain: How the personal got political* (Manchester: Manchester University Press, 2013).
9 Pilcher, "The Gender Significance," 498.
10 Ibid., 499.
11 Webster, *Not a Man to Match Her*, 68.
12 Zweiniger-Bargielowska, *Women in Twentieth Century Britain*, 285.
13 Pilcher, "The Gender Significance of Women in Power," 500.
14 Zweiniger-Bargielowska, *Women in Twentieth Century Britain*, 285.
15 Ann Nolan, "The Gay Community Response to the Emergence of AIDS in Ireland: Activism, Covert Policy, and the Significance of an 'Invisible Minority'," *Journal of Public Policy* 30, no. 1 (2018): 106.
16 Cristophe Broqua, "AIDS Activism from North to Global," in *The Ashgate Research Companion to Lesbian and Gay Activism*, trans. Sharon Calandra, ed. David Paternotte and Manon Tremblay (New York: Routledge, 2015), 59; Jeffrey Weeks, *Making Sexual History* (Malden, MA: Polity Press, 2000), 195.
17 Weeks, *Making Sexual History*, 195.
18 Broqua, "AIDS Activism from North to Global," 64.

19 Claire E. Ernst, "Activisme à l'américaine ["American-style activism"]? The Case of Act Up-Paris," *French Politics and Society* 15, no. 4 (Fall 1997): 24–5.
20 Broqua, "AIDS Activism from North to Global," 59; Weeks, *Making Sexual History*, 195.
21 Nolan, "The Gay Community Response," 106, 108.
22 Ibid., 107.
23 Ibid., 110.
24 Ibid., 111.
25 Ibid.; Broqua, "AIDS Activism from North to Global," 59; Weeks, *Making Sexual History*, 195.
26 Natalie Adler, "The Real Story of ACT UP: A New Book by Sarah Schulman Spotlights the Women Who Unleashed Power," *Lux Magazine*, August 2021, https://lux-magazine.com/article/the-real-story-of-act-up-sarah-schulman/, accessed September 21, 2025.
27 Emily Scharf and Sue Toole, "HIV and the Invisibility of Women: Is There a Need to Redefine AIDS?" *Feminist Review* 41 (1992): 65.
28 Ibid., 64.
29 James Chin, "Current and Future Dimensions of the HIV/AIDS Pandemic in Women and Children," *The Lancet* 336 (1990): 221.
30 J. Chin, "Current and Future Dimensions," 221.
31 Sue O'Sullivan and Kate Thompson eds., *Positively Women: Living with AIDS* (London: Sheba Feminist Press, 1992), 3, 9.
32 Ibid., 17.
33 Ibid., 89.
34 Ibid., 37.
35 Ibid., 38, 48.
36 Justyna Struzik, "Disentangling the 1980s and 1990s in Poland: Milestones and Framework of HIV/AIDS Policies," in *Disentangling European HIV/AIDS Policies: Activism, Citizenship and Health (Europach)*, Working Paper no. 17–001/5. https://europach.phils.uj.edu.pl/project-outcomes/library/workingpapers/, accessed February 3, 2025, 9.
37 Samuel Clowes Huneke, *States of Liberation: Gay Men Between Dictatorship and Democracy in Cold War Germany* (Toronto: University of Toronto Press, 2022), 212–13.
38 Mihály Riszovannij, "Self-Articulation of the Gay and Lesbian Movement in Hungary after 1989," in *Pink, Purple, Green: Women's, Religious, Environmental and Gay/Lesbian Movement in Central Europe Today*, ed. Helena Flam (New York: Columbia University Press, 2001), 150.
39 Jill Owczarak, "Defining Democracy and the Terms of Engagement with the Postsocialist Polish State: Insights from HIV/AIDS," *East European Politics and Societies* 23, no. 3 (2009): 427.
40 Owczarak, "Defining Democracy," 427.
41 "Breast Cancer," *World Health Organization*, March 26, 2021. https://www.who.int/news-room/fact-sheets/detail/breast-cancer, accessed February 2, 2022.
42 Philippe Autier, Mathieu Boniol, Anna Gavin, and Lars Vatten, "Breast Cancer Mortality in Neighbouring European Countries with Different Levels of Screening but Similar Access to Treatment: Trend Analysis of WHO Mortality Database," *British Medical Journal* 343 (2001): 1.

43. Ibid.
44. Ibid.
45. Vakhtang M. Merabishvili, Vladimir F. Semiglazov, L.S. Serova, and M. M. Buslayeva, "Geographical Distribution of Breast Cancer in the USSR," *International Journal of Cancer* 34 (1984): 71–2.
46. Louise Krasniewicz, *Nuclear Summer: The Clash of Communities at the Seneca Women's Peace Encampment* (Ithaca: Cornell University Press, 1992), 2.
47. Petra Karin Kelly, "Green Politics in New Europe: Hope or Change," (Tenth Annual Ava Helen Pauling Memorial Lecture for World Peace, Special Collections and Archives Research Center, Oregon State University ,OR, October 30, 1991).https://scarc.library.oregonstate.edu/events/1991kelly/speakers.html.
48. Petra Karin Kelly, *Fighting for Hope*, trans. Marianna Howarth (Cambridge, MA: South End Press, 1984), 39.
49. Ibid., 103.
50. Andrew S. Tompkins, *Better Active than Radioactive! Anti-Nuclear Protest in 1970s France and West Germany* (Oxford: Oxford University Press, 2016), 212.
51. Kelly, *Fighting for Hope*, 19, 30.
52. Laura Branciforte, "The Women's Peace Camp at Comiso, 1983: Transnational Feminism and the Anti-nuclear Movement," *Women's History Review* (October 2021): 1–29.
53. Tompkins, *Better Active*, 62.
54. Ibid., 63.
55. Astrid Mignon Kirchhof, *Pathways into and out of Nuclear Power in Western Europe: Austria, Denmark, Federal Republic of Germany, Italy, and Sweden* (Munich: Deutsches Museum, 2020), 21.
56. Cornelia Frey, "Wachsam in Holzpalästen: Im Gorlebener Friedensdorf leisten Atomkraftgegner Widerstand" ["Vigilant in wooden palaces: Nuclear power opponents are resisting in the Gorleben Peace Village"], *Die Zeit*, May 30, 1980. https://www.zeit.de/1980/23/wachsam-in-holzpalaesten/komplettansicht, accessed September 22, 2025.
57. Tompkins, *Better Active*, 187, 124.
58. Frey, "Wachsam in Holzpalästen."
59. Women's antimilitarist campaigns have been active for over two centuries. See Margaret L. Laware, "Circling the Missiles and Staining them Red: Feminist Rhetorical Invention and Strategies of Resistance at the Women's Peace Camp at Greenham Common," *NWSA Journal* 16, no. 3 (2004): 18.
60. Laware, "Circling the Missiles," 18.
61. Ibid., 19.
62. Belinda A. Stillion Southard, "Rhetorical Legacies of the National Women's Party: Shuttling Rhetorics, Endurance, and Survival," *Quarterly Journal of Speech* 106, no. 3 (2020): 264.
63. Wilmette Brown, *Black Women and the Peace Movement* (London: Calvert's Press, 1983), 5.
64. Brown, *Black Women*, 5.

65 Hazel Z. Carby, "White Women Listen! Black Feminisms and the Boundaries of Sisterhood," in *The Empire Strikes Back: Race and Racism in 70s Britain*, ed. Centre for Contemporary Culture (London: Hutchinson, 1982), 112.
66 Nanette Funk, "A Very Tangled Knot: Official State Socialist Women's Organizations, Women's Agency and Feminism in Eastern European State Socialism," *European Journal of Women's Studies* 21, no. 4 (2014): 345.
67 Zsófia Lóránd, "Feminism as Counterdiscourse [sic] in Yugoslavia in Two Different Contexts," (MA Thesis, Central European University History Department, Budapest, 2007), 26.
68 Weissbort, "The Ordeal," 576–7.
69 Lóránd, "Feminism as Counterdiscourse [sic] in Yugoslavia," 20.
70 Henry P. David and Joanna Skilogianis, "The Woman Question," in *From Abortion to Contraception: A Resource to Public Policies and Reproductive Behavior in Central and Eastern Europe from 1917 to the Present*, ed. Henry P. David (Greenwood, CT: Greenwood Press, 1999), 44.
71 Bolton, *Worlds of Dissent*, 115.
72 Ibid., 192.
73 M. Martin, "The Growth of Czech Feminism, 38–9.
74 Bolton, *Worlds of Dissent*, 248.
75 Ibid.
76 Helena Flam, "Dissenting Intellectuals and Plain Dissenters," in *Intellectuals and Politics in Central Europe*, ed. Andr Bozcki (New York: Central European University Press, 1999), 21.
77 Frauen für Frieden, "Christen und Pazifisten in der DDR—Staatsfeinde?" ["Women for Peace, Christians, and Pacifists in the GDR—Enemies of the State?"] (Autumn 1983), reprinted in Berhard Pollmann ed., *Lesebuch zur deutsche Geschichte, vom deutschen Reich bis zur Gegenwart*, Vol. 3 (Dortmund: Chronik, 1984), 268–70.
78 Flam, "Dissenting Intellectuals," 21.
79 Kim Lane Scheppele and Didier Fassin, "Responses and Discussion," in *The Humanities and Public Life*, ed. Peter Brooks (New York: Fordham University Press, 2014), 124–5.
80 Kenney, "The Gender Resistance," 408–9.
81 Magdalena Kubow, "The Solidarity Movement in Poland: Its History and Meaning in Collective Memory," *The Polish Review* 58, no. 2 (2013): 10.
82 Ibid.
83 Penn, *Solidarity's Secret*, 5–6.
84 Ibid., 10.
85 Kenney, "Gender Resistance," 416, 419.
86 Judt, *Postwar*, 597–8.
87 Ibid., 598.
88 Kate Brown, *Plutopia: Nuclear Families, Atomic Cities, and the Great Soviet and American Plutonium Disasters* (Oxford: Oxford University Press, 2013), 286.
89 Silvia Meybatyan, "Nuclear disasters and displacement," *Forced Migration Review* 45 (February 2014): 63–5.
90 Alla Yaroshinskaya, *Chernobyl: The Forbidden Truth*, trans. Michèle Kahn and Julia Sallabank (Lincoln: University of Nebraska Press, 1995).

91 Kate Brown, *Manual for Survival: An Environmental History of the Chernobyl Disaster* (New York: W. W. Norton, 2019), 241–4.
92 Brown, *Plutopia*, 283.
93 Ibid., 325–6.
94 Ibid.
95 Ibid., 328.
96 "Transcript of Barbara Labuda. Interviewer: Sławomira Walczewsak," Warsaw, November 2003, trans. Kasia Kietlińska, Global Feminisms: Comparative Case Studies of Women's Activism and Scholarship, Site: Poland, Rundacja Kobieca, eFKa Women's Foundation, https://sites.lsa.umich.edu/globalfeminisms/wp-content/uploads/sites/787/2020/05/Labuda_P_E_102806.pdf, accessed January 31, 2025.
97 Clair Apodaga, "Global Economic Patterns and Personal Integrity Rights After the Cold War," *International Studies Quarterly* 45, no. 4 (2001): 594.
98 Donna J. Sullivan, "Women's Human Rights and the 1993 World Conference on Human Rights," *The American Journal of International Law* 88, no. 1 (1994): 156, 160–3.
99 During the Cold War era, the socialist republics that made up the Socialist Federal Republic of Yugoslavia were Bosnia–Herzegovina, Croatia, Macedonia, Montenegro, Serbia, and Slovenia. Serbia also had two autonomous socialist provinces, Kosovo and Vojvodina. Yugoslavia was always nonaligned and never a Soviet satellite state.
100 Jacques Semelin, "Analysis of a Mass Crime: Ethnic Cleansing in the Former Yugoslavia, 1991–1999," in *The Specter of Genocide: Mass Murder in Historical Perspective*, ed. Robert Gellately and Ben Kiernan (Cambridge: Cambridge University Press, 2003), 368; Ann Petrila and Hasan Hasanović, *Voices from Srebrenica: Survivor Narratives of the Bosnian Genocide* (Jefferson, NC: McFarland, 2021), 218.
101 After the 1948 UN Convention on the Prevention and Punishment of the crime of genocide, it became, oddly enough, more difficult to define genocide. Scholars have disagreed on the scope of genocide's definition with some declaring it too narrow and others too broad. See Semelin, "Analysis of a Mass Crime," 353.
102 Jennifer Turpin and Lois Ann Lorentzen, eds., *The Gendered New World Order: Militarism, Development, and the Environment* (New York: Routledge, 1996), 6; Petrila and Hasanović, *Voices from Srebrenica*, 201.
103 Lynda E. Boose, "Crossing the River Drina: Bosnian Rape Camps, Turkish Impalement, and Serb Cultural Memory," *Signs: Journal of Women in Culture and Society* 28, no. 1 (2002): 71.
104 Semelin, "Analysis of a Mass Crime," 353.
105 Véronique Nahoum-Grappe, "L'usage politique de la cruauté: L'épuration ethnique (ex-Yugoslavie 1991–1995)" ["The political use of cruelty: Ethnic cleansing (former Yugoslavia 1991–1995)"], in *De la violence*, ed. Séminaire de Françoise Héritier (Paris, 1996): 273–323, quoted in Semelin, "Analysis of a Mass Crime," 369; Petrila and Hasanović, *Voices from Srebrenica*, 205; Semelin, "Analysis of a Mass Crime," 355, 361.
106 Semelin, "Analysis of a Mass Crime," 361; See also, Mirko Grmek, "Un mémoricide," ["a memorycide"] in *Le Figaro*, December 19, 1991.
107 Semelin, "Analysis of a Mass Crime," 355, 361.

108 Elma Leydesdorff, *Surviving the Bosnian Genocide: The Women of Srebrenica Speak*, trans. Kay Richardson (Bloomington: Indiana University Press, 2011), 61.
109 Ibid., 61.
110 Ibid., 2. About 8,000 Muslim men and boys were massacred near Srebrenica in Bosnia–Herzegovina by Bosnian Serb troops in July 1995. In 2017, the International Criminal Court in The Hague ruled that Dutch UN Peacekeepers were partly liable for 300 of these deaths, since the area had been declared a UN safe zone. Daniel Boffey, "Srebrenica massacre: Duch soldiers let 300 Muslims die, court rules," *The Guardian*, June 27, 2017.
111 Leydesdorff, *Surviving*, 8.
112 Ibid., 22.
113 Daubié, "A Women's Therapy Center in Zenica, Bosnia," in *Lives and Voices* (February 23, 1995), 623.
114 "Report of the International Tribunal for the Prosecution of persons responsible for serious violations of international humanitarian law committed in the territory of the former Yugoslavia since 1991," *United Nations*, General Assembly Security Council, August 29, 1994; "Innovative Procedure: Hearing, protecting and counseling survivors of sexual violence," *United Nations International Criminal Tribunal for the former Yugoslavia*, https://www.icty.org/en/features/crimes-sexual-violence/innovative-procedures, accessed November 15, 2021.
115 "Landmark Cases," *United Nations International Criminal Tribunal for the former Yugoslavia*, https://www.icty.org/en/features/crimes-sexual-violence/landmark-cases, accessed November 15, 2021.
116 "Report of the International Tribunal for the Prosecution"; "Innovative Procedure," https://www.icty.org/en/features/crimes-sexual-violence/innovative-procedures, accessed November 15, 2021.
117 Leydesdorff, *Surviving*, 8.
118 Ibid., 22.
119 "Bosnia and Herzegovina: 'Whose justice?': The Women of Bosnia and Herzegovina Are Still Waiting," *Amnesty International*, September 20, 2009, Index Number: EUR 63/006/2009. https://www.amnesty.org/en/documents/eur63/006/2009/en/, accessed September 21, 2025.
120 Scott, *Politics of the Veil*, 22.
121 Ibid., 52.
122 Ayaan Hirsi Ali, *Caged Virgin: An Emancipation Proclamation for Women and Islam* (New York: Atria, 2015), 7.
123 Scott, *Politics of the Veil*, 21.
124 Tiffany N. Florvil, "Connected Differences: Black German Feminists and Their Transnational Connections in the 1980s and 1990s," in *Gendering Post-1945 German History: Entanglements*, ed. Karen Hagemann, Donna Harsch, and Frederike Brühöfener (New York: Berghahn, 2019), 229–30.
125 Ibid.
126 Ibid., 230, 233.
127 Ibid., 233.
128 Tiffany Florvil, Dagmar Schults, and the Free University of Berlin Archive, https://feminismandthemedia.co.uk/stories/audre-lorde-and-afro-german-feminisms/, accessed January 26, 2022.

129 May Ayim, Katharina Oguntoye, and Dagmar Schultz, eds., *Showing our Colors: Afro-German Women Speak Out* (Amherst: University of Massachusetts Press, 1991); See also, Akwugo Emejulu and Francesca Sobande, eds., *To Exist is to Resist: Black Feminism in Europe* (London: Pluto Press, 2019) 288, 3 fn 1.

8 The New Millennium

1 Fluehr-Lobban and Mancici Billson, *Female Well-Being*, 374.
2 Christiane Krieger-Boden and Alina Sorgner, "Labor market opportunities for women in the digital age," *Economics* 12 (2018): 1.
3 Geeta Rao Gupta, "Globalization, Women and the HIV/AIDS Epidemic," *Peace Review* 16, no. 1 (2004): 79.
4 Fluehr-Lobban and Mancici Billson, *Female Well-Being*, 375.
5 Turpin and Lorentzen, *The Gendered New World Order*, 2, 3, 7, 17–19, 41, 131–3, 187; Fluerh-Lobben and Mancici Billson, *Female Well-Being*, 5–7; Gerben Bruinsma ed., *Histories of Transnational Crime* (New York: Springer, 2015).
6 Tiantian Zheng ed., *Sex Trafficking, Human Rights, and Social Justice* (London: Routledge, 2010), 102.
7 Timm and Sanborn note European mass culture has seized on the Eastern European prostitute: "The figure of the East European sex slave proved irresistible for cultural producers. Television shows, movies and novels repeated this story ... so often that it became a staple theme of contemporary European mass culture" in *Gender, Sex, and The Shaping of Modern Europe*, 225.
8 Siddharth Kara, *Sex Trafficking: Inside the Business of Modern Slavery* (New York: Columbia University Press, 2009), 84.
9 Kara, *Sex Trafficking*, 85.
10 Ibid.
11 Kara, *Sex Trafficking*, 86.
12 Ibid.; TAMPEP is the European Network for the Promotion of Rights and Heath among Migrant Sex Workers and was founded in 1993 in response to the needs of migrant sex workers across Europe. It has operated in twenty-five different countries and reached over eighty different nationalities since it began. https://tampep.eu.
13 Timm and Sanborn, *Gender, Sex, and the Shaping of Modern Europe*, 256.
14 Ibid., 256–7.
15 Ibid., 253.
16 Nicholas Denysenko, "An Appeal to Mary: An Analysis of Pussy Riot's Punk Performance in Moscow," *Journal of the American Academy of Religion* 81, no. 4 (2013): 1085.
17 Marina Yusupova, "Pussy Riot: Feminist Band Lost in History and Translation," *Nationalities Papers: Journal of Nationalism and Ethnicity* 42, no. 4 (2014): 604.
18 Yusupova, "Pussy Riot," 605.

19 Emily Channell, "Is Sextremism the New Feminism? Perspectives from Pussy Riot and Femen," *Nationalities Papers: Journal of Nationalism and Ethnicity* 42, no. 4 (2014): 611.
20 Karina Eileraas, "Sex(t)ing Revolution, Femen-izing the Public Square: Aliaa Magda Elmahdy, Nude Protest, and Transnational Feminist Body Politics," *Signs: Journal of Women in Culture and Society* 40, no. 1 (2014): 40–52.
21 Theresa O'Keefe, "My Body is My Manifesto! Slutwalk, FEMEN and Femmenist Protest," *Feminist Review* 107, no. 1 (2014): 1–19; Mariam Betlemidze, "Mediated Controversies of Feminist Protest: FEMEN and Bodies as Affective Events," *Women's Studies in Communication* 38 (2015): 374–9.
22 O'Keefe, "My Body," 47–48. Despite FEMEN's claims to be "new feminism," a 2013 documentary about the group advances the idea that political scientist Victor Svyatski is the "male mastermind" and potential funder of the groups, further complicating their bodily protests; see O'Keefe, 48.
23 Channell, "Is sextremism the new feminism?," 612.
24 Hajer Naili, "Femen's Islam-Bashing Disregards Muslim Feminism," *Women's eNews*, April 10, 2013, https://womensenews.org/2013/04/femens-islam-bashing-disregards-muslim-feminism/, accessed March 18, 2022.
25 Naz Akyol, "The Topless Imperialists: FEMEN's Brand of Feminism is Silencing Muslim Women," *Brown Political Review*, November 6, 2015, https://brownpoliticalreview.org/the-topless-imperialists-femens-brand-of-feminism-is-silencing-muslim-women/.
26 FEMEN Response on "Silencing Muslim Women" Insinuation, *FEMEN Official Blog*, November 17, 2015. https://brownpoliticalreview.org/the-topless-imperialists-femens-brand-of-feminism-is-silencing-muslim-women/, accessed September 22, 2025.
27 See, for example, Anna Korteweg and Gökçe Yurdakul, *Islam, Gender, and Immigrant Integration: boundary drawing in discourses on honour killing in the Netherlands and Germany* (New York: Routledge, 2012).
28 Rita Chin, *The Crisis of Multiculturalism in Europe: A History* (Princeton: Princeton University Press, 2017), 276.
29 Scott, *The Politics of the Veil*, 4–10, 17, 22, 32, 35, 45, 63, 71.
30 Fadela Amara and Sylvia Zappi, *Breaking the Silence: French Women's Voices from the Ghetto*, trans. Helen Harden Chenut (Berkeley: California University Press, 2006), 15, 112–13.
31 Amara and Zappi, *Breaking the Silence*, 2–3.
32 "Muslim Girl Shaves Head Over Ban," *BBC News*, October 1, 2004. http://news.bbc.co.uk/2/hi/europe/3708444.stm, accessed February 19, 2022.
33 Ibid.
34 Katherine Pratt Ewing, *Stolen Honor: Stigmatizing Muslim Men in Berlin* (Stanford: Stanford University Press, 2008), 4–5, 17–19, 53–4, 166; Carolin Wildt, *Kann Morden Ehre Sein? Ursachen von Ehrenmorden in Deutschland am Beispiel Hatun Sürücü* (Hamburg: Diplomica Verlag, 2014), 3.
35 Anna Korteweg and Gökçe Yurdakul, "Islam, Gender, and Immigrant Integration: Boundary Drawing in Discourses on Honour Killing in the Netherlands and Germany," *Ethnic and Racial Studies* 32, no. 2 (2009): 218–19.
36 Korteweg and Yurdakul, "Islam, gender and immigrant integration," 222.
37 Ibid.

38 Esra Özyürek, "Convert Alert: German Muslims and Turkish Christians as Threats to Security in the New Europe," *Comparative Studies in Society and History* 51, no. 1 (2009): 98.
39 Ibid., 99; Astrid Geisler, "Sicherheit in Zeiten von Terroralarm: Angst macht Angst" ["Security in Times of Terror Alert: Fear breeds Fear"] *Taz*, November 29, 2010.
40 Ibid.
41 Ibid.
42 Timm and Sandborn, *Gender, Sex, and the Shaping of Modern Europe*, 262.
43 Achim Hildebrandt, "Routes to Decriminalization: A Comparative Analysis of the Legalization of Same-sex Sexual Acts," *Sexualities* 17, no. 1/2 (2014): 245; See also, Council of the European Union, "Guidelines to Promote and Protect the Enjoyment of All Human Rights by Lesbians, Gay, Bisexual, Transgender and Intersex (LGBTI) Persons," Foreign Affairs Council Meeting, Luxembourg, June 24, 2013. https://www.eeas.europa.eu/sites/default/files/07_hr_guidelines_lgbti_en.pdf, accessed September 22, 2025.
44 Ibid.
45 Anne Lise Ellingsaeter and Ragnhild Steen Jensen, "Politicising Women's Part-Time Work in Norway: A Longitudinal Study of Ideas," *Work, Employment, and Society* (2019): 4.
46 Stokes, *Fear of the Family*, 219–21.
47 "Why Swedish Men Take so Much Paternity Leave," *The Economist*, July 23, 2014. https://www.economist.com/the-economist-explains/2014/07/22/why-swedish-men-take-so-much-paternity-leave, accessed July 9, 2024.
48 Ásdís A. Arnalds, Guðný Björk Eydal, and Ingólfur V. Gíslason, "Equal Rights to Paid Parental Leave and Caring Fathers-the Case of Iceland," *Icelandic Review of Politics and Administration* 9, no. 2 (2013): 323–44; Carmen Castro-García and Maria Pazos-Moran, "Paternal Leave Policy and Gender Equality in Europe," *Feminist Economics* 22, no. 3 (2016): 5, 7.
49 Gunhild R. Farstad, "Difference and Equality: Icelandic Parents' Division of Parental Leave within the Context of a Childcare Gap," *Community, Work, and Family* 18, no. 3 (2015): 354.
50 Ibid., 359.
51 Ibid., 357.
52 The states were known under the pejorative acronym PIGS, for Portugal, Ireland, Greece, and Spain.
53 Roberta Guerrina and Annick Masselot, "Walking into the Footprint of EU Law and the Gendered Consequences of Brexit," *Social Policy and Society* 17, no. 2 (2018): 320.
54 Johanna Kantola and Emanuela Lombardo, eds., *Gender and the Economic Crisis in Europe: Politics, Institutions, and Intersectionality* (New York: Palgrave Macmillan, 2017), 195.
55 Josep Maria Antentas and Esther Vivas, "Scissors of Debt: Comments from Southern Europe," *Women's Studies Quarterly* 42, no. 1 and 2 (2014): 53; Francesca Bettio, Marcella Corsi, Carlo D'Ippoliti, Antigone Lyberaki, Manuela Samek Lodovici and Alina Verashchagina, "The Impact of the Economic Crisis on the Situation of Women and Men and on Gender Equality Policies," December 2012, Report prepared for European Commission Directorate-General for Justice, Unit D2.

56 Quoted in Antentas and Vicas, "Scissors of Debt," 59.
57 Devaki Jain, *Women, Development, and the UN: A Sixty-Year Quest for Equality and Justice* (Bloomington: Indiana University Press, 2005), 136.
58 "UN Women: United Nations Entity for Gender Equality and the Empowerment of Women," https://www.un.org/youthenvoy/2013/07/un-women-the-united-nations-entity-for-gender-equality-and-the-empowerment-of-women/, accessed February 2, 2025; UN Women, 2010, https://www.unwomen.org/en/about-us/about-un-women; United Nations Human Rights Office launched the Free and Equal, 2013, https://www.unfe.org/.
59 Anthony King, "Women in Combat," *The Royal United Services Institute Journal* 158, no. 1 (2013): 4–11.
60 "Women in the NATO Armed Forces, Year-in-Review, 1999–2000," The Office on Women in the NATO Forces, International Military Staff, NATO Headquarters, Brussels, Belgium.
61 "Norway Extends Mandatory Military Service To Women," *Deutsche Welle*, June 24, 2013, https://p.dw.com/p/18qMU.
62 "Women Join German Fighting Forces," *BBC News*, January 2, 2001. http://news.bbc.co.uk/1/hi/world/europe/1097492.stm, accessed March 14, 2022.
63 Nina Werkhäuser, "Germany Marks Five Years of Women in Armed Forces," *Deutsche Welle*, January 2, 2006. https://p.dw.com/p/7jLq, accessed September 22, 2025.
64 Allan Hall, "German Troops Taught How To Treat Women," *The Telegraph*, December 17, 2000.
65 "Women join German Fighting Forces," *BBC News*, January 2, 2001.
66 "Row over frontline Women Troops," *BBC News*, December 24, 2000. http://news.bbc.co.uk/2/hi/uk_news/1086226.stm, accessed September 22, 2025.
67 Paul Cawkill, Alison Rogers, Sarah Knight, and Laura Spear, "Women in Ground Close Combat Roles: The Experiences of other Nations and a Review of the Academic Literature," Defense Science and Technology Laboratory, Human Systems Group, Grenville Building Information Management Department, DSTL Portsdown West Fareham, Hants, P017 6 AD, September 29, 2009, (Crown Copywrite, DSTL, 2010), 1.
68 Northern Ireland was an exception, choosing to remain within the European Single Market and in the EU Customs Union.
69 Niall Ó Dochartaigh, Kay Hayward, and Elizabeth Meehan, *Dynamics of Political Change in Ireland: Making and Breaking a Divided Island* (New York: Routledge, 2017), 4; Guerrina and Masselot, "Walking into the Footprint of EU Law and the Gendered Consequences of Brexit," 319–30.
70 Dochartaigh, Hayward, and Meehan, *Dynamics of Political Change in Ireland*, 3–4.
71 Guerrina and Masselot, "Walking in the Footprint of EU Law," 321.
72 Ibid.
73 "Black Lives Matter," https://blacklivesmatter.com/.
74 Madeleine Kennedy and Dubravka Zarkov, "Black Lives Matter in Europe," *European Journal of Women's Studies Special Open Forum* (December 2021), S3–S5.
75 Ibid.

76 "Adama Traoré: French anti-racism protests defy police ban," *BBC*, June 3, 2020, https://www.bbc.com/news/world-europe-52898262, accessed February 28, 2022.
77 Haroon Siddique and Clea Skopeliti, "BLM protesters topple statue of Bristol Slave Trader Edward Colston," *The Guardian*, June 7, 2020.
78 Alex Finnis, "Who is Jen Reid? The Black Lives Matter activist whose statue replaced Edward Colston's in Bristol, before it was taken down." The iPaper, July 19, 2020. https://inews.co.uk/news/uk/jen-reid-blm-activist-statue-colston-bristol-539776, accessed February 28, 2022.
79 Haroon Siddique and Clea Skopeliti, "BLM protesters topple statue of Bristol Slave Trader Edward Colston," *The Guardian*, June 7, 2020.
80 "Transcript: Greta Thunberg's Speech at the UN Climate Action Summit" *National Public Radio (NPR)*, September 23, 2019. https://www.npr.org/2019/09/23/763452863/transcript-greta-thunbergs-speech-at-the-u-n-climate-action-summit, accessed February 28, 2022.
81 Kate Lyons, "'She seems very happy': Trump appears to mock Greta Thunberg's emotional speech," *The Guardian*, September 24, 2019.
82 Damian Carrington, "'Blah, Blah, Blah': Greta Thunberg lambasts leaders over climate crisis," *The Guardian*, September 28, 2021.
83 "Global Roadmap for Accelerated SDG7 Action in Support of the 2030 Agenda for Sustainable Development and the Paris Agreement on Climate Change," High-Level Dialogue on Energy, United Nations, New York, September 2021. General Assembly resolution 74/225.
84 Ibid.
85 Ibid.

Conclusion

1 Marion Moncrieffe, "Young Powerful Women in Cycling: Advancing Anti-Racism in Cycling," *Science in Sport*, February 9, 2021. https://www.scienceinsport.com/sports-nutrition/advancing-anti-racism-in-cycling-powerful-young-women/, accessed September 22, 2025; "Track Cycling: The 'Crazy' Rise of Taky Marie-Divine Kouamé," Union Cycliste Internationale (UCI), May 6, 2025. https://www.uci.org/article/track-cycling-the-crazy-rise-of-taky-marie-divine-kouame/2ZcOCXjRGmoKghzpgUyh7M, accessed September 22, 2025; See also, Marlon Moncrieffe, *New Black Cyclones: Racism, Representation and Revolutions of Power in Cycling* (Bloomsbury, 2024), 76–81, 131, 146.
2 In 2004, the BBC released a poll for the "100 Greatest Britons" that included no Black Britons. In response, British historians Patrick Vernon, Officer of the Order of the British Empire (OBE) appointed in 2012, and Dr. Angelina Osborne released a poll for the Greatest Black Britons and Seacole topped the list. 100 Great Black Britons, https://www.100greatblackbritons.co.uk/.

BIBLIOGRAPHY

Abandan-Unat, Nermin. *Turks in Europe: From Guest Worker to Transnational Citizen*. Translated by Caterine Campion. New York: Berghahn, 2011.

Abbate, Janet. *Recoding Gender: Women's Changing Participation in Computing*. Cambridge, MA: The MIT Press, 2012.

Adamson, Maria, and Erika Kispeter. "Gender and Professional Work in Russia and Hungary." In *Gender in Twentieth-Century Eastern Europe and the USSR*. Edited by Catherine Baker. New York: Palgrave Macmillan, 2017. 214–27.

Akçam, Taner. *The Young Turks' Crimes against Humanity: The Armenian Genocide and Ethnic Cleansing in the Ottoman Empire*. Princeton: Princeton University Press, 2012.

Akgündüz, Ahmet. "Guest Worker Migration in Post-war Europe (1946–1974): An Analytical Appraisal." In *An Introduction to International Migration Studies*. Edited by Marco Martiniello and Jan Rath. Chicago: University of Chicago Press, 2012. 181–209.

Alexievich, Svetlana. *The Unwomanly Face of War: An Oral History of Women in World War II*. Translated by Richard Pevear and Larissa Volokhonsky. New York: Random House, 2017.

Allen, Ann Taylor. *Women in Twentieth-Century Europe*. New York: Palgrave Macmillan, 2008.

Amara, Fadela, and Sylvia Zappi. *Breaking the Silence: French Women's Voices from the Ghetto*. Translated by Helen Harden Chenut. Berkeley: California University Press, 2006.

Åmark, Klas. "Women's Labour Force Participation in the Nordic Countries during the Twentieth Century." In *The Nordic Model of Welfare: A Historical Reappraisal*. Edited by Niels Finn Christiansen, Klaus Petersen, Nils Edling, and Per Have. Copenhagen: Museum Tusculanum Press, 2005. 299–334.

Amerian, Stephanie M. "The Fashion Gap: The Cold War Politics of American and Soviet fashion, 1945–1959." Journal of Historical Research in Marketing 8, no. 1 (2016): 65–82.

Anderson, Bonnie. *Joyous Greetings: The First International Women's Movement, 1830–1860*. Oxford: Oxford University Press, 2000.

Anitha, Sundari, Ruth Pearson, and Linda McDowell. "Striking Lives: Multiple Narratives of South Asian Women's Employment, Identity and Protest in the UK." Ethnicities 12, no. 6 (2012): 754–75.

Antentas, Josep Maria, and Esther Vivas. "The Scissors of Debt: Comments from Southern Europe." Women's Studies Quarterly 42, no. 1/2 (2014): 49–64.

Anton, Lorena. "On Memory Work in Post-communist Europe: A Case Study on Romania's Ways of Remembering Its Pronatalist Past." Anthropological Journal of European Cultures 18, no. 2 (2006): 106–22.

Apodaca, Clair. "Global Economic Patterns and Personal Integrity Rights after the Cold War." *International Studies Quarterly* 45, no. 4 (2001): 587–602.

Arnalds, Ásdís A., Guðný Björk Eydal, and Ingólfur V. Gíslason. "Equal Rights to Paid Parental Leave and Caring Fathers-the Case of Iceland." *Icelandic Review on Politics & Administration* 9, no. 2 (2013): 323–44.

Audoin-Rouzeau, Stéphane, and Annette Becker. *14–18: Understanding the Great War*. Translated by Catherine Temerson. New York: Hill and Wang, 2002.

Autier, Philippe, Mathieu Boniol, Anna Gavin, and Lars Vatten. "Breast Cancer Mortality in Neighbouring European Countries with Different Levels of Screening but Similar Access to Treatment: Trend Analysis of WHO Mortality Database." *British Medical Journal* 343 (2001): 1–10.

Ayim, May, Katharina Oguntoye, and Dagmar Schultz, eds. *Showing Our Colors: Afro-German Women Speak Out*. Amherst: University of Massachusetts Press, 1991.

Baader, Meike S. "Childhood and Happiness in German Romanticism, Progressive Education and in the West German Anti-authoritarian *Kinderläden* Movement in the Context of 1968." *Paedagogica Historica* 48, no. 3 (June 2012): 485–99.

Barany, Zoltan. "The East European Gypsies in the Imperial Age." *Ethnic and Racial Studies* 24, no. 1 (2001): 50–63.

Barry, Kathleen. *Femininity in Flight: A History of Flight Attendants*. Durham: Duke University Press, 2007.

Batinić, Jelena. *Women and Yugoslav Partisans: A History of World War II Resistance*. Cambridge: Cambridge University Press, 2015.

Bauer, Yehuda. *Rethinking the Holocaust*. New Haven: Yale University Press, 2002.

Beiner, Guy. *Pandemic Re-awakenings: The Forgotten and Unforgotten "Spanish Flu" of 1918–1919*. Oxford: Oxford University Press, 2022.

Berenson, Edward. *Europe in the Modern World: A New Narrative History since 1500*. Oxford: Oxford University Press, 2017.

Bergen, Doris L. *War and Genocide: A Concise History of the Holocaust*, 3rd ed. New York: Rowman and Littlefield, 2016.

Bernhard, Pollmann. *Lesebuch zur deutschen Geschichte: Texte und Dokumente aus zwei Jahrtausend*, Vol 3. Dortmund: Chronik, 1984.

Bessel, Richard. "The Shadow of Death in Germany at the End of the Second World War." In *Between Mass Death and Individual Loss: The Place of the Dead in Twentieth-Century Germany*. Edited by Alon Confino, Paul Betts, and Dirk Schumann. New York: Berghahn Book, 2008. 51–68.

Biess, Frank. *Homecomings: Returning POWS and the Legacies of Defeat in Postwar Germany*. Princeton: Princeton University Press, 2006.

Birkett, Dea. "Wartime Women at Work." *Engineering & Technology* 9, no. 6 (2014): 52–5.

Bock, Gisela, and Pat Thane, eds. *Maternity and Gender Policies: Women and the Rise of the European Welfare States, 1880s-1950s*. New York: Routledge, 1994.

Bock, Gisela. "Racism and Sexism in Nazi Germany: Motherhood, Compulsory Sterilization, and the State." In *When Biology Becomes Destiny: Women in Weimar and Nazi Germany*. Edited by Bridenthal, Atina Grossmann, and Marion Kaplan. New York: Monthly Review Press, 1984. 271–96.

Bohachevsky-Chomiak, Martha. *Feminists Despite Themselves: Women in Ukrainian Community Life, 1884–1939*. Toronto: University of Toronto Press, 1988.

Boittin, Jennifer A. *Colonial Metropolis: The Urban Grounds of Anti-imperialism and Feminism in Interwar Paris*. Lincoln: University of Nebraska Press, 2010.

Bonham, Jennifer, and Kat Jungnickel. "Cycling and Gender: Past, Present and Paths Ahead." In *The Routledge Companion to Cycling*. Edited by Glen Norcliffe, Una Brogan, Peter Cox, Boyang Gao, Tony Hadland, Sheila Hanlon, Tim Jones, Nicholas Oddy, and Luis Vivanco. London: Routledge, 2022. 24–32.

Boose, Lynda E. "Crossing the River Drina: Bosnian Rape Camps, Turkish Impalement, and Serb Cultural Memory." *Signs: Journal of Women in Culture and Society* 28, no. 1 (2002): 71–96.

Borgos, Anna. "Secret Years: Hungarian Lesbian Herstory, 1950s–2000s." *Aspasia* 9, no. 1 (2015): 87–112.

Boxer, Marilyn J., and Jean H. Quataert, eds. *Connecting Spheres: European Women in a Globalizing World*. New York: Oxford University Press, 2000.

Brack, Maud Anne. "Between the Transnational and the Local: mapping trajectories and contexts of the Wages for Housework Campaign in 1970s Italian Feminism." *Women's History Review* 22, no. 4 (2013): 607–24.

Branciforte, Laura. "The Women's Peace Camp at Comiso, 1983: Transnational Feminism and the Anti-nuclear Movement." *Women's History Review* 31, no. 2 (2022): 316–43.

Bren, Paulina. "1968 East and West: Visions of Political Change and Student Protests from across the Iron Curtain," In *Transnational Moments of Change: Europe 1945, 1968, 1989*. Edited by Gerd-Rainer Horn and Padraic Kenney. New York: Rowan and Littlefield Publishers, 2004.

Brittain, Vera. *Chronicle of Youth: War Diary 1913–1917*. London: Fontana Collins, 1982.

Broqua, Cristophe. "AIDS Activism from North to Global." In The *Ashgate Research Companion to Lesbian and Gay Activism*. Edited by David Paternotte and Manon Tremblay. Translated by Sharon Calandra. New York: Routledge, 2015.

Brown, Kate. *Manual for Survival: An Environmental History of the Chernobyl Disaster*. New York: W. W. Norton, 2019.

Brown, Kate. *Plutopia: Nuclear Families, Atomic Cities, and the Great Soviet and American Plutonium Disasters*. Oxford: Oxford University Press, 2013.

Brown, Wilmette. *Black Women and the Peace Movement*. London: Calvert's Press, 1983.

Bruinsma, Gerben, ed. *Histories of Transnational Crime*. New York: Springer, 2015.

Bucur, Maria. "Romania." In *Women, Gender, and Fascism in Europe, 1919–45*. Edited by Kevin Passmore. New Brunswick, NJ: Rutgers University Press, 2003. 57–78.

Burgess, Colin, and Rex Hall. *The First Soviet Cosmonaut Team: Their Lives, Legacy, and Historical Impact*. New York: Springer, 2009.

Caldwell, Peter C., and Karrin Hanshew. *Germany since 1945: Politics, Culture, and Society*. New York: Bloomsbury, 2018.

Callaghan, Marie Hammond. "Women's Responses to State Violence: Peace Women and Peacebuilding in Northern Ireland." *Canadian Women's Studies* 22, no. 2 (2003): 28–35.

Campani, Giovanna. "Immigrant Women in Southern Europe: Social Exclusion, Domestic Work and Prostitution in Italy." In *Eldorado or Fortress? Migration in Southern Europe*. Edited by Russell King, Gabriella Lazaridis, and Charalambos Tsardanidis. London: Palgrave Macmillan, 2000.

Canning, Kathleen. "Social Policy, Body Politics: Recasting the Social Question in Germany, 1875–1900." In *Gender and Class in Modern Europe*. Edited by Laura L. Frader and Sonya O. Rose. Ithaca, NY: Cornell University Press, 1996. 211–37.

Caravantes, Peggy. *The Many Faces of Josephine Baker Dancer, Singer, Activist, Spy*. Chicago: Chicago Review Press, 2015.

Carby, Hazel Z. "White Women Listen! Black Feminisms and the Boundaries of Sisterhood." In *The Empire Strikes Back: Race and Racism in 70s Britain*. Edited by Centre for Contemporary Culture. London: Hutchinson, 1982.

Carden-Coyne, Ana, and Laura Doan. "Gender and Sexuality." In *Gender and the Great War*. Edited by Susan R. Grazel and Tammy M. Proctor. New York: Oxford University Press, 2017. 91–114.

Castro-García, Carmen, and Maria Pazos-Moran. "Parental Leave Policy and Gender Equality in Europe." *Feminist Economics* 22, no. 3 (2016): 51–73.

Channell, Emily. "Is Sextremism the New Feminism? Perspectives From Pussy Riot and Femen." *Nationalities Papers* 42, no. 4 (2014): 611–14.

Chase, William J. *Workers, Society, and the Soviet State: Labor and Life in Moscow*. Urbana, IL: University of Illinois Press, 1987.

Chauncey Jr., George. "From Sexual Inversion to Homosexuality: The Changing Medical Conceptualization of Female Deviance." *Passion and Power: Sexuality in History* 109 (1989): 1890–940.

Chin, James. "Current and Future Dimensions of the HIV/AIDS Pandemic in Women and Children." *The Lancet* 336, no. 8709 (1990): 221–4.

Chin, Rita. *The Crisis of Multiculturalism in Europe: A History*. Princeton: Princeton University Press, 2017.

Church, Emily Musil. "In Search of Seven Sisters: A Biography of the Nardal Sisters of Martinique." *Callaloo* 36, no. 2 (2013): 375–90.

Clark, Anna. *Desire: A History of European Sexuality*. New York: Routledge, 2008.

Clark, Anna. *The Struggle for the Breeches: Gender and the Making of the British Working Class*. Berkeley: University of California Press, 1995.

Clark, Linda. *Women and Achievements in Nineteenth-Century Europe*. Cambridge: Cambridge University Press, 2008.

Cohen, Jean, Alan Trounson, Karen Dawson, Howard Jones, Johan Hazekamp, Karl Gösta Nygren, and Lars Hamberger. "The Early Days of IVF outside the UK." *Human Reproduction Update* 11, no. 5 (2005): 439–60.

Comiscioli, Elisa. "Trafficking Histories: Women's Migration and Sexual Labor in the Early Twentieth Century." *Deportate, esuli, profughe. Rivista telematica de studi sulla memoria femminile* 40 (2019): 1–13.

Cook, Barnard A., ed. *Women and War: A Historical Encyclopedia from Antiquity to the Present*, Vol. 2. Ann Arbor: University of Michigan, ABC-CLIO, 2006.

Cook, Hera. *The Long Sexual Revolution: English Women, Sex, and Contraception: 1800–1975*. Oxford: Oxford University Press, 2007.

Cravinho, Pedro. "The 'Black Angel' in Lisbon: Josephine Baker Challenges Salazar, Live on Television." *EU-topias: revista de interculturalidad, comunicación y estudios europeos* 18 (2019): 121–31.

Dahlerup, Drude. "Denmark: High Representation of Women without Gender Quotas." In *Breaking Male Dominance in Old Democracies*. Edited by Drude Dahlerup and Monique Leyenaar. Oxford: Oxford University Press, 2013. 146–71.

David, Henry P., and Adriana Baban. "Women's Health and Reproductive Rights: Romanian Experience." *Patient Education and Counseling* 28, no. 3 (1996): 235–45.

David, Henry P., and Joanna Skilogianis. "The Woman Question." In *From Abortion to Contraception: A Resource to Public Policies and Reproductive Behavior in Central and Eastern Europe from 1917 to the Present*. Edited by Henry P. David. Greenwood, CT: Greenwood Press, 1999.

Davis, Belinda J. *Home Fires Burning: Food, Politics, and Everyday Life in World War I Berlin*. Chapel Hill: University of North Carolina Press, 2000.

De Beauvoir, Simone. *The Second Sex*. Translated by H. M. Parshley. New York: Vintage Books, 1989.

De Bock, Jozefien. *Parallel Lives Revisited: Mediterranean Guest Workers and Their Families at Work and in the Neighbourhood, 1960–1980*. New York: Berghahn, 2018.

De Grazia, Victoria. *How Fascism Ruled Women: Italy, 1922–1945*. Berkeley: University of California Press, 1992.

De Jonge, Alex. *The Weimar Chronicle, Prelude to Hitler*. New York: New American Library, 1979.

Denysenko, Nicholas. "An Appeal to Mary: An Analysis of Pussy Riot's Punk Performance in Moscow." *Journal of the American Academy of Religion* 81, no. 4 (2013): 1061–92.

De Zordo, Silvia, Joanna Mishtal, and Lorena Anton, eds. *A Fragmented Landscape: Abortion Governance and Protest Logics in Europe*. New York: Berghahn Press, 2018.

DiCaprio, Lisa, and Merry E. Wiesner, eds. *Lives and Voices: Source in European History*. Boston: Houghton Mifflin, 2001.

Dochartaigh, Niall Ó., Katy Hayward, and Elizabeth Meehan, eds. *Dynamics of Political Change in Ireland: Making and Breaking a Divided Island*. New York: Routledge, 2017.

Doughty, Frances. "Lesbians and International Women's Year: A Report on Three Conferences." In *Our Right to Love: A Lesbian History Resource Book*. Edited by Ginny Vida Englewood Cliffs. NJ: Prentice Hall, 1978. 144–9.

Draper, Elizabeth. *Birth Control in the Modern World: The Role of the Individual in Population Control*, 2nd ed. Baltimore: Penguin, 1972.

Drapikowska, Barbara. "The Military Participation of Women in the Polish Armed Forces." *National Defence University Scientific Quarterly* 91, no. 2 (2013): 127–41.

Drucker, Donna J. *Contraception: A Concise History*. Massachusetts Institute of Technology Press, 2020.

Eileraas, Karina. "Sex (t) ing Revolution, Femen-izing the Public Square: Aliaa Magda Elmahdy, Nude Protest, and Transnational Feminist Body Politics." *Signs: Journal of Women in Culture and Society* 40, no. 1 (2014): 40–52.

Einarsdóttier, Thorgerdur. "Women in Iceland: Strong Women—Myths and Contradictions." In *Female Well-Being: Toward a Global Theory of Social Change*. Edited by Janet Mancini Billson and Carolyn Fluehr-Lobban. New York: Zed Books, 2005.

Einhorn, Barbara. *Cinderella Goes to Market: Citizenship, Gender and Women's Movements in East Central Europe*. New York: Verso, 1993.

Ellis, Havelock. *Studies in the Psychology of Sex: Sexual Inversion*. Philadelphia: F. A. Davis Company, 1901.

Ellingsæter, Anne Lise, and Ragnhild Steen Jensen. "Politicising Women's Part-Time Work in Norway: A Longitudinal Study of Ideas." *Work, Employment and Society* 33, no. 3 (2019): 444–61.

Engel, Barbara Alpern. *Women in Russia, 1700–2000*. Cambridge: Cambridge University Press, 2004.

Engel-Di Mauro, Salvatore A. "Citizenship, Systemic Change, and the Gender Division of Labor." In *Women and Citizenship in Central and Eastern Europe*. Edited by Jasmina Lukić, Joanna Regulska, and Darja Zaviršek. Burlington, VT: Ashgate, 2006. 61–80.

Engelstein, Laura. *Russia in Flames: War, Revolution, Civil War, 1914–1921*. Oxford: Oxford University Press, 2018.

Ernst, Claire E. "Activisme à l'américaine? The Case of Act Up-Paris." *French Politics and Society* 15, no. 4 (Fall 1997): 22–31.

Erskine, Ralph. "The First Naval Enigma Decrypts of World War II." *Cryptologia* 21, no. 1 (1997): 42–6.

Evans, Sara M. "Sons, Daughters, and Patriarchy: Gender and the 1968 Generation." *The American Historical Review* 114, no. 2 (2009): 331–47.

Everett, Suzanne. *Handbook of Contraception and Sexual Health*. New York: Routledge, 2014.

Ewing, Katherine Pratt. *Stolen Honor: Stigmatizing Muslim Men in Berlin*. Stanford: Stanford University Press, 2008.

Fara, Patricia. *A Lab of One's Own: Science and Suffrage in the First World War*. Oxford: Oxford University Press, 2018.

Farstad, Gunhild R. "Difference and Equality: Icelandic Parents' Division of Parental Leave within the Context of a Childcare Gap." *Community, Work & Family* 18, no. 3 (2015): 351–67.

Feinberg, Melissa. *Communism in Eastern Europe*. New York: Routledge, 2022.

Feinberg, Melissa. "Dumplings and Domesticity: Women, Collaboration, and Resistance in the Protectorate of Bohemia and Moravia." In *Gender and War in Twentieth-Century Eastern Europe*. Edited by Nancy W. Wingfield and Maria Bucur-Deckard. Bloomington: University of Indiana Press, 2006. 95–110.

Feinberg, Melissa. *Elusive Equality: Gender, Citizenship, and the Limits of Democracy in Czechoslovakia, 1918–1950*. Pittsburg: University of Pittsburg Press, 2006.

Fernandes, Tiago. "Rethinking Pathways to Democracy: Civil Society in Portugal and Spain, 1960s–2000s." *Democratization* 22, no. 6 (2015): 1074–104.

Fidelis, Malgorzata. "Participation in the Creative Work of the Nation: Polish Women Intellectuals in the Cultural Construction of Female Gender roles, 1864–1890." *Journal of Women's History* 13, no. 1 (2001): 108–25.

Fitzpatrick, Shelia, and Yuri Slezkine. *In the Shadow of Revolution: Life Stories of Russian Women from 1917 to the Second World War*. Princeton: Princeton University Press, 2000.

Flam, Helena. "Dissenting Intellectuals and Plain Dissenters." In *Intellectuals and Politics in Central Europe*. Edited by Andr Bozęki. New York: Central European University Press, 1999.

Florvil, Tiffany N. "Connected Differences: Black German Feminists and Their Transnational Connections in the 1980s and 1990s." In *Gendering Post-1945 German History: Entanglements*. Edited by Karen Hagemann, Donna Harsch, and Frederike Brühöfener. New York: Berghahn, 2019. 229–52.

Forcucci, Lauren E. "Battle for Births: The Fascist Pronatalist Campaign in Italy 1925–1938." *Journal for the Society for the Anthropology of Europe* 10, no. 1 (2010): 4–13.

Frader, Laura L., and Sonya O. Rose, eds. *Gender and Class in Modern Europe*. Ithaca, NY: Cornell University Press, 1996.

Freidenvall, Lenita, and Marian Sawer. "Framing Women Politicians in Old Democracies." In *Breaking Male Dominance in Old Democracies*. Edited by Drude Dahlerup and Monique Leyenaar. Oxford: Oxford University Press, 2013. 260–74.

Frevert, Ute. *Women in German History: From Bourgeois Emancipation to Sexual Liberation*. Translated by Stuart McKinnon-Evans, Terry Bond, and Barbara Norden. Washington, DC: Berg, 1990.

Friedlander, Henry. *The Origins of Nazi Genocide: From Euthanasia to the Final Solution*. Chapel Hill: University of North Carolina Press, 1995.

Fuchs, Rachel G., and Victoria E. Thompson. *Women in Nineteenth Century Europe*. New York: Palgrave Macmillan, 2005.

Funk, Nanette. "A Very Tangled Knot: Official State Socialist Women's Organizations, Women's Agency and Feminism in Eastern European State Socialism." *European Journal of Women's Studies* 21, no. 4 (2014): 344–60.

Gelb, Joyce. *Feminism and Politics: A Comparative Perspective*. Berkeley: University of California Press, 1989.

Gellately, Robert. *Backing Hitler: Consent and Coercion in Nazi Germany*. Oxford: Oxford University Press, 2001.

Gibson, Mary. *Prostitution and State in Italy, 1860–1915*. Columbus: Ohio State University Press, 2000.

Gildea, Robert. *Barricades and Borders: Europe 1800–1914*. Oxford: Oxford University Press, 2003.

Godayal, Pilar. "Feminism and Translation in the 1960s: The Reception in Catalunya of Betty Friedan's The Feminine Mystique." Translated by Sheila Waldeck. *Translation Studies* 7, no. 3 (2014): 267–83.

Göktürk, Deniz, David Gramling, and Anton Kaes, eds. *Germany in Transit: Nation and Migration, 1955–2005*. Berkeley: University of California Press, 2007.

Goldstein, Joshua S. *War and Gender: How Gender Shapes the War System and Vice Versa*. Cambridge: Cambridge University Press, 2003.

Goldstein, Robert Justin, and Andrew M. Need, eds. *Political Censorship of the Visual Arts in Nineteenth-Century Europe*. London: Palgrave Macmillan, 2015.

Gorbanevskaya, Natalya. "Writing for 'Samizdat'." *Index on Censorship* 6, no. 1 (1977): 229–39.

Grayzel, Susan R. *Women's Identities at War: Gender Motherhood, and Politics in Britain and France during the First World War*. Chapel Hill: University of North Carolina Press, 1999.

Grossman, Atina. *Jews, German, and Allies: Close Encounters in Occupied Germany*. Princeton: Princeton University Press, 2007.

Guerrina, Roberta, and Annick Masselot. "Walking into the Footprint of EU Law: Unpacking the Gendered Consequences of Brexit." *Social Policy and Society* 17, no. 2 (2018): 319–30.

Gullace, Nicoletta F. "War Crimes or Atrocity Stories? Anglo-American Narratives of Truth and Deception in the Aftermath of World War I." In *Sexual Violence in*

Conflict Zones: From the Ancient World to the Era of Human Rights. Edited by Elizabeth D. Heineman. Philadelphia: University of Pennsylvania Press, 2011. 105–21.

Gupta, Geeta Rao. "Globalization, Women and the HIV/AIDS Epidemic." *Peace Review* 16, no. 1 (2004): 79–83.

Hagemann, Karen, and Sonya Michel, eds. *Gender and the Long Postwar: The United States and the Two Germanies, 1945–1989.* Baltimore: Johns Hopkins University Press, 2014.

Hamer, Emily. *Britannia's Glory: A History of Twentieth-Century Lesbians.* New York: Bloomsbury, 2016.

Hamilton, Carrie. *Women and the ETA: The Gender Politics of Radical Basque Nationalism.* New York: Manchester University Press, 2007.

Hanson-DeFusco, Jessi. "Comparative Analysis of the Gendered Effects of Newly-Emergent Outbreaks on Women: Case Study of the 1918–20 Spanish Influenza, 2014/15 Ebola Pandemic, and 2019 / 20 Covid-19." *Women's Health Research* 2, no. 2 (2020): 1–8.

Harfield, Alan. "The Women's Auxiliary Corps (India)." *Journal of the Society for Army Historical Research* 83 (2005): 243–54.

Harsh, Donna. "Society, the State, and Abortion in East Germany, 1950–1972," *The American Historical Review*, 102, no. 1 (1997): 53–84.

Healy, Maureen. *Vienna and the Fall of the Hapsburg Empire: Total War and Everyday Life in World War One.* Cambridge: Cambridge University Press, 2004.

Hearne, Siobhán. "Sex on the Front: Prostitution and Venereal Disease in Russia's First World War." *Revolutionary Russia* 30, no. 1 (2017): 102–22.

Heineman, Elizabeth. "The Hour of the Woman: Memories of Germany's 'Crisis Years' and West German National Identity." *The American Historical Review* 10, no. 2 (1996): 354–95.

Hellbeck, Jochen. *Revolution on My Mind: Writing a Diary under Stalin.* Cambridge, MA: Harvard University Press, 2006.

Herzog, Dagmar. *Sexuality in Europe: A Twentieth-Century History.* Cambridge: Cambridge University Press, 2012.

Hicks, Seymour. *Difficulties: An Attempt to Help*, 3rd ed. London: Duckworth, 1923.

Higonnet, Margaret R., and Patrice L. R. Higonnet. "The Double Helix." In *Behind the Lines: Gender and the Two World Wars.* Edited by Margaret Randolph Higonnet, Jane Jenson, Sonya Michel, and Margaret Collins Weitz. New Haven: Yale University Press, 1987. 31–48.

Hildebrandt, Achim. "Routes to Decriminalization: A Comparative Analysis of the Legalization of Same-sex Sexual Acts." *Sexualities* 17, no. 1–2 (2014): 230–53.

Hilevych, Yuliya, and Chizu Sato. "Popular Medical Discourses on Birth Control in the Soviet Union during the Cold War: Shifting Responsibilities and Relational Values." In *Children by Choice? Changing Values, Reproduction, and Family Planning in the 20th Century.* Edited by Ann-Katrin Gembries, Theresia Theuke, and Isabel Heinemann. Boston: De Gruyter Oldenbourg, 2018. 99–122.

Hinds, Donald. "The West Indian Gazette: Claudia Jones and the Black Press in Britain." *Race and Class* 50, no. 1 (2008): 89–97.

Hirsi Ali, Ayaan. *Caged Virgin: An Emancipation Proclamation for Women and Islam.* New York: Atria, 2015.

Hobson, Barbara. "Feminist Strategies and Gendered Discourses." In *Mothers of a New World: Maternalist Politics and the Origins of Welfare States*. Edited by Seth Koven and Sonya Michel. New York: Routledge, 1993. 396–429.

Hubbard-Hall, Claire, and Adrian O'Sullivan. "Wives of Secret Agents: Skyscapes of the Second World War and Female Agency." *International Journal of Military History and Historiography* 39 (2019): 181–207.

Humphries, Jane, and Carmen Sarasúa. "Off the Record: Reconstructing Women's Labor Force Participation in the European Past." *Feminist Economics* 18, no. 4 (2012): 39–67.

Huneke, Samuel Clowes. *States of Liberation: Gay Men between Dictatorship and Democracy in Cold War Germany*. Toronto: University of Toronto Press, 2022.

Ingham, Mary. *Now We Are Thirty: Women of the Breakthrough Generation*. London: Eyre Methuen, 1981.

Inglis, Lucy. "The Art of Medicine: Elsie Inglis, the Suffragette Physician." *The Lancet* 384 (2014): 1664–5.

Jain, Devaki. *Women, Development, and the UN: A Sixty-Year Quest for Equality and Justice*. Bloomington: Indiana University Press, 2005.

James, Selma. *Sex, Race and Class, the Perspective of Winning: A Selection of Writings, 1952–2011*. Oakland, CA: PM Press, 2012.

Jansz, Ulla. "Women or Workers? The 1889 Labor Law and the Debate on Protective Legislation in the Netherlands." In *Protecting Women: Labor Legislation in Europe, The United States, and Australia, 1880–1920*. Edited by Ulla Wikander, Alice Kessler-Harris, Jane E. Lewis. Champaign, IL: University of Illinois Press, 1995. 188–209.

Jennings, Rebecca. *Tomboys and Bachelor Girls: A Lesbian History of Post-War Britain 1945–71*. Manchester: Manchester University Press, 2007.

Jepsen, Thomas C. *My Sisters Telegraphic: Women in the Telegraph Office, 1846–1950*. Athens: Ohio University Press, 2000.

Jones, Harriet. "The State and Social Policy." In *Women in Twentieth Century Britain: Social, Cultural and Political Change*, 1st ed. Edited by Ina Zweiniger-Bargielowska. New York: Routledge, 2001. 321–35.

Judt, Tony. *Postwar: A History of Europe Since 1945*. New York: Penguin Press, 2005.

Jütte, Robert. *Contraception: A History*. Malden, MA: Polity Press, 2008.

Kaes, Anton, Martin Jay, and Edward Dimendberg, eds. *The Weimar Republic Sourcebook*. Berkeley: University of California Press, 1994.

Kantola, Johanna, and Emanuela Lombardo, eds. *Gender and the Economic Crisis in Europe: Politics, Institutions, and Intersectionality*. New York: Palgrave Macmillan, 2017.

Kaplan, Gisela. *Contemporary Western European Feminism*. Edited by Gisela Kaplan. New York: Routledge, 2014.

Kaplan, Marion A. *Between Dignity and Despair: Jewish Life in Nazi Germany*. New York: Oxford University Press, 1998.

Kara, Siddharth. *Sex Trafficking: Inside the Business of Modern Slavery*. New York: Columbia University Press, 2009.

Karcher, Katharine. *Sisters in Arms: Militant Feminisms in the Federal Republic of Germany since 1968*. New York: Berghahn, 2017.

Karlsson, Lynn. "The Beginning of a 'Masculine Renaissance': The Debate on the 1909 Prohibition against Women's Night Work in Sweden." In *Protecting*

Women: Labor Legislation in Europe, The United States, and Australia, 1880–1920. Edited by Ulla Wikander, Alice Kessler-Harris, and Jane E. Lewis. Champaign, IL: University of Illinois Press, 1995. 210–35.

Katz, M. Barry. "The Women of Futurism." *Women's Art Journal* 7, no. 2 (1986): 3–13.

Kelly, Petra Karin. *Fighting for Hope*. Translated by Marianna Howarth. Cambridge, MA: South End Press, 1984.

Kenealy, Arabella. *Feminism and Sex-Extinction*. London: Fisher Unwin, 1920.

Kennedy-Macfoy, Madeleine, and Dubravka Zarkov. "Black Lives Matter in Europe–EJWS Special Open Forum: Introduction." *European Journal of Women's Studies* 30, no. 1 (2023): 3S–5S.

Kenney, Padraic. "The Gender of Resistance in Communist Poland." *The American Historical Review* 104, no. 2 (1999): 399–425.

Keown, Bridget E. "Nurses' Friendships, Trauma and Resiliency during WWI." *Family and Community History* 21, no. 3 (2018): 151–65.

Khan, Yasmin. "Women and War in the British Empire." *War and Society* 39, no. 3 (2020): 227–31.

Kiblitskaya, Marina. "Russia's Female Breadwinners." In *Gender, State, and Society in Soviet and Post-Soviet Russia*. Edited by Sarah Ashwin. New York: Routledge, 2000. 55–70.

King, Anthony. "Women in Combat." *The Royal United Services Institute Journal* 158, no. 1 (2013): 4–11.

Kirchhof, Astrid Mignon. *Pathways into and out of Nuclear Power in Western Europe: Austria, Denmark, Federal Republic of Germany, Italy, and Sweden*. Munich: Deutsches Museum, 2020.

Kochanski, Halik. *The Eagle Unbowed: Poland and the Poles in the Second World War*. Cambridge, MA: Harvard University Press, 2012.

Kollwitz, Käthe. *The Diary and Letters of Käthe Kollwitz*. Edited by Hans Kollwitz. Translated by Richard and Clara Winston. Evanston, IL: Northwestern University Press, 1988.

Korteweg, Anna, and Gökçe Yurdakul. "Islam, Gender, and Immigrant Integration: Boundary Drawing in Discourses on Honour Killing in the Netherlands and Germany." *Ethnic and Racial Studies* 32, no. 2 (2009): 218–38.

Kovály, Heda Margolius. *Under A Cruel Star: A Life in Prague 1941–1968*. Translated by Franci Epstein and Helen Epstein. New York: Homes and Meier, 1986.

Koven, Seth. *Slumming: Sexual and Social Politics in Victorian London*. Princeton: Princeton University Press, 2004.

Koven, Seth. *The Match Girl and the Heiress*. Princeton: Princeton University Press, 2014.

Kramer, Alan. "Combatants and Noncombatants: Atrocities, Massacres, and War Crimes." In *A Companion to World War I*. Edited by John Horne. Malden, MA: Blackwell, 2012. 188–201.

Krasniewicz, Louise. *Nuclear Summer: The Clash of Communities at the Seneca Women's Peace Encampment*. Ithaca, NY: Cornell University Press, 1992.

Kravetz, Melissa. *Women Doctors in Weimar and Nazi Germany: Maternalism, Eugenics, and Professional Identity*. Toronto: Toronto University Press, 2019.

Kreisel, Cynthia. "Happy Motherhood and Lesbian Spaces." In *Women and Gender in Postwar Europe: From Cold War to European Union*. Edited by Joanna Regulska and Bonnie G. Smith. New York: Routledge, 2012. 122–38.

Kubow, Magdalena. "The Solidarity Movement in Poland: Its History and Meaning in Collective Memory." *The Polish Review* 58, no. 2 (2013): 3–14.

Kurimay, Anita. *Queer Budapest, 1873–1961*. Chicago: University of Chicago Press, 2020.

Krieger-Boden, Christiane, and Alina Sorgner. "Labor Market Opportunities for Women in the Digital Age." *Economics* 12, no. 1 (2018): 1–8.

Krylova, Anna. *Soviet Women in Combat: A History of Violence on the Eastern Front*. Cambridge: Cambridge University Press, 2010.

Laska, Vera, ed. *Women in the Resistance and the Holocaust: The Voices of Eyewitnesses*. Westport, CT: Greenwood Press, 1983.

Lawrence, Dorothy. *Sapper Dorothy Lawrence: The Only English Woman Soldier, Late Royal Engineers, 51st Division 179th Tunnelling Company, B.E.F.* New York: John Lane Company, 1919.

Lazaridis, Gabriella. "Filipino and Albanian Women Migrant Workers in Greece: Multiple Layers of Oppression." In *Gender and Migration in Southern Europe: Women on the Move*. Edited by Flora Anthias and Gabriella Lazaridis. New York: Berg, 2000.

Lee, Julia. "Mary Seacole and the Virtual Nation." *Anthurium: A Caribbean Studies Journal* 15, no. 1 (2019): 1–7.

Leidinger, Christiane. "'Anna Rüling': A Problematic Foremother of Lesbian Herstory." *Journal of the History of Sexuality* 13, no. 4 (2004): 477–99. http://www.jstor.org/stable/3704535.

Lengyel, Olga. *Five Chimneys: A Woman Survivor's True Story of Auschwitz*. Chicago: Academy Chicago Publishers, 1995.

Levine, Joshua. *Forgotten Voices of the Blitz and the Battle for Britain: A New History in the Words of Men and Women on Both Sides*. New York: Random House, 2007.

Levine, Philippa. *Prostitution, Race, and Politics: Policing Venereal Disease in the British Empire*. New York: Routledge, 2003.

Lévy-Hass, Hanna. *Diary of Bergen-Belsen*. Translated by Sophie Hand. Chicago: Haymarket Books, 2009.

Leydesdorff, Elma. *Surviving the Bosnian Genocide: The Women of Srebrenica Speak*. Translated by Kay Richardson. Bloomington: Indiana University Press, 2011.

Lóránd, Zsófia. "Feminism as Counterdiscourse in Yugoslavia in Two Different Contexts." MA Thesis. Central European University History Department, Budapest, 2007.

Loughnan, Naomi. "Munition Work." In *Women War Workers: Accounts Contributed by Representative Workers of the Work Done by Women in the More Important Branches of War Employment*. Edited by Gilbert Stone. London: G.G Harrap and Company, 1917. 25–45.

Lower, Wendy. *Hitler's Furies: German Women in the Nazi Killing Fields*. New York: Mariner, 2013.

Lualdi, Katharine, ed. *Sources of the Making of the West: Peoples and Cultures*, 5th ed. Boston: Bedford St Martin, 2012.

Magyari-Vincze, Enikő. "Romanian Gender Regimes and Women's Citizenship." In *Women and Citizenship in Central and Eastern Europe*. Edited by Jasmina Lukić, Joanna Regulska, and Darja Zaviršek. Burlington, VT: Ashgate, 2006. 21–38.

Mamelund, Svenn-Erik. "Profiling a Pandemic: Who Were the Victims of the Spanish Flu?" *Natural History* 125, no. 9 (2017): 6–10.

Marhoefer, Laurie. *Sex and the Weimar Republic: German Homosexual Emancipation and the Rise of the Nazis*. Toronto: University of Toronto Press, 2015.

Marinetti, Filippo Tommaso. *Critical Writings: New Edition*. Edited by Günter Berghaus. Translated by Doug Thompson. New York: Farrar, Straus and Giroux, 2006.

Marrus, Michael. *The Unwanted: European Refugees in the Twentieth Century*. New York: Oxford University Press, 1985.

Martin, Megan R. "The Growth of Czech Feminism: Analyzing Resistance Activities Through a Gendered Lens, 1968 to 1993." *Gender, Equal Opportunities, Research* 10, no. 1 (2009): 37–44.

Martin, Tara. "The Beginning of Labor's End? Britain's 'Winter of Discontent' and Working-Class Women's Activism." *International and Labor and Working-Class History* 75 (2009): 49–67.

Martineau, Harriet. *Heath, Husbandry, and Handicraft*. London: Bradbury and Evans, 1861.

Matera, Marc. *Black London: The Imperial Metropolis and Decolonization in the Twentieth Century*. Berkeley: University of California Press, 2015.

Mazower, Mark. *Dark Continent: Europe's Twentieth Century*. New York: Vintage, 1998.

McLellan, Josie. "'Even Under Socialism, We Don't Want to do Without Love': East German Erotica." In *Pleasures in Socialism: Leisure and Luxury in the Eastern Bloc*. Edited by David Crowley and Susan E. Reid. Chicago: Northwestern University Press, 2010. 219–38.

McBride, Thereas. "A Woman's World: Department Stores and the Evolution of the Women's Employment, 1870–1920." *French Historical Studies* 10, no. 4 (1978): 664–83.

McDonough, Frank. *Sophie Scholl: The Real Story of the Women Who Defied Hitler*. Stroud, Gloucestershire: History Press, 2009.

McFadden, Margaret H. "Borders, Boundaries, and the Necessity of Reflexivity: International Women Activists, Rosika Schwimmer (1877–1948), and the Shadow Narrative." *Women's History Review* 20, no. 4 (2011): 533–42.

McHugh, Paul. *Prostitution and Victorian Social Reform: The Campaign against the Contagious Diseases Act*. New York: St. Martin's Press, 1980.

Melzer, Patricia. *Death in the Shape of a Young Girl: Women's Political Violence in the Red Army Faction*. New York: New York University Press, 2015.

Merabishvili, Vakhtang M., Vladimir F. Semiglazov, L. S. Serova, and M. M. Buslayeva. "Geographical Distribution of Breast Cancer in the USSR." *International Journal of Cancer* 34, no. 1 (1984): 71–5.

Meybatyan, Silvia. "Nuclear Disasters and Displacement." *Forced Migration Review* 45 (2014): 63–5.

Meyer, Sibylle, and Eva Schultz. *Wie wir das Alles geschafft haben: Alleinstehende Frauen berichten über ihr Leben nach 1945*. Munich: Beck, 1985.

Michaels, Paula A. "Comrades in the Labor Room: The Lamaze Method of Childbirth Preparation and France's Cold War Home Front, 1951–1957." *The American Historical Review* 115, no. 4 (2014): 1031–60.

Miller, Jennifer A. *Turkish Guest Workers in Germany: Hidden Lives and Contested Borders, 1960s to 1980s*. Toronto: University of Toronto Press, 2018.

Mitchell, Juliet. *The Longest Revolution*. New York: Pantheon Books, 1984.

Moeller, Robert G. "The Homosexual is a 'Man,' the Homosexual Woman is a 'Woman'": Sex, Society, and the Law in Postwar West Germany." *Journal of the History of Sexuality* 4, no. 3 (1994): 395–429.

Moncrieffe, Marlon. *New Black Cyclones: Racism, Representation and Revolutions of Power in Cycling*. Bloomsbury, 2024.

Morgan-Collins, Mona, and Grace Natusch. "At the Intersection of Gender and Class: How Were Newly Enfranchised Women Mobilized in Sweden?" *Comparative Political Studies* 55, no. 7 (2022): 1063–94.

Morris, Felicia. "Beautiful Monsters." *Legacy* 11, no. 1 (2011): 59–70.

Morrison, Lynn. "Ceausescu's Legacy: Family Struggles and Institutionalization of Children in Romania." *Journal of Family History* 29, no. 3 (2004): 168–82.

Müller, Simone M. "Telegraphy and the 'New Woman' in Late-Nineteenth-Century Europe." In *Connecting Women: Women, Gender and the ICT in Europe in the Nineteenth and Twentieth Century*. Edited by Valérie Schafer and Benjamin G. Thierry. New York: Springer, 2015. 27–46.

Murray, Hallie. *The Role of Female Spies in World War II*. New York: Cavendish Square Publishing, 2019.

Naughton, Lindie. *Markievicz: A Most Outrageous Rebel*. Newbridge, Ireland: Merrion Press, 2016.

Neuheiser, Jörg, and Stefan Wolff. *Peace at Last? The Impact of the Good Friday Agreement on Northern Ireland*. New York: Berghahn Books, 2004.

Nocita, Nick. "Politics and the Olympics." *Harvard International Review* 41, no. 2 (2020): 24–8.

Nolan, Ann. "The Gay Community Response to the Emergence of AIDS in Ireland: Activism, Covert Policy, and the Significance of an 'Invisible Minority'." *Journal of Policy History* 30, no. 1 (2018): 105–27.

Nordstrom, Justin. "The 'Kitchen Debate' Revisited: Abundance and Anti-domesticity in Cold War America." *Global Food History* 10, no. 3 (2024): 375–7.

Notz, Gisela. *Warum flog die Tomate? Die autonomen Frauenbewegungen der Siebzigerjahr*. Neu-Ulm: AG SPAK Bücher, 2018.

Nunn, Heather. *Thatcher, Politics and Fantasy: The Political Culture of Gender and Nation*. London: Lawrence and Wishart, 2002.

Ogilvie, Marilyn Bailey. "Sciences: Natural Sciences." In *The Oxford Encyclopedia of Women in World History*, Vol 1. Edited by Bonnie G. Smith. Oxford: Oxford University Press, 2008, 657–61.

O'Keefe, Theresa. "My Body is My Manifesto! SlutWalk, FEMEN and Femmenist Protest." *Feminist Review* 107, no. 1 (2014): 1–19.

O'Keefe, Theresa. "Policing Unruly Women: The State and Sexual Violence during the Northern Irish Troubles." *Women's Studies International Forum* 62 (2017): 69–77.

Oldfield, Sybil. "Mary Sheepshanks Edits an Internationalist Suffrage Monthly in Wartime: *Jus Suffragii* 1914–1919." *Women's History Review* 12, no. 1 (2003): 119–34.

Olwig, Karen Fog. "The Timescape of Post-WWII Caribbean Migration to Britain: Historical Heterogeneity as Challenge and Opportunity." In *Migration, Temporality, and Capitalism*. Edited by Pauline Gardiner Barber and Winnie Lem. New York: Palgrave Macmillan, 2018.

Oram, Alison, and Annmarie Turnbull. *The Lesbian History Sourcebook: Love and Sex between Women in Britain from 1780–1970*. London: Routledge, 2001.

Orloff, Ann. "Gender and the Welfare State." *Annual Review of Sociology* 22 (1996): 51–78.

O'Sullivan, Sue, and Kate Thomson, eds. *Positively Women: Living with AIDS*. London: Sheba Feminist Press, 1992.

Overy, Richard. *The Battle of Britain: The Myth and the Reality*. New York: W. W. Norton and Company, 2002.

Owczarzak, Jill. "Defining Democracy and the Terms of Engagement with the Postsocialist Polish State. Insights from HIV/AIDS." *East European Politics and Societies* 23, no. 3 (2009): 421–45.

Özyürek, Esra. "Convert Alert: German Muslims and Turkish Christians as Threats to Security in the New Europe." *Comparative Studies in Society and History* 51, no. 1 (2009): 91–116.

Pantelić, Ivana. "Yugoslav Female Partisans in World War II." *Cahiets Balkaniques* 41 (2013): 239–50.

Parker, Rachel, Jonathan Garcia, and Robert M. Buffington, "Sexuality in the Contemporary World." In *A Global History of Sexuality: The Modern Era*. Edited by Robert M. Buffington, Eithne Luibhéid, and Donna J. Guy. Malden, MA: Wiley Blackwell, 2014.

Parush, Iris. *Reading Jewish Women: Marginality and Modernization in Nineteenth Century Eastern European Jewish Society*. Translated by Saadya Sternberg. Lebanon, NH: University Press of New England, 2004.

Paterson, Michael. *Voices of the Codebreakers: Personal Accounts of the Secret Heroes of World War II*. Barnsley, S. Yorkshire: Greenhill Books, 2018.

Pattinson, Juliette. *Behind Enemy Lines: Gender, Passing and the Special Operations Executive in the Second World War*. Manchester: Manchester University Press, 2007.

Pauer, Jan. "Czechoslovakia." In *1968 Europe: A History of Protest and Activism, 1956–1977*. Edited by Martin Klimke and Joachim Scharloth. New York: Palgrave Macmillan, 2008.

Pesotta, Rose. *Days of Ours Lives*. Boston: Excelsior, 1958.

Petrila, Ann, and Hasan Hasanović. *Voices from Srebrenica: Survivor Narratives of the Bosnian Genocide*. Jefferson, NC: McFarland, 2021.

Picq, Manuela Lavinas, and Markus Thiel. *Sexualities in World Politics: How LGBTQ Claims Shape International Relations*. New York: Routledge, 2015.

Pierce, Rachel M., and Griselda Rowntree. "Birth Control in Britain, Part II: Contraceptive Methods Used by Couples Married in the Last Thirty Years." *Population Studies* 15, no. 2 (1961): 121–60.

Pilcher, Jane. "The Gender Significance of Women in Power: British Women Talking About Margaret Thatcher." *European Journal of Women's Studies* 2, no. 4 (1995): 493–508.

Potter, Jane. "Valiant Heroines or Pacific Ladies? Women in War and Peace." In *The Routledge History of Women in Europe since 1700*. Edited by Deborah Simonton. New York: Routledge, 2006. 250–98.

Prata, Ana. "Finding a Voice: Abortion Claim-making during Portuguese Democratization." *Women's Studies International Forum* 33, no. 6 (2010): 579–88.

Proctor, Tammy M. *On My Honour: Guides and Scouts in Interwar Britain.* Philadelphia: American Philosophical Society, 2002.

Proctor, Tammy M. "Women, Popular Culture and Leisure." In *Women in Europe Since 1700.* Edited by Deborah Simonton. New York: The Routledge, 2006. 299–340.

Pugh, Martin. *Women and the Women's Movement in Britain since 1914.* New York: Bloomsbury, 2015.

Purvis, Jane. *Christabel Pankhurst: A Biography.* New York: Routledge, 2018.

Randall, Amy E. "'Abortion will Deprive You of Happiness!' Soviet Reproductive Politics in the Post-Stalin Era." *Journal of Women's History* 23, no. 3 (2014): 13–38.

Rappaport, Erika. "'The Halls of Temptation': Gender, Politics, and the Construction of the Department Store in Late Victorian London." *Journal of British Studies* 35, no.1 (1996): 58–83.

Raw, Louis. *Striking a Light: The Bryant and May Matchwomen and Their Place in Labour History.* London: Continuum, 2009.

Reader, Keith A., and Khursheed Wadia, eds. *The May 1968 Events in France: Reproductions and Interpretations.* London: Palgrave Macmillan, 1993.

Regulska, Joanna, and Bonnie G. Smith, eds. *Women and Gender in Postwar Europe: From Cold War to European Union.* New York: Routledge, 2012.

Reid, Susan E. "Cold War in the Kitchen: Gender and the De-Stalinization of Consumer Taste in the Soviet Union under Khrushchev." *Slavic Review* 61, no. 2 (2002): 211–52.

Richie, Alexandra. *Warsaw 1944: Hitler, Himmler, and the Warsaw Uprising.* New York: Farrar, Straus and Giroux, 2013.

Ringelheim, Joan. "Women and the Holocaust: A Reconsideration of Research." *Signs* 10, no. 4 (Summer 1985): 741–61.

Riszovannij, Mihály. "Self-Articulation of the Gay and Lesbian Movement in Hungary after 1989." In *Pink, Purple, Green: Women's, Religious, Environmental and Gay/Lesbian Movement in Central Europe Today.* Edited by Helena Flam. New York: Columbia University Press, 2001.

Roberts, Mary Louis. *Civilization without Sexes: Reconstructing Gender in Postwar France, 1917–1927.* Chicago: University of Chicago Press, 1994.

Roberts, Mary Louis. *Disruptive Acts: The New Woman in Fin-de-Siècle France.* Chicago: University of Chicago Press, 2002.

Roberts, Mary Louis. *What Soldiers Do: Sex and the American GI in World War II France.* Chicago: University of Chicago Press, 2013.

Robinson, Jane. *Mary Seacole: The Charismatic Black Nurse Who Became a Heroine of the Crimea.* London: Constable and Robinson, 2005.

Robinson, Lucy. *Gay Men and the Left in Post-war Britain: How the Personal Got Political.* Manchester: Manchester University Press, 2013.

Rodgers, Rebecca. "Learning to be Good Girls and Women." In *The Routledge History of Women in Europe Since 1700.* Edited by Deborah Simonton. New York: Routledge, 2006. 93–133.

Röger, Maren, and Emmanuel Debruyne. "From Control to Terror: German Prostitution Policies in Eastern and Western European Territories during both World Wars." *Gender and History* 28, no. 3 (2016): 687–708.

Ross, Andrew Israel. "Josephine Butler in Paris: Sex and Race in the Early Campaign to Abolish Regulated Prostitution, 1870–1880." *Journal of Women's History* 36, no. 2 (2024): 51–71.

Rupp, Leila J. "Constructing Internationalism: The Case of Transnational Women's Organizations, 1888–1945." *American Historical Review* 99, no. 5 (1994): 1571–600.

Rupp, Leila J. *Mobilizing Women for War: German and American Propaganda, 1939–1945*. Princeton: Princeton University Press, 1978.

Salt, John, and James Clarke. "Europe's Migrant Groups." In *The Demographic Characteristics of Immigrant Populations*. Edited by Werner Haug, Paul Compton, Youssef Courbage. Strasbourg, France: Council of Europe Publishing, 2002.

Sanborn, Joshua. "The Genesis of Russian Warlordism: Violence and Governance during the First World War and the Civil War." *Contemporary European History* 19, no. 3 (2010): 195–213.

Sanders, Lisa. *Consuming Fantasies: Labor, Leisure, and the London Shopgirl, 1880s–1920*. Columbus: Ohio State University Press, 2006.

Scharf, Emily, and Sue Toole. "HIV and the Invisibility of Women: Is There a Need to Redefine AIDS?" *Feminist Review* 41, no. 1 (1992): 64–7.

Scholl, Inge. *The White Rose: Munich 1942–1943*, 3rd ed. Translated by Arthur R. Schultz. Middletown, CT: Wesleyan University Press, 2012.

Scheppele, Kim Lane. "Responses and Discussion." In *The Humanities and Public Life*. Edited by Peter Brooks. New York: Fordham University Press, 2014. 123–5.

Schwenkel, Christina. "Rethinking Asian Mobilities." *Critical Asian Studies* 46, no. 2 (2014): 235–58.

Scott, Joan W. *The Politics of the Veil*. Princeton: Princeton University Press, 2007.

Seacole, Mary. *Wonderful Adventures of Mrs. Seacole in Many Lands*. New York: Oxford University Press, 1988. Reprint of London: J. Blackwood, 1857.

Semelin, Jacques. "Analysis of a Mass Crime: Ethnic Cleansing in the Former Yugoslavia, 1991–1999." In *The Specter of Genocide: Mass Murder in Historical Perspective*. Edited by Robert Gellately and Ben Kiernan. Cambridge: Cambridge University Press, 2003. 353–72.

Shaw, Flora Luisa. *The Work of the War Refugees Committee: An Address Given by Lady Lugard to the Royal Society of Arts, March 25th, 1915*. London: G. Bell and Sons, 1915.

Shepherd, Ben. *Terror in the Balkans: German Armies and Partisan Warfare*. Cambridge, MA: Harvard University Press, 2012.

Shivers, Lynne. "There is SOME Nonviolent Action in Northern Ireland." *Fellowship* 39, no. 13 (1973): 4–5.

Siegel, Mona. *Peace on Our Terms: The Global Battle for Women's Rights After the First World War*. New York: Columbia University Press, 2020.

Silies, Eva-Maria. "Taking the Pill after the 'Sexual Revolution': Female Contraceptive Decisions in England and West Germany in the 1970s." *European Review of History—Revue europeenne d'histoire* 22, no. 1 (2015): 41–59.

Simić, Ivan. "Gender and Youth Work Actions in Post-War Yugoslavia." In *Gender in Twentieth-Century Eastern Europe and the USSR*. Edited by Catherine Baker. New York: Palgrave Macmillan, 2017. 143–56.

Simonton, Deborah, ed. *The Routledge History of Women in Europe Since 1700*. London: Routledge, 2006.

Simpson, Clare S. "Capitalizing on Curiosity: Women's Professional Cycle Racing in the Late-Nineteenth Century." In *Cycling and Society*. Edited by Dave Horton, Paul Rosen, and Peter Cox. New York: Routledge, 2016. 47–65.

Sjögren, Åsa Karlsson. "Matrimony, Property and Power: Marriage Settlements in Sweden 1870–1920." *Scandinavian Journal of History* 36, no. 4 (2001): 443–61.

Slaughter, Jane M. "'What's New' and Is it Good for You? Gender and Consumerism in Postwar Europe." In *Women and Gender in Postwar Europe: From Cold War to European Union*. Edited by Joanna Regulska and Bonnie G. Smith. New York: Routledge, 2012. 104–121.

Smith, Bonnie G. *Women in World History: 1450 to the Present*. New York: Bloomsbury, 2020.

Smith, Bradley F., and Agnes F. Peterson, eds. *Heinrich Himmler Geheimreden 1933 bis 1945*. Frankfurt Main: Propylaen, 1972. 162–183.

Smith, Harold L. "The Women's Movements, Politics and Citizenship: 1960s–2000." In *Women in Twentieth Century Britain: Social, Cultural and Political Change*, 1st ed. Edited by Ina Zweiniger-Bargielowska. New York: Routledge, 2001. 278–91.

Steel, Flora Annie, and Grace Gardiner. *The Complete Indian Housekeeper and Cook*. Edited by Ralph Crane and Anna Johnston. Oxford: Oxford University Press, 2010.

Stillion Southard, Belinda A. "Rhetorical Legacies of the National Woman's Party: Shuttling Rhetorics, Endurance, and Survival." *Quarterly Journal of Speech* 106, no. 3 (2020): 258–68.

Stloukal, Libor. "Understanding the 'Abortion Culture' in Central and Eastern Europe." In *From Abortion to Contraception: A Resource to Public Policies and Reproductive Behavior in Central and Eastern Europe 1917 to the Present*. Edited by Henry P. David and Joanna Skilogianis. Westport, CT: Greenwood Press, 1999. 23–38.

Stokes, Lauren. *Fear of the Family: Guest Workers and Family Migration in the Federal Republic of Germany*. New York: Oxford University Press, 2022.

Stockdale, Melissa K. "'My Death for the Motherland is Happiness': Women, Patriotism, and Soldiering in Russia's Great War, 1914–1917." *The American Historical Review* 109, no. 1 (2004): 78–116.

Stoler, Ann. "Making Empire Respectable: The Politics of Race and Sexual Morality in 20th-Century Colonial Cultures." *American Ethnologist* 16, no. 4 (1989): 634–60.

Strobel, Margaret. "Gender, Race, and Empire in Nineteenth- and Twentieth-Century Africa and Asia." In *Becoming Visible: Women in European History*, 3rd ed. Edited by Renate Bridenthal, Susan Mosher Stuart, and Merry Wiesner. Boston: Houghton Mifflin Company, 1998. 389–416.

Sullivan, Donna J. "Women's Human Rights and the 1993 World Conference on Human Rights." *American Journal of International Law* 88, no. 1 (1994): 152–67.

Takács, Judit. "Listing Homosexuals since the 1920s and under State Socialism in Hungary." In *Gender in Twentieth-Century Eastern Europe and the USSR*. Edited by Catherine Baker. New York: Palgrave Macmillan, 2017. 157–70.

Terras, Melissa, and Elizabeth Crawford, eds. *Millicent Garrett Fawcett: Selected Writings*. London: University College London Press, 2022.

Thane, Pat. "Women in the British Labour Party and the Construction of State Welfare, 1906–1939." In *Mothers of a New World: Maternalist Politics and the Origins of Welfare States*. Edited by Seth Koven and Sonya Michel. New York: Routledge, 1993. 343–77.
Thompson, Ceri. *From the Cradle to the Coalmine: The Story of Children in Welsh Mines*. Cardiff: University of Wales Press, 2014.
Timm, Annette F., and Joshua A. Sanborn, eds. *Gender, Sex and the Shaping of Modern Europe: A History from the French Revolution to the Present Day*, 2nd ed. New York: Bloomsbury, 2016.
Todd, Alex J. "The Protestor's Playground: Throughout the 1970s, the Feminist Group Dolle Mina Combined Radical Protests with Conceptual Art." *History Today* 69, no. 6 (June 2019): 15–17.
Tompkins, Andrew S. *Better Active Than Radioactive! Anti-nuclear Protest in 1970s France and West Germany*. Oxford: Oxford University Press, 2016.
Townsend, Colin, and Eileen Townsend, eds. *War Wives: A Second World War Anthology*. London: Grafton Books, 1989.
Tröger, Annemarie. "A Female Assembly-Line Proletariat." In *When Biology Becomes Destiny: Women in Weimar and Nazi Germany*. Edited by Bridenthal, Atina Grossmann, and Marion Kaplan. New York: Monthly Review Press, 1984. 237–70.
Trott, Magda. "Frauenarbeit, ein Ersatz für Männerarbeit?" *Die Frau* 3 (1915): 277–9.
Trgovčević, Ljubinka. "The Professional Emancipation of Women in 19th Century Serbia." *Serbian Studies: Journal of the North American Society for Serbian Studies* 25, no. 1 (2011): 7–21.
Tristan, Flora. *The Workers' Union, 1843*. Translated by Beverly Livingston. Urbana Champaign: University of Illinois Press, 1983.
Turpin, Jennifer, and Lois Ann Lorentzen, eds. *The Gendered New World Order: Militarism, Development, and the Environment*. New York: Routledge, 1996.
Tyrer, Louise. "Introduction of the Pill and Its Impact." *Contraception* 59, no. 1 (Supplement 1, 1999): 11S–16S.
Umoren, Imaobong D. *Race Women Internationalists: Activists-Intellectuals and Global Freedom*. Oakland: University of California Press, 2018.
Van de Walle, Étienne. "Birth Prevention Before the Era of Modern Contraception." *Population and Societies* 418 (December 2005): 1–4.
Van Heyningen, Elizabeth B. "The Social Evil in the Cape Colony 1986–1902: Prostitution and the Contagious Diseases Acts." *Journal of Southern African Studies* 10, no. 2 (1984): 170–97.
Velling, Johannes. "Determinants of Family Reunification among German Guest-Workers." *Vierteljahrshefts zur Wirtschaftsforschung* 63, no. 1(1994): 126–32.
Vincendeau, Ginette. *Brigitte Bardot*. New York: Palgrave Macmillan, 2013.
Vromen, Suzanne. *Hidden Children of the Holocaust: Belgian Nuns and their Daring Rescue*. New York: Oxford University Press, 2008.
Wade, Rex A. *The Russian Revolution, 1917*, 3rd ed. Cambridge: Cambridge University Press, 2017.
Walkowitz, Judith. *City of Dreadful Delight: Narratives of Sexual Danger in Late-Victorian London*. Chicago: University of Chicago Press, 1992.

Waxman, Zoë. *Women in the Holocaust: A Feminist History*. Oxford: Oxford University Press, 2017.
Webster, Wendy. *Not a Man to Match Her: Feminist View of Britain's First Woman Prime Minister*. London: The Women's Press, 1990.
Webster, Wendy. "'Race', Ethnicity and National Identity." In *Women in Twentieth Century Britain: Social, Cultural and Political Change*, 1st ed. Edited by Ina Zweiniger-Bargielowska. New York: Routledge, 2001. 292–306.
Weeks, Jeffery. *Making Sexual History*. Malden, MA: Polity Press, 2000.
Weeks, Jeffery. *Sex, Politics and Society: The Regulation of Sexuality since 1880*, 3rd ed. New York: Routledge, 2012.
Weissbort, Daniel. "The Ordeal of Natalya Gorbanevskaya." *Index of Censorship* 1, no. 1 (1972): 117–23.
Weitz, Eric D. *Weimar Germany: Promise and Tragedy*. Princeton: Princeton University Press, 2007.
Wildenthal, Lora. *German Women for Empire, 1884–1945*. Durham: Duke University Press, 2001.
Wildt, Carolin. *Kann Morden Ehre Sein? Ursachen von Ehrenmorden in Deutschland am Beispiel Hatun Sürücü*. Hamburg: Diplomica Verlag, 2014.
Wilson, Duncan. "In Vitro Fertilization, Infertility, and the 'Right to a Child' in 1970s and 1980s Britain." In *The Palgrave Handbook of Infertility History: Approaches, Contexts and Perspectives*. Edited by Gayle Davis and Tracey Loughran. London: Palgrave Macmillan, 2017. 565–86.
Wingfield, Nancy M. "The Enemy Within: Regulating Prostitution and Controlling Venereal Disease in Cisleithanian Austria during the Great War." *Central European History* 46 (2013): 568–98.
Wingfield, Nancy M., and Maria Bucur, eds. *Gender and War in Twentieth-Century Eastern Europe*. Bloomington: Indiana University Press, 2006.
Wojtyńska, Anna. "Black Protesters in Iceland: Transnational Flows and Entanglements." In *Mobility and Transnational Iceland: Current Transformations and Global Entanglements*. Edited by Kristín Loftsdóttir, Unnur Dís Skaptadóttir, and Sigurjón Baldur Hafsteinsson. Reykjavik: University of Iceland Press, 2020.
Woollacott, Angela. *Gender and Empire*. New York: Palgrave Macmlillan, 2006.
Yaroshinskaya, Alla. *Chernobyl: The Forbidden Truth*. Translated by Michèle Kahn and Julia Sallabank. Lincoln: University of Nebraska Press, 1995.
Yusupova, Marina. "Pussy Riot: A Feminist Band Lost in History and Translation." *Nationalities Papers* 42, no. 4 (2014): 604–10.
Zahra, Tara. *Against the World: Anti-Globalism and Mass Politics between the World Wars*. New York: W. W. Norton, 2023.
Zahra, Tara. *The Great Departure: Mass Migration from Eastern Europe and the Making of the Free World*. New York: W. W. Norton, 2016.
Zektin, Clara. *The Emancipation of Women: From the Writings of V. I. Lenin*. New York: International Publishers, 1966.
Zheng, Tiantian, ed. *Sex Trafficking, Human Rights, and Social Justice*. London: Routledge, 2010.
Zimmerman, Susan. "The Changing Politics of Women's Work and the Making of Extended Childcare Leave in State-Socialist Hungary, Europe, and Internationally: Shifting the Scene." In *Life Course, Work, and Labour in Global*

History. Edited by Josef Ehmer and Carola Lentz. Boston: Walter de Gruyter, 2023. 225–58.

Zimmerman, Susan, and Borbala Major. "Róza Schwimmer." In *A Biographical Dictionary of Women's Movements and Feminisms: Central, Eastern, and South Eastern Europe, 19th and 20th Centuries*. Edited by Francisca de Haan, Krassimira Daskalova, and Anna Loutfi. New York: Central European University Press, 2006. 484–90.

INDEX

Note: Figures are indicated by page number followed by "f."

Abbate, Janet 82
Abbott, Diane 151
abortion
   in Albania 135–6
   and birth control 69
   in Britain 134
   in Bulgaria 135–6
   decriminalizing 127, 145
   in Denmark 134
   and divorce 153
   in Eastern Europe 135–7
   and homosexuality 67
   illegal 134, 137
   laws during 1950s and 1960s in USSR 105
   in the Netherlands 134–5
   rights 124
   in Romania 135–6
   in Soviet Union 135
   in Spain 135
   in Western Europe 132–5
ACT-UP Paris, in 1989 152
Action Council for the Liberation of Women (ACLW) 131
actions, 1968 125, 131, 139, 142, 146, 160
   gay rights movements 141
activism 3–4, 146–8
   climate 188–90
   HIV/AIDS 152–5
   for labor and civil rights 124
   by student and global revolution 138–40
   women's labor 141–3
advertising 100, 115, 128
   mass culture and 53
   media and 127

Afghanistan, rigid gender regime in 184–5
Africa 2, 21, 22, 33
   communities 57
   decolonization in 112, 138
   national liberation movements in 138
African American 59, 96, 187
   music and culture 57
Afro-British women 120
Afro-feminism 119, 150, 196
   activism 121
   in the 1980s and 1990s 171–2
Afro-French
   public 59
   writers 59
Afro-German Women (ADEFRA) 171–2
Albania 135
   pronatalist program 136
   Women's inequality in 136
alcoholism 55, 62, 67
   in slums and working-class residents 12
Alexeivich, Svetlana 163
Algeria 2, 110, 178
   decolonization in 111–12
   National Liberation Front (NLF) 112
Algerian War for Independence (1954–62) 111
All-Russian Congress of Working Women 50
Altvater, Johanna 94
Amara, Fadela 178, 195
American suffrage organization 19–20
Anisimova, Nadezhda Vasilyevna 83

anti-Muslim sentiment 149–50, 180
anti-natalism 70
antinuclear movements and feminism 155–7, 196
anti-pornography Law, 1953 128
antiracism 157
antisemitic policies 41, 72, 84–5, 94
Arena Three (Mary L.) 130
Argentina 138
Armand, Inessa 50
Armenia 36, 61
arms race 105–6, 156, 157
Asia 16, 20, 23
　decolonization in 112, 138
　national liberation movements in 138
Association of Women Workers in Hungary 34
Astakhova, Larisa 164
athletes 193–4
Auclert, Hubertine 18
Auschwitz 89, 93
Austria 31, 52, 60, 61, 154
　promoting women's employment 102
Austro-Hungarian 8, 9, 16, 33, 35, 39, 42, 48, 50, 54
authoritarianism 68, 73
Auxiliary Territorial Service (ATS) 78, 80f, 81, 81f

Bachelet, Michelle 183
Bainić, Jelena 88
Baker, Josephine 57, 58f, 75, 76, 83, 196
Bang, Nina 61
Bardot, Bridget 114, 116f, 196
Basque Homeland and Liberty/Euskadi Ta Askatasuna (ETA) 145–6
battleground of women's bodies 165–7
Beiner, Guy 44
Belarus 174
Belgium 23, 35, 37f, 38, 41, 42, 43, 52, 88, 108, 111, 112, 117, 156
　abortion not legal in 134–5
Belgrade 14, 159, 167
Belorussia 60
Berlin Wall in 1961 110, 154, 164

Berliner Illustrirte Zeitung 53
Besant, Annie 27
birth control 25, 26, 27–8, 34, 56, 69, 100, 105, 123–5, 127, 135, 136, 137
　abortion 27, 56, 67, 69, 71, 105, 110, 124, 125, 127, 132–5, 137, 145, 148, 153, 194, 196
　condoms 27, 41, 123, 136, 137, 152, 153, 155
　diaphragms 26–7, 123
　IUD 123
　the pill 124–5, 127, 134, 166
　practices 123
　sterilization 70, 71, 72, 123, 155
　technological advancement in 25, 26, 27, 123
birth rates 43, 62, 71, 99, 105
Björk 176
Black anti-imperial 57
Black feminist movement 120, 171
Black Friday 32
Black Lives Matter (BLM) 4, 187–8
Black women 57, 59, 119, 120, 145, 157, 158, 171–2, 187
The Black World Review 59
Bletchley Park 79
"Blitz" 78
Blondel, Lucienne 69
Bock, Gisela 70
Bodichon, Barbara 18
Bogoraz, Larisa 140
Bohachevsky-Chomiak, Martha 19
Bohley, Bärbel 164
Bolshevik Revolution, 1917 135
Bosnia–Herzegovina 167
Bradlaugh, Charles 27
breast cancer 155
Brexit 186–7
Britain 111
　abortion right in 134
　National Health Service (NHS) in 100
　"the Pill" in 124–5
British Auxiliary Territorial Service (ATS) 78–9, 80f, 81f
British House of Commons 55
British Labour Party 62
British Ten Hours Act, 1847 13

British Women's Social and Political
    Union 31
Brittain, Vera 43, 48
Bröring, Ria 87
Brown, Kate 164
Brown, Louise Joy 126
Brown, Wilmette 157, 195
Browne, Stella 25
Bulgaria 105, 117, 135
Butler, Josephine 13

cancer, research 155
Cape Verde 108
capitalism 54, 105, 113, 114, 116–17,
    164, 165
  versus communism 99–100
  gendered policies 100
Carby, Hazel 158
career advancement 6, 17, 20, 24, 65,
    119, 131, 149
  for European women 14–16
Caribbean communities 57
Carmen Alvarado, Ceylin del 193
Carpenter, Edward 25
casual racism 195
Catholic Church 145
  on birth control and abortion 125
  on "The Pill" 125
Catholicism 76
Cauer, Minna 18–19
Cavour Law of 1860 12
Cavour, Camillo 12
Ceaușescu, Nicolae 136
  regressive policies 136–7
Central America
  decolonization in 138
  national liberation
    movements in 138
Channell, Emily 177
Charter 77, 139, 160
Chernobyl nuclear disaster, 1986
    149, 162–4
childbirth 43, 56, 84, 99–100, 103,
    123, 136, 144
  Lamaze method 99
Chin, Rita 178
Clarke, Joan 81
climate activism 188–90
Cold War 1, 4, 123, 174–5

colonial bodies, fetishizing 57–60
colonial resistance 111
colonialism 2, 15, 20, 22
communism 56, 61, 76, 101, 103, 104,
    106, 113, 121, 136, 143, 151,
    159, 160, 162, 197
  gendered policies 100
communist 4, 68
  countries 103
Communist Manifesto 11
Communist Party 136
"communist scientific technique" 99
"community feminism" 19
Comprehensive Equality Act 1976 144
computer science 82, 194
concentration camps 71, 85–86, 89,
    93, 96, 128–9
conflict 3, 33, 35
Conservative Party 151
conservative women 4
Contagious Diseases Act (CDA) 12,
    13, 194
Crimean War (1853–56) 5
"crisis of masculinity" 76, 95
Croatia 165, 167
Cuba 110
cultural contributions 60
culture 3, 21, 26, 36
Cummings, Constance 60
Czech Republic 184
  women in military troops 184
Czech women 65
Czechoslovakia 60, 70, 105, 135,
    138–40, 149, 160

Darwin, Charles 20
Daubié, Julie-Victoire 8, 12
de Beauvoir, Simone 118, 123
de Saint-Point, Valentine 29
Dean, James 115
decolonization 1, 2, 120, 121, 138,
    174, 178
  and gender 111–13
democracy 11, 48, 54, 57, 68, 101,
    112, 114, 137, 138, 143, 145,
    149, 150, 162, 170, 172
Denmark 112
  homosexuality and LGBTQ+
    communities 129, 180–1

legalized abortion in 134
  promoting women's
    employment 102
department store 10
Der Spiegel (German magazine) 154
Deraismes, Maria 18
"de-Stalinization" 139
Difficulties: An Attempt to Help 56
"Digital Age" 173
Dior, Christian 114
"displaced persons" (DPs) 96
  Nuremberg 76, 95, 96, 167
divorce rates 56, 95
Dohm, Hedwig 18
Dolle Mina (Mad Mina) 132, 133f, 175, 198
domestic violence 112–13
domesticity 8, 10, 21, 54, 69, 72, 100, 101, 105, 108, 114, 117, 118, 149, 150
Drozd 164
Dubçek, Alexander 139
Dublin Lesbian and Gay Men's Collective 153
Dumas, Alexandre 16

East Asia 111
East Germany 104, 105, 110, 128, 135, 154, 161, 164
Eastern Bloc 105, 110, 117, 149
  "abortion culture" in 135–6
  reproductive rights
    restrictions in 136
  women's experiences in 103
  women's lives at work and home in 103–7
Eastern Europe 14, 17, 19, 32–3, 46
  HIV/AIDS in 154
  legal abortion and reproductive autonomy in 135–7
Ecofeminism 157
education
  reform for European women 14–16
Edwards, Robert 126, 126f
Einsatzgruppen (mobile killing units) 86, 87f
Electric Telegraph Company 15
Ellis, Havelock 25, 26
Employment Protection Act, 1975 150

England 159
  on homosexuality 129
Enigma Machine 79, 81
entertainers 56, 58f, 75
environmental movements and feminism 4, 155–7
environmentalism 157
equal pay 50, 52, 79, 104, 124, 130, 142
Equal Pay Act, 1970 142
equality and gender roles 181–2
Eritrea 108
Erteltová, Zdena 161
Estonia 60
Ethiopia 68
"ethnic cleansing" 166
eugenics 20, 54, 57, 62, 70–2, 194
Europe 59, 68, 70
  African American music and culture influence in 57
  wartime recruitment 57
European Commission in Belgium 155
European Economic Community 186
"European feminism" 119
European imperialism 20
European Jewry 86
European Social Charter of 1961 109
European society
  First World War impact on 31
European Union (EU) 149, 172, 173, 180–1, 186
  2010 Equity Act 186–7
"European women" 2–3, 11, 21
  changing roles and experiences of 29, 31
  into full-time employment 77
eurozone crisis 182
Euskadi Ta Askatasuna (ETA; Basque Homeland and Liberty) 145–6
expanded rights, fighting for 123
  gay and lesbian communities and identity 128–30, 140–1
  international advocacy in the 1970s 143–5
  legal abortion and reproductive autonomy in eastern Europe 135–7

legal abortion and reproductive
  autonomy in western
  Europe 132–5
 second-wave feminism 130–2
 sexual revolution 127–8
 student activism and global
  revolution 138–40
 technology and fertility 124–7
 violent protest and terrorism
  145–7
 women's labor activism 141–3
extermination camps 85–6, 91

far right, rise of 169–71
Fasci Femminili 69
fascism 68, 69–70, 76
 and communism 101
fascist leaders 68
Fawcett, Millicent 18
February Revolution 49–50
female contract workers 110
female literacy rate
 in Europe 14
female spy 83
FEMEN 175, 177, 179
Feminine Mystique 118
femininity 26, 53, 83, 102, 114, 117
feminism 1, 2, 6, 16, 19, 29, 34, 55, 61,
  119, 124, 130–1, 138, 143, 146,
  147, 150, 155–7, 157–60, 162,
  171, 175–7, 196
 first wave of 17, 46, 112, 120
 history of 2
 "second-wave" of 124
 third wave of 159, 177
feminist critiques 117–19
"feminization" 102
Ferdinand, Franz 33
Finland 10
 women full voting rights in 32
First International Congress on
  Women's Rights 18
first wave feminism 17, 46, 112, 120
First World War 1, 27–8, 31, 33, 34,
  35, 36, 38, 40, 43, 46–51, 53–5,
  57, 60–5, 82, 101
Flappers, *see* Modern Woman
Fleischmann, Gisela "Gisi" 89
food riots 196

France 2, 14, 15, 69, 88, 95, 111, 112,
  117, 138, 159, 193
 against homosexuals 129
 on homosexuality 129
 Islamic women in 178
 legalized abortion in 134
 "the Pill" in 124–5
 promoting women's
  employment 101
 sécurité social (social security) in 100
Franco, Francisco 125
French feminist groups 59
French Revolution (1789–99) 1, 18, 169
 towards equal rights 6
French West Africa 59
Freud, Sigmund 57
Friedan, Betty 118
Fuden, Regina 90
Futurism 29, 31, 40
Futurist Manifesto of Lust (1913) 29
Futurist movement 29, 31

Gagarin, Yuri 106
Gardiner, Grace 21
Garvey, Amy Ashwood 60
Garvey, Marcus 60
gay and lesbian
 communities and identity 128–30
 liberation 140–1
Gay Health Action (GHA) 153
gay liberation 130, 131, 141
gay rights 4
gender and sex 3, 20, 25, 26, 31, 85
 and biopolitics 99
 history of 2
 violence 35–8
Geneva Conventions of 1949 168
genocide 76, 87, 90, 93, 94, 97, 166,
  168, 196
German Democratic Republic (GDR)
  104, 110, 111
German Girls' League 72
German Green Party 155
German Revolution 51
German Social Democratic Party 32
German Weimar Republic (1918–
  33) 56
Germany 13, 21, 26, 33, 36, 38, 46,
  54, 61, 68, 70, 86, 88, 169

equality and gender roles 184
in vitro fertilization (IVF) in 127
Islamic women in 179–80
mothers in 1930s 73f
1923 inflation 56
"The Pill" in 124–5
socialist feminists in 17
Gestapo 85
Glajtman, Masha 90
global economic depression 54
globalization 4, 173–4, 190–1, 197
Goncharova, Natalia Sergeevna 29, 30f, 196
Good Friday Agreement of 1998 146
Gooder, Sarah 8
Goodyear, Charles 27
Gorbachev, Mikhail 162
Gorbanevskaya, Natalya 140
Great Britain 114, 150, 156, 169
in vitro fertilization (IVF) in 126–7
promoting women's employment 102
Great Depression 54, 62, 68, 73
Great War 31, 33–5
Greece 110, 112, 117, 156
Greenham Common and Women's Peace Camps 157–9
Greenham Common 157, 158f, 171, 198
Grmek, Mirko 166
Guerrina, Roberta 182
guest workers 109
and "contract workers" 108, 109, 110
see also immigrant workers
Gupta, Geeta Rao 173
Gustavsen, Laila 183–4

Harlem Renaissance in America 57
HeHalutz movement 90
Heineman, Elizabeth 95
Helsinki Accords 160
"heroine of Crimea" 195
Hicks, Seymour 56
Himmler, Heinrich 86
Hirsi Ali, Ayan 171
Hitler, Adolf 69, 71, 72, 79, 127
eugenic ideas 136–7

HIV/AIDS 137, 152–5, 196
epidemic and women's healthcare 152–5, 196
Holocaust 73, 75, 76, 97
genocide of 87
and resistance 86–93
women and 84–6
home 6, 8, 10, 12, 31, 40, 50, 62, 64, 69, 76, 78, 101, 103
technological advancement in 114
homophobia 196
Homosexual Action West Berlin (HAW) 141
Homosexual Front for Revolution Action in Paris (FHAR) 141
Homosexual Law Reform Society 129
homosexuality and LGBTQ+ communities, decriminalizing 180–1
homosexuality 55, 56
Hughes, Langston 59
human biology and politics 99
Hungary 60, 70, 103, 105, 110, 159, 160
on homosexuality 129
laws for women political and legal equality 104
women in labor force 104

Iberia 108
Iceland 112, 131, 144
equality and gender roles 182
paternity leave policies 182
Ida Grese, Irma Ilse 93
illegitimacy rates 9
in slums and working-class residents 12
immigrant women 108
immigrant workers 108
abuse of 112
see also guest workers
immigration/migration 108, 110, 112, 142, 150, 169–71, 172, 174, 177, 178
imperialism 6, 20, 21, 111
in vitro fertilization (IVF) 125–7
technological advancement in 126
Indochina 59

Industrial Revolution (1760–1848)
  exploitation of women and children 6, 8–9
industrialization
  towards high imperialism 20
  and urbanization 8
  and women's greater participation 194
Ingham, Mary 134
Inglis, Elsie 42
international advocacy in the 1970s 143–5
International Black Liberation Movements 187–8
International Congress of Women 34
International Council of Women 19–20, 34
International Criminal Tribunal for the former Yugoslavia (ICTY) 167–8
International Labour Organization 52
International Research and Training Institute for the Advancement of Women (INSTRAW) 143
International Telegraphic Union (ITU) 15
International Tribunal at Nuremberg 94, 143
International Wages for Housework Campaign (IWFHC) 144, 145
International Woman Suffrage Association (IWSA) 32, 51
International Women's Suffrage Alliance Congress 34
International Women's Suffrage Association 51
International Women's Year 1975 143
intersectional feminism 119–21
intersectionality 3, 119, 177
interwar Modern Girl 55
  versus conservative women 55
interwar Period 52, 53, 60–3, 70, 72, 196
interwar sexuality 54–7
Ireland 60, 112, 146
Irish Republican Army (IRA) 146
Islamic women in Europe 177–80
  after September 11, terrorist attack 178
Islamophobia 195

Italy 59, 68, 78, 101, 108, 111, 117, 156, 159, 184
  divorce rates in 131
  on homosexuality 129
  legalized abortion in 134
  women in military troops 184, 185f

Jacobs, Alette 27, 34
Japan 138
"Jewish-Bolshevistic system" 78
Jewish ghettos 32, 85, 87, 89
Joffre, Joseph 38, 39
Johnson, Boris 186
Jones, Claudia 120
Judaism 76

Kamanin, Nikolai 105–6
Kaplan, Marion 71, 84
Kayser, Marie-Elise 63–4
Kelly, Petra Karin 155
Kenealy, Arabella 55
Kergomard, Pauline 11
Key, Ellen 25
Khrushchev era 117
Khrushchev, Nikita 113
Kiblitskaya, Marina 103
killing centers, see extermination camps
Kinder, Katja 171
kitchens 85, 150, 157
  technological advancement in 113–14
Kollontai, Alexandra 50, 65
Kollwitz, Käthe 47
  "The Parents" 47f
Koonz, Claudia 70
Kosovo War 167
Kouamé, Taky Marie-Divine 193
Kruseman, Mina 16
Krylova, Anna 82
Kutepova, Nadezhda 164

La Revue du Monde Noir (The Black World Review) 59
labor camps 85–6, 89
Labor Unions 63, 64, 142
  and strikes 51, 138, 142–3
Ladies National Association 13
Lamaze, Fernand 99

Latvia 61
Law for the Prevention of Hereditarily
    Diseased Offspring 71
Lawrence, Dorothy 44, 45f
Le Pen, Jean-Marie 169
League of Nations 52, 59
Lebensraum "superior German
    race" 86
legal abortion and reproductive
    autonomy
  in eastern Europe 135–7
  in western Europe 132–5
leisure and consumption 23, 27, 72,
    100, 113–17, 154
Lengye, Olga l 93
Lenin 50, 67
lesbianism 25, 26, 55–7
Lévy-Hass, Hanna 89
LGBTQ+ liberation 180–1, 196
liberalism 76
liberation 48
Lithuania 60, 61
Lord Beveridge 101
Lorde, Audre 171
Lotta Femminista 144
Lower, Wendy 94
Lubetkin, Zivia 90
Luxembourg 60, 61

Macedonia 167
Malta 117
Maltby, Margaret 14
Man, Marlboro 115
managerial class 6
The Manifesto of the Futurist Women
    (1912) 29
Manzurova, Natalia 164
Marinetti, F. T. 29
Marital Health Law 71
Markievicz, Constance 48, 49
Married Woman Property
    Association 19
Married Women's Property Act 18
Marson, Una 60
Martineau, Harriet 18
Marxist 160
masculinity 53
mass culture 53
Masselot, Annick 182

maternalism and interwar politics 60–3
maternalism 60–3, 68, 72
maternity leave 50, 64, 101, 104–5,
    139, 186
May, Theresa 186
"medically infertile patients" 127
Meier, Liselotte 94
"memorycide" 166
midcentury reform 11–14
middle class 9–10, 11, 17, 19, 25
Middle East countries
  decolonization in 112, 138
  international labor programs
    in 108
  national liberation
    movements in 138
migrant 195
  communities 57
  families 181
  sex workers 175
  women labor 102, 108
migration 2, 3, 11, 31–3, 175, 186, 190
  European countries 108
military intelligence
  European women crucial roles
    in 79–80
military service 161, 184, 194
Milošević, Slobodan 165, 167
minerki patrols 91
Minister of Education in Denmark 61
Misme, Jane 53
Mitchell, Juliet 119
modern warfare
  and medical care 42–4
Modern Woman 29, 53, 69, 72,
    82, 112
modern woman and rise of extremist
    politics 53
Moraczewska, Zofia 48
Morrison, Majbritt 120
Morrison, Raymond 120
Moscow 65, 140
  Red Square 156
Mozambique 110
Muslim populations
  Serbian civil law for 104
  Sharia law for 104
  women 172, 196
Mussolini 68

Nardal, Paulette 59, 60
National Fascist Party 68
National Health Service (NHS) 102
National Liberation Front (NLF) 112
National Socialist ideology 77
National Union of Women's Suffrage Societies 18
nationalism 19, 33, 35, 46, 48, 70, 99, 100, 169, 170
nationality 2, 20, 36
Nazi camps 76, 84, 93
  concentration camps 71, 85–6, 89, 93, 96, 128–9
  extermination camps 85–6, 91
  labor camps 85–6, 89
Nazi Germany 70, 71, 72
  military campaign 85
Nazi racial state 86
Nazi regime 70–2
  against gay people 129
Nazism 93, 116
Negritude Movement 59, 195
  in Paris 57
Neoliberalism 149, 150, 172
the Netherlands 9, 13, 16, 60, 101, 111, 112, 156, 171, 193
  abortion not legal in 134–5
  homosexuality and LGBTQ+ communities 129, 180–1
Neumann, Elsa 14
New Caledonia 59
New Economic Policy (NEP) 65
new middle class 10
New Millennium 173
  Black Lives Matter 187–8
  Brexit 186–7
  climate activism 188–90
  equality and gender roles 181–2
  homosexuality and LGBTQ+ communities, decriminalizing 180–1
  International Black Liberation Movements 187–8
  Islamic women in Europe 177–80
  sex trafficking and gendered exploitation 174–5
  twenty-first century feminisms 175–7
  women in UN and military 183–6
new social classes 9–11

New Soviet woman 65–8, 66f
New Woman 23, 25, 53, 54, 63
Ni Putes ni Soumises (Neither Whores nor Submissives) 178
Nigerian Women's League (NWL) 120
Nightingale, Florence 5, 6
Nikolayeva-Tereshkova, Valentina 106, 107f
Nixon, Richard 113
North Africa 111
North Atlantic Treaty Organization (NATO) 178, 183
Northern Ireland Women's Rights Movement (NIWRM) 147
Northern Ireland 146
Northwestern Europe
  international labor programs in 108
Norway 112
  equality and gender roles 183
  legalized abortion in 134
  women full voting rights in 32
Now women 54
nursing 5, 8, 9, 15, 21, 50
  and other professions 63, 77, 85, 102, 112

Oguntoya, Katharine 171
Origuel, Concepción 109
Orley, Marian 79
Ottoman Empire 23, 36, 54

pacifism 34
Pan Africanism 57, 59, 195
Pankhurst, Christabel 34
Pankhurst, Sylvia 60
Paris Colonial Exhibition 59
Paris 138
  Black women in 57, 59
  Negritude movement in 57
paternity leave 181–2
Pavlov, Ivan 99
Pavlovna Chudayeva, Valentina 82–3
peace movements and feminism 4, 155–7
Peisoty, Rakhel 195
People's Liberation Army of Yugoslavia 88
Pereira-James, Imani 193
Pesotta, Rose 32, 33

Petri, Erna 94
philanthropy, women involvement in 11, 14
Philippines 108
Phillips, Marion 62
physical violence
  against women 85
"The Pill" 124–5
pink collar jobs 63
Poland 60, 61, 88, 86, 105, 110, 140, 159, 161, 165
policies and legistation
  impacting women
  property 18
  on voting 11, 31, 32
policing women's bodies 13, 38, 40, 41, 57, 99, 100, 117, 123, 131, 137, 165–7, 172, 174, 190, 194, 197
political activism
  and feminism 196
politics 3, 32, 47
pornography 27, 127–8
Portugal 60, 61, 108, 112, 145, 196
  abortion not legal in 134–5
  women's movements 135
positively women collective 153–4
post-Cold War Eastern Europe
  economic collapse of 174
  gendered exploitation 174–5
  sex trafficking 174–5
  women into Western Europe 174
postwar guest worker
  migration 108–11
postwar labor migration 110
Prague 138, 160
pregnancy and childbirth 84
Presley, Elvis 115
Princip, Gavril 33
pronatalism 54, 62, 67, 68, 69, 70, 71, 100–2, 105, 136
  motherhood and 101
  and women's roles in western welfare states 100–2
Pross, Helge 119
prostitution 12, 17, 40, 41, 51, 55, 57, 60, 96, 160, 194
  laws to regulate, in mid-1800s 12–13
  in slums and working-class residents 12
Protestant and Catholic Encounter (PACE) 146
protestors 4
psychoprophylaxis method (PPM) 99
Purdy, Jean 126, 126f
Pussy Riot 4, 175, 176f, 177, 196

Quinn, Marc 187–8

race 2, 3, 20, 22, 55, 71, 84, 100, 101, 120, 141, 157, 169, 171, 194, 195
racial hygiene 70–2
racial nationalism 70–2
racism 2, 20, 54, 57, 70, 71, 73, 88, 100, 113, 120, 158, 171, 187, 188, 195
  Black Lives Matter 4, 187
radical protest and revolutions 46–51
Rappaport, Erica 10
Ravensbrück 93
Red Army Faction in West Germany 132, 147
Red Square 140
Red Zora 132
Reeder, Linda 109–10
Reich 86, 93
Reid, Jen 187–8, 195
Reid, Susan 117
"Remember Belgium" poster 36–8, 37f
reproductive autonomy 123, 124, 132, 135
reproductive freedom 196
reproductive rights 123, 130, 134, 135, 143, 148, 160
resistance movements 10, 139, 143, 145, 196
resistance 10, 63, 75, 85, 86–93, 111, 124, 131, 139, 145, 147–8, 159, 160, 171, 196–7
revolutions and rebirth 149
  Afro-feminism in the 1980s and 1990s 171–2
  battleground of women's bodies 165–7
  Chernobyl Nuclear disaster 162–4

feminism meets environmental,
    antinuclear, and peace
    movements 155–7
Greenham common and women's
    peace camps 157–9
HIV/AIDS epidemic and women's
    healthcare 152–5
immigration 169–71
rise of far right 169–71
"thatcherism" and neoliberal
    turn 150–1
war crimes tribunal and women's
    testimonies 167–9
women's activism in Eastern
    Europe 159–62
xenophobia 169–71
Yugoslav Wars 165–7
Reynolds, Tessie 23, 24f, 193
Richer, Leon-Pierre 18
Ricken, Käthe 78
Ringelblum, Emanuel 90
rise of extremist politics 68–70
Roma 84
Romania 61, 68, 117, 123, 135
    abortion right in 136
    contraceptives use in 137
"Rubble Women" 95
Rudneva, Evgenia 67
Russia 174
Russian Eugenics Office 71
Russian Revolution, 1917 61, 103
Russian 54

Samizdat 140
Sander, Helke 131
Sarajlic, Zejneba 167
Scandinavia 61, 70, 108, 156
    women in 64
Scholl, Sophie 88
Schulman, Sarah 153
Schwimmer, Roza 34
scientific racism 2, 20, 54, 57, 70, 71, 73
scientists 19, 26, 149, 162, 163
Scott, Joan 170
"Scramble for Africa" 20
Seacole, Mary Jane 5, 7f, 195
Second International socialist
    conference, 1907 32, 204 n.7
The Second Sex 118

second wave feminism 124, 130–2,
    141, 147, 159, 172
Second World War 73, 75–7, 96, 111
    Caribbean women
        contribution in 79
    complexity of women's lives 76
    Dominions women
        contribution in 79
    European women at war 76–84
    and holocaust 75
    India women contribution in 79
    and Nazism 116
    perpetrators 93–4
    postwar Germany 94–5
    resistance 87–93
    West Indian women in 79, 81f
    women and holocaust 84–6
    women's equality after 97
second-wave feminism 130–2
Senegal 59
Senegalese poets 59
September 11, terrorist attack 178
Serbia 35, 42, 159, 165, 167
    female literacy rate 14
Serbian women's movement 14, 46
sex trafficking 194, 196
    and gendered exploitation 174–5
sex work 12, 13, 33, 40, 41, 55, 56, 85,
    158, 174, 175
sexism 54, 70
sexology 25, 26, 27, 55–7, 72, 195
"sextremism" 177
sexual liberation 2, 3
sexual revolution 127–8
    media and advertising in 127–8
sexual violence 85, 146, 174–5
sexuality 25–7, 53, 54–5, 100, 127,
    128, 134, 160, 177, 193
Siberia 82
Sinti 84
Slavova, Kornelia 119
Slovak Central Refugee Committee 89
Slovak women 65
Slovakia 89
Slovenia 165, 167
"slumming" 12
Social Darwinism 20, 71
social democracy
    policies of 101

socialism 128, 151
socialist 4
Socialist Federal Republic of
    Yugoslavia 160
socialist feminists 11, 17, 19, 50, 196
Socialist Republic of Vietnam 110
"socially infertile patients" 127
Solidarity Movement in Poland
    161–2
Solovieva, Antonina 67
South America 108
South Asia 111
Southern Europe
  promoting women's
    employment 102
Soviet Bloc 196
Soviet Red Army soldiers 96
Soviet Socialist Republic (SSR) 117
Soviet Union 54, 65, 86, 95, 103,
    138, 139
  abortion laws during 1950s 105
  abortion restrictions in 135
  laws for women political and legal
    equality 104
  women into combat 82
space race 105–6, 156, 157
Spain 60, 61, 70, 101, 108, 123, 135,
    145, 156, 184, 196
  abortion not legal in 134–5
  equality and gender roles 182
  paternity leave policies 182
  women in military troops 184
Spanish Civil War 196
Sprüngli, Theodora Anna 26
Sputnik I 105
Stalin, Joseph 67, 135, 138, 160
Steel, Flora Annie 21
Steptoe, Patrick 126
Stroop, Jürgen 90
student activism and global
    revolution 138–40
Sub-Saharan Africa 111
suffrage 14, 19–20, 31, 32, 48, 50
  campaigns 34
  movement 40
suffragettes 4, 16–17, 18, 40, 51, 61,
    175, 198
A Surge of Power (Jen Reid) 2020
    187–8, 189f

"surplus women" 21–2
Sweden 13, 60, 62, 112, 120
  against homosexuals 129
  on homosexuality 129
  promoting women's
    employment 102
Swedish Marriage Code 19
Swedish Social Democratic Party 64
Switzerland 14, 15, 16
  on homosexuality 129
Szeliga, Maria 48
Szochur, Stefania 90

technology and fertility 124–7
telegraphy
  women in 15–16
Teodoroiu, Ecaterina 46
Thatcher, Margaret 150, 155
"thatcherism" and neoliberal
    turn 150–1
third wave feminism 159, 177
Thunberg, Greta Tintin Eleonora
    Ernman 188, 190
thyroid cancer 162–3
Tomšič, Vida 160
trafficking women 33
Tristan, Flora 11
Trump, Donald 190
Tubal ligation 70
Tunisia 108
twentieth century 1–2, 5
  beginnings of 5
  educational and career
    advances 14–16
  field of sexology, development
    of 25–7
  midcentury reform 11–14
  new social classes 10–11
  political action and migration in 31–3
  women's movements and activism 16
twenty-first century feminisms 1, 4,
    112, 171, 183, 175–7

UK 14, 16–17, 23, 49, 60, 63, 77, 112,
    117, 130, 146, 184, 185, 186–7
  BLM movement in 187–8
  on homosexuality 129
UK 1967 Abortion Act 134
UK Education Act 63

Ukraine 197
  sex tourism in 175
  trafficked woman in Western Europe 174–5
UN Climate Action Summit, 2019 188
UN World Congress of Women 143
United Kingdom, see UK
United Nations Development Fund for Women (UNIFEM) 143, 183
United Nations Entity for Gender Equality and the Empowerment of Women (UN Women) 183
United Nations Human Rights Office 183
United Nations (UN) 143, 167, 172, 183
United States and the USSR during Cold War 105
United States 14, 15, 32, 75, 97
  international labor programs in 108
  "The Pill" in 124–5
  stock market crash of 1929 54
Universal Workers' Union 11
US Eugenic Record Office 71
USSR 61, 67, 70, 94, 97, 105, 117–18, 140, 155, 162
  contraceptive method 125
  legalized abortion in 135

Vaincre le Sida (Defeat AIDS) 152
"Velvet Revolution" 149
Victims and Witnesses Section (VWS) 168
Vietnam 110
Vincendeau, Ginette 114
violence against women 197
violent protest and terrorism 145–7
Vitková-Kuněticka, Božena 32
von Alemann, Marianne 157
von Gizycki, Lily 18–19
von Krafft-Ebing, Richard 25
Von Reichenau, Walter 78

Wake, Nancy 83
Walentynowicz, Anna 143, 161
Wales
  on homosexuality 129
Wannsee Conference 85–6
war 5, 6, 29, 33, 35–8
  crimes tribunal and women's testimonies 167–9
  European understandings of 35
  propaganda and gendered violence 35–8
  and prostitution 40–1
  protest and revolutions against 46–51
  women in 44, 46
Warsaw Ghetto in Poland 90
Warsaw Uprising of 1944 91
wealthy upper class 10–11, 12, 17, 26, 39, 42, 46
Weimar Germany
  sexual culture 57
welfare 1, 11, 13, 53, 54, 61
West Berlin 131
West Germany 101, 108, 110, 116–17, 150, 156
  commercialization of sex in 128
  legalized abortion in 134
  1953 anti-pornography Law 128
  Socialist German Student Union (SDS) 131
West German Law, 1952 101
West versus East nations 99
  gendered policies 100
Western Bloc 118
  promoting women's employment 102
Western countries
  in vitro fertilization (IVF) in 126
Western Europe 108
  legal abortion and reproductive autonomy in 132–5
white-collar jobs 10, 63, 150
Williams, Henria 32
Williams, Lance Corporal Adina Henrietta 79
Wilson, Woodrow 34, 51
Winter, Jay 41
Woman Question 1, 16, 18, 19
Women for Peace 161, 164
women in divided Europe 99
  decolonization and gender 111–13
  feminist critiques 117–19
  intersectional feminism 119–21
  leisure and consumption 113–17

postwar "guest worker"
  migration 108–11
pronatalism and women's roles in
  western welfare states 100–2
women's lives at work and at home
  in the eastern bloc 103–7
women
  activism in Eastern Europe 159–62
  birth control practices 123
  in cabinets 61
  on capitalist versus communist
    nations 99–100
  as cheap labor 77
  in colonial holdings 20–2
  in combat 44–6
  cycling 23, 24f, 25, 27, 35, 53, 193
  economic development 174
  in education 10, 14–15, 21, 22,
    40, 65, 69, 138, 146, 147, 152,
    170, 172
  employment growth 101–2
  equal rights 62
  in Europe 77
  experiences with migration 33
  as industrial labor 38–9
  Jewish and non-Jewish 86
  labor activism 141–3
  medical corps 42
  movements and activism, in
    Europe 16–20
  in Nazi Germany 77–8
  into new political power 54
  political and social campaigns for
    emancipation 48
  political participation in 1920s and
    1930s 62
  protest and revolutions against
    war 46–51
  reproductive rights 123
  as researchers 153, 163, 173, 174
  role change after Second World
    War 76–7
  as student activists 138–40
  as students 131, 138–9, 157

suffrage 18
transition from old tradition 22–5
UN and military 183–6
wartime employment of 77
on West versus East nations 99–100
workforce 38, 39, 40, 53, 63–4, 194
Women's Auxiliary Air Force
  (WAAF) 79, 81
Women's Day Off Strike in
  Iceland 144
Women's International League for
  Peace and Freedom 34
Women's Peace Camps 157–9
Women's Royal Naval Service
  (WRNS) 81
Women's Social and Political Union
  (WSPU) 31
Woodstock, Ena Collymore 79
working class 9–10, 16, 17, 23, 26
World Health Organization (WHO)
  141, 163
  breast cancer survival rates 155
  Special Programme on AIDS 152
WWI, see First World War
WWII, see Second World War
Wyszogrodzka, Bluma 90, 91f, 92f
Wyszogrodzka, Rachela 90, 91f, 92f

xenophobia 112–13, 121, 150, 154,
  169–71, 195

Yaroshinskaya, Alla 163
Yelverton, Juliet 158
Youth4Climate 190
Yugoslav Wars 149, 165–7, 197
Yugoslavia 89, 104, 105, 117, 135,
  159, 172

Zdrojewicz, Małka 90, 91f, 92f
Žena-Žrtva Rata (Women Victims of
  War) 167
Zetkin, Clara 32, 204 n.7
Zhenotdel (Women's Department of
  the Central Committee) 67